Portraiture and Friendship in Enlightenment France

Studies in Seventeenth- and Eighteenth-Century Art and Culture

SERIES EDITOR: Sarah R. Cohen,
University at Albany, State University of New York

SERIES ADVISORY BOARD: Wendy Bellion, University of Delaware; Martha Hollander, Hofstra University; Christopher M. S. Johns, Vanderbilt University; William Pressly, University of Maryland; Amelia Rauser, Franklin and Marshall College; Michael Yonan, University of Missouri

Marika Takanishi Knowles · *Realism and Role-Play:
The Human Figure in French Art from Callot to the Brothers Le Nain*

Julia A. Sienkewicz · *Epic Landscapes:
Benjamin Henry Latrobe and the Art of Watercolor*

Tilden Russell · *Theory and Practice in Eighteenth-Century Dance:
The German-French Connection*

Paula Radisich · *Pastiche, Fashion, and Galanterie in Chardin's Genre Subjects:
Looking Smart*

Christine A. Jones · *Shapely Bodies:
The Image of Porcelain in Eighteenth-Century France*

Jean-François Bédard · *Decorative Games: Ornament, Rhetoric, and Noble Culture
in the Work of Gilles-Marie Oppenord (1672–1742)*

Amelia Rauser · *Caricature Unmasked:
Irony, Authenticity, and Individualism in Eighteenth-Century English Prints*

Alden Cavanaugh, ed. · *Performing the "Everyday":
The Culture of Genre in the Eighteenth Century*

William L. Pressly · *The Artist as Original Genius:
Shakespeare's "Fine Frenzy" in Late Eighteenth-Century British Art*

Charles A. Cramer · *Abstraction and the Classical Ideal, 1760–1920*

Susan M. Dixon · *Between the Real and the Ideal:
The Accademia degli Arcadi and Its Garden in Eighteenth-Century Rome*

Dorothy Johnson, ed. · *Jacques-Louis David: New Perspectives*

Amy S. Wyngaard · *From Savage to Citizen:
The Invention of the Peasant in the French Enlightenment*

Mark Reinberger · *Utility and Beauty:
Robert Wellford and Composition Ornament in America*

Martha Mel Stumberg Edmunds · *Piety and Politics:
Imaging Divine Kingship in Louis XIV's Chapel at Versailles*

Elise Goodman, ed. · *Art and Culture in the Eighteenth Century:
New Dimensions and Multiple Perspectives*

Portraiture and Friendship in Enlightenment France

JESSICA L. FRIPP

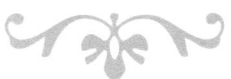

University of Delaware Press · Newark, Delaware

Distributed by the University of Virginia Press

University of Delaware Press
Copyright © 2020 by Jessica L. Fripp
All rights reserved
Printed in the United States of America on acid-free paper

First published 2020

ISBN 978-1-64453-201-0 (casebound)
ISBN 978-1-64453-202-7 (e-book)

1 3 5 7 9 8 6 4 2

Library of Congress Cataloging-in-Publication Data
is available for this title.

Publication of this book has been aided by a grant from the
Robert and Mary Jane Sunkel Art History Endowment,
Texas Christian University

Book design by Robert L. Wiser, Silver Spring, Maryland

For Lyn and Raymond

Table of Contents

List of Illustrations ... ix

Acknowledgments ... xv

INTRODUCTION
1

Chapter 1
FRIENDSHIP IN THE ACADEMY
11

Chapter 2
CELEBRATING CELEBRITY
35

Chapter 3
RE-EVALUATING RIVALRY
81

Chapter 4
FRIENDSHIP ABROAD
123

EPILOGUE
183

Endnotes ... 191

Bibliography ... 233

Index ... 247

List of Illustrations

Fig. 2.1. Étienne Ficquet after Maurice Quentin de La Tour, *Voltaire à 41 ans*. 1762. Engraving, 5⅜ × 3⁷⁄₁₆ in. (13.6 × 8.7 cm). Bibliothèque Nationale de France, Département des Estampes.

Fig. 2.2. Maurice Quentin de La Tour, *Portrait of the Sculptor Jean-Baptiste II Lemoyne*, 1763. Pastel, 18¼ × 15¼ in. (46.4 × 38.8 cm), post 2017 restoration. Musée du Louvre, Paris, France. Photo: Michel Urtado. © RMN-Grand Palais/Art Resource, NY.

Fig. 2.3. Maurice Quentin de La Tour, *Portrait of the Painter Jean Restout*, 1746. Reception piece for the Académie Royale, Sept. 24, 1746. Pastel on gray paper, 42½ × 35¼ in. (108 × 89.5 cm). Musée du Louvre, Paris, France. Photo: Gérard Blot. © RMN-Grand Palais/Art Resource, NY.

Fig. 2.4. Maurice Quentin de La Tour, *Portrait of the Painter Claude Dupouch*, 1739. Pastel, 23⅝ × 19⅝ in. (60 × 50 cm). Photo: Mathieu Rabeau. Musee Antoine Lecuyer, Saint-Quentin, France. © RMN-Grand Palais/Art Resource, NY.

Fig. 2.5. Maurice Quentin de La Tour, *Portrait of the Sculptor René Frémin*, salon of 1743. Pastel, 35⅞ × 28¾ in. (91 × 73 cm), post 2017 restoration. Musée du Louvre, Paris, France. Photo: Michel Urtado. © RMN-Grand Palais/Art Resource, NY.

Fig. 2.6. Jean-Baptiste II Lemoyne, *Bust of Maurice Quentin de la Tour*, salons of 1748 and 1763. Terracotta, h. 25⅝ in. (65 cm). Photo: Agence Bulloz. Musee Antoine Lecuyer, Saint-Quentin, France. © RMN-Grand Palais/Art Resource, NY.

Fig. 2.7. Maurice Quentin de La Tour, *Portrait of the Painter Charles Parrocel*, 1743. Pastel, 22 × 17⅜ in. (56 × 44 cm). Photo: Mathieu Rabeau. Musee Antoine Lecuyer, Saint-Quentin, France. © RMN-Grand Palais/Art Resource, NY.

Fig. 2.8. Maurice Quentin de La Tour, *Portrait of Jean Le Rond d'Alembert*, 1753. Pastel, 21⅝ × 18 in. (55 × 45.8 cm). Photo: R. G. Berizzi. Musée du Louvre, Paris, France. © RMN-Grand Palais/Art Resource, NY.

Fig. 2.9. Maurice Quentin de La Tour, *Portrait of Jean-Jacques Rousseau*, 1753. Pastel on blue paper, 17¾ × 14 in. (45 × 35.5 cm). Musee Antoine Lecuyer, Saint-Quentin, France. Photo: Mathieu Rabeau. © RMN-Grand Palais/Art Resource, NY.

Fig. 2.10. Maurice Quentin de La Tour, *Portrait of Marquis Marc-René de Voyer d'Argenson*, 1753. Pastel, 25¼ × 20½ in. (64 × 52 cm). Musee Antoine Lecuyer, Saint-Quentin, France. Photo: Mathieu Rabeau. © RMN-Grand Palais/Art Resource, NY.

Fig. 2.11. Maurice Quentin de La Tour, *Portrait of Louis de Silvestre*, 1753. Pastel, 24¾ × 20⅛ in. (63 × 51 cm). Musee Antoine Lecuyer, Saint-Quentin, France. Photo: Mathieu Rabeau. © RMN-Grand Palais/Art Resource, NY.

Fig. 2.12. Louis-Michel Vanloo, *Portrait of the Marquis de Marigny and His Wife*, 1769. Oil on canvas, 51 × 38½ in. (129.6 × 97.5 cm). Musée du Louvre, Paris, France. Photo: Tony Querrec. © RMN-Grand Palais/Art Resource, NY.

Fig. 2.13. Jean-Baptiste Greuze, *Portrait of Claude-Henri Watelet*, 1765. Oil on canvas, 45¼ × 34½ in. (115 × 88 cm). Musée du Louvre, Paris, France. Photo: Michel Urtado. © RMN-Grand Palais/Art Resource, NY.

Fig. 2.14. Jean Valade, *Portrait of the Painter Louis de Silvestre*, 1754. Oil on canvas, 51 × 38½ in. (129.5 × 98 cm). Chateaux de Versailles et de Trianon, Versailles, France. Photo: Franck Raux. © RMN-Grand Palais/Art Resource, NY.

Fig. 2.15. Maurice Quentin de La Tour, *Portrait of the Painter Jean Baptiste Chardin*, 1760. Pastel on paper, 17⅜ × 13¾ in. (44 × 35 cm), post-restoration. Musée du Louvre, Paris, France. Photo: Michel Urtado. © RMN-Grand Palais/Art Resource, NY.

Fig. 2.16. Charles-Nicolas Cochin *fils*, *Portrait de Chardin*, n.d. Black chalk, diam. 4 in. (10 cm). Musée du Louvre, Paris, France. Photo: Michel Urtado. © RMN-Grand Palais/Art Resource, NY.

Fig. 2.17. Laurent Cars, after Cochin, *Portrait of Jean-Siméon Chardin*, ca. 1755. Engraving, 7 9/16 × 5⅝ in. (19.2 × 14.2 cm). Bibliothèque nationale de France, Département des estampes et de la photographie, Paris.

Fig. 2.18. Hubert Robert, *Le déjeuner de Madame Geoffrin*, ca. 1770–72. Oil on canvas, 26 × 22⅞ in. (66 × 58 cm). Private Collection. Photo: Erich Lessing/Art Resource, NY.

Fig. 2.19. Hubert Robert, *Présentation d'un tableau à Madame Geoffrin*, ca. 1770–72. Oil on canvas, 26 × 22⅞ in. (66 × 58 cm). Private Collection. Photo: Bridgeman-Giraudon/Art Resource, NY.

Fig. 2.20. Gerard Edelinck, *Pierre Mignard*, in Charles Perrault, *Les Hommes illustres qui ont paru en France pendant ce siècle, avec leurs portraits au naturel* (Paris: Antoine Dezallier, 1696–1700).

Fig. 3.1. Élisabeth-Vigée Lebrun, *Portrait of Jean-Baptiste II Lemoyne*, 1772. Oil on canvas, 14¾ × 17⅜ in. (37.4 × 44.1 cm). Cleveland Museum of Art.

Fig. 3.2. Adélaïde Labille-Guiard, *Augustin Pajou Modeling the Bust of His Teacher, Lemoyne*, 1783. Pastel on paper, 28 × 22⅞ in. (71 × 58 cm). Musée du Louvre, Paris, France. Photo: Michel Urtado. © RMN-Grand Palais/Art Resource, NY.

Fig. 3.3. Augustin Pajou, *Portrait Bust of Jean-Baptiste II Lemoyne*, 1759. Terracotta, 23⅜ × 14⅛ in. (59.5 × 36 cm). Musee des Beaux-Arts. Photo: Gérard Blot. © RMN-Grand Palais/Art Resource, NY.

Fig. 3.4. Augustin Pajou, *Portrait Bust of Jean Baptiste II Lemoyne*, 1758. Bronze, 24½ × 12¼ × 8 in. (62 × 31 × 20.5 cm). Musée du Louvre, Paris, France. Photo: Gerard Blot/Christian Jean. © RMN-Grand Palais/Art Resource, NY.

Fig. 3.5. Élisabeth Louise Vigée Le Brun, *Portrait of Madame Grand (Noël Catherine Vorlée)*, 1783. Oil on canvas, 36¼ × 28½ in. (92.1 × 72.4 cm). Metropolitan Museum of Art, NY.

Fig. 3.6. Adélaïde Labille-Guiard, *Portrait of Joseph-Marie Vien*, 1783. Pastel on paper, 23 × 18 in. (58.5 × 48.2 cm). Musée Fabre, Montpellier. Photo: Frédéric Jaulmes. © Musée Fabre de Montpellier Méditerranée Métropole.

Fig. 3.7. Adélaïde Labille-Guiard, *Portrait of Jean-Jacques Bachelier*, 1782. Pastel on paper, 22½ × 17¾ in. (57 × 45 cm). Musée du Louvre, Paris, France. Photo: Martine Beck-Coppola. © RMN-Grand Palais/Art Resource, NY.

Fig. 3.8. Adélaïde Labille-Guiard, *Portrait of Joseph-Benoît Suvée*, 1783. Pastel on paper, 23⅞ × 19⅞ in. (60.5 × 50.5 cm). Ecole nationale supérieure des Beaux-Arts, Paris, France. © Beaux-Arts de Paris, Dist. RMN-Grand Palais/Art Resource, NY.

Fig. 3.9. Adélaïde Labille-Guiard, *Portrait of François-André Vincent*, 1782. Pastel on blueish-grey paper, 19⅝ × 18½ in. (50 × 47 cm). Musée du Louvre, Paris, France. Photo: Martine Beck-Coppola. © RMN-Grand Palais/Art Resource, NY.

Fig. 3.10. Adélaïde Labille-Guiard, *Self-Portrait with Two Pupils*, 1785. Oil on canvas, 83 × 59½ in. (210.8 × 151.1 cm). Metropolitan Museum of Art, NY.

Fig. 3.11. Augustin Pajou, *Portrait Bust of Claude-Edmé Labille*, 1785. Marble, 24⅝ × 8¼ × 10⅞ in. (62.5 × 21 × 27.5 cm). Musée du Louvre, Paris, France. Photo: Franck Raux. © RMN-Grand Palais/Art Resource, NY.

Fig. 3.12. *Marcus Tullius Cicero (106–43 B.C.)*. Roman Greek Islands, 1st century B.C.; bought by the Duke of Wellington in 1816. Marble, h. 36⅝ in. (93 cm). Victoria and Albert Museum. Photo: V&A Images, London/Art Resource, NY.

Fig. 3.13. Adélaïde Labille-Guiard, *Portrait of the Painter Charles-Amédée-Philippe Vanloo*, 1785. Oil on canvas, 51¼ × 38½ in. (130 × 98 cm). Musée des châteaux de Versailles et de Trianon. Photo: Christophe Fouin. © RMN-Grand Palais/Art Resource, NY.

Fig. 3.14. Adélaïde Labille-Guiard, *Portrait of Joseph Vernet*, 1785. Oil on canvas, 21⅝ × 18⅜ in. (55 × 46.5 cm). Musée Calvet, Avignon.

Fig. 3.15. Elisabeth-Louise Vigée-Lebrun, *Portrait of Charles-Alexandre de Calonne*, 1784. Oil on canvas, 61¼ × 51¼ in. (155.5 × 130.3 cm). Royal Trust. © Her Majesty Queen Elizabeth II 2019.

Fig. 3.16. Abraham Bosse, *Touch* from *The Five Senses*, ca. 1638. Etching, 10³⁄₁₆ × 12⅞ in. (25.8 × 32.7 cm). Metropolitan Museum of Art, NY.

Fig. 3.17. Élisabeth Vigée-Lebrun, *Portrait of Hubert Robert*, 1788. Oil on wood, 41½ × 33 in. (105 × 84 cm). Musée du Louvre, Paris, France. Photo: Jean-Gilles Berizzi. © RMN-Grand Palais/Art Resource, NY.

Fig. 3.18. Augustin Pajou, *Portrait Bust of Hubert Robert*, 1787. Terracotta, 22 × 20½ in. (56 × 52 cm). Ecole nationale supérieure des Beaux-Arts, Paris, France. © Beaux-Arts de Paris, Dist. RMN-Grand Palais/Art Resource, NY.

Fig. 4.1. François-André Vincent, *Caricature of the Painter Pierre-Charles Jombert*, 1774. Pen and brown ink, brown wash, color crayons, 48¾ × 155½ in. (124 × 395 cm). Musée du Louvre, Paris, France. Photo: Madeleine Coursaget. © RMN-Grand Palais/Art Resource, NY.

Fig. 4.2. Moricaud Franconville after Jean-Baptiste Stouf, *Caricatures*, early 1770s. Etching. Nationalmuseum, Stockholm. Photo: Erik Cornelius/Nationalmuseum.

Fig. 4.3. Jean-Simon Berthélemy, *Caricature of François-André Vincent*, 1770. Sanguine on paper, 18⁵⁄₁₆ × 14⁵⁄₁₆ in. (46.5 × 36.3 cm). Musée Atger, Montpellier. Photo: BIU de Montpellier, Service photographique.

Fig. 4.4. Joseph-Barthélemy Le Bouteux, *Portrait-charge of François-André Vincent*, 1773. Sanguine on paper, 18⁵⁄₁₆ × 14⁵⁄₁₆ in. (46.5 × 36.3 cm). Musée Atger, Montpellier. Photo: BIU de Montpellier, Service photographique.

Fig. 4.5. François-André Vincent, *Portrait-charge of the painter Le Bouteux*, 1774. Pen and ink, with traces of pen and pencil on used paper, 7⅝ × 3¹¹⁄₁₆ in. (19.4 × 9.3 cm). Nationalmuseum, Stockholm.

Fig. 4.6. Michel-Honoré Bounieu, *La Gaîté*, 1762. Sanguine, 17¹³⁄₁₆ × 13⅛ in. (45.3 × 33.3 cm). École nationale supérieure des beaux-arts, Paris. Photo © RMN-Grand Palais/ Art Resource, NY.

Fig. 4.7. François-André Vincent, *Portrait-charge of the Painter Suvée*, 1774. Black chalk on paper, 16⅛ × 22¹¹⁄₁₆ in. (41 × 22.1 cm). Musée Atger, Montpellier. Photo: BIU de Montpellier, Service photographique.

Fig. 4.8. François-André Vincent, *Portrait-charge of the Painter Suvée*, 1774. Black chalk on paper, counterproof, 16¾ × 9⁵⁄₁₆ in. (42.6 × 23.7 cm). Gift of Jean-Pierre Selz, 1986. Metropolitan Museum of Art, NY.

Fig. 4.9. François-André Vincent, *Portrait-charge of the Painter Lemonnier*, 1774. Black chalk on paper, 16³⁄₁₆ × 8¾ in. (41.1 × 22.2 cm). Musée Atger, Montpellier. Photo: BIU de Montpellier, Service photographique.

Fig. 4.10. François-André Vincent, *Portrait-charge of the Painter Le Bouteux*, 1774. Black chalk on paper, 14¼ × 7¹¹⁄₁₆ in. (36.2 × 19.6 cm). Bibliothèque municipal de Rouen. Photo: Bibliothèque municipale de Rouen.

Fig. 4.11. François-André Vincent, *Portrait-charge of the Painter Jombert*, 1774. Black chalk on paper, 16¾ × 8¾ in. (42.5 × 22.2 cm). Musée Atger, Montpellier. Photo: BIU de Montpellier, Service photographique.

Fig. 4.12. Moricaud Franconville after Jean-Baptiste Stouf, *Caricatures*, early 1770s. Etching. Nationalmuseum, Stockholm. Photo: Erik Cornelius/Nationalmuseum.

Fig. 4.13. François-André Vincent, *Portrait-charge of the Architect Rousseau*, 1774. Black chalk on paper, 16⁵⁄₁₆ × 8¾ in. (41.5 × 22.2 cm). Musée Atger, Montpellier. Photo: BIU de Montpellier, Service photographique.

Fig. 4.14. François-André Vincent, *Portrait-charge of the Sculptor Boquet*, 1774. Black chalk on paper, 17³⁄₁₆ × 11⅛ in. (43.7 × 28.2 cm). Musée Atger, Montpellier. Photo: BIU de Montpellier, Service photographique.

Fig. 4.15. François-André Vincent, *Portrait de trois hommes*, 1774. Oil on canvas, 31⅞ × 38½ in. (81 × 98 cm). Musée du Louvre, Paris, France. Photo: Daniel Arnaudet. © RMN-Grand Palais/Art Resource, NY.

Fig. 4.16. François-André Vincent, *Portrait of Pierre Rousseau*, 1774. Oil on canvas, 32¼ × 26¾ in. (82 × 68 cm). Musée de l'Hôtel Sandelin, Saint-Omer. © Ph. Beurtheret.

Fig. 4.17. Louis-Michel Vanloo, *Portrait of Carle Vanloo and His Family*, 1757. Oil on canvas, 78¾ × 61½ in. (200 × 156 cm). Musée du Louvre, Paris, France. Photo: Gérard Blot. © RMN-Grand Palais/Art Resource, NY.

Fig. 4.18. Jean-Marc Nattier, *Portrait of the Artist and His Family*, 1732–62. Oil on canvas, 58¾ × 65 in. (149 × 165 cm). Musée national des châteaux de Versailles et de Trianon, Versailles. Photo: Gérard Blot. © RMN-Grand Palais/Art Resource, NY.

Fig. 4.19. Giuseppe Baldrighi, *Triple Portrait of Artists*, 1751. Oil on canvas, 20¾ × 25¾ in. (52.7 × 65.4 cm). National Gallery of Canada, Ottawa.

Fig. 4.20. James Barry, *Self-Portrait with James Paine and Dominique Lefèvre*, 1767. Oil on canvas, 23⅞ × 19⅝ in. (60.5 × 50 cm). National Portrait Gallery, London. © National Portrait Gallery, London.

Fig. 4.21. Jean-François Rigaud, *Portrait of Francesco Bartolozzi, Agostino Carlini, and Giovanni Battista Cipriani*, 1777. Oil on canvas, 39½ × 49½ in. (100.3 × 125.7 cm). National Portrait Gallery, London.

Fig. 4.22. Jacopo Pontormo, *Portrait of Two Friends*, ca. 1521–24. Oil on panel, 34¾ × 26¾ in. (88.2 × 68 cm). Fondazione Giorgio Cini, Venice, Italy. Photo: Cameraphoto Arte, Venice/Art Resource, NY.

Fig. 4.23. Peter Paul Rubens, *Self-Portrait in a Circle of Friends from Mantua*, ca. 1602–5. Oil on canvas, 30½ × 39¾ in. (77.5 × 101 cm). Wallraf-Richartz-Museum-Fondation Corboud, Cologne, Germany. Photo: HIP/Art Resource, NY.

Fig. 4.24. Anthony van Dyck, *Portrait of George Gage with Two Servants*, 1622–23. Oil on canvas, 45¼ × 44½ in. (115 × 113.5 cm). National Gallery of Art, London. © The National Gallery, London.

Fig. 4.25. Simon de Vos, *Artists' Portraits as Smokers and Drinkers*, 1626. Oil on canvas, 24⅜ × 36¼ in. (62 × 92 cm). Musée du Louvre, Paris, France. Photo: Stéphane Maréchalle. © RMN-Grand Palais/Art Resource, NY.

Fig. 4.26. Adrien Brouwer, *The Smokers*, ca. 1636. Oil on wood, 18¼ × 14½ in. (46.4 × 36.8 cm). Metropolitan Museum, NY.

Fig. 4.27. Eustache Le Sueur, *Réunion d'amis*, 1640–44. Oil on canvas, 53½ × 76¾ in. (136 cm. × 195 cm). Musée du Louvre, Paris, France. Photo: Erich Lessing/Art Resource, NY.

Fig. 4.28. Charles Algernon Tomkins, after Joshua Reynolds, *Members of the Society of Dilettanti*, mid-nineteenth century. Mezzotint, 11 1/16 × 8⅜ in. (28.1 cm × 21.3 cm). National Portrait Gallery, London.

Fig. 4.29. Charles Algernon Tomkins, after Joshua Reynolds, *Members of the Society of Dilettanti*, mid-nineteenth century. Mezzotint, 11⅛ × 8 5/16 in. (28.3 cm × 21.1 cm). National Portrait Gallery, London.

Fig. 4.30. François-André Vincent, *Self-Portrait*, 1766. Oil on canvas, 28 × 21¼ in. (71 × 54 cm). Musée du Louvre, Paris, France. Photo: Franck Raux. © RMN-Grand Palais/Art Resource, NY.

Fig. 4.31. Jean-Honoré Fragonard, *Portrait of Louis Richard de La Bretèche*, ca. 1769. Oil on canvas, 31½ × 25⅝ in. (80 × 65 cm). Musée du Louvre, Paris, France. Photo: Franck Raux. © RMN-Grand Palais/Art Resource, NY.

Fig. 4.32. Carle Vanloo, *A Pasha Having a Mistress's Portrait Painted*, 1737. Oil on canvas, 26 × 29⅞ in. (66 × 76 cm). Virginia Museum of Fine Arts.

Fig. 4.33. Carle Vanloo, *La conversation espagnole*, 1754. Oil on canvas, 64½ × 50¾ in. (164 × 129 cm). The State Hermitage Museum, St. Petersburg. Photo: Vladimir Terebenin, Leonard Kheifets, Yuri Molodkovets. © The State Hermitage Museum.

Fig. 4.34. Carle Vanloo, *La lecture espagnole*, salon of 1761. Oil on canvas, 64½ × 50¾ in. (164 × 129 cm). The State Hermitage Museum, St. Petersburg. Photo: Vladimir Terebenin, Leonard Kheifets, Yuri Molodkovets. © The State Hermitage Museum.

Fig. 4.35. Joseph Marie Vien, *Le Grand Visir (The Grand Vizir)*, from the series *Caravane du Sultan à la Mecque*, 1748. Etching, 7 15/16 × 5¼ in. (20.2 × 13.4 cm). Metropolitan Museum, NY.

Fig. 4.36. Anicet-Charles-Gabriel Lemonnier, *Portrait of the Artist's Brother in Fancy Dress*, n.d. Pencil and white chalk on paper, 12 5/16 × 8⅜ in. (31.2 × 21.2 cm). Musée des beaux-arts de Rouen. © C. Lancien, C. Loisel/Réunion des Musées Métropolitains Rouen Normandie.

Fig. 5.1. Simon-Charles Miger after Adélaïde Labille-Guiard, *Joseph Vien*, in or after 1790. Engraving on heavy laid paper, 18 7/16 × 13 1/8 in. (46.9 × 33.4 cm). Ailsa Mellon Bruce Fund. National Gallery of Art, Washington, DC.

Fig. 5.2. Marie-Gabrielle Capet, *Studio Scene: Adélaïde Labille-Guiard Painting the Portrait of Joseph-Marie Vien*, 1808. Oil on canvas, 27 1/8 × 32 7/8 in. (69 × 83.5 cm). Neue Pinakothek, Munich. Photo: bpk-Bildagentur/Art Resource, NY.

Fig. 5.3. Louis-Léopold Boilly, *A Gathering of Artists in the Studio of Isabey*, 1798. Oil on canvas, 28 1/8 × 43 3/4 in. (71.5 × 111 cm). Musée du Louvre, Paris, France. Photo: Adrien Didierjean. © RMN-Grand Palais/Art Resource, NY.

List of Tables

Table 1.1. Frequency per 10,000 words of *ami* and *amitié*, 1600–1789. (Data from the ARTFL-FRANTEXT database).

Table 1.2. Occurrences of *ami* and *amitié* in works by genre, 1600–1789. (Data from the ARTFL-FRANTEXT database).

Table 2.1. Portraits displayed at the Salon as percentage of total works displayed, 1737–89.

Acknowledgments

THIS IS A BOOK ABOUT FRIENDSHIP—professional, personal, familial—and I have many individuals to thank that represent the diverse relationships that fall under the umbrella of friendship. The late Mary Vidal, who advised my undergraduate thesis at the University of California San Diego, inspired my love of the eighteenth century. During my time in the master's program at Williams College and the Clark Art Institute, Mark Ledbury encouraged me to think about the connection between social networking and eighteenth-century portraiture. Susan Siegfried helped me develop these initial ideas into a dissertation at the University of Michigan that eventually became this book. I am eternally grateful for her generosity as an adviser, and her thoughtful commentary on this project over the years. She continues to go above and beyond in her role as mentor. Dena Goodman provided an important introduction to the intellectual and cultural history of the Enlightenment when I was a graduate student. This book would be poorer without her numerous insights. Patricia Simons sent me many portraits relevant to this study during her travels, and has been a welcomed sounding board over the years.

Laura Auricchio, Daniella Berman, Kenneth Loiselle, Katie Hornstein, Melissa Hyde, Elizabeth Mansfield, and Andrew Ross generously provided feedback on various chapters. I would like to thank my colleagues at Texas Christian University: Babette Bohn, Frances Colpitt, Lori Diel, Sara-Jayne Parsons, Richard Lane, Rachel Livedalen, and Mark Thistlethwaite for their encouragement. Hannah Plank served as an invaluable research assistant. Other members of the Metroplex art history community, including Denise Amy Baxter, Amy Freund, Nicole Myers, and George Shackelford, have made North Texas a welcoming and intellectually stimulating place to live and work. I am truly grateful to be part of the Historians of Eighteenth-Century Art and Architecture, whose members—too many to list here—are a continuous source of support and make conferences productive, interesting, and fun.

Funding for this project came from a number of generous sources. A Samuel H. Kress Foundation Travel Grant and a Bourse Chateaubriand allowed me to begin my initial research at the Institut national d'histoire de l'art in Paris with the support of Philippe Bordes and Anne Lafont. The Rackham Graduate School at the University of Michigan also provided funding for research. At Texas Christian University, a Junior Faculty Summer Research Fellowship, the Research and Creative Activity Fund, and the Robert and Mary Jane Sunkel Art History Endowment allowed me to finalize my research and helped finance the book's production. None of this work would have been possible without access to works of art and archives provided by the Kungliga Bibliothek in Stockholm, the Bibliothèque nationale de France, the Centre de documentation and the Département des arts graphiques at the Musée du Louvre, and the library of the Institut national d'histoire de l'art in Paris. I spent many hours in the collection of the Musée Atger in Montpellier aided by Hélène Lorblanchet. In Besançon, Marie-Claire Waille at the Bibliothèque d'étude et de conservation and Ghislaine Courtet at the Musée des beaux-arts et d'archéologie guided me through the enormous amount of material on Pierre-Adrien Pâris. Nadine Lopez at the Musée des beaux-arts of Marseille allowed me to see works in the collection even though the museum was closed for renovation. Martin Olin and Ulf Cederlöf provided access to the drawing collection at the Nationalmuseum, Stockholm. Denis Reynaud introduced me to the Académie des sciences, belles lettres et arts de Lyon, so that I could consult the *discours* of Donat Nonnotte. Portions of the book have been read at many conferences over the years. Parts of the Introduction and Chapter 2 were published in the volume I co-edited with Amandine Gorse, Nathalie Manceau, and Nina Struckmeyer, *Artistes, savants et amateurs: art et sociabilité au XVIIIe siècle (1715–1815)* (Paris: Mare et Martin, 2016). Part of Chapter 4, on François-André Vincent's caricatures, was published in *Eighteenth-Century Studies* 52, no. 1 (Fall 2019).

Caroline Weaver's astute editorial eye helped get the original manuscript into presentable shape. I would like to thank Julia Oestreich, the director of the University of Delaware Press, Sarah Cohen, director of the Studies in Seventeenth- and Eighteenth-Century Art and Culture series, and the series editorial board for their support of this project; and my reviewers for their feedback. Finally, thank you to the team at Delaware and designer Robert Wiser for their hard work to bring it to fruition.

My most heartfelt thanks go to Christopher Leichtnam, who has been a dinner companion, conversation partner, translator, editor, and generous host over the years. Describing the friendship of the following people, formed over years and continents, would require a book in and of itself: Kate Anderson and Ross O'Connell, Catherine Clark and Brian Jacobson, Daniella Berman, Bonnie Blackwell and Rachel Gollay, Heather Burns and Ray Darmstadt, Amanda and Scott D'Aquila, Elisa Foster, Graeme Hind and Sara-Jayne Parsons, Katie Hornstein and Viktor Witkowski, Charles Kang, Becca Krecek, Sean Kramer, Jacob Lewis and Melissa Dean, Rachel and Tim Livedalen, Tyson Leuchter, Katy and Matthew Pennington, Carolyn Purnell, Kathryn Sederberg, Pam Stewart, Andrew Ross, Jessica Spuehler, Michael Yonan and Jim Quinn, and the folks at the Boiled Owl.

My cats, Colbert and Stewart, have provided adorable distraction and probably created some typos along the way. Last, but not least, thank you to my family: Nicolette, Heather, Connor, Ryan, Brooklyn, Tanner, Matthew, and the Fripps, Packingtons, and Dovetons in South Africa and the UK. I dedicate this book to my parents, Lyn and Raymond, living proof that "immigrants . . . get the job done." I would be nowhere without your love and support.

Author's Note

All translations are my own, unless otherwise noted.

References to Salon criticism in the Deloynes collection include the stable URL to the digitized version in the collection of the Bibliothèque nationale de France when available.

INTRODUCTION

DURING A VISIT to the 1765 Salon exhibition of the Royal Academy of Painting and Scupture, a Swedish man asked the critic Charles-Joseph Mathon de La Cour, "are all Royal Academies required to present their work to the public in the same manner as [the Royal Academy of Painting and Sculpture]?"[1] Mathon de La Cour reflected on this surprising question in his *Lettres à Monsieur *** sur les peintures, les sculptures, et les gravures, exposées au Sallon du Louvre en 1765*, considering at length the differences between the Academy of Painting and Sculpture and the Académie française.

He began his musings discussing competition for the highest positions in the Academy of Painting and Scupture, from the drawing *concours* (contests) of the young students to the attainment of the position of *recteur*, one of the highest offices in the institution's hierarchy, and explained the various steps an artist must take to attain them.[2] This arrangement, he maintained, was "wonderful for stimulating emulation."[3] Intriguingly, Mathon de la Cour compared this to the art of love: "It's like watching a clever coquette play the field with her lovers: by means of progress and skill, she inflames desires and pushes passions to their highest pitch."[4] He noted that such intense competition inspired intrigue and disputes in literary societies, but that among visual artists, "[i]n spite of this, nothing bothers their association. They are supportive of each other. They praise with pleasure the good works of their colleagues. Finally, they are friends, albeit rivals, rare advantage much more precious than all talents."[5] This was counterintuitive, the critic claimed, because although nothing prevents an author from penning a book, when an artist wins a commission, his competitors are left with idle hands.[6]

The critic considered this unusual aspect of Academic relationships at length. He concluded that the Academy's artists could remain "friends" in the face of continual competition because of their shared education and communal living arrangements. The "communal education and life" of the Academy made the artists a "single family," like the ancient Spartans. "Raised in the breast of the Academy," they studied under the same masters and under the same roof before going to Rome together. Upon returning to Paris, the close habitation continued; the artists lived and worked at the Louvre.[7] Mathon de la Cour concluded: "They see each other constantly and consult each other on their works, they relax together after work. Consequently, the men that dare to have gathered together come to love each other like brothers. If reasons of interest cause dissent among them, it is a cloud that dissipates in a moment, and friendship always triumphs."[8] For him, such close and continuous contact "mellow[ed] morals" of visual artists and allowed competition to bring them together rather than divide them. Community was for Mathon de la Cour a central feature of the Royal Academy.

In defining Academic life this way, Mathon de La Cour situated the relationships between the members of the Academy firmly within classical definitions of friendship drawn from Aristotle and Cicero. Friendship, according to Aristotle, required frequent contact and thrived when friends were in proximity to one another. Perfect friendship formed between men who were the same or similar in virtue. It was based on disinterested and reciprocal acts driven by love, specifically *philia*; in other words, affection, not desire. Because the principle of "sameness" in virtue and interests brought people together, friendship was thought to be a source of stability and thus had a civic and political dimension.[9] Furthermore, because of this civic dimension, ideal friendship was based on the virtues of reason and was thus perceived as possible only between men, something Mathon de La Cour highlighted in his claim that men of letters "hate each other like pretty women" ("Nos Auteurs se haïssent mutuellement comme les jolies femmes ...").[10]

Yet Mathon de la Cour's explanation of friendship in the Royal Academy was highly idealized. The critic painted in broad strokes the typical experience of an Academician. Not all artists were "raised from a young age at its breast," and even those who began their training with an Academician were not guaranteed a trip to Rome. Moreover, after their return to Paris, not all of them were given housing at the Louvre. And while the critic claimed that members rose through the ranks only when they earned it because of the competitive nature of artistic training, he conveniently ignored the fact that not all members could rise to the highest ranks, which were reserved for history painters.¹¹

Mathon de La Cour's idealization of friendship in the Royal Academy of Painting and Sculpture was not unique. The Academy, since its creation in 1648, consistently described the relationships between its members as based in amicability. In doing so, it made use of a classical understanding of friendship to promote itself as a smoothly run, politically stable, and productive body. There was, and still is, however, a large gap between the classical ideals lauded by philosophers and moralists, and the practice of friendship in everyday life.¹² This book traces how the rhetoric of friendship was invoked and materialized—in both the written word and visual art—by the Academy, critics, and artists, from the founding of the Royal Academy in 1648 until the 1789 Revolution, exploring artists' multifarious friendships in eighteenth-century France. It is the objective of this study to bring out the tension between the Academy's classical notion of friendship and artists' practice of friendship in their personal and professional lives, which often ran counter to idealized versions of amicability.

Enlightenment Friendship

From Michel de Montaigne's "De l'amitié" to Madame de Lambert's *Traité sur l'amitié*, to Jean-Jacques Rousseau's *Émile*, friendship was a hot topic during the Enlightenment. In the first edition of the *Dictionnaire de l'Académie française* of 1694, the word *ami*, or friend, was defined as "a mutual, reciprocal affection between two persons more or less equal," but it was used in a variety of contexts including, but not limited to, business relationships, kin, and in certain cases it could be used as a derogatory term when employed in interactions between two individuals of different social status.¹³ By the mid-eighteenth century, *encyclopédiste* the abbé Claude Yvon defined friendship in Denis Diderot's and Jean le Rond D'Alembert's *Encyclopédie* first and foremost as "nothing other than the practice of maintaining a decent and pleasant commerce with someone," situating friendship clearly within Enlightenment theories of sociability, an abstract concept that explained the desire humankind has to participate in a society based on the idea of reciprocal exchange.¹⁴

Little attention has been paid to the crucial role friendship played in artists' lives in eighteenth-century France.¹⁵ It is the goal of this study to address this lacuna. Scholarship on Enlightenment friendship in history and literature is abundant, focusing on textual sources such as epistolary correspondence, novels, and political and philosophical discourse in both the English and French contexts.[16] Scholars have considered friendship as both a historical and sociological relationship through questions about exchange, reciprocity, and gift-giving.[17] Their analyses of the written word and the circulation of physical objects have demonstrated that friendship operated simultaneously as fact and fiction, in both private and public life.[18]

Many of the existing studies have demonstrated that Enlightenment understandings of friendship were driven by broader changes in sociability and in the public sphere: growing secularism, the rise of merchant capitalism, and new sites of voluntary association—including coffeehouses, literary societies, and masonic lodges—that created increasing criticism of *ancien régime* hierarchies. Like many forms of eighteenth-century sociability, friendship was met with scrutiny in the decades leading up to the French Revolution.[19] New definitions of friendship were used to criticize both society and government, and, as Adam Sutcliffe argues, French *philosophes* in particular looked to Epicurean, skeptical, and materialist ideas to question the ideals that had dominated how men understood their relationships with other men since the classical era.[20] In 1789, *fraternité* began to replace *amitié*, but the easy slippage between friendship and family relationships remained. Jean-Paul Marat, for example, may have fashioned himself as the "Friend of the People" (*L'ami de peuple*), but his assassination made him one of the martyr-brothers celebrated by the Jacobins.[21]

For all the criticism of friendship in public life, amicability remained central to private life, and, as Naomi Tadmor and Emrys Jones have argued, it is difficult to fully understand the differences between friendship in public life and private life as they would have been experienced by individuals in the eighteenth century.[22] This is especially true when trying to consider what friendship between artists, both inside and outside of the Academy, meant to them and how it was enacted. Numerous artists' biographies and catalogues raisonnés mention the individuals with whom they interacted as their "friends" in passing, but what it might have meant for artists to be "friends" is rarely considered. Scholars of the history of collecting and patronage have examined the idea of friendship to fruitfully consider the role new conceptions of friendship played in the cultivation of patronage circles.[23] Charlotte Guichard, influenced by Pierre Bourdieu's theories of the unconsciously interested gift, has demonstrated that friendship was central to the rise of the *amateur*—a new type of patron-collector that developed in the eighteenth century—which disguised an interested, unequal patronage relationship as a disinterested, egalitarian one, and furthermore, she has shown that the word "friend" was employed consciously and purposefully.[24] Like Guichard, I am interested in the confluence of economic and social capital that was a product of adapting friendship to the new public role of sociability.

The point of this study is not to claim that certain artists were "true" friends while others were not. Instead, my starting point is how the rhetoric of friendship was employed in artists' professional and personal lives. I focus on three cornerstones of classical friendship—disinterestedness, equality, and masculine reason—to examine both the role of friendship and its rhetorics in artists' careers in the eighteenth century and how new conceptions of friendship were made evident in the creation, display, and circulation of portraits.

Portraiture is a particularly useful genre for analyzing relationships. Portraits serve, on one level, as documents of social interactions, helping us to reconstruct the milieus in which artists circulated; but these encounters, both friendly and professional, are only part of the story. As objects that moved fluidly between public and private spaces, portraits can teach us not only about their subjects but also about the social currency of their display and exchange. By situating portraiture within larger social practices of exchange—both in private and in the public venue of the Academy's exhibitions—I argue that artists and viewers were well-aware of its social value. The sheer number of extant portraits of artists, the wide variety of formats artists chose when depicting each other, and the way these objects circulated suggest that the significance of friendship was more complex than binary oppositions of interestedness and disinterestedness and of public versus private allow. It is the objective of this book to bring out that complexity.

Friendship and Portraiture

At the beginning of the eighteenth century, portraiture was awarded a relatively high and respected position in the hierarchy of genres. However, over the course of the century, the genre became increasingly derided as a symbol of selfishness, a sign of vanity in a sitter and a display of avarice in the artist.[25] The only exceptions were portraits of *grands hommes*, individuals whose actions could be an example to Salon viewers.[26] By the eve of the Revolution, a portrait's value was determined by the greatness of the artist and the importance of the sitter.[27]

Since the publication of Thomas Crow's *Painting and Public Life in Eighteenth-Century France* in 1985, art historians have taken an interest in the role of art in the public sphere, but that interest remains heavily biased toward history painting.²⁸ As Tony Halliday has noted, portraiture's seemingly private and particular interest was at odds with the newly public role of art described by Crow, which may explain why art historical scholarship on portraiture was long influenced by eighteenth-century biases.²⁹ The last thirty years have seen studies of French portraiture of the *ancien régime* with an eye toward the performance and representation of the self to others, focusing on issues as varied as political power, gender politics, and psychology.³⁰ These works have often taken the form of monographic studies of artists, focusing particularly on large-scale portraits commissioned by members of the court—in other words, the portraits that were the most publicly visible during the eighteenth century.³¹ More recent scholarship has examined the social and economic importance of portraiture.³² Hannah Williams, for example, has demonstrated the importance of portraiture to the Royal Academy: portraits made visible its history and hierarchy, and provided evidence of the various social bonds of family, friendship, and rivalry that made up the Academic body.³³

The present study considers a range of portrait formats—including small, drawn medallion portraits, pastels, oil portraits, caricatures, and ambitious group portraits—to be the primary documentary evidence of friendship, but with the understanding that the word "friend" was just as self-conscious a construction of social interactions in the eighteenth century as the portraits that supposedly represented them were. The creation, display, and exchange of friendship portraits under examination here implicated a diversity of artistic milieus, from those of celebrated artists working in minor genres, such as Maurice Quentin de La Tour and Charles-Nicolas Cochin, and of women artists such as Adélaïde Labille-Guiard and Élisabeth Vigée-Lebrun, to that of history painters such as François-André Vincent. I treat these artists as "hubs" of social networks because of the sheer number of portraits they produced that can be used to trace the social connections between individuals. However, it is not enough to map out social networks by describing who depicted whom. It is equally important to consider the role of these different but frequently intersecting networks in artists' careers and their effects on artistic production. I pair formal analyses of various portrait typologies with attention to the circumstances of specific portraits' creation, their subsequent circulation among artists, and between artists and patrons, and their display to a viewing public.

A major interest in this study is how easily these objects could move between public and private spaces. Not all of the works of art addressed in this book were intended, from their inception, to have a public life. Certainly, some of the portraits were destined for the Salon or other exhibition venues from the start. Other works moved from intimate viewing spaces—such as the homes of artists or patrons—to the walls of the Louvre's *salon carré* well after they were created. Finally, a number of portraits never circulated beyond the original group of men and women who were depicted in them.

The range of portrait formats, presented to different intended or unintended audiences, are the primary form of evidence of the multifarious relationships between artists that fell under the umbrella of "friendship." I analyze these paintings, pastels, and drawings alongside Academic lectures, Salon criticism, philosophical discussions and treatises, and, when available, personal correspondences and memoirs to uncover the role portraits played in friendship networks in the eighteenth century and the social value that those networks had for artists.

Chapter Descriptions

Chapter 1 analyzes the Royal Academy of Painting and Sculpture's construction of friendship, as defined in its official discourse. The Academy, as a royally sponsored institution for the production of visual art, touted the ideal friendship among its members to define itself as an elite and exclusive community. The changing social and political landscape of the eighteenth century challenged those ideals. This was most obvious in the Academy's discussion of criticism. Academic discourse framed criticism as something that was best given by artists who were also friends: men of equal talent who put the glory of the Academy before their own. Importantly, corrective advice was supposed to be given behind closed doors. By the eve of the Revolution, however, the language of friendship was co-opted by the authors of clandestine, published art criticism in response to the Academy's Salon exhibition. Critics claimed they were "friends" of artists to justify their harsh commentary about works of art and the institution of the Academy, aligning with Enlightenment thinkers' use of friendship to criticize both society and government. The chapters that follow call attention to the numerous ways that artists took advantage of the mutability of friendship to navigate the changing social world of the eighteenth century.

When the Royal Academy's public exhibition became a regular event in 1737, the friendships—between artists and between artists and patrons—that the Academy claimed were at the core of Academic sociability were made visible to the growing viewing public in the portraits displayed at the exhibition. These relationships could be, and were, celebrated or criticized, depending on the author or subject of a portrait, and on the type of friendship the portrait was thought to display. Chapter 2 considers portraits of artists and intellectuals that both circulated in the semiprivate sphere of Enlightenment society and were also exhibited to a wider audience in the Royal Academy's exhibitions. My choice of the word "semiprivate" owes a debt to Dena Goodman's work on complicating notions of public and private in the eighteenth century.[34] While Goodman's argument focuses on intellectual exchange, her acknowledgment of a liminal space between spheres is relevant to how works of art were viewed. Many of the portraits discussed in this book were displayed in the homes of individuals who opened their doors to a select audience, and also appeared in the Academy's exhibitions. A number of critics saw those works both in their domestic and public displays. In both venues, these portraits served the personal and professional gain of the artists who created them and the sitters who were represented. I examine how Charles-Nicolas Cochin and Maurice Quentin de La Tour used portraits for self-promotion at a moment when portraits were increasingly criticized as products of greed and vanity. These artists reoriented discussion of their works to center on social rather than economic capital through portraits that were created in the intellectual circles in which they participated. When we examine the display of these portraits and the criticism written about them within the context of Enlightenment debates about celebrity, disinterestedness, and friendship, we see that portraits were interpreted by critics to have been created out of friendship, and not for profit.

During the eighteenth century, there were major philosophical debates about the possibility of women experiencing friendship with men or other women.[35] Chapter 3 examines portraits by Adélaïde Labille-Guiard and Élisabeth Vigée-Lebrun in relation to their particular paths to acceptance into the Royal Academy of Painting and Sculpture. The combination of celebrity and friendship, discussed in Chapter 2, had a largely positive impact on male artists' careers. Labille-Guiard's and Vigée-Lebrun's attempts to reveal and display in public their famous friendships resulted in very different conversations about their portraits. The literature on the two women almost always discusses them in tandem and, furthermore, presents them as rivals. This imagined rivalry was framed around their unusual status as female Academicians. I posit that it was also deeply rooted in debates and anxieties about women's ability to experience friendship, particularly in the context of the supposedly homosocial community of the Royal Academy.

The last chapter shifts from portraits that were displayed at the Salon to focus on works destined for a more limited audience: caricatures and group portraits created by student-artists in Rome in the early 1770s. The importance of Rome in eighteenth-century artistic education cannot be overstated. The cosmopolitanism of the city drew male artists from all over Europe who worked and socialized together, and these men fostered lifelong ties and established career-changing patronage networks. Rome was a particularly homosocial city, and the intense bonds male foreign-born artists formed in this environment are apparent in the caricatures and painted portraits of François-André Vincent, his fellow student-artists, and other foreign artists in Rome. The caricatures these men produced were copied and circulated among their group and responded to their shared experiences. Shortly after leaving Rome, Vincent continued to explore themes of male friendship in his ambitious and enigmatic *Portrait de trois hommes*, a triple portrait of himself with two acquaintances from Rome. The triple portrait was an unusual format for a French painter, but its deeply rooted association with male bonding and traveling artists was employed by a number of men studying in their work abroad. Together, their caricatures and group portraits demonstrate how male intimacy fostered in private provided space for experimenting with the genre of portraiture.

The epilogue addresses the new challenges friendship and portraiture faced during the French Revolution. The Academy's biennial exhibition, previously limited exclusively to members of the Academy, was opened to all artists and quickly filled up with portraits. Many of them celebrated the heroes of the Revolution. The new emphasis on fraternity and public association in the early years of the Revolution led to distrust of private friendship networks, which were seen as self-serving remnants of the previous regime and possibly counterrevolutionary. The distrust of friendship was not solely the product of heady Revolutionary politics but also a continuation of new questions, concerns, and ideas about friendship that developed over the course of the eighteenth century.

Artists profited from as much as they were hindered by changing definitions of friendship in the eighteenth century. In the twenty-first century, social media allows us to display our social connections in an unprecedented manner. Our "friends" or followers on Facebook, Instagram, or Twitter can range from individuals we have known since childhood to a sheer massing of numbers that turns popularity into financial profit. The various understandings of "friendship" that social media takes advantage of illustrate the same malleability of friendship that Enlightenment thinking was trying to parse in the eighteenth century, within a new set of social and political conditions. Friendship was the guise that permitted a new form of art criticism to flourish while at the same time serving as the vehicle by which artists shored up personal and professional connections that advanced their careers. Artists clearly valued—and needed—friendship, but in the midst of debates that put a new emphasis on the individual, they found that "friendship," broadly defined, could also be at odds with a new understanding of human relationships driven by Revolutionary politics.

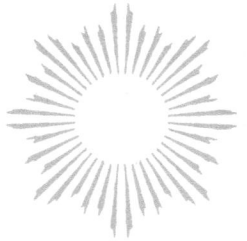

Chapter 1

FRIENDSHIP IN THE ACADEMY

THE 1648 STATUTES of the Royal Academy of Painting and Sculpture made it clear that the bonds between the members of the newly formed institution were a primary concern. The ninth statute declared: "There will be close and friendly relations among the members of the Academy, there being nothing so antithetical to virtue as envy, malicious gossip and discord. If any should be incline thereto, and should be unwilling to amend after reprimand by an Elder, he shall be excluded from the Academy."[1]

Versions of the same statement appeared in the revisions to the statutes in 1664 and 1777.[2] Along with the mandate that Academicians maintain positive relations, the words *ami* (friend) and *amitié* (friendship) appeared frequently in the *Procès verbaux*, or minutes, of the Royal Academy's meetings over the next 145 years. The diverse contexts in which friendship was employed reflect the many meanings it carried in early modern society. For example, in correspondences with foreign academies, the French Royal Academy referred to these institutions as "friends," demonstrating that the Academy was connected to the broader European community of art-making, and mirroring friendship as a display of loyalty across intellectual communities and the Republic of Letters.[3] As was the case for early modern academy members across France, the word *ami* appeared frequently in the eulogies for deceased Academicians, to highlight their moral qualities as a "good friend."[4]

The word *ami* was also used in the lectures on artistic theory that opened the *conférences*, monthly meetings for the Academy's members to discuss artistic questions.[5] These lectures give a view into the Academicians' ideas and theories about painting, which, as Christian Michel and Jacqueline

Lichtenstein point out, did not create the rigorous and strict system the nineteenth-century historiographers of the Academy passed on to art historians of the twentieth and twenty-first centuries. The lectures avoided defining what might be the "perfect" artist or "perfect" work of art in any strict homogeneous terms.[6] They did, however, offer examples of specific behaviors that would help artists attain an abstract idea of greatness.

Friendship was a theme that frequently arose in these lectures. In particular, those read by Antoine and Charles Coypel in the first half of the century made it clear that amity mattered to artistic creation just as much as a practical knowledge of color, space, and human expression did. The Coypels drew from the classical model of friendship described by Cicero and Aristotle, which emphasized virtue and claimed that friendship played an important role in both private and civic life.[7] Virtuous friendship in private naturally extended into the public realm, providing political stability.[8] Reliance on friendship was based in the belief in men's rational choices and ethical behavior, and, as such, it was a part of civic life, inspiring individuals to sacrifice their personal desires to the needs of the greater whole.[9] In contrast to love, friendship required sustained and controllable passions. By presenting the Academicians as virtuous friends in the model of Aristotle and Cicero, the Coypels promoted the stability of the Academy as a social body, justified its existence, and increased its social prestige.[10] But as much as the Academy tried to maintain ideal friendship as a central feature of the institution, the development of a politicized—and more inclusive—public sphere called friendship's role into question.[11]

The Academic ideal of friendship was most explicitly challenged by the clandestine criticism published in response to the Royal Academy's exhibitions held in the *salon carré* of the Louvre, which were regularized in 1737. As Thomas Crow has argued, the success of the Salon exhibition and the art criticism it spurred ushered in a larger debate about who exactly made up the art-viewing public, what its role in artistic production was, and importantly, who had the right to speak for that public.[12] Unofficial commentary on the Salon, particularly that which spoke disparagingly about the Academy and its artists' works, was always contested. The Academy argued that the often-anonymous critics were not speaking to the Salon audience's true desires. Despite the Academy's attempts to stop criticism through censorship and the seizure of published pamphlets, the criticism reached its height in the 1770s and 1780s. It was at precisely that moment that critics began to use friendship to justify their commentary.

This chapter focuses on three key moments, roughly dated to 1712, 1747, and 1779, to examine the relationship between friendship and criticism, as discussed by both the Academy and its critics. The *conférences* relied heavily on three traditional cornerstones of friendship—disinterestedness, sameness, and masculinity—in defining the role of friendship in criticism, framing it as a social exchange restricted to individuals who possessed the sufficient knowledge about art to comment on it. This served to define Academicians and *amateurs honoraires*, patrons who were given membership in the Academy, as artistic authorities and as members of an exclusive community.[13] Salon critics' appropriation of friendship challenged the Academy's authority by engaging with eighteenth-century questions about friendship, including discussions of virtue, *amour-propre* (self-love), gender, and friendship's place in public life.

Antoine Coypel's Épître à mon fils: *Criticism and Ideal Friendship*

On January 7, 1708, the history painter and future director of the Royal Academy Antoine Coypel read a poem dedicated to his son Charles at the Academy's general assembly. The poem, *Épître à mon fils, sur la peinture*, was published that same year.[14] On May 7, 1712, Coypel reread the poem at the Academy; according to the *procès verbaux*, the Academicians "unanimously begged Monsieur Coypel to continue the commentary that he started with the Letter in verse to his son, and wanted him to read it to the Company on meeting days."[15] Coypel complied, and over the next eight years he divided the poem's 186 lines into twenty-one lectures on various subjects, which were read at nineteen different *séances*, or meetings, of the Academy.[16] Coypel's poem and the subsequent lectures it inspired covered a range of topics, from formal and technical aspects of artistic practice (such as color, drapery, and proportion) to theoretical ideas that resonated with those discussed in the *conférences* read previously by the theorist and *amateur honoraire* Roger de Piles.[17]

Along with practical discussions of painting, Coypel also presented substantial discussions of what might be called the morals and behavior of painters. His first three lectures, on July 2, 1712, focused on the three parties involved in the lifespan of a work of art: the painter (*peintre*); those who advise the painter (*conseillers*); and the spectator-viewer for whom the work is destined (*spectateur*). The discussions of the *spectateur*, as Lichtenstein and Michel note, introduced for the first time the idea of not merely a viewing public, but a critical public.[18]

From the outset, Coypel's lectures suggested a close connection between friendship and criticism. The second one, "A Painter's Advisers" (*Les conseillers d'un peintre*), corresponded to the sixth verse of *Épître à mon fils*—"But listen my son, to a father who loves you" ("Mais écoutez mon fils, un père qui vous aime")—and focused on those who might help the painter to succeed, while also including discussions of "taste" (*goût*), who was qualified to judge works of art and how to do so, and bias (*prévention*).[19] All three concepts were intricately linked to friendship as it was understood by the Academy. In the poem, Coypel's ideas are framed as advice from a loving father to his son. The lecture that expands on the verse, however, clearly advises on friendship, not familial love. Slipping between friend and family would not have been counterintuitive in the early modern period, as kinship was often discussed using the language of friendship. From the medieval period through the eighteenth century, French law considered friendship synonymous with kinship; the phrase *parents et amis* referred to both relatives and friends in law codes. Catholic moralist literature similarly described parent-child relations in terms of friendship, not love.[20]

Coypel's choice to move away from the bonds of blood points to a second, evolving form of friendship. The period during which this group of lectures was delivered coincided with the increasing prominence of the role of honorary amateurs (*amateurs honoraires*), which Coypel was keen to cultivate in order to bolster the social status of the Academy.[21] The relationship between these patrons and Academic artists drew heavily on a language of friendship.[22] This was an extension of earlier, seventeenth-century descriptions of "friendship" that delineated the relationship between patrons and artists, and helped to put order to political and social life rather than portray intimate relationships between men.[23] As a number of scholars have noted, during the eighteenth century, artists and patrons began to socialize in unprecedented ways, which significantly altered traditional patron-artist friendships.[24]

Coypel's *conférences* were, however, equally concerned with friendship between artists, and his discussion provided a baseline for how Academic relationships would be framed throughout the century. He began by claiming that an artist would be most inspired by advice that came from a friend: "The advice that we are given by the people with whom we know friendship surely makes more of an impression on us than that of others. For much self-interest enters in the desire to give advice. How many people persuade themselves to deserve all the honor of a work on which they have given a favorable critique, from which the same author himself would profit!"[25] Coypel is intriguingly generic in his description of friendship in this quote; one must look for a person (*personne*) who knows friendship (*amitié*). While he avoids using the word friend (*ami*) directly, he clearly contrasts this type of individual with the unhelpful people who lack a principal element of friendship: disinterestedness.

People who offer advice outside of friendship should not be trusted, according to Coypel, because some of those individuals seek to profit from convincing others that a work has merit, or they enjoy the satisfaction of having others agree with them. A critic's self-serving actions are especially dangerous—ultimately, the critic has little to lose compared to the artist himself: "Happenstance gives them the liberty to always criticize, it is introduced in society for the connoisseurs and the sole arbiters of good taste alone. As such the decisions no longer cost them anything; they make them even without seeing what they criticize and without examining it; simpletons listen to them; ignorant people admire them and the appalled artists are always the victims."[26] Eventually, an abundance of advice, often offered out of self-interest, becomes so tiresome for an artist that he might not accept any advice at all.[27]

Such a scenario could be frustrating for the painter. Happily, Coypel offered one test to help an artist determine if he was receiving appropriate counsel: "How easy it is to distinguish what friendship advises from what vain pride decides! The true friend praises in public that which can be praised and criticizes in private what appears weak or defective. The vain and sumptuous man lauds face-to-face and becomes cold or a ruthless censor when surrounded."[28] In describing to whom precisely an artist should turn for advice, Coypel switched from the generic friendly "person" to the specific "true friend" (*véritable ami*). Importantly, he placed the true friend within a particular social context. Negative criticism was reserved for private settings (*en particulier*)—one envisions the studio—implying that an artist should seek advice when a work was still in process, and errors and infelicities could be corrected. Yet praise belonged in public, presumably when the work was finished and accessible to a larger audience. According to Coypel, artists could benefit from the criticisms of those who hated them ("de ceux qui nous haïssent"), but this required finding the truths buried in their bad advice, which was inspired by passion and jealousy. Ultimately, the best solution was to find "a faithful friend, fair critic, who points out to us sincerely the faults in our works, who knows how to enlighten us in our doubts and rekindles our ideas."[29]

In his description of an artist's advisers, Coypel drew on two qualities—virtue and disinterestedness—that had long been considered necessary components of friendship that defined how friendship functioned in private and in public. Coypel's first belief, that friendship is based in virtue, finds its origin in Aristotle, who claimed that perfect friendship requires two men who are similar or equal in virtue. Virtuous individuals sacrifice their personal desires to the needs of the greater whole, and ideal friendship pushes men to be more virtuous.³⁰ In the early modern period, the idea of virtue was employed to promote friendship as belonging to the realm of the elite, and, as Marisa Linton has argued, in the early decades of the eighteenth century, virtue was frequently used in the context of asserting authority. It bestowed on the nobility power and social prestige that was (theoretically) not based on birth or wealth alone.³¹

The Academy had several reasons to emphasize the virtue of its constituents. As Reed Benhamou has argued, the idea that Academicians were morally, socially, and artistically superior to their counterparts in the painters' guild, the Académie de Saint-Luc, was a key aspect of the Academy's self-description when it was founded in 1648. The Academy's statutes explicitly forbade medieval guild practices of initiation and participation in the commerce of art, and encouraged other "civilizing processes." The Academy continued throughout the eighteenth century to differentiate itself from, and eventually abolished, its rival.³² Emphasizing friendship also circumvented a number of issues within the Royal Academy that were caused by the inherent inequalities in the Academic structure. The claim that the Academicians were equal to each other in virtue, if not also in their talent or social status, deemphasized an internal hierarchy that was, in fact, constructed around seniority, medium, genre, and social status. This last point was most obvious in the case of artistic family dynasties such as the Coypels, the Silvestres, and the Vanloos, among others, and in the fact that children of Academicians were often given special privileges.³³

Finally, and most relevant here, virtue helped dictate the public and private behavior of artists. As mentioned above, Coypel saw the true friend as someone who offered criticism *en particulier*, while the vain man incapable of friendship did so in front of other people. The juxtaposition between public and private within the context of friendship finds reinforcement in lawyer, translator, and member of the Académie française Louis de Sacy's *Traité d'amitié*: "The advice that one gives in public can only have a bad effect. They irritate those who receive it. Rancor takes away trust and acquiescence: besides, shame compels him to apologize so as to not be taken over by the malignity of those who are present. Thus, one gains nothing from such an inappropriate opinion other than upsetting one's friend and often delighting his enemies."³⁴ Again, the issue of public and private in both Coypel's and de Sacy's constructions of useful advice finds its origins in classical ideas of friendship. For instance, Cicero, drawing heavily from Aristotle, wrote about his friendship with Scipio: "In it I found agreement on public questions; in it counsel in private business, and in it, too, a leisure of unalloyed delight."³⁵ A true friend maintained continuity between public and private behavior, while the false friend acted differently depending on the context.

The continuity that virtue-based friendship provided was a means to organize the Academy into a unified social body, one that guaranteed its artists would receive productive advice and united them in the common goal of working toward the greater good of French art. Similar beliefs about friendship structured a number of the other institutions of "voluntary association," to use Daniel Roche's term, of the eighteenth century, such as the Republic of Letters and masonic lodges.³⁶ As will be discussed below, friendship became increasingly important to the Royal Academy of Painting and Sculpture as a stabilizing force in the middle of the century, when rivalries spurred by the Academy's dependence on competition and emulation threatened its public reputation as a sociable institution.

Coypel's belief about classical friendship was that it should be disinterested. Generosity, moderation, and kindness in friendship were expected, and a good friend demonstrated their virtue by refusing to act merely in their own self-interest. Rather, their actions were motivated by the good they could do for their friend.³⁷ Some people, according to Coypel—namely "vain and sumptuous" men—offered criticism in a self-serving way, seeking to ride the coattails of artists: "How many people persuade themselves to deserve all the honor of a work on which they have given a favorable critique, from which the same author himself would profit!"³⁸

The idea of disinterestedness in friendship was, and still is, one of the most hotly debated aspects of amicability—particularly in the early modern period, when the language of friendship was used to mask decidedly interested relationships, such as patronage.³⁹ Coypel, however, framed the "interestedness" that prevented good criticism through eighteenth-century beliefs about *amour-propre*, which are worth considering at length. Simply translated, *amour-propre* is pride or self-love, and often had negative connotations related to egoism and selfishness. It played a central role in philosophers' discussions of the role of passion in social order, and as such, *amour-propre* was often discussed in relationship to, if not directly connected to, friendship.⁴⁰

The concept of *amour-propre* influenced the moralist François de La Rochefoucauld's generally pessimistic ideas of friendship being "nothing but an alliance, a reciprocal accommodation of interests."⁴¹ This negative view of friendship was greatly debated in the seventeenth and eighteenth centuries, and contrary to La Rochefoucauld's views, other moralists saw friendship as a force for moderation, virtue, and social order, and importantly, proposed it as a solution to *amour-propre*. For de Sacy, *amour-propre* was inherent to mankind, but it could be a force for either good when "cultivated and polished" (*cultivé et poli*) or bad when "raw and uncultivated" (*brute et inculte*). The former state allowed an individual to balance self-respect and consideration for others, while the latter caused one to be unjust and selfish.[42] Left unchecked, *amour-propre* was friendship's worst enemy.[43]

Coypel's references to *amour-propre* stayed in line with more positive philosophical discussions of it. Notably, the intersection between *amour-propre*, friendship, and criticism in his commentary suggests that friendship was a cure for *amour-propre*. Artists needed not only to watch out for *amour-propre* in others, but they also needed to watch out for it in themselves. In his discourse "The Idea of the Perfect Painter" ("L'idée du peintre parfait"), read on June 2, 1713, Coypel described *amour-propre* as a vice as detrimental to artistic greatness as any technical fault: "It is the flaw of *amour-propre* that usually stops the progress of our studies. As one always loves one's self too much, one is always easily flattered, and one is often satisfied with oneself when one is furthest from pleasing others."[44] Constructive criticism was key, according to Coypel, to avoid the faults that were brought on by excessive *amour-propre*. He recommended young artists avoid anything that might give them a sense of self-importance, explaining that in his own practice, he "worked to humble his self."[45] By claiming that listening to others tempered one's own sense of *amour-propre*, Coypel argued that the feedback of honest friends was necessary to cultivate artistic talent. This meant avoiding bad connoisseurs (*mauvais connoisseurs*) and ignorant zealots (*ignorants zélés*).[46] Instead, an artist should listen to those who have demonstrated a measured response to his work; paraphrasing Horace's *Ars poetica*, Coypel informed his audience that "flatterers are far more moved than sincere friends."[47]

Friendship, however, also had its pitfalls. In the "Critique of Bias" ("Critique de la prévention"), of August 6, 1712, Coypel warned of friendship's ability to inspire cabals:

It comes about without our perceiving the personal friendship we have for artists and the amour-propre *that one has for oneself, as many people, unable to distinguish themselves through their own talents, seek to stand out via the reputation of their friends. So, to flatter themselves, they embrace with enormous warmth the parts of those they love, seeking to destroy all that they believe might oppose their glory; even those who can share it become odious. And so cabals are formed. One confines oneself to the parterre, inserting admirers for friends, and critics against others, and audacious injustice usurps through domination the very place of reason.*[48]

Bias (*prévention*), in Coypel's view, was a social as well as an individual problem. In its best version, it was a desire to protect one's friends; in its worst, it served one's own self-interest. He demonstrated this point through a discussion of a series of famous cabals. Those who believed in the supposed supremacy of Michelangelo over all other painters, and a cardinal who treated Domenichino unjustly because he "supported other painters" instead of Domenichino are but two of his examples. Coypel also expressed fears that, in the context of Academic education, bias could corrupt students, as teachers could pass on their own prejudices.[49] The fear of cabals demonstrated a serious concern about friendship that would only grow over the course of the eighteenth century. The Academy would be forced to confront this growing suspicion of friendship as the institution became a more prominent part of public life in the 1730s and 1740s, under the directorship of Antoine Coypel's son, Charles Coypel.

Friendship in the Aftermath of the Concours *of 1727*

In November 1730, eighteen years after Antoine Coypel began reading his commentaries on the *Épitre à mon fils* to the Academy, the son to which the poem was dedicated read his own lecture, "Discourse on the Necessity of Receiving Advice" ("Discours sur la nécessité de recevoir des avis"). Charles Coypel continued many of the themes his father had addressed: friendship, advice, and cabals. The "Discours" came in the wake of the *concours* of 1727, a competition to encourage history painting that was organized by the *directeur des bâtiments* (the royal arts administrator), the duc d'Antin. Twelve artists participated. Each submitted a history painting on a subject of his choosing, and all were displayed publicly in the Louvre's Apollo gallery. In announcing the competition, the duc d'Antin explained that he would seek the opinions of both the Academy's members and the general public when deciding who should receive the prize.[50]

The *concours* had a long tradition in early modern academies, and the Royal Academy of Painting and Sculpture was no exception.[51] Unlike those of the Académie française and other literary academies in France, however, the Royal Academy's competitions were open only to members of the Academy, and most of them were for students engaged with the academic curriculum, for example, the competitions for the quarterly life-drawing prize, known as the Prix de quartier, and the Prix de Rome.[52] The 1727 *concours* was somewhat exceptional in that it was not a student competition, but instead was open only to full members of the Academy.

A number of scholars have paid rapt attention to what the competition signified for the relationship between public opinion and art, but internal politics—what Antoine Coypel referred to as *cabales*—resulted in a competition that rewarded politicking as much as merit.[53] Charles Coypel's discourse demonstrates that the rivalry between two of the Academy's rising stars, Jean-François de Troy and François Lemoyne, created a rift in the Academic body.[54] Lemoyne was the protégé of the duc d'Antin and, from the start, it was presumed that he would win the *concours*. By most accounts, the competition was meant to solidify Lemoyne's place as heir apparent to the Academy's highest accolades—*premier peintre du roi* (First Painter to the King) and director of the Academy—two positions often, but not always, held jointly.[55] The stacked deck did not deter the equally ambitious de Troy from launching his own campaign. Ultimately, the competition ended in a tie, and the prize was split between the two artists. The decision was not well received. De Troy refused to accept the prize in person, declaring that he was indisposed. He continued to demonstrate his dissatisfaction by irregularly attending the Academy's meetings, finally abandoning them altogether in 1737 when Lemoyne was finally named *premier peintre du roi*, and not reappearing until after Lemoyne's suicide in December of that year.[56]

Coypel's lecture suggests that the hostility over this prize spilled over to the larger Academic body.[57] While he did not specifically name Lemoyne and de Troy, he did talk at length about the type of unsociable behavior that they were demonstrating. The first part of the lecture was concerned with the difficulty of finding good, valid criticism, given the wide-ranging expertise—in such subjects as drawing color, costume, and composition—required to judge painting properly. As Jacqueline Lichtenstein has noted, Coypel claimed that, first and foremost, it should be friends who give advice; of these, he described several types that fell into different categories. The first category comprised "men of taste" (*gens de goût*), "men of letters" (*gens de lettres*), and "connoisseurs." The second category included other painters. Finally, in the last category, one could turn to both living and dead artists and look to their completed works for guidance.[58]

Criticizing the works of living artists, however, posed some serious problems. "Unfortunately," Coypel explained, "this is the most difficult for us; we find it difficult to admit that in our day there are people who possess in our art perfections that we have not been able to attain: we forgive the old masters, it seems they have expiated this offense by ceasing to live."[59] Coypel went on at length about why it was so difficult to criticize living artists, noting that it was far more common for an artist to criticize others for how they did something he himself did well than to praise someone else for skills he himself did not possess. Ultimately, pride (*orgeuil*) was to blame for artists' inability to criticize each other in a just manner: "Let's not fool ourselves: the pride which causes different emotions pierces even the discussions that seem to us the most modest. We praise others sometimes, but we don't talk about them long, if those who listen to us don't have the politeness to disagree with us."[60]

Coypel's concern about the difficulties of fair criticism within the Academy was not only about the problems that self-interest and pride created amongst the institution's members. Importantly, he simply did not think that such hard feelings between artists were necessary. He highlighted an example of competitive artists who did not engage in such petty behavior. Reverting back to the familial role of friendship, he described how Hyacinthe Rigaud, Nicolas de Largillière, and François de Troy were "united brothers" (*frères unis*) despite the rivalry between them:[61]

For a long time, it was hard for the public to understand that they could preserve these noble sentiments, all three eminent parties possessing the same talent; but having never rushed to the one without hearing him praise the productions of others, this formidable public, whose suggestions are almost always divided, was compelled to unite them in their favor, and to admit that all three were equally revered by a high-minded way of thinking, that they were admired by excellence of their brush.[62]

The three artists were excellent models because they displayed their virtue publicly by praising each other, and demonstrated that they were capable of moving beyond competition and rivalry for the greater good of the Academy. This, in turn, raised the public's esteem not only of their works, but also of them as sociable people, and of the friendly "brotherhood" of the Academy more broadly, as well. By bringing the idea of public opinion into his commentary on Academic rivalries, Coypel demonstrated that he was not only concerned by the tensions between Academicians but also well aware of how infighting spilled beyond Academy walls. Unseemly behavior among Academicians could cause the public to turn against artists, so Academicians had much to gain from demonstrating that they were friends.

"Friendly" Advice Goes Public

Perhaps one of the most interesting aspects of Charles Coypel's discourse on advice is the frequency with which it was repeated. The text of his *conférence* was published in 1732, under the title *Discours sur la peinture*.[63] Coypel then reread it in front of the Academy two more times: in 1744, with some corrections and additions, and again in 1747.⁶⁴ The latter reading of Coypel's discourse followed a substantial rewrite, including a new conclusion to the work that served as a defense of the Salon exhibition, and referenced the upcoming *concours* of 1747 that had been announced by the new *surintendant des bâtiments* Lenormant de Tournement and the recent decision to increase the price paid by the crown for history paintings.⁶⁵ As Coypel explicitly stated in the final sentences of his *conférence*, these actions were part of a larger program to return French art to the glory it held at the time of the Grand Colbert.⁶⁶

Between 1730 and 1747, much had changed with regard to the advice artists were receiving. Coypel's decision to repeat his lecture in 1747 followed the publication of Étienne La Font de Saint-Yenne's seminal *Réflexions sur quelques causes de l'état présent de la peinture en France*, written in response to the Salon of 1746.⁶⁷ If both the Coypels championed the amicable relationships between artists as a cornerstone of criticism and of Academic sociability as a whole, La Font saw those close relationships as a hindrance to the progress of art. Most pertinent, he challenged the Academy's dependence on friendship in the artistic process by calling into question the possibility of disinterestedness. For both Coypels, the supposed disinterestedness that friendship provided was what guaranteed a good critique. While interested outside parties might turn to criticism for their own personal gain, the expected friendship between the artists and amateurs of the Academy meant that they could depend on each other for generous, rather than self-serving, advice. Disinterestedness meant that the artist-critic or amateur-critic was not looking for fame or profit, but rather sought to help Academicians attain greatness in their practice by uniting them in a common goal linked to the perfection and promotion of French art. Simultaneously, it tamed the *amour-propre* that threatened not only the Academy's sociability but also its members' own practice.

La Font claimed, quite to the contrary, that artists were not the best judges of each other's works precisely because they were too close to their *métier*, or profession. The investment in their friendships and in their profession made them incapable of impartiality. While in the *Refléxions* he hinted at the problem, suggesting that critics should have "no personal interest" ("*aucun intérêt personnel*") in the arts, he was more emphatic in the follow-up letter to his work: "It is only in the mouths of those firm and equitable men who make up the Public, and who do not relate to the Authors, either by blood, friendship, or profession, that we can find the language of truth."⁶⁸ As Lichtenstein notes, this comment has a "republican accent" in its description of an egalitarian public that is truly disinterested, and foreshadows the politically oriented criticism of the 1780s, which will be discussed below.[69] It is also suggestive of a growing distrust in the eighteenth century of friendship as aristocratic, with its links to patronage and favoritism.[70]

La Font was not the only one who questioned whether friendship could corrupt criticism. The abbé Leblanc's 1747 pamphlet *Lettre sur l'exposition des ouvrages de peinture, sculpture etc.... à Monsieur R. D. R.* talks at length about the eleven portraits Maurice Quentin de La Tour displayed that year, which included a portrait of Leblanc.[71] The fact that a portrait of Leblanc himself was included in the works he praised so highly did not go unnoticed. A copy of the pamphlet in the Deloynes Collection includes a handwritten note by Pierre-Jean Mariette, which informs us that "some evil tongues have dared to propose that this work was made for M. de La Tour and that he paid for it with the portrait of M. l'abbé Le Blanc: others have said that if this was the case, they found it badly paid for."[72] Similarly, in 1759, the anonymous author of the *Lettre critique à un ami sur les ouvrages de MM de l'Académie exposés au Sallon du Louvre* claimed that Joseph-Marie Vien's friendship with critics was the reason his works received positive reviews.[73] The suggestion that a critic could be "bought" for a portrait, or that friendship with a critic was enough to garner that critic's praise, called into question the whole practice of criticism and raised serious misgivings about the misuse of amity.

La Font and other critics' claims that a proper judge of art could not have any connection with the art world—that he should be completely disinterested—was a long-running theme in eighteenth-century art criticism, as Richard Wrigley has noted. On one side, critics thought positive criticism was rooted in cronyism; on the other, the Academy and its supporters accused critics of betraying their principles.[74] If criticism had been conceived by Antoine Coypel as a private exchange between artists and educated amateurs, and was linked to Academic sociability, then La Font's publication, and others like it, decisively moved criticism from the private realm of the studio into the public sphere, open to anyone who had something to say about the works on display at the Salon exhibition. This shift corresponded with art historians' analyses of the debate about criticism, during which the Academy drew upon its own network of approved critics—amateurs and connoisseurs who were part of the sociable communities in which artists participated—and a politicization of Salon criticism that commented on the broader institutions of the *ancien régime*.[75]

Taste, Criticism, and Friendship

Considering the central role that friendship played in the Academy's construction of criticism, it is curious that scant attention has been paid to the way it was similarly employed in published Salon criticism. The appearance of the word "friend" in published critical pamphlets was not entirely new. Given the epistolary form that criticism often took, such pamphlets were often published under some variation of the title of "a letter to a friend." The increasing use of "friend" in these publications was in line with similar trends in French literature at the time. According to the Project for American and French Research on the Treasury of the French Language ARTFL-FRANTEXT database, the use of the word *ami* doubled over the course of the eighteenth century (Table 1.1). The increased frequency with which that word appeared was largely due to the proliferation of epistolary novels, as 96 percent of the eighteenth-century novels in the database contain the word *ami*, while only 31 percent of the novels from the seventeenth century do (Table 1.2).

By the end of the 1770s, Salon pamphlets began not only to use the word "friend" in the form of letters, but also to use it to justify or call into question public criticism. *Le visionnaire, ou Lettres sur les Ouvrages exposés au Sallon*, written by "a friend of the arts" ("*un Ami des Arts*"), published in response to the Salon of 1779, is structured (like many pamphlets) as letters to the author's friend, in which the author describes an accidental and fantastic visit to the galleries of the Louvre.[76] Walking through the Jardin de l'Infante,

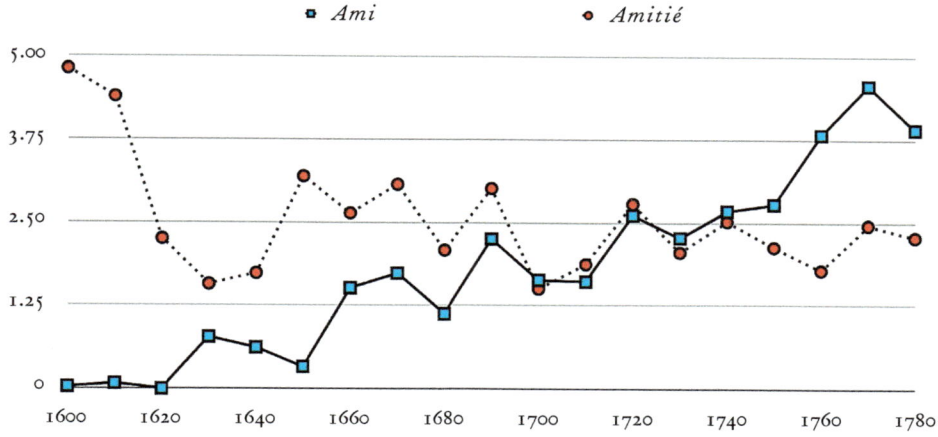

Table 1.1. Frequency per 10,000 words of *ami* and *amitié*, 1600–1789.

he finds his curiosity piqued at the sight of men carrying paintings. Upon entering the exhibition, he laments that he is not knowledgeable enough to understand the strengths and weaknesses of the works he sees, and instead begins to listen to the conversations of the people around him.[77] He encounters two beautiful and fashionably dressed young people, who reveal themselves to be the God of Taste and his sister, the Goddess of Criticism.

The two deities offer to guide him through the Salon, explaining that they will be visible only to him. This does not surprise him, and he comments to Criticism, "You are very much feared there."[78] Criticism, for her part,

··· 1600–1699 ···

GENRE	NUMBER OF WORKS	*Ami*	PERCENTAGE	*Amitié*	PERCENTAGE
Correspondence	33	13	39%	24	73%
Published Speeches	22	6	27%	10	45%
Literary Mélanges	11	7	64%	8	73%
Memoires	8	8	100%	8	100%
Poetry	67	20	30%	50	75%
Novels	41	13	32%	36	88%
Theater	118	70	60%	98	83%
Treatises and Essays	69	33	48%	50	72%

··· 1700–1789 ···

GENRE	NUMBER OF WORKS	*Ami*	PERCENTAGE	*Amitié*	PERCENTAGE
Correspondence	16	15	94%	16	100%
Published Speeches	5	2	40%	3	60%
Literary Mélanges	35	31	89%	24	69%
Memoires	11	11	100%	10	91%
Poetry	37	26	70%	19	51%
Novel	127	122	96%	118	93%
Theater	108	99	92%	88	81%
Treatises and Essays	112	84	75%	74	66%

Table 1.2. Occurrences of *ami* and *amitié* in works by genre, 1600–1789.

understands that she may be seen as a persona non grata to artists, but explains to the narrator that that is not exactly the case. Rather, she knows many artists who do not fear her, and look to her for advice. Her bad reputation, she claims, comes from the fact that there is another goddess, Satire, who dresses up as Criticism and dishes out cruel and unjust commentary.[79] The god's and goddess's invisibility creates the opportunity for a private conversation in the very public venue of the Salon. It is, of course, ironic that the author ultimately makes the conversation public by publishing it in the form of a letter to a friend.

Throughout the pamphlet, the discussion between Taste and Criticism is framed by the deities' personal relationships with the creators of the works they are viewing. The first work they encounter, Augustin Pajou's portrait of Jacques Bénigne Bossuet, a sculpture commissioned for the duc d'Angiviller's *Grands hommes* project, is praised by Taste, who claims that the sculptor is one of his favorites. Criticism responds with the backhanded compliment, "He is very much my friend as well ... I join you with all my heart in the praise you give him."[80] Criticism is far harsher in her judgments than her counterpart Taste is, and she increasingly forces him on the defensive. In response to her comments on Clodion's plaster model for his portrait of Montesquieu—another contribution to the *Grands hommes*—he reminds her, "My sister ... this artist has merit, you should not discourage him with your severity."[81] Criticism justifies her response by declaring that, because this is a preparatory work, there is still time to offer "useful observations."[82] Up to this point, the pamphlet does not stray too far from Antoine Coypel's idea that criticism was best offered when a work was still in progress.

As the trio continues to wander the Salon, the combination of friendship and criticism becomes increasingly complicated. Criticism prefaces her comments by acknowledging that Taste is personally invested in the artists, implying that he will take issue with the commentary she is about to give. Regarding Louis Jean-Jacques Durameau's works, she notes, "I know how much you like him," before commenting on the inaccuracy of the clothing worn by the figures.[83] In the same discussion, she insists that one must criticize one's friends as much as anyone else: "You are hurt, my brother ... but rest assured that I am just as much his friend as you are: truthfully, I am more difficult with regard to my friends than I am on others; this is why I continue."[84] Criticism's comments bring to mind the overlap between friendship and critique that was outlined earlier in the century, recalling Coypel's claim that an artist needs "a faithful friend, fair critic, who points out to us sincerely the faults in our works, who knows how to enlighten us in our doubts and rekindles our ideas."[85]

It becomes clear in *Le visionnaire* that Criticism is not, in fact, compatible with friendship, and the pamphlet simultaneously highlights Taste's place—and his amicability—within aristocratic communities. As Charlotte Guichard notes, in the eighteenth century, taste had a discernible social function.[86] The language of taste served to frame social relationships and functioned as a social bond for societies. To quote Guichard: "The language of taste relied on an ideal of communication and socialization of one's likings: 'Everyone' here does not refer to the general public, but to small societies, structured by interpersonal relationships, civility, and forms of sociability, within which artistic and erudite judgments could be exchanged and discussed."[87] As she notes, the rise in prominence of amateurs during the period was due in no small part to their integration within the Academic community, and other opportunities they were given for socializing with artists. Thus, it is unsurprising that Taste's positive comments are consistently prefaced by his own personal experience with the artists, even going as far as to claim he was a witness to one of the works' creation.[88] Taste's insistence that he knows the artists is clearly in line with the important role sociability played in the development of taste.

At the end of his rope, Taste throws himself into the arms of the narrator, complaining, "You see how she treats one of my best friends."[89] The intrepid narrator responds: "Women are cruelly demanding ... but we often do well in following their advice."[90] The claim that women are demanding—yet often give good advice—has the effect of gendering taste, criticism, and friendship in a particularly forceful way. It might seem logical that the masculine word *goût* would be personified in the form of a man. Criticism's gender, on the other hand, is more problematic. The 1762 edition of the *Dictionnaire de l'Académie française* does not assign a unifying gender to the noun *critique*. In its masculine form, *le critique* is "Someone who examines works of the mind, to judge them, explain them, elucidate them, etc. It signifies as well a critic, someone who manages to repeat everything to everyone."[91] When employed as a feminine noun, however, *la critique* does not denote the person who criticizes, but rather the ability or skill to criticize: "Criticism, feminine. The art, the ability (*faculté*) to judge an artwork."[92] In the context of *Le visionnaire*, the goddess is not a critic; she is the practice of criticism itself, and she personifies the worst aspect of it, "malicious censorship" (*une censure maligne*).[93]

Paradoxically, the Goddess of Criticism lacks the *faculté* to judge works of art in the same manner as Taste does because she fixates on problematic details of the works under discussion. In discussing François-Guillaume Ménageot's

La justification de Suzanne, for example, Taste praises the painting's "great effect," while Criticism demands they discuss the issues with its perspective.[94] Criticism's attention to detail and neglect of the whole would have been seen, in the eighteenth century, as characteristic of women's judgment, as Jennifer Jones has addressed in her work on women and fashion. She quotes Boudier de Villemert, who edited the fashion journal the *Courrier de la mode ou journal du goût*: "Women's imaginations continually nourish themselves on the details of jewels, clothing, etc.; these so fill up their heads with colors that there does not remain any attention for objects which might merit it more.... The mind of the woman glides over essential qualities and only attaches itself to the drapery."[95] The "essential qualities" of fashion evoked here correspond to the qualities that true connoisseurs—those who, presumably, had taste—would focus on when looking at a painting. This is apparent in Taste's use of specific language as he discusses the effect of a work's composition or the overall impact of color, and comments on artists' *facilité* (facility) or the *chaleur* (passion) of execution—language, as Mary Sheriff has noted, that was commonly used by those considered true connoisseurs to describe an artist's genius.[96] Women were viewed as incapable of seeing the genius in a painting because they fixated on detail, and this is clearly the problem that plagues the Goddess of Criticism. She gets caught up in the proportion of a thigh, the whiteness of drapery, the particular shape of a head; in short, she does not speak the language of Taste.

Criticism is particularly dangerous in *Le visionnaire* because, by countering Taste's opinions, she is interfering with the naïve narrator's education. Moreover, Criticism's bad influence correlates to broader ideas about women's effect on men's taste. Jean-Jacques Rousseau, among others, blamed women, particularly the Parisian *salonnières*, for having a negative effect on creative men. In the *Discourses on the Sciences and the Arts*, he claimed:

Every artist wants to be applauded. The praises of his contemporaries are the most precious part of his reward. What then will he do to obtain praise if he has the misfortune to be born among a people and a time when learned men, having become fashionable, have placed a frivolous youth in a position to set the tone; when men have sacrificed their taste to the tyrants of their liberty; when because one of the sexes dares approve only what is a match for the other's pusillanimity, masterpieces of dramatic poetry are dropped and harmonic prodigies rejected?[97]

These lady "tyrants" pushed men into making things that would garner immediate praise, rather than encouraging them to create lasting works of genius.

Women similarly distracted painters and sculptors from making great works of art in favor of luxury goods:

Carle, Pierre; the moment has come when that brush destined to enhance the majesty of our temples with sublime and saintly images will either fall from your hands or be prostituted to embellish carriage panels with lascivious pictures. And you, rival of the likes of Praxiteles and Phidias, you whose chisel the ancients would have employed to make the gods capable of excusing their idolatry in our eyes; inimitable Pigalle, either your hand will be determined to rough out the belly of a grotesque or it will have to remain idle.[98]

Rousseau's ideas about women's judgment were taken up by other Salon critics. The author of the 1782 pamphlet *Sur la peinture* addressed women's poorly formulated judgment, citing Rousseau's comment in the *Lettre à M. D'Alembert* that women "in general love no art, know nothing and have no genius."[99]

Le visionnaire frames the debate about masculine taste and feminine criticism around how well both the god and goddess know the artists, around the fact that they are all "friends," thereby raising another long-debated question about friendship: whether it is indeed possible for men and women to be friends. As we have seen, ideal friendship had long been considered a masculine endeavor, which will be addressed further in Chapter 3. Criticism's consistent willingness to betray artists, despite her claims that she is their "friend," demonstrates a certain fickleness that would seem to illustrate women's inability to participate in true friendship.

Le visionnaire's second letter demonstrates that the male narrator does, in the end, learn the language of Taste. He praises works in ways that parrot Taste's descriptions. Criticism, however, continues to disagree with both men's assessments by nitpicking the details. Intriguingly, the second letter includes a moment in which Criticism encounters a work by the only woman artist exhibiting at the Salon, Anne Vallayer-Coster. The narrator notes:

We saw with the greatest satisfaction several pictures by Mademoiselle Vallayer. They are painted with truth, with taste and with ease. Criticism could not conceal from us how much she was flattered to see in this Salon the works of a person of her sex. She agreed with the usefulness of encouraging those who have enough virtue to sacrifice the pleasures that are offered from everywhere in their young age with this honor, to those that engage in the hard work required by the study of such difficult arts. She expressed the greatest displeasure at not seeing any companions in this place, and yet, she added, many others are worthy: and if I count correctly, there are only three that I could cite.... She stopped, and I did not ask her to explain herself more clearly, for she seemed to say no more.[100]

Criticism's unhappiness about the lack of women exhibited, and her ability to cite only three other women artists, is a reference to Jean-Baptiste Marie Pierre's decision, in 1770, to limit the number of female Academicians to four.[101] Criticism's comment that there were other women who were capable of exhibiting at the Salon, but were not permitted to do so due to their gender, highlights that the cultural communities that the God of Taste personifies, and that the Coypels trusted, were—at least in theory—homosocial networks. The Academy's antagonism toward women artists has been discussed by scholars at length, but the institution was also inconsistent in its application of rules regarding women members. Furthermore, women artists had always been part of the Academy's social networks, as a number of Academicians' wives, daughters, and sisters were practicing artists in their own right, even if they never were accepted into the Academy.[102] Undoubtedly, they participated in the type of private, friendly conversations that the Coypels believed generated good criticism. In short, women would have been part of the private, "friendly" circles of criticism that the Academy had long championed.

The gendering of friendship, and of academic and taste communities, is worth further consideration. *Le visionnaire*'s narrator, in the first letter, claimed that women were "cruelly demanding," yet he followed his negative remark with the caveat that men "might do well to follow their [women's] advice."[103] This comment raises the question of under what circumstances a man should follow a woman's advice. As much as Rousseau blamed women's love of fashion and luxury for corrupting men's taste, he also believed that women had an innate, natural taste that was trustworthy as long as it had not been corrupted by society.[104] In the dedication to the *Discourse on Inequality*, he praised the virtues of the women of Geneva: "What barbarous man could resist the voice of honor and reason in the mouth of a gentle wife."[105] Unlike Parisian women, they rejected luxury for a "simple and modest dress," and exercised their power "solely within the marriage bond."[106] Rousseau situated feminine reason squarely within the realm of the domestic.

In *Le visionnaire*, the Goddess of Criticism operates in the public realm, clearly overstepping the boundaries of femininity circumscribing women to the private sphere. In this way, she personifies the type of criticism the Academy, and its network of amateurs, was fighting against, by individuals outside of established taste circles, who were perceived as being antagonistic to artists. This is apparent in the final words of advice that the God of Taste passes on to the narrator:

Beware of concluding from what you have heard, the works about which Criticism has developed her feelings are nevertheless worthy of esteem, otherwise she would not have focused upon them; thus, do not diminish the consideration you owe to the artists who produced them. Painting is an extremely difficult art; it embraces a great quantity of parts, which would be necessary to unite in order to escape Criticism. Therefore, she must not aim to depress the artist but to warn him.[107]

Taste returns to the Coypels' and others' claims about the difficulty of painting that an artist must find an adviser, or multiple advisers, to help navigate the various components that make a painting truly great. The Goddess of Criticism's failure—like that of all Salon criticism—is that she moved that collaboration from behind closed doors to out in the open, from the private to the public realm.

The problematic relationship between friendship and criticism raised in *Le visionnaire* only became more complex over the course of the 1780s, and "friendly" critics often attacked the taste communities that the God of Taste personified. For instance, the anonymously authored *Le pourquoi ou l'ami des artistes*, published in 1781, begins with a discussion of the various merits and failings of criticism. Before going on to review the quality of several critical pamphlets, the author discusses the characteristics and qualifications of a fair critic; the conclusions are not particularly promising. For example, amateurs and older artists are disqualified, because they are too close, too personally invested in the process: "The amateur who, because he pays for paintings (whose value he most often does not grasp), believes he has a right to judge artists.... There will still be one or two old artists who, because they respect those who have likewise spent their whole lives in the Arts, focus their anger on their young associates, whom they think they are teaching, and do so with such confidence in their own brilliance that they seem to say: Imitate me."[108] While in theory, men who had studied and practiced art would be the best judges of finished works, this pessimistic author points out that artists who have been rejected by the Academy might use criticism as vengeance, and those who have been admitted might be cruel to artists they see as rivals.[109] He also questions if a young artist can judge the works of the master who trained him.

Finally, he concludes that it is not up to him to judge criticism good or bad, stating, "[I] leave it to the artists to whom I submit my observations, to judge if the Critics are more useful than dangerous,"¹¹⁰ and circles back to the long-standing problem of economic interest in Salon criticism: "How many of these writings owe their existence to the author's need for money! So, they are amusing, pleasant; sacrifice reason and justice to a funny quip, or even make a cold critique, which will only be read by the artists interested in them."¹¹¹ With this final statement, this author claims that criticism can never be truly disinterested. Amateurs want their paintings to be valuable. Artists, young or old, are too jealous of each other to comment on each other's work objectively. Critics outside of networks of production are in it for profit. Artists cannot possibly have a friend to trust.

Satirical appropriations of "friendship" to justify criticism rooted themselves in older, more familiar uses of the term. The author of 1783's *Messieurs, ami de tous le monde* writes in the introduction:

*The epigraph that I have chosen conveys all my feelings. Friends of the arts, I come neither to destroy you, nor with a perfidiously malignant hand to give mortal wounds. Nor do I come, with cowardly complaisance, to palliate defects or erect them into beauties. Excess is above all a flaw. But as a true friend, in praising virtue, rails without weakness against the vices of his friends, even when praising the numerous beauties in the Salon, I will be ruthless towards the defective products that appear next to masterpieces of genius.*¹¹²

This particular author comes back to classical ideals of friendship, in which true friendship corrects bad or unvirtuous behavior.¹¹³ Yet, at the same time, he takes the aspects of friendship lauded by the Coypels that, in private, were a force that helped stabilize the Academy in the face of competition, and pushes them into the public realm. His claim that he will be "ruthless" in his criticism of bad works that appear next to great ones flies in the face of the Coypels' assertion that negative criticism should be shared only behind closed doors. The injustice of using friendship as a defense of harsh criticism was noted by the author of *L'impartialité au Sallon*, who criticized this pamphlet: "This new Jupiter then promises to thunder without weakness on the vices of his friends, and he sticks to his word. His badly aimed lightning almost always strikes indiscriminately."¹¹⁴

Whether satirizing friendship or drawing on its classical ideals to defend their comments, critics in the 1770s and 1780s were influenced by conflicted and even contradictory notions of friendship. The Academy's reliance on the private nature of friendship to promote the stability of the institution and defend its authority was called into question by critics who claimed that friendship promoted favoritism and impeded artistic progress. If French art was to thrive, then the private discussions fostered by friendship had to be made public. The conflict over friendship's role in private and public life was spurred by the increasingly public role of art created by the Salon. The next two chapters demonstrate how artists engaged with the public/private binary created by this debate through displaying portraits of fellow artists and patrons. The motivations behind these displays were often at odds with the Academy's reliance on ideal friendship, particularly in regard to self-promotion, disinterestedness, and its supposedly homosocial nature. These portraits, and the friendships they were interpreted to represent, were met with varying degrees of approval.

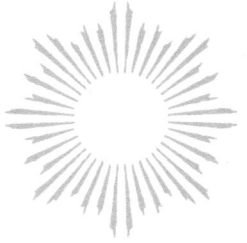

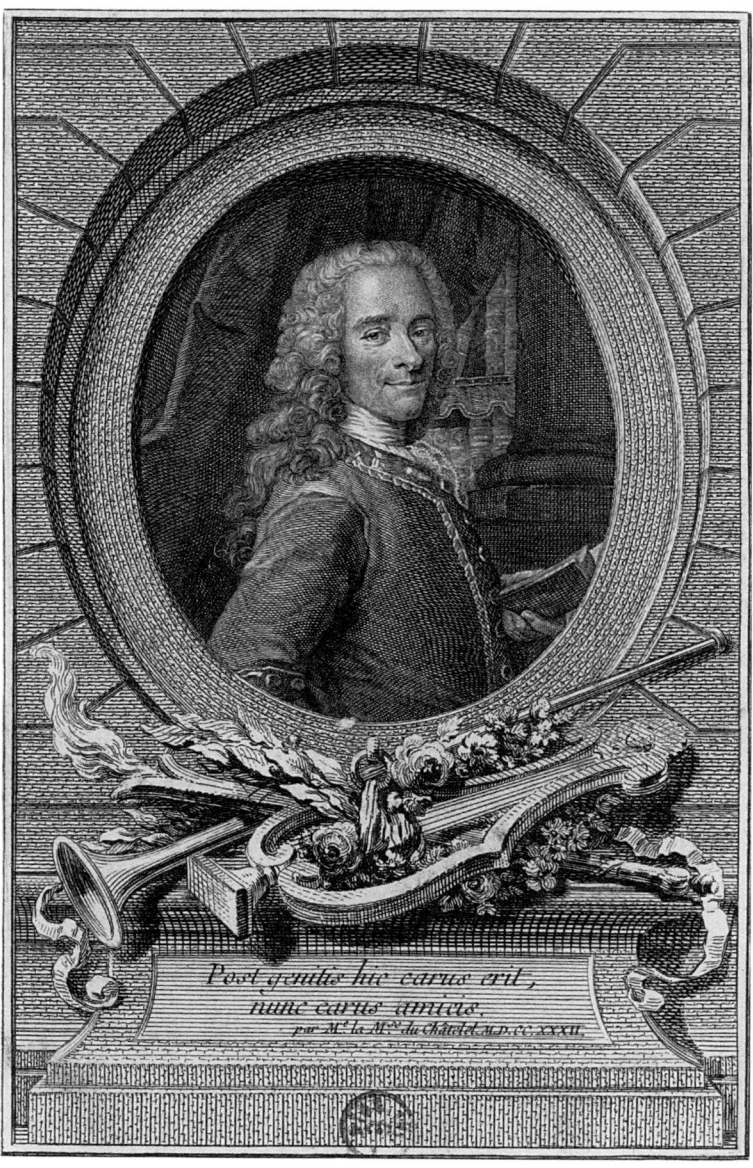

Fig. 2.1. Étienne Ficquet after Maurice Quentin de La Tour, *Voltaire à 41 ans*. 1762.

Chapter 2

CELEBRATING CELEBRITY

La Tour and Cochin at the Salon of 1753

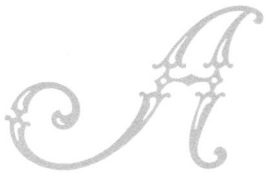S AN INSTITUTION, the Royal Academy of Painting and Sculpture struggled with the shift of friendship from a private to a public affair over the course of the eighteenth century. Individual artists, however, found that they had a lot to gain by publicizing relationships that could be construed as friendships in the public venue of the Salon through displaying portraits. The works exhibited by the pastellist Maurice Quentin de La Tour and the engraver Charles-Nicolas Cochin at the Salon of 1753 give insight into the use-value of the social practice of portraiture. While these portraits had currency in the personal lives of both La Tour and Cochin, representing the artistic and intellectual networks in which they participated, both men cleverly used them to depict their extra-Academic social lives to gain public recognition.

Born to a family of engravers in 1715, Charles-Nicolas Cochin *fils* was an ever-present figure in both Academic and intellectual life in eighteenth-century Paris.[1] At various points in his career, he worked for the *Menu plaisirs du roi*, which organized royal ceremonies and festivals, was in charge of the Crown's drawing collection as *garde des dessins du Roi*, served as the permanent secretary of the Royal Academy, and was an arts administrator. He was a prolific writer, penning obituaries, art theory, and art criticism. He also illustrated the frontispiece to Denis Diderot and Jean le Rond d'Alembert's *Encyclopédie* and participated in numerous salon circles, such as that of Marie-Thérèse Geoffrin. As Christian Michel has argued, Cochin connected himself to an "academic clan" that worked in the so-called "minor" genres and media—pastel, engraving, still life, portraiture, and the larger, poorly defined category of genre painting.² Although these artists had achieved a certain level of renown within the art world, they were restricted from attaining the highest offices of the Royal Academy, which were reserved for history painters.³

La Tour, born in 1704, was also a member of this group. One of few artists accepted into the Royal Academy who worked exclusively in the medium of pastel, he took advantage of the popularity and legitimacy of the practice, which was cultivated by the visit of the Italian painter Rosalba Carriera to Paris in 1720–21.⁴ La Tour rode the vogue for having one's portrait painted in pastel, and paired the fashionable new medium with depictions of famous faces. He launched his career with a portrait of Voltaire painted in the spring of 1735.⁵ Although the original was not exhibited publicly, the engraving of the portrait generated a demand for the artist's services (Fig. 2.1). Over the course of his career, La Tour earned recognition by attaching his name to figures that were already well known to the public, displaying portraits of other artists as well as of prominent or up-and-coming intellectuals and musicians. Like Cochin, he met many of these individuals by attending salon gatherings, including those held by Madame Geoffrin and Alexandre-Jean-Joseph Le Riche de la Pouplinière.

While both artists consistently promoted their involvement in important intellectual networks over the course of their careers, the Salon of 1753 particularly stands out in the sheer number of portraits that these men presented to the public. The Salon of 1753 represented a boom year for portraits of all kinds: paintings, sculpted busts, and engraved and drawn portraits made up 39 percent of all the exhibited works, the highest percentage of such works displayed at any Salon between 1737 and 1789 (Table 2.1). Combined, Cochin and La Tour were responsible for sixty-four of the 118 portraits displayed that year, with Cochin contributing forty-six drawings, and La Tour eighteen pastels.⁶

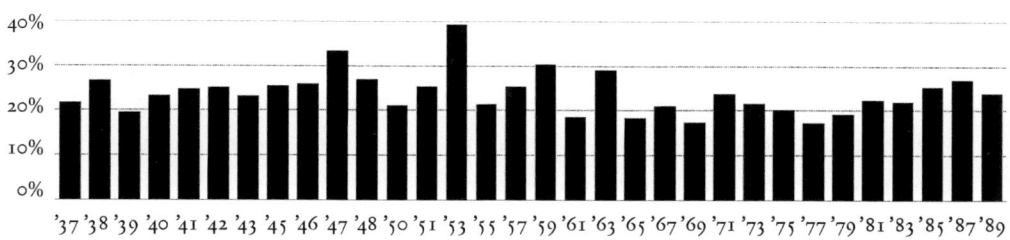

Table 2.1 Portraits displayed at the Salon as percentage of total works displayed, 1737–89.

The artists' choice to display an exceptionally large number of portraits at the Salon of 1753 came on the heels of two significant developments: a critical attack on portraiture and a resurgent emphasis on history painting in the Academy. Both created intense discussion about the value of portraits in the Salon in the 1750s. Thus, the Salon of 1753 was in many ways exceptional, and brings to light how La Tour and Cochin used a public demonstration of their intense involvement with the sociable world of the eighteenth century as a defense of portraiture.[7] La Tour and Cochin positioned themselves and the subjects of their portraits within a new concept of celebrity, and reoriented the discussion of their works at the Salon exhibition to highlight the social uses of portraiture. The particular formats and medium of each artist—La Tour's bust-length pastels and Cochin's drawn medallion portraits—created an intimate viewing experience for Salon visitors, giving the illusion of personal access to famous people, a cornerstone in the development of the modern idea of the celebrity, through their works. The idea of intimacy is apparent in the Salon critics' repeated claims that La Tour and Cochin created their portraits for friends and, in doing so, neglected commissions from wealthy (and therefore paying) customers. Those portraits were praised for their value to the posterity of France and contributed to a growing interest in "great men" (*grands hommes*), individuals who were celebrated for their contribution to French culture and history.[8] Finally, the emphasis on the male sitters, coupled with the relative dearth of commentary on the women Cochin and La Tour depicted, demonstrates the highly gendered conception of the value of portraits and the public role of friendship.

Portraiture at Midcentury

Over the course of the 1740s, portraiture was increasingly linked to greed and vanity. Economic gain was becoming part of the very definition of the genre. As early as 1723, lexicographer Pierre Richelet defined a portraitist as "someone who easily earns what he needs in order to bring home the bacon, because there is no lack of flirtatious and well-to-do women who want to have their portrait done."[9] With the appointment of Charles-François Le Normand de Tournehem to lead the king's arts administration as the *directeur-général des bâtiments du Roi* in 1745, an overhaul of the Royal Academy was undertaken to revive history painting.[10] In 1747, Tournehem lowered the price for portrait commissions and increased the fees for history paintings in an effort to encourage artists toward the more prestigious but less profitable history painting genre. Not coincidentally, this move followed the art critic Étienne La Font de Saint-Yenne's description of portraiture as "the most lucrative" genre. In his discussion of the Salon of 1746, he listed the increasing number of portraits at the Salon as a reason for the decline of history painting in France.[11]

In response to these attacks, the promotion of a sociable side of portraiture became increasingly present in lectures on portraiture presented by artists in the Academy. In his *discours* on portraiture read at the assembly of the Royal Academy in 1750, the successful portraitist Louis Tocqué made the following recommendation to young artists: "Be gentle, read, speak little, listen a lot, seek out friendship with those who combine the great customs of society with the purity of morals. Acquire from them the noble tone so necessary to be admitted into good company. Only good company can put us in a position to express—nobly, vividly, and delicately—the passions of the soul so difficult to render adequately in painting."[12] For Tocqué, friendship was a way for artists to be socialized. It taught them the proper behavior that allowed them to enter into "good" company. Sociability was also a means for the betterment of an artist's work, as it allowed them to get to know a sitter and thus to capture more skillfully the sitter's individuality.

A decade later, the Lyonnais portraitist Donat Nonnotte saw other benefits to artists from participating in *bonne compagnie* (good company): profit and social elevation. In "Les avantages du portrait et la manière de le traiter," a *discours* on portraiture that he gave at the Academy of Fine Arts in Lyon in 1760, he recognized the role of sociability in the career of Pierre Mignard, one of the most celebrated portraitists during the reign of Louis XIV: "I will go further and say that it is only because of his portraits that M. Mignard, first painter to the King, received such elevation. He painted them superbly, and it was for him a sure way to earn a living and to make friends."[13] Nonnotte argued that Mignard's portraits were alone responsible for his promotion to the highest position an artist could achieve, that of First Painter to the King (*Premier peintre du Roi*). Portraiture was a way of earning a living and making friends, and these two aspects were intricately linked when the "friends" in question were the same individuals who provided the artist with his living. In fusing friendship, profit, and social elevation together in this passage, Nonnotte relied on an older rhetoric of friendship in the context of patronage. A patron and an artist could be "friends" on the basis of an equality of virtue, even if they were not equal in social status. Casting patronage in terms of friendship allowed the patron to seem generous and helped elevate the artist's social position.[14] Here, Nonnotte adapted this rhetoric to eighteenth-century sociability by tying portraiture to the social commerce of friendship. Equal exchange, not equal virtue, was the basis for friendship between two individuals of differing social and economic positions. The social exchange inherent to friendship as it was defined by sociability was used to deemphasize the economic exchange of portraiture. In Nonnotte and Tocqué's descriptions alike, sociability, not profit, was both an impetus for and product of portraiture.

Nonnotte's *discours* addressed at length how the most famous history painters—Titian, Rubens, and Van Dyck, among others—had produced a number of important portraits of significant people. The list of works emphasized that portraiture had an important role to play in history, promoting the usefulness of the genre. In his explanation of the history of portraiture, he pointed to friendship as one of the primary motivating factors in the production of portraits:

From its beginning this art excited a universal enthusiasm. Gradually achieving its perfection, one employs it to represent all that can touch the heart and please the mind. Friendship, respect, recognition erected monuments to the memory of parents, friends, great men. The sublime talent of making lively and spiritual likenesses generated astonishing feats. The great princes, philosophers, heads of families, virtuous men, beauty and the graces, became models whose images we believed we needed to leave for posterity.[15]

Friendship remained intricately linked to fame.

La Tour tapped into the genre's relationship to friendship and fame early in his career. In 1747, he exhibited a portrait of the sculptor Jean-Baptiste II Lemoyne (Fig. 2.2). It is a closely cropped bust-length portrait. Lemoyne is shown without a wig, in an unbuttoned grey coat, with a blue cravat casually tied around his neck. The portrait differs greatly from the portraits of artists La Tour had previously sent to the Salon, such as those of Jean Restout (Fig. 2.3), Claude Dupouch (Fig. 2.4), and René Frémin (Fig. 2.5), which were substantially larger, half-length portraits that referenced their sitters' occupations. Devoid of any reference to Lemoyne's artistic practice, even his hands, it is a portrait of the man, not the famous sculptor. The simplicity of this portrait is perhaps one reason why the work did not receive any known critical commentary until the following year, when Louis-Guillaume Baillet de Saint-Julien, in his discussion of Lemoyne's reciprocal portrait of La Tour (Fig. 2.6), noted: "By [this portrait of] M. La Tour, M. Le Moine wanted to pay back the debt of his pastel portrait, exhibited at the preceding Salon and received with applause by all the Public. How M. Le Moine has paid it in full and oh how few in the world have such good credit!"[16]

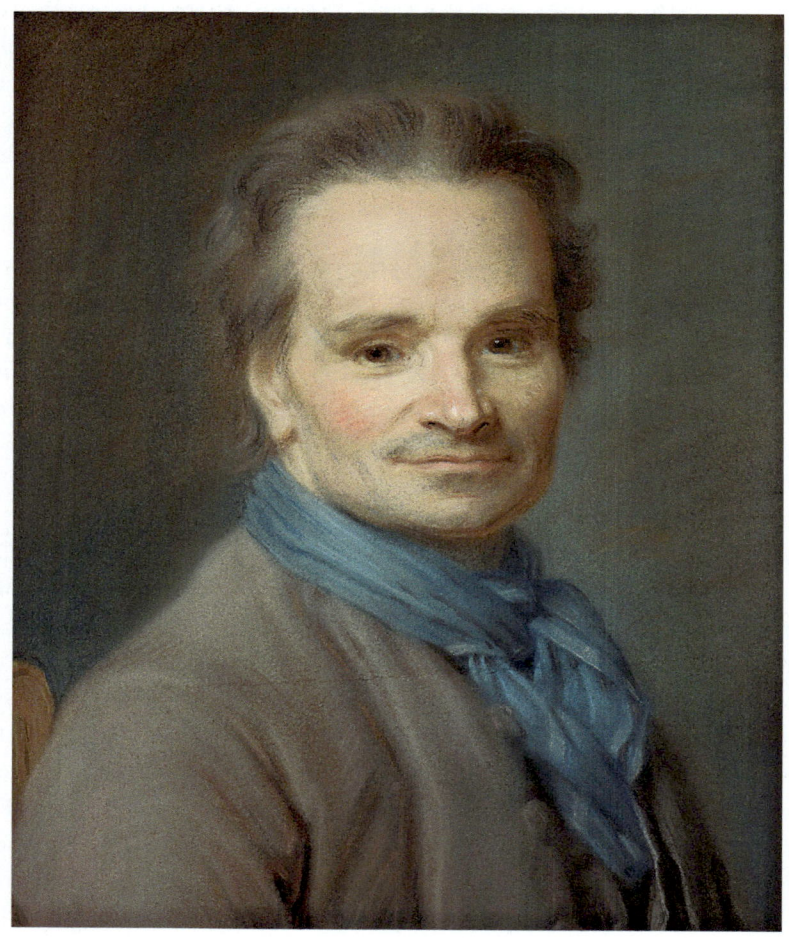

Fig. 2.2. Maurice Quentin de La Tour, *Portrait of the Sculptor Jean-Baptiste II Lemoyne*, 1763.

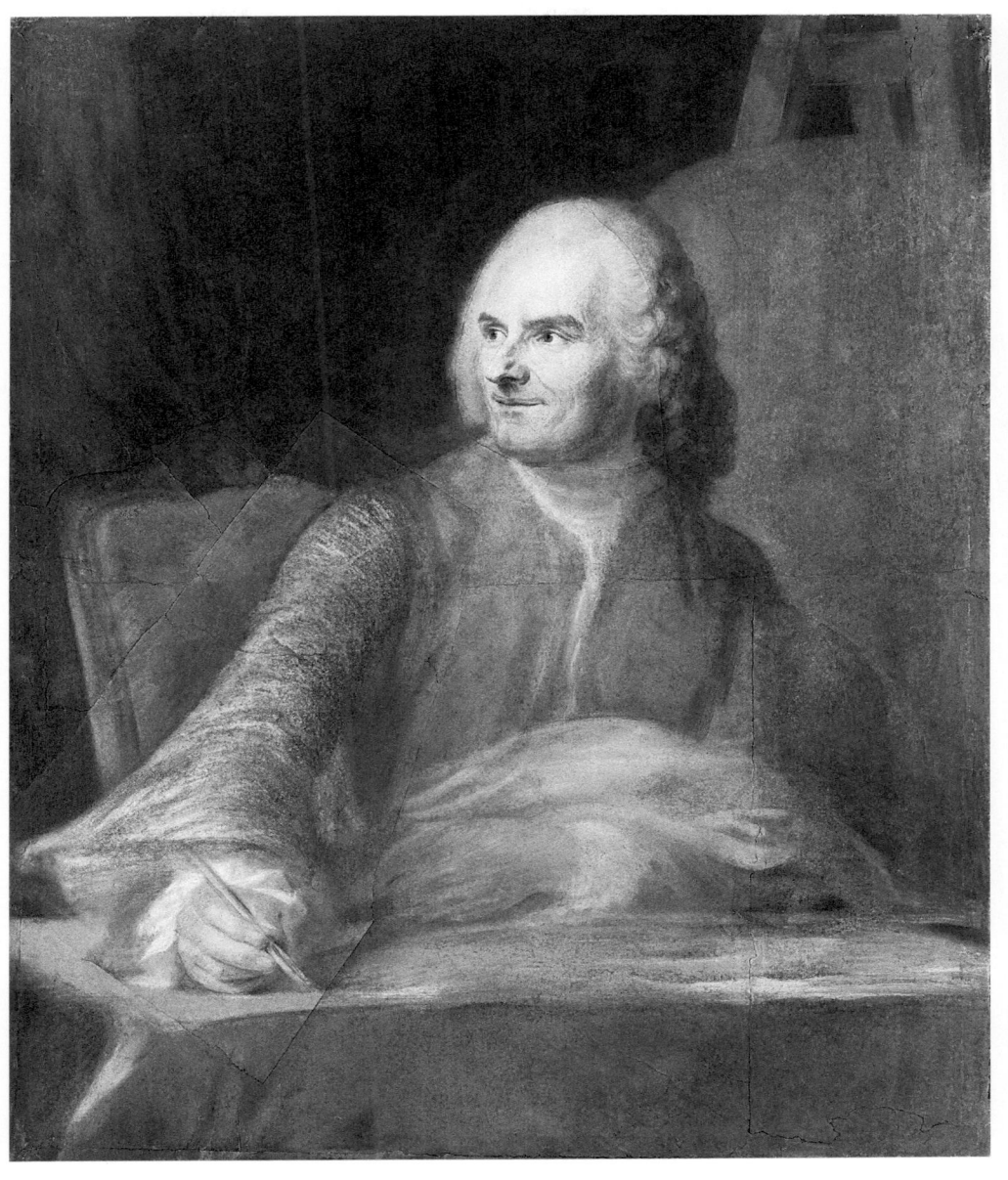

Fig. 2.3. Maurice Quentin de La Tour, *Portrait of the Painter Jean Restout*, 1746.

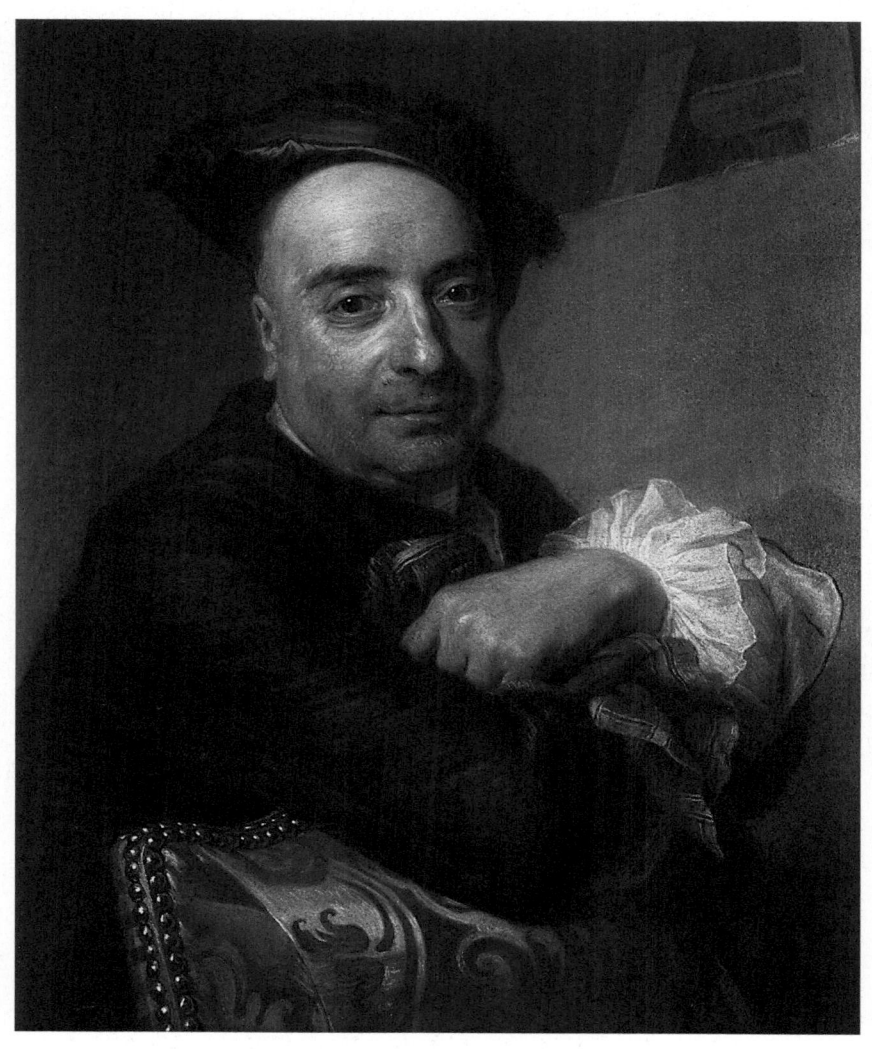

Fig. 2.4. Maurice Quentin de La Tour, *Portrait of the Painter Claude Dupouch*, 1739.

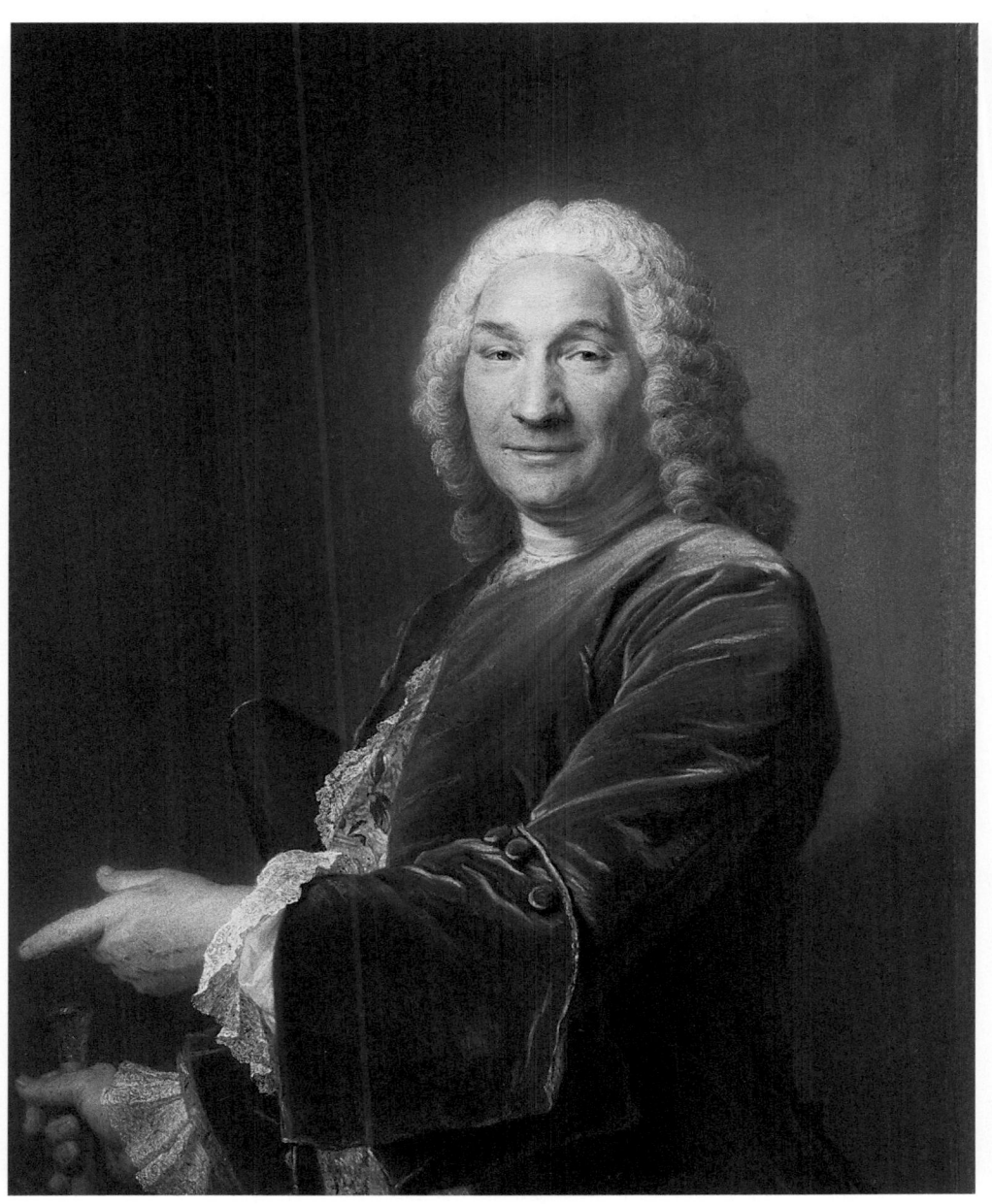

Fig. 2.5. Maurice Quentin de La Tour, *Portrait of the Sculptor René Frémin*, salon of 1743.

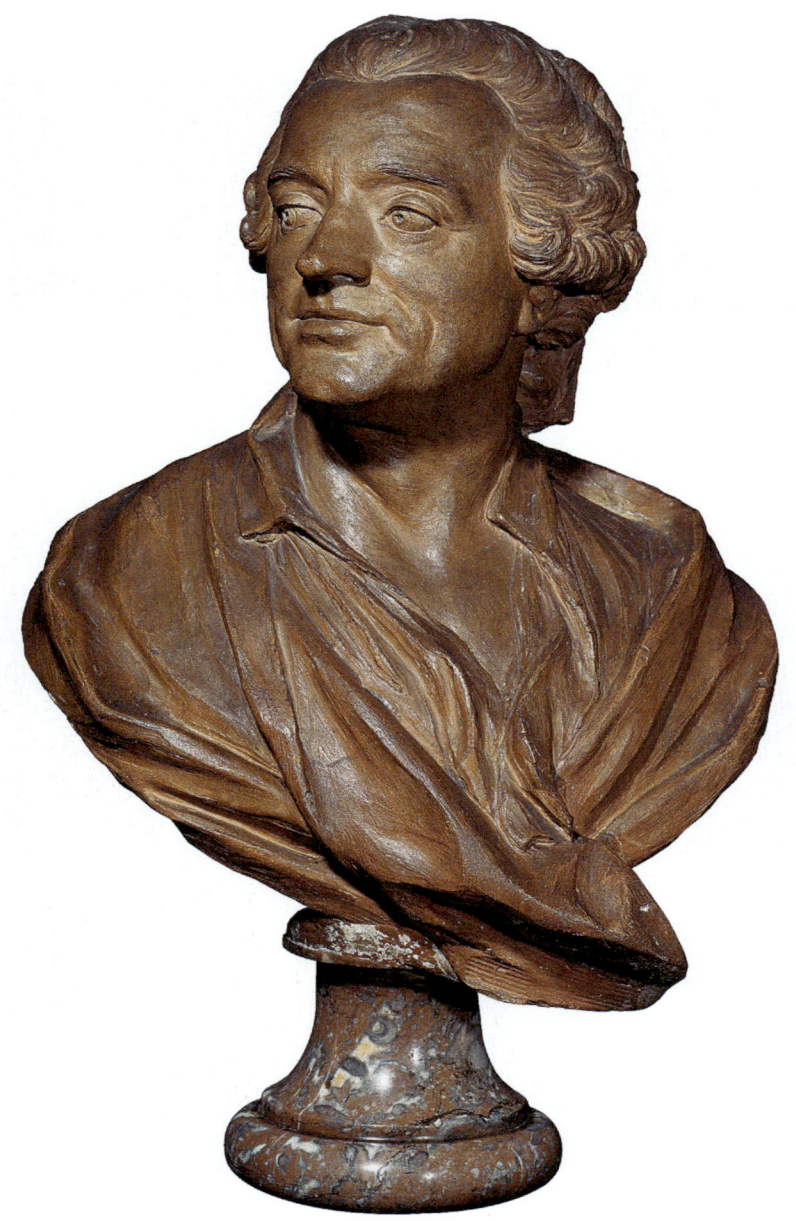

Fig. 2.6. Jean-Baptiste II Lemoyne, *Bust of Maurice Quentin de la Tour*, salons of 1748 and 1763.

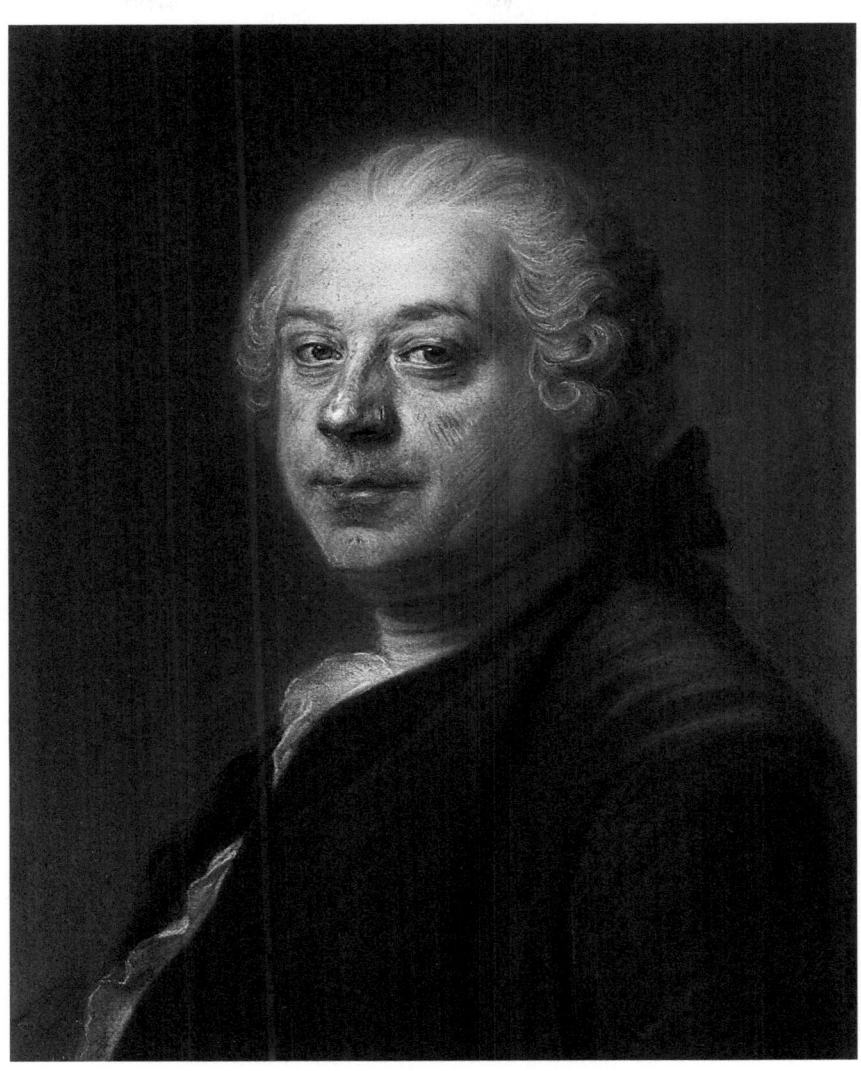

Fig. 2.7. Maurice Quentin de La Tour, *Portrait of the Painter Charles Parrocel*, 1743.

Although La Tour's portrait of Lemoyne was greeted with appreciation by the public in 1747, it appears not to have been worth mentioning in published criticism until it was recognized as part of a reciprocal exchange. La Tour's only other portrait of a fellow artist with such a simple format from the 1740s, his 1743 portrait of Charles Parrocel (Fig. 2.7), was similarly exhibited without comment, not even mentioned by name in the Salon *livret*.[17]

The exchange between La Tour and Lemoyne was between two unequal Academicians, as Hannah Williams notes. The pastellist had recently been accepted into the Royal Academy; the sculptor had been an Academician for ten years. Salon viewers were accustomed to seeing portraits of established artists painted by newly accepted artists as *morceaux de réception*, the works they submitted to gain admission to the Academy, but it was highly unusual for an established artist to return the favor and paint a portrait of the new Academician that painted them.[18] The unusual inequality of the exchange may indicate that a close and voluntary relationship existed between the two artists, a conclusion further supported by the fact that the exchange was repeated at the Salon of 1763, where the artists re-exhibited their portraits.[19]

Baillet de Saint-Julien described Lemoyne's portrait of La Tour and its display in terms of commerce between two men ("M. le Moine a voulu acquitter la dette de son portrait"). Particularly striking is the fact that a discussion of a portrait exchange in these terms happened in 1748, when criticism of portraiture as the most profitable genre was coming to the forefront. While commerce is largely associated today with systems of market exchange, in the eighteenth century, any form of exchange was considered a form of commerce, including social exchanges such as letter writing, conversation, and friendship. The *Encyclopédie* defined commerce rather broadly, as "that reciprocal dependency of men, by way of the variety of commodities they may provide, extending to actual needs or those one believes one has."[20] Dena Goodman has demonstrated, for example, the serious nature of correspondence in the eighteenth century, when the agreement to correspond implied reciprocal responsibilities.[21] Letter writing necessitated replies in order for a relationship to be maintained.

Social commerce was key to eighteenth-century understandings of sociable practice. As the definition of *société* shifted in the eighteenth century from the notion of pleasurable company to that of a large-scale, basic unit of human organization, *sociabilité* became an abstract philosophical idea that tried to explain mankind's desire to participate in *société*.[22] The adjective *sociable* underwent a similar shift, from describing a personal quality of someone who was polite and pleasant company to, as Daniel Gordon states, "an anthropological fact, an element of national character, and an individual psychological trait."[23]

The separation of sociable commerce from economic commerce rested largely on the principle of disinterestedness. A belief in equal exchange was crucial to sociable practice. One's ability to reciprocate signaled their civility. As noted by Gordon, the Marquis de Mirabeau, one of the pioneers of liberal economics, insisted on there being a difference between *cupidité* (greed) and *sociabilité*, and "[b]y employing commerce to denote the entire field of sociable relations, [Mirabeau] made commerce synonymous with *société*. In this way, he suggested that economic production and trade were not acquisitive activities but civilized activities based on the rational quest for happiness within a field of human interdependence."[24] The allusion to a transaction is clear in Baillet de Saint-Julien's comment: La Tour's pastel portrait created a debt that Lemoyne felt obliged to pay. But between two artists, such a debt could only be paid in the form of another portrait, not with currency as in a typical transaction with a patron. The author also emphasized that the reciprocal public display of the portraits was part of the payment of the debt. Baillet de Saint-Julien showed that the reciprocity of Lemoyne and La Tour's portrait transaction made it an equal exchange, a form of sociable and friendly commerce rather than an economic exchange driven by greed.

Celebrity at the Salon: The Salon of 1753

Following his successful display of friendship in 1747 and 1748, La Tour exhibited portraits of other men and women with whom he engaged in sociable commerce, and simultaneously took advantage of a new interest that grew among Salon audiences in the 1750s: portraits of celebrities. In 1753, he exhibited eighteen pastels at the Salon, the largest number of works the artist had ever shown at one exhibition.[25] This group included portraits of the director of the Royal Academy, Louis de Silvestre; three *associés-libres* of the Royal Academy—the Marquis de Voyer, Claude-Henri Watelet, and the Marquis de Montalembert; two members of the French Academy—dramatist Pierre-Claude Nivelle de la Chaussée and author Charles Pinot Duclos; three members of the Royal Academy of Sciences—the abbé Nollet, the Marquis de la Condamine, and Jean le Rond d'Alembert; and portraits of writer Louis Petit de Bachaumont, Jean-Jacques Rousseau, and Italian singer Pietro Manelli. La Tour also included portraits of six women: Marguerite Lecomte, Madame de Geli, Madame de Mondonville, Madame Huet, Mademoiselle Ferrand, and Mademoiselle Gabriel.[26] He had encountered these sitters through his regular participation in salon gatherings, including those held by Madame Geoffrin and Madame Le Riche de la Pouplinière. Clearly, as Rena Hoisington notes, La Tour's involvement in private salons where he could mingle with famous clients was a ploy to fashion himself as the artist of the *philosophes*.[27]

The same year La Tour displayed this large group of portraits, La Font de Saint-Yenne reiterated his problems with their proliferation, claiming that the Salon was once more plagued by "the mass of obscure men, without name, without talent, without reputation, even without physiognomy."[28] Portraiture was still a distraction for France's best painters, but he allowed that it had become a "necessary" part of the spectacle of the Salon, because the French were a proud people.[29] Unlike in his 1747 commentary, in 1753, La Font de Saint-Yenne distinguished between portraits made out of vanity and those he saw as acceptable for display, which included those of "good Kings, virtuous Queens, and all our kind and generous Rulers," ministers who "have zeal for the honor of the nation, and even more for the tranquility, abundance and ease of the people," "heroes of valor and humanity," "irreproachable magistrates with integrity," ambassadors (both foreign and French), and, finally, "our excellent authors whose morals, genius, vast and useful knowledge illuminate their country either in the sciences, Literature or the Fine Arts."[30]

La Font's distinction was tied to the increasing emphasis on the Salon as a place of edification for the public, but he also acknowledged these portraits' public appeal. The public's desire to see representations of the sitters went beyond learning from the sitters' deeds. It was also part of the development of the modern idea of celebrity that began to emerge in the eighteenth century. As Antoine Lilti has argued, celebrity is a form of renown that exists on a spectrum: reputation is situated at the local level, while glory is elevated to the universal.[31] And while, in the eighteenth century, glory was linked to being posthumous, celebrity was about contemporaneity—it was based on a person's ability to captivate the public and required interest in that person's private life.[32] The eighteenth-century French writer Nicolas Chamfort, for example, defined celebrity as "the privilege of being known by people who do not know you."[33] As the status of an individual began to depend more on achievements than on birth, celebrity emerged as a new form of social recognition. In France, the appearance of the word *célébrité* in writings reached a peak between the 1760s and 1780s.[34] To be *célèbre* was to be famous, and this word, as well as its synonyms *fameux* and *illustre*, was sprinkled liberally throughout the salon criticism that discussed portraits.[35]

As many scholars have noted, the rise of the celebrity was directly tied to important social and cultural shifts brought about by the growth of publishing, the rise of literacy, and the development of newspapers.[36] These provided new forums for the dissemination and consumption of portraits, both written and visual, and new ways for the public to learn about people of note and to possess images of them, thanks to developments in engraving and other forms of intaglio prints. The proliferation of imagery of famous or notorious individuals was a driving force behind the increasing importance of these individuals in the public consciousness.[37] Viewers or collectors of images of famous individuals no longer wanted stereotyped, interchangeable portraits but "real" ones, as Lilti has demonstrated in the case of Voltaire.[38]

The new category of celebrity emerged not only because of the rise of politicized conversation in the public sphere, as described by Jürgen Habermas, but also because of the development of public consumption and commercialized leisure, which led to a public interest in famous figures.[39] The eighteenth century offered unprecedented opportunities for the visual consumption of celebrity portraits at public exhibitions. As historians of British art have noted, commissioning a portrait from a famous artist to be shown to the public in London's Royal Academy exhibitions was an important means of self-construction and self-presentation, particularly for actresses. A successful portrait could act as an advertisement for the artist's services and for the actress's talents.[40] La Font's description of the Paris Salon as a "spectacle," which forced him to acquiesce to the number of portraits on display, demonstrates that Salon exhibitions served a similar purpose in the formation of the French celebrity.

The role of the Salon in displaying celebrity is clear in the discussion of the eighteen portraits La Tour displayed in 1753. The *livret* of 1753 identified every one of La Tour's sitters, listing their titles and professional affiliations. The numerous commentaries on this notable group of portraits focused both on their value for posterity and on La Tour's selflessness in creating them. These commentaries, however, primarily focused on the male sitters. The Comte de Caylus declared that, "[La Tour] prefers the consolation of making portraits of illustrious men over those of wealthy people."[41] The claim is an exaggerated one. Increasingly in demand as a portraitist over the course of the 1750s, La Tour became notorious for charging outrageous sums for his portraits, primarily because he could afford to do so. His normal fee was twelve hundred livres, but in some cases, he charged as much as five thousand livres. Wealthy individuals were willing to pay high prices to be depicted by an artist known for his paintings of the royal family and nobility, because it was a display of personal wealth to be able to pay such prices.[42] The impressive number of portraits of important people that La Tour exhibited at the Salon of 1753 successfully distracted critics from the pecuniary aspect of the artist's practice. They discussed these portraits as if the subjects had been chosen by La Tour himself and were not commissioned, as if, in other words, they were unpaid works. The abbé Leblanc, for example, claimed that La Tour had painted the portraits displayed in the 1753 Salon purely for his own "pleasure."[43] Even La Font de Saint-Yenne claimed, "to the immortality of our illustrious authors' writings, he adds the immortality of their portraits, brought about by his love and zeal for the nation's honor. These portraits will transmit to posterity both the spirit of their physiognomies and the life of their features which he has engraved to preface their works."[44]

Jacques La Combe, like other critics, claimed that La Tour's portraits possessed significance because of the importance of the sitters. But he also acknowledged the fact that La Tour's choice to represent these figures was equally important: "This celebrated artist exhibited at the Salon several of these masterpieces of Art which we cannot stop admiring. He seems to have wanted to give double value to his works; the curious ... will seek [the portraits] out one day, because they are by M. La Tour and because they represent the Illustrious Men of our century."[45] La Tour had much to gain from his works being discussed as selfless contributions to the recording of France's celebrated men; a certain generational split in the group, however, suggests that La Tour's use of the new category of celebrity also profited his sitters.

Half of the men he painted were born around 1700 and were well established in society. Louis de Silvestre (b. 1675) was the recently appointed director of the Royal Academy and painter to the king of Poland. Writers Pierre-Claude Nivelle de la Chaussée (b. 1692), Charles Pinot Duclos (b. 1704), and Bauchaumont (b. 1690), and the physicist the abbé Nollet (b. 1700), had produced a number of well-known works; the Marquis de la Condamine (b. 1704) was a famed explorer. The remaining six men, however, were of a slightly later generation, and had only recently completed, or were just about to complete, the projects that would garner them the most attention. The collector the Marquis de Voyer (b. 1722) had his chateau, designed by Hardoiun-Mansart, completed in 1752. Watelet (b. 1718) had published his *Vies des premiers peintres du roi, depuis M. Le Brun jusqu'à présent* in 1753. The Marquis de Montalembert (b. 1714) had successfully petitioned to create a canon foundry in 1750, which was founded in 1753. The Italian singer Manelli had arrived in Paris in 1752 with a comic troop of actors known as the *bouffons*.⁴⁶

The inclusion of d'Alembert (b. 1717) (Fig. 2.8) and Rousseau (b. 1712) (Fig. 2.9), in particular, suggests La Tour's strategy was not one-sided: of all the men on display, these two had the most to gain from publicity at the Salon. Watelet was a wealthy tax-farmer (*fermier général*) and well-known amateur, the Marquis de Voyer was an ennobled military hero, and Manelli was a performer at the center of a musical debate about the superiority of Italian opera. D'Alembert and Rousseau, however, had more on the line. D'Alembert was a member of the Royal Academy of Sciences, but in the early 1750s was concentrating on the *Encyclopédie*. In February 1752, the first two volumes of the *Encyclopédie* were suppressed by royal decree after several articles in it were denounced as heretical.⁴⁷ The third volume of the *Encyclopédie* was published in October 1753, only a few months after the Salon opened. The publication of this third volume was thus an important renewal of the project after its forced hiatus, and the display of d'Alembert's portrait at the Salon would have been welcome publicity for it. Indeed, in December of 1753, the *Correspondance littéraire* described La Tour's portraits and the *Encyclopédie* as "immortal" works.⁴⁸ D'Alembert would be elected to the Académie française the following year, a victory for the *encyclopédistes*.⁴⁹ Rousseau had attracted public attention for his *Discours sur les sciences et les arts* in 1750. The *Discours sur l'inégalité*, published in 1755, would appear shortly after the Salon of 1753, but he would not reach the height of his fame until 1761 with the publication of *Julie, ou la nouvelle Héloïse*.

Both d'Alembert and Rousseau were on the cusp of fame, and the young *philosophes* were undoubtedly enthusiastic to have an artist who could promote their importance in the public venue of the Salon, and to be included among the portraits of well-established men with whom they mingled. The Salon of 1753 offered them an opportunity to present their faces to the public through La Tour's talents, on the heels of having published works that established their places in the Republic of Letters. Jacques Lacombe's and other critics' inclusion of these young *philosophes* in a group of "illustrious men" validated and endorsed their work.⁵⁰

Friendship was central to this practice of mutual self-promotion. Author Jean-François Marmontel wrote verses on the portrait of Rousseau that firmly fixed the portrait's creation in friendship: "At these features traced by zeal and friendship / Stop, wise men; move on, fashionable people." Salon critics did not fail to notice this inscription.⁵¹ The idea that Rousseau's features

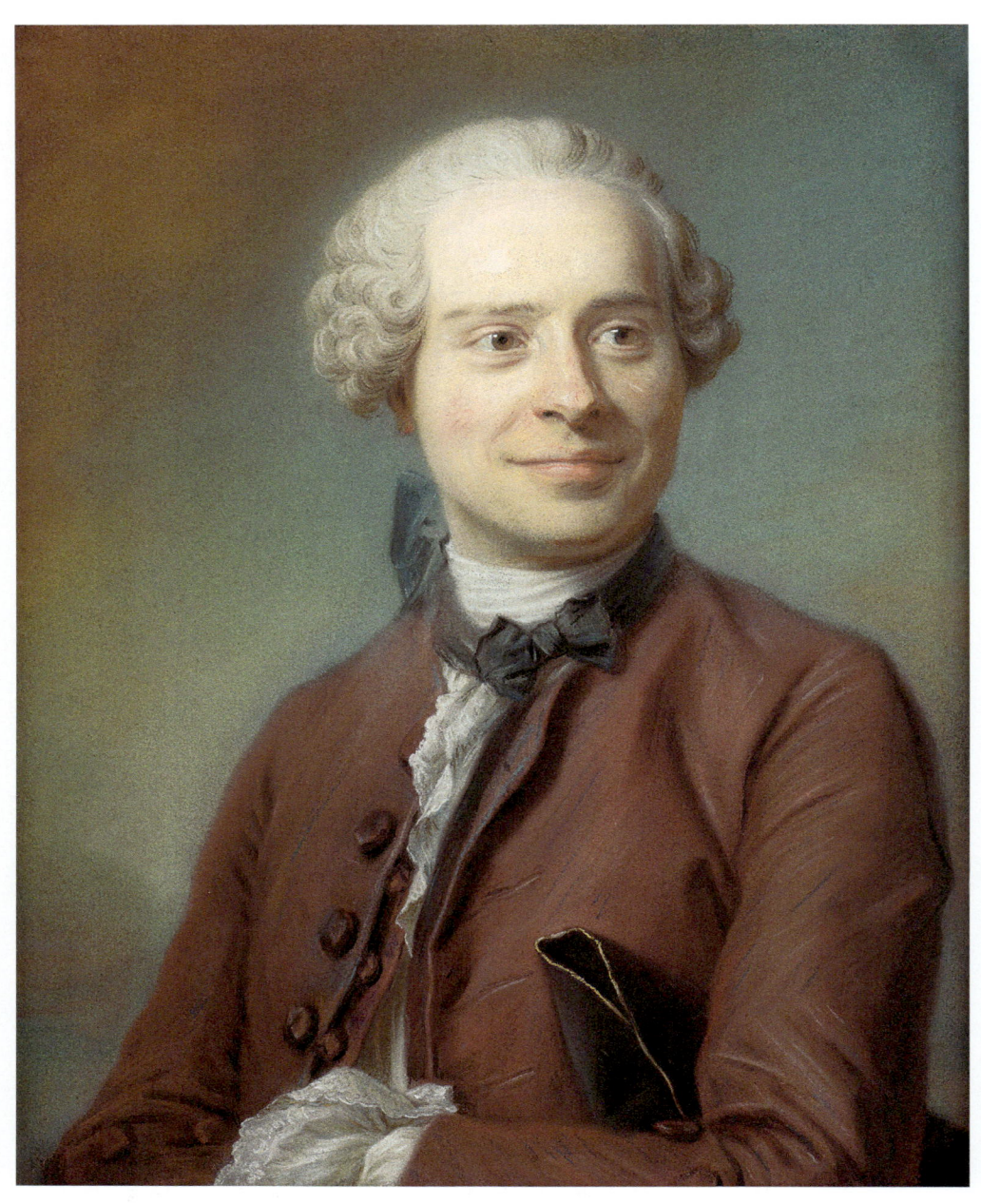

Fig. 2.8. Maurice Quentin de La Tour, *Portrait of Jean Le Rond d'Alembert*, 1753.

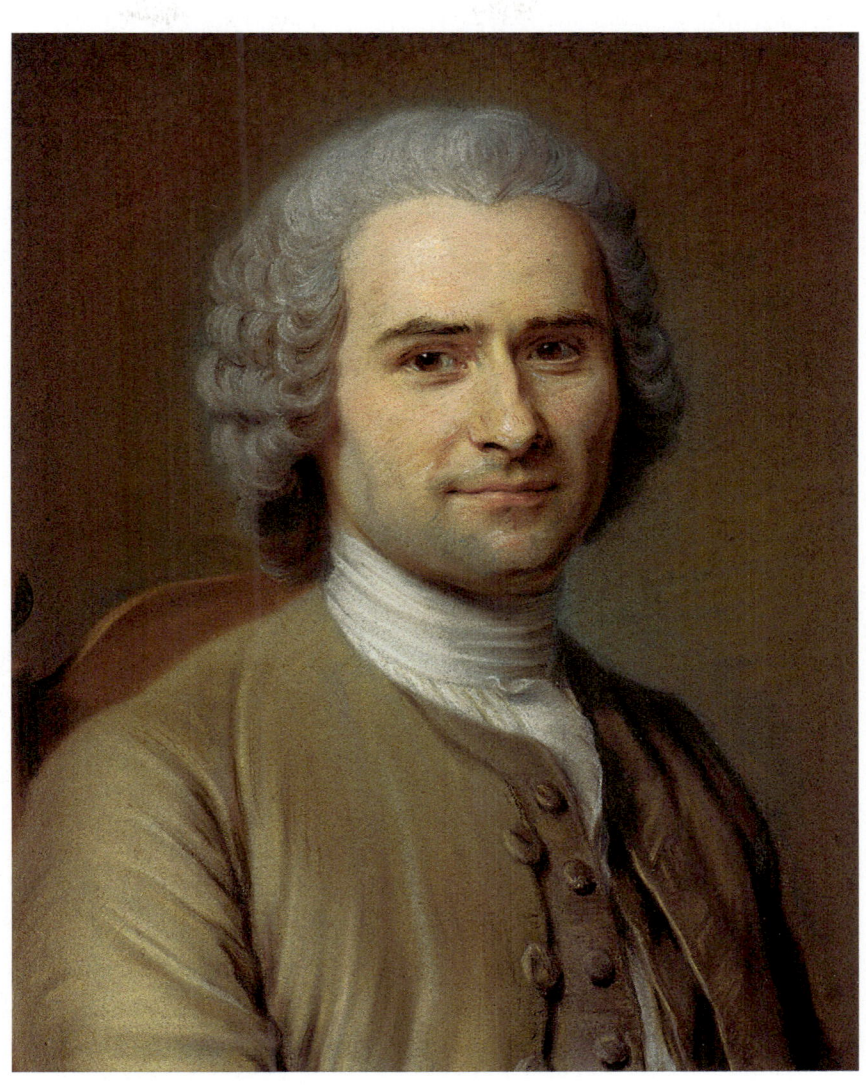

Fig. 2.9. Maurice Quentin de La Tour, *Portrait of Jean-Jacques Rousseau*, 1753.

had been "traced by friendship" was perhaps not entirely an exaggeration. La Tour intended his portrait to be a gift when he painted it. Writing about the events of 1759 in the *Confessions*, Rousseau described his portrait by La Tour:

Sometime after my return to Mont-Louis, La Tour, the painter, came to see me and brought my portrait in pastel, which had been exhibited at the Salon a few years before. He wanted to give me the portrait, but I did not accept it. But madame d'Épinay, who had given me her portrait and wanted to have La Tour's portrait of me, requested that I ask him for it again. He took sometime to retouch it. In the interval came my break with madame d'Épinay. I gave her portrait back; with no reason to give her mine, I put it in my room at the petit château.[52]

Eventually, Rousseau gave the portrait to the Maréchal de Luxembourg.

La Tour, in turn, created a second portrait of Rousseau, which Rousseau also tried to refuse at first, but finally accepted.[53] He wrote to La Tour in 1764 on the subject of this new work:

Yes, sir, I accept my second portrait. You know that I gave the first one a purpose as honorable to you as to me, and very dear to my heart. Monsieur le Maréchal de Luxembourg deigned to accept it: Madame la Maréchale deigned to keep it. This monument of your friendship, your generosity, your rare talents, occupies a place worthy of the hand from whence it came ... it shall remain before me each day of my life; it speaks ceaselessly to my heart. It will be passed down in my family, and what flatters me the most about that is that it will allow our friendship to be remembered forever.[54]

Beyond the Salon, the portrait took on an important role: Rousseau offered it to his patron, most likely as a gesture of appreciation. In Rousseau's description of these events to La Tour, he insisted that giving the portrait to the Maréchal was just as much an honor for La Tour, as the artist, as it was for Rousseau, as the subject. By extending the gift to the Maréchal, Rousseau paid forward La Tour's initial gift of showing his portrait at the Salon, which presented Rousseau's face to the public, and placed him among a group of *hommes illustres*, free of charge. It is ironic, then, as Leo Braudy and Lilti have demonstrated, that Rousseau had an incredibly hard time reconciling himself with his own celebrity. His understanding of the difference between his "natural" self and that seen by the public ultimately caused a sort of paranoid breakdown, made evident in *Rousseau, juge de Jean-Jacques* and the *Confessions*.[55]

The Celebrity Artist Undressed

Critics were impressed by the ambitious number of La Tour's portraits at the Salon of 1753 and by the cultural importance of the men and women depicted. They noted, however, a distinct shift in La Tour's style: "We count in this Salon up to eighteen portraits by M. de La Tour. Among this great number, there is only that of M. Bachaumont which is done in the taste that you have already seen from this artist. All the other portraits are in a new manner. The colors are less blended, and one should not look at them up close. Despite this criticism, we cannot help but recognize in the pastels of this master a freshness that erases all that is done in oil."[56] Within this stylistic shift, critics also noted that not all of La Tour's sitters were painted the same way. His portraits of artists differed from his portraits of military men, aristocrats, and the royal family. The abbé Leblanc observed the following: "Those of the Marquis de Voyer [Fig. 2.10] and M Silvestre [Fig. 2.11] are no less perfect each in their own way. As the latter is a portrait of a painter, we could say that M. de La Tour has made it for painters, and in effect those who know best the difficulties of art are those who will admire it the most. In this portrait there are imperceptible passages of light in the shadows, and shadows in the light, which give it all the relief and fullness of nature."[57] In this discussion of La Tour's style, Leblanc intriguingly suggests that there was a distinction between works created for painters and those directed at the general public, which was tied to the changing status of artists. By the 1750s, artists, both as creators of and sitters for portraits, were increasingly included in the category of celebrity.[58] As noted earlier, La Font included in his list of acceptable portrait subjects "our excellent authors whose morals, genius, vast and useful knowledge illuminate their country either in the sciences, Literature or the Fine Arts."[59] Salon critics identified the artists depicted in portraits in their pamphlets, even when these artists were not named in the Salon *livret*, suggesting that these men were identifiable and that their identity was viewed as worth sharing with the larger public.[60]

The stylistic shift perceived in La Tour's 1753 submissions was described as *moins fonduës*—a looser use of pastels than in his earlier work that was less dependent on the blending of pigment.[61] This style emphasized strong individual strokes of pastels so that "one should not look at them up close."[62] It also emphasized the physical traces of the artist's own hand. The tactility of pastel was seen as one of its defining traits. Watelet, in his poem *L'Art de peindre*, emphasized the tactile nature of the medium: "Without [the] brush,

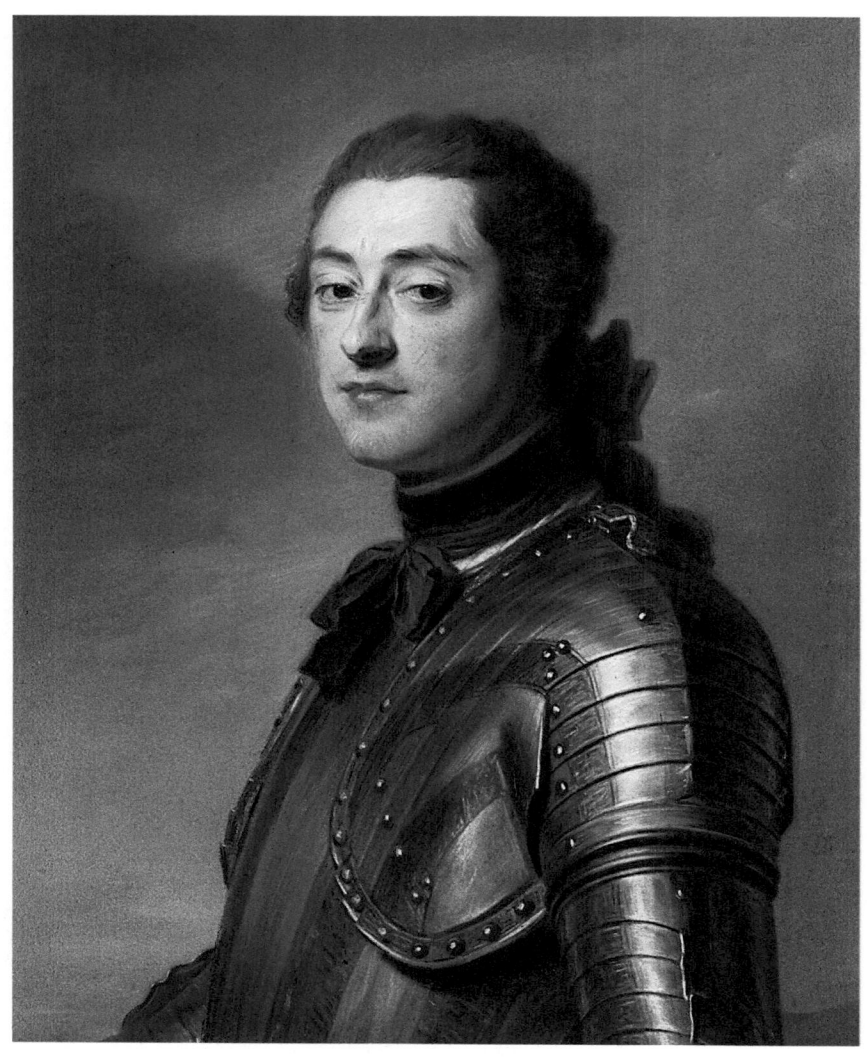

Fig. 2.10. Maurice Quentin de La Tour, *Portrait of Marquis Marc-René de Voyer d'Argenson*, 1753.

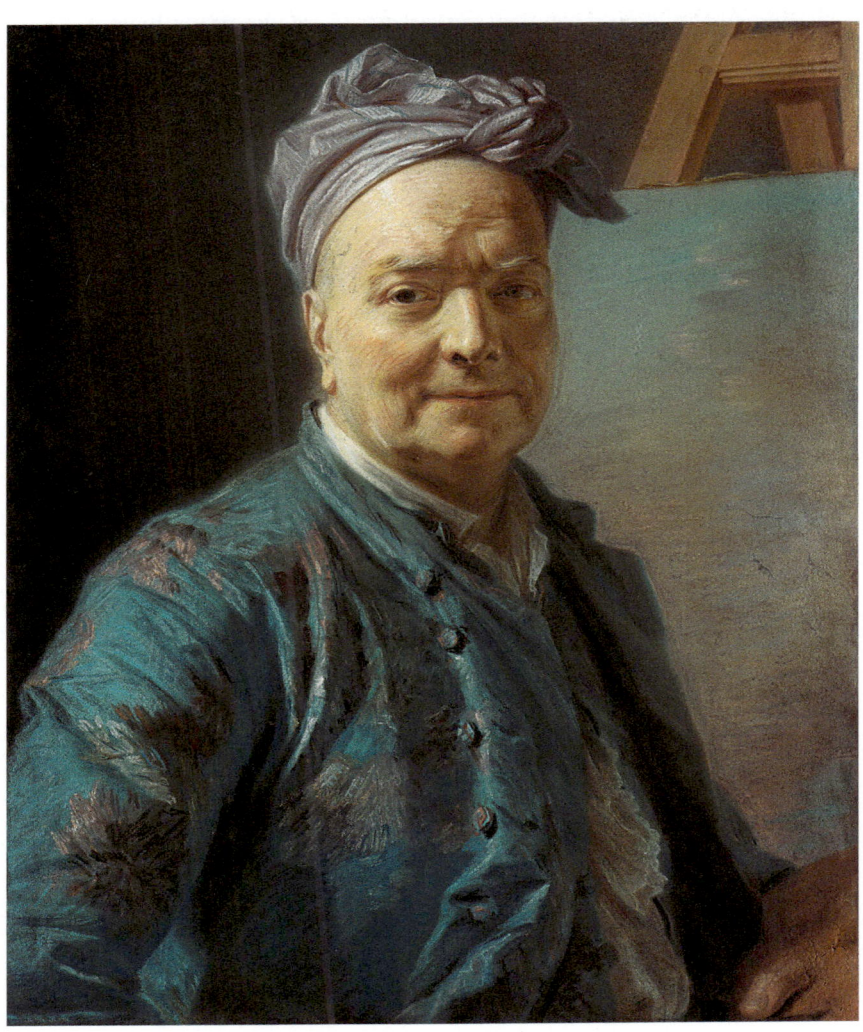

Fig. 2.11. Maurice Quentin de La Tour, *Portrait of Louis de Silvestre*, 1753.

the finger alone places and starts each shade."⁶³ After placing and blending large areas of color, often with the use of fingers, small details—contours, reflections of light, embroidered lace—would be formed by leaving heavy lines of unblended color on top of smooth areas, producing a layered surface.

The expressive display of *touche*, the artist's touch, was loaded with meaning in the eighteenth century, as many art historians have noted.⁶⁴ According to Watelet, touch was a tool for both representation and expression. The artist used it to make an image as well as to display how he felt at the moment of its creation. Over the course of the eighteenth century, *touche* was increasingly seen as a mark of an artist's individuality. Amateurs' and theorists' interest in touch was a product of the recognition of the connection between paint—or in this case, pastel—and the artist.

The looser style La Tour developed in the 1750s brought his viewers closer to his portraits' sitters and to himself as the artist who created the portraits. Joseph Roach has described what he calls the rise of a "publicly intimate genre of personal effigy-making" as an important part of the development of the modern concept of celebrity. He notes that the production and distribution of personal images, begun in the seventeenth century, underwent a continuous, growing expansion over the course of the eighteenth century, and soon became part and parcel of celebrity culture. This provided everyone, not just heads of state or men of the Church, with the opportunity to publicize themselves by making their faces public.⁶⁵ As Roach has stated, "along with such premeditated appearances came a concomitant desire to appear spontaneous. This required readiness on the part of the performers to adopt an air of 'life-like' informality, which actors call public intimacy and portraitists *déshabille*."⁶⁶

Public intimacy and *déshabille* are separate but equivalent ideas in Roach's assessment; both suggest a sort of personal closeness between the actor-sitter and the viewer. Their relationship to a notion of lifelike informality became increasingly important to La Tour, who critics frequently claimed was an artist who captured his sitters' souls (*âmes*). In La Tour's portraits, artists do not appear in *déshabille* in the traditional sense that was associated with portraits of ladies at their *toilette*, such as Louis-Michel Vanloo's portrait of Madame de Marigny and her husband (Fig. 2.12), or with those of collector-amateurs, such as Jean-Baptiste Greuze's portrait of Watelet (Fig. 2.13). But they have as their goal the representation of their sitters in the frame of lifelike informality. They abandon much of the pomp and circumstance of portraits of artists from the late seventeenth and early eighteenth centuries, a tradition that was integral to the Royal Academy's public identity.

As the Academy became a fixed institution in the last quarter of the seventeenth century, the image of its members, created through the *morceaux de réception* portraits, became standardized. Artists who sought acceptance to the Academy were required to paint two portraits, the subjects of which were usually assigned by the Academy. By the middle of the eighteenth century, these portraits were always of high-ranking members of the institution. The vast majority of the artists depicted their sitters in an elaborate, three-dimensionally conceived space, either at work or holding artistic attributes such as brushes, palettes, and chisels.[67] This sort of painting is exemplified by one of Jean Valade's 1754 *morceau de réception*, a portrait of Louis de Silvestre (Fig. 2.14). Silvestre is represented at work. He wears a luxurious blue velvet coat and a rose-colored silk *gilet* that is elegantly embroidered with gold, appropriate to a man of his position. He is seated next to a blank canvas with a loaded palette and brushes, a maulstick in his left hand; in his right hand, he holds a brush, as if he is about to dab the paint on his palette and make the first stroke on his canvas.

La Tour, by contrast, eschewed the full-length format in his portrait of Silvestre, preferring a barely half-length format (Fig. 2.11). Frequently, his portraits of artists disregarded the standard inclusion of the tools of the trade, such as palettes, brushes, or chisels. Even if tools were included, as in his portrait of Silvestre, the sitters were shown in an indeterminate space, rather than in an elaborately depicted studio. La Tour presented Silvestre in a traditional form of artistic *déshabille*: rather than wearing his wig and powder, the painter wears a kerchief on his head, seemingly more appropriate dress for painting than the finery he wears in Valade's portrait.

La Tour's use of *déshabille* is reflected in more than just the dress and pose we find in the representation of Silvestre. La Tour made little or no attempt to smooth the powdery medium in a way that mimicked the sheen of silk or satin to mask the lines he drew. In Silvestre's face, the obvious lines of pastel are even more striking. Strokes of pink, yellow, white, and black build up the curves and crevices of Silvestre's face. The colors lie on top of each other and side-by-side, unblended. In the lower right section of the canvas, the painter holds an empty palette rendered so roughly that it would be indistinguishable were it not for the flesh-toned blob that is his thumb. Looking at the pastel as a whole, we see that La Tour's technique lends a certain softness to the portrait. Far from being a fixed image, Silvestre seems to quiver with life.

Among La Tour's different styles, the one used here emphasized the trace of his hand on the paper, and best expressed an idea of a firsthand encounter between artist and sitter. His *touche* appears to have been used most commonly

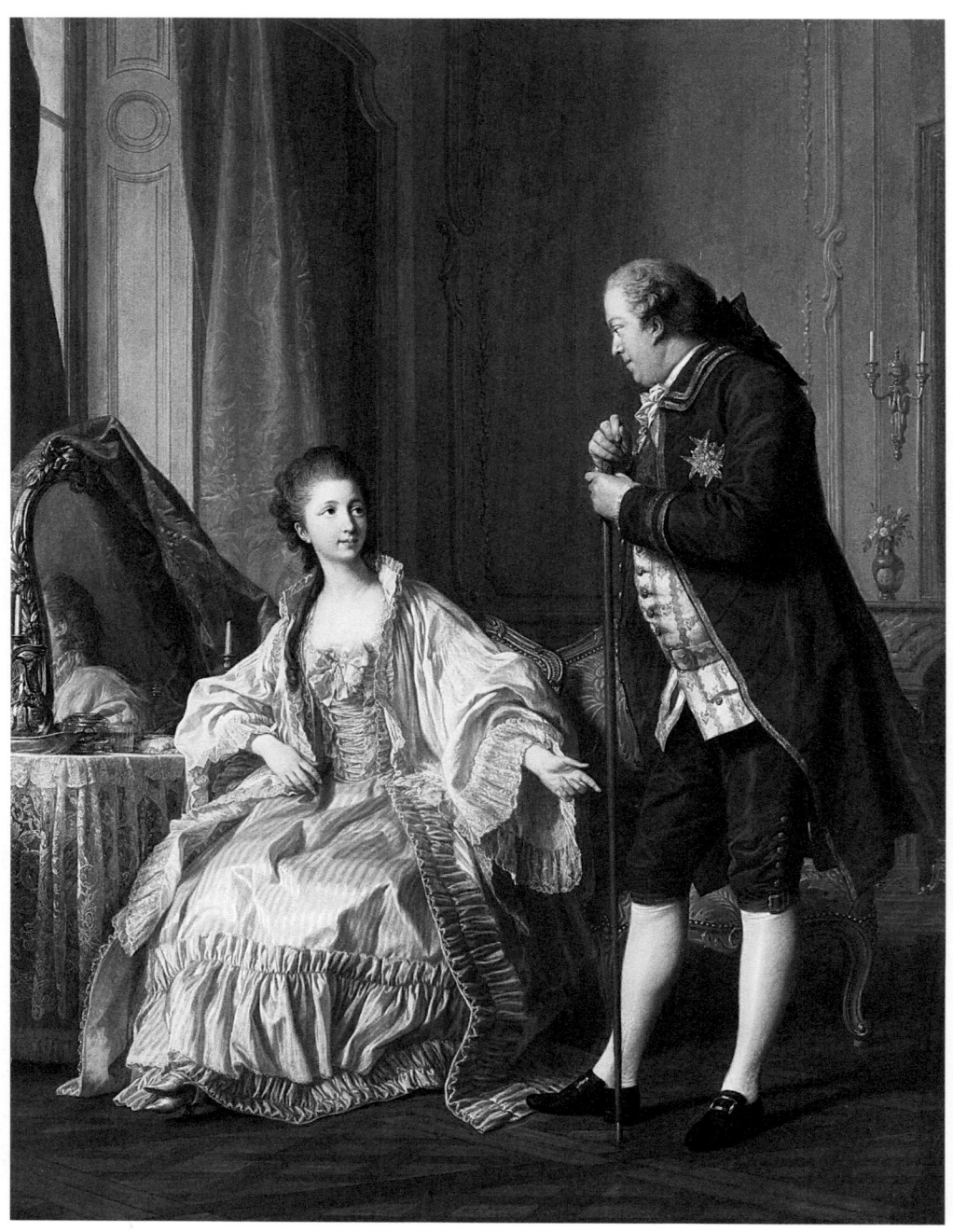

Fig. 2.12. Louis-Michel Vanloo, *Portrait of the Marquis de Marigny and His Wife*, 1769.

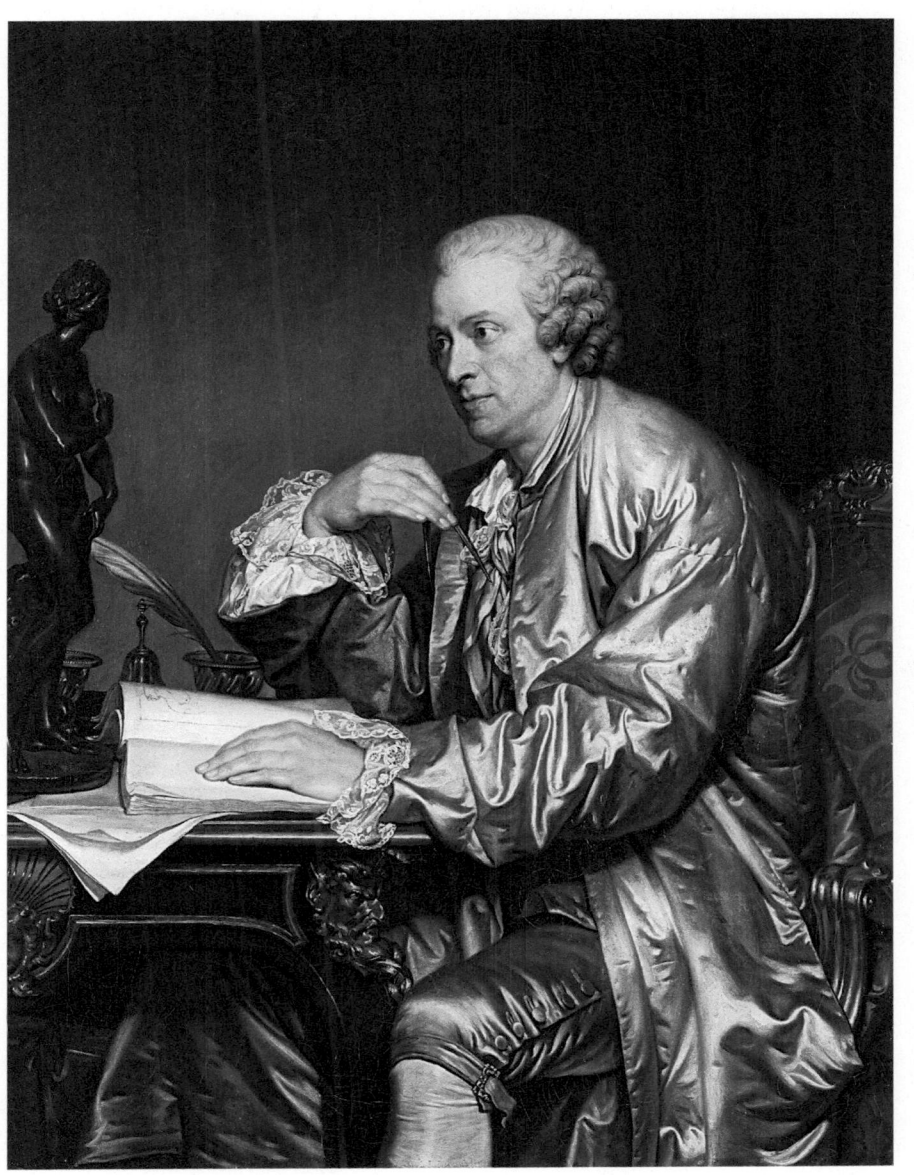

Fig. 2.13. Jean-Baptiste Greuze, *Portrait of Claude-Henri Watelet*, 1765.

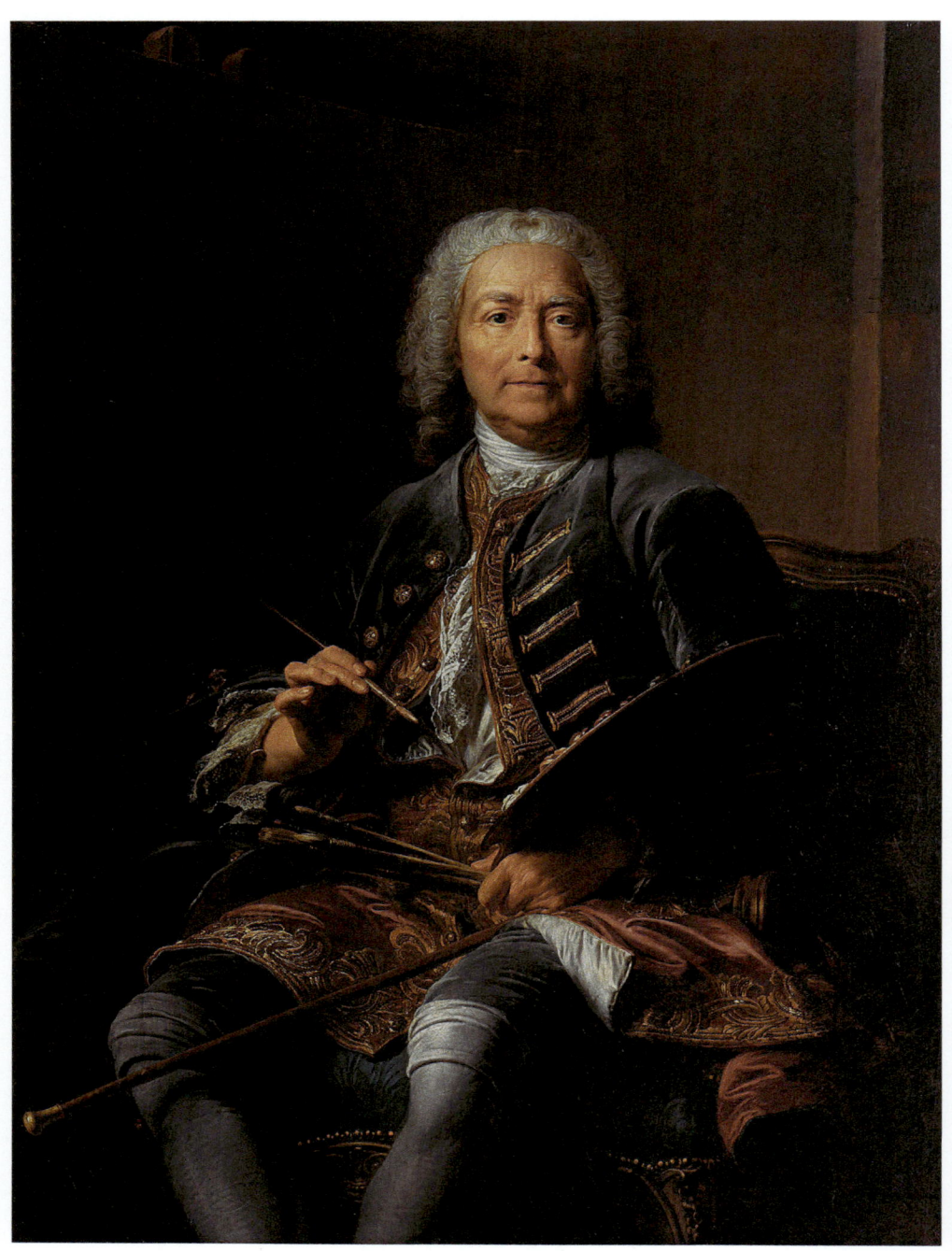

Fig. 2.14. Jean Valade, *Portrait of the Painter Louis de Silvestre*, 1754.

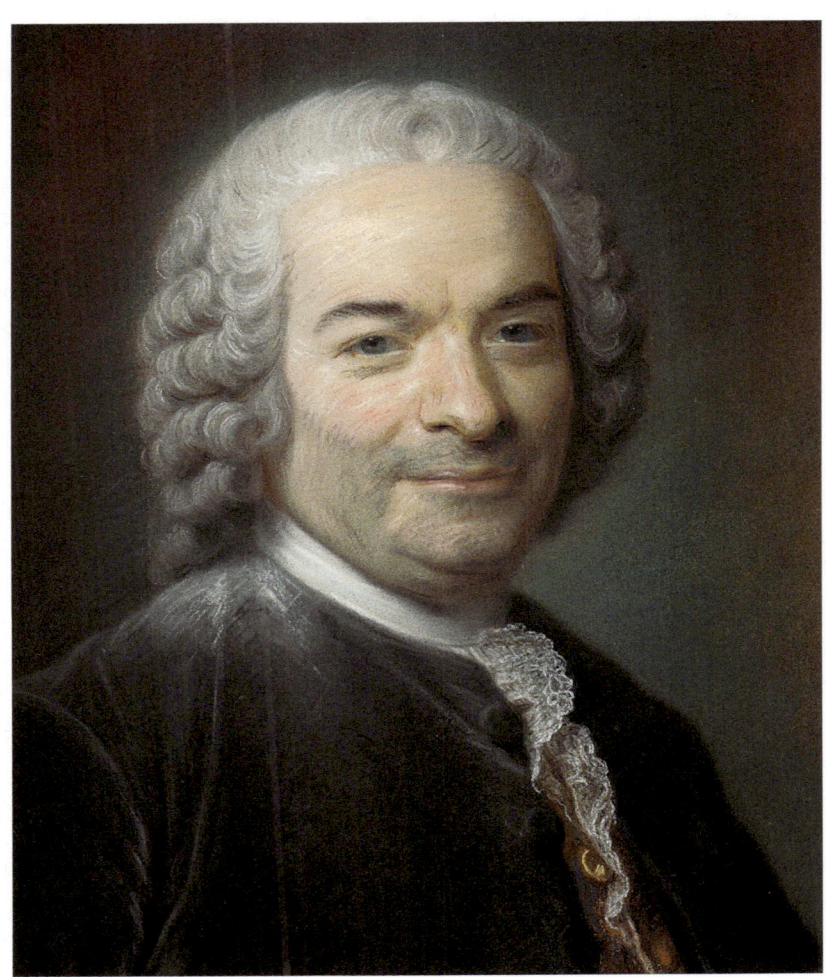

Fig. 2.15. Maurice Quentin de La Tour, *Portrait of the Painter Jean Baptiste Chardin*, 1760.

on those men who were counted among his closest allies, and particularly his professional colleagues. La Tour would continue this looser painting style throughout the 1760s, when he depicted artists in an increasingly informal manner. The appearance of this *touche* is strikingly evident in his portraits of Jean-Siméon Chardin (Salon of 1761; Fig. 2.15) and Jean Baptiste II Lemoyne (Salon of 1747 and 1763; Fig. 2.2). Unlike the half-length format La Tour used for his portraits of René Frémin and Silvestre, he shows Chardin and Lemoyne bust length, in tightly cropped frames. La Tour's handling in both these pastels is startlingly loose. The works lack the finish of the artist's earlier portraits of the royal family and members of the court. Broad areas of color, such as those on the sitters' clothing, lack the heightened definition of fabric texture so often praised in La Tour's early work. Lemoyne's coat comes across as surprisingly flat, the buttons not so much clearly defined as suggested. La Tour's attention to detail increases, however, as the portraits focus on the sitters' faces, and it is precisely in this area where his handling of the pastel is most evident. When viewed closely, we can see that both Lemoyne's and Chardin's faces are made up of easily distinguished strokes of the pastel crayon. Heavy strokes of red create the ruddiness of Lemoyne's cheeks, and his brushy eyebrows are formed by individual strokes of black. The corner of Chardin's right eye is delineated by sepia pastel, and thick patches of black create the effect of wrinkles and bags under the aging painter's eyes. It is impossible to view the faces of these artists without thinking of the hand that painted them. La Tour extended the idea of *déshabille* from the sitters' dress and attitude to the physical nature of the portrait: his portraits of artists constantly display his particular *touche* to signify that that they are his. The works' style is as informal as the attitude of their subjects is.

Charles-Nicolas Cochin: From Salon to the Salon

La Tour alone was not responsible for the extraordinary number of portraits at the Salon of 1753. That same year, Charles-Nicolas Cochin exhibited forty-six portrait drawings, described in the Salon *livret* as "small portraits in medallion form."[68] An earlier version of the *livret*, in the Collection Deloynes, mentions only twenty-five portraits, implying that Cochin added more portraits to the group than he originally intended to show, possibly because the original twenty-five were well received. The official catalogue of the Salon does not give us a precise list of the people represented in these portraits. There are at least twenty-five portraits in Cochin's oeuvre that likely existed before 1754, and there is overlap between the subjects of the portraits La Tour and Cochin displayed, including the Marquis de Voyer, Watelet, d'Alembert, Marguerite Lecomte, and Silvestre.[69] A few critics give us a sense of the personalities Cochin included. The abbé Garrigues described the international nature of the people depicted: "enclosed in two large frames are portraits of many of our most famous masters and several illustrious men of Italy."[70] According to Jacques-Gabriel Huquier, the drawings represented "the illustrious modern men among whom are with good reason almost all artists whose works we see at the Salon."[71] The abbé Leblanc gave some precise names, including "Doctor Lami, Doctor Cocchi, M. le Baron Stoch, M. Bouchardon, De Troy and le Père Jacquier," as well as describing "men of letters, painters, sculptors and amateurs."[72]

The forty-six drawings displayed at the Salon of 1753 represent a small fraction of the number of portraits Cochin produced over the course of his career. A complete inventory of these drawings has yet to be made, but at least 150 of his portrait drawings were engraved over the course of the century.[73] Each sitter is represented at bust length, in profile (Figs. 2.16 and 2.17). The shape and the profile view in each are based on the tradition of antique medals, a point that will be addressed later in this chapter. At first glance, the formulaic and classical approach to these drawings might seem the opposite of the very personal, and literal, touch present in La Tour's pastels. But their small size—about ten centimeters in diameter—and conventional format made these portraits easy to produce quickly, suggesting brief but intense encounters between the artist and his sitters, which were, in turn, passed on to the viewer.

While the creation of the portraits may have been brief, Cochin would have seen his sitters fairly regularly. That there were repeated personal encounters between the artist and his sitters is supported by the history of these portraits. The idea for them originated in the Monday salons held at the home of Madame Geoffrin in the 1740s.[74] Hugues-Adrien Joly, the curator of prints for the king's library, wrote of their creation:

Cochin, during the time that the amateurs and artists assembled at Mad. Geoffrin's one day a week, drew them in profile in the form of a medallion. He promised to engrave them all and to give them to us to be placed in front of this Collection of M. le Comte de Caylus. Cochin drew many of the amateurs and artists who were received and very well hosted every Monday. Madame Geoffrin held at her place a dinner called the dinner of the Arts and while they conversed, Cochin amused himself by drawing either his colleagues or the amateurs, with the intention of having them all engraved to make a suite of portraits.[75]

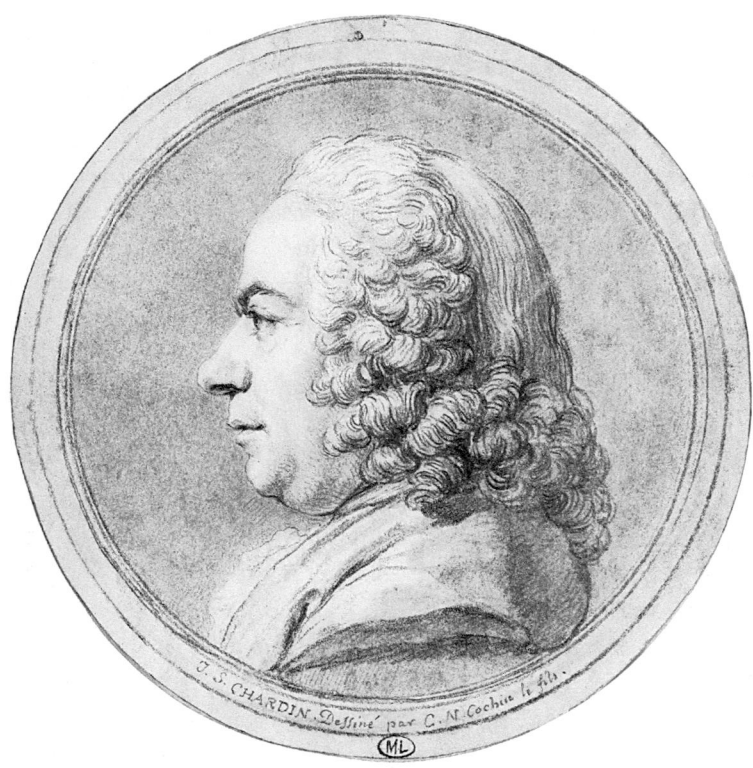

Fig. 2.16. Charles-Nicolas Cochin *fils*, *Portrait de Chardin*, n.d.

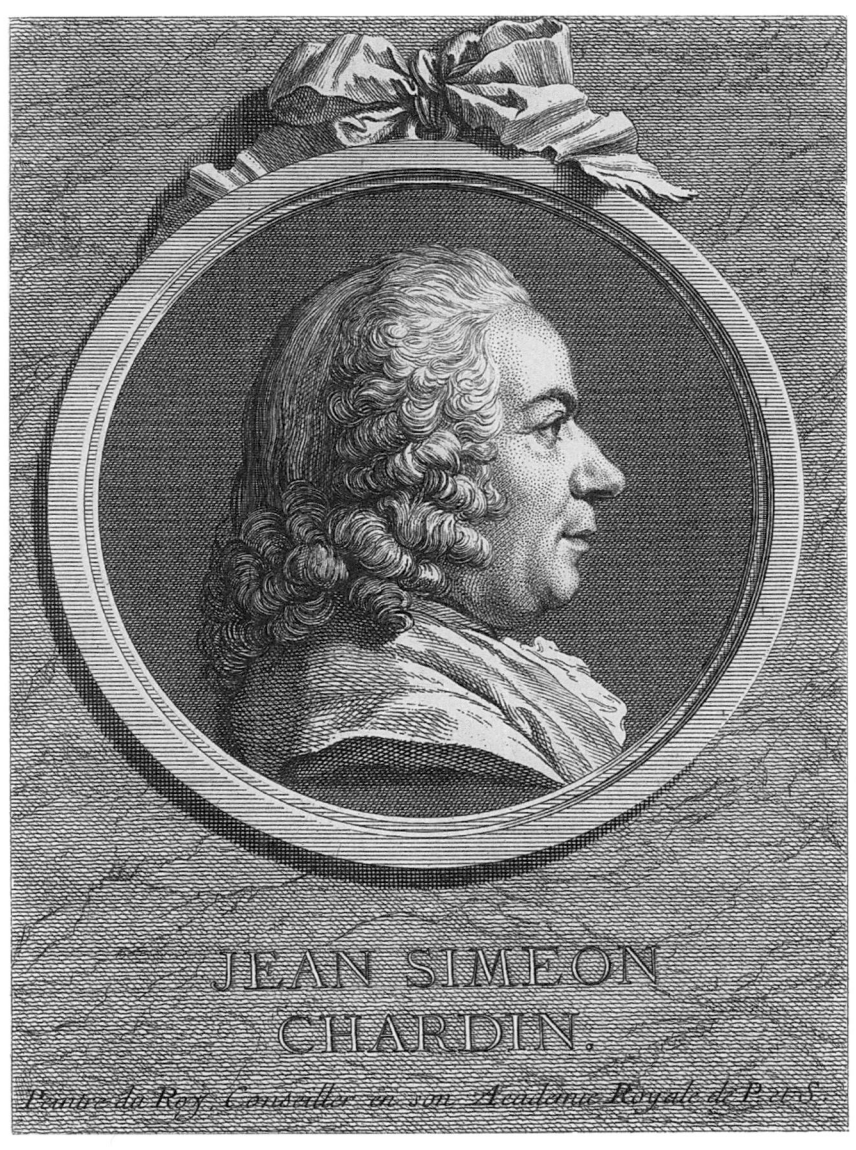

Fig. 2.17. Laurent Cars, after Cochin, *Portrait of Jean-Siméon Chardin*, ca. 1755.

Joly's description of these drawings as a form of personal amusement (*se recrée*) belies their importance. What Joly recounted was the act of recording a social network in visual form. That these drawings were intended to function this way was made apparent in their use: Geoffrin had at least forty-three medallion portraits in her collection, several of which dated to after 1753, including portraits of François Boucher, Chardin, Jean-Baptiste Pierre, Joseph-Marie Vien, Claude-Joseph Vernet, and Étienne Charles Le Guay, who attended her Monday salon, which was dedicated to the discussion of the visual arts.[76] We have no direct record of where exactly in Geoffrin's home they were displayed, but one imagines that they would have been shown together, at least in small groups. Hubert Robert's paintings of the inside of Geoffrin's home in the 1770s (Figs. 2.18 and 2.19) support this idea: in the background, several clusters of medallion frames decorating the walls are visible.

Viewed as a group, the medallion portraits operate as a *galerie de grands hommes*. The idea that these objects may have been intended to do just that is suggested by their format: they are two-dimensional versions of the medals that had long been used to disseminate the images of rulers and other great men, and were collected by numismatists. This was noted by the abbé Leblanc, who described them as "heads dignified enough to be cast as medallions, either because of the celebrity of the people they represent or because of the art in which their resemblance is rendered."[77]

Leblanc's connection of Cochin's works to the older tradition of collecting "great men" in medal form took on new significance, however, with his and other critics' use of the word "celebrity." As Lilti has argued, there is a distinct difference between the *grand homme* and the celebrity: the former was traditionally dead, the latter living.[78] Yet, critics' discussion of Cochin's portraits emphasized the fact that the men presented were alive, that one could compare their likenesses, and that Cochin's project was a sort of monument. Lacombe described the works as "pencil portraits of many celebrated men, the majority very good likenesses, all perfectly drawn."[79] As noted earlier, the abbé Garrigues claimed they represented "our most famous masters," and Baillet de Saint-Julien wrote:

This clever artist has never shined more than in these works ... Posterity cannot fail to applaud his noble and generous enterprise that gives us the portraits of our most illustrious artists and fellow citizens in medallion form. [Posterity] will one day be able to contemplate these celebrated monuments which will make them immortal, when they might not have already been so by their works, and be assured to find them as real, as similar as if they were actually in front of its eyes.[80]

Compiling collections of *grands hommes* was not a new phenomenon. Prior to Cochin's display of portraits, the most famous compendium of them was Charles Perrault's *Les Hommes illustres qui ont paru en France pendant ce siècle*, first published in 1697 (Fig. 2.20).[81] About a dozen collections of engravings of great men of France were produced in the eighteenth century, many inspired by Perrault's book. At least one of these projects was tied to Geoffrin's salon: Ange-Laurent La Live de Jully began his own compendium of *grands hommes* with the intent of updating Perrault's work in 1752.[82] At the Salon of 1753, Cochin's works were the largest group of *grands hommes* portraits to have been shown at the Salon to date, and they appear to have started something of a vogue for these types of portraits in the public venue of the Salon. After Cochin's portraits were exhibited, the number of medallion formats at the Salon, including engravings and medals, increased substantially and began to be categorized differently in the Salon *livret*. In the first years of the Salons, prints and medals were listed in the catalogue interspersed among the paintings and sculptures, but not numbered. After 1753, engravings were separated into their own category and numbered. In the 1760s, artists began to be listed specifically as *graveurs des médailles*. Commemorating *grands hommes* reached a pinnacle in the late 1770s and 1780s, when the *surintendant des bâtiments*, the Comte d'Angiviller, commissioned a series of large-scale, full-length sculptures of the great men of France.

The use of the word "celebrity" in reference to Cochin's portraits signals an important shift in the public consideration of these men, and the broader appreciation for collections of great men in the eighteenth century, as discussed by David Bell. Perrault's *Hommes illustres* and the establishment of the reading of eulogies at the Académie française were offshoots of the quarrel of the ancients and the moderns. These collections, and others like them, tried to highlight the greatness of modern men. They made a distinction, however, between "illustrious" men and "great" men; the former were tied to heroic deeds, while the latter were seen as having noble qualities in every aspect of their lives. As Bell notes, by the end of the eighteenth century, greatness was to be found not in public life, but in private actions, and biographers "prefer[red] to capture the great man in the bosom of his family instead of on the battlefield, in the courtroom, or any other public arena."[83] Furthermore, newer compilations of great men moved away from the court and disregarded social hierarchy, often including men of low birth (painters, playwrights, doctors, jurists, novelists, architects, and astronomers) and not organizing them by social class.[84] In short, new standards of fame

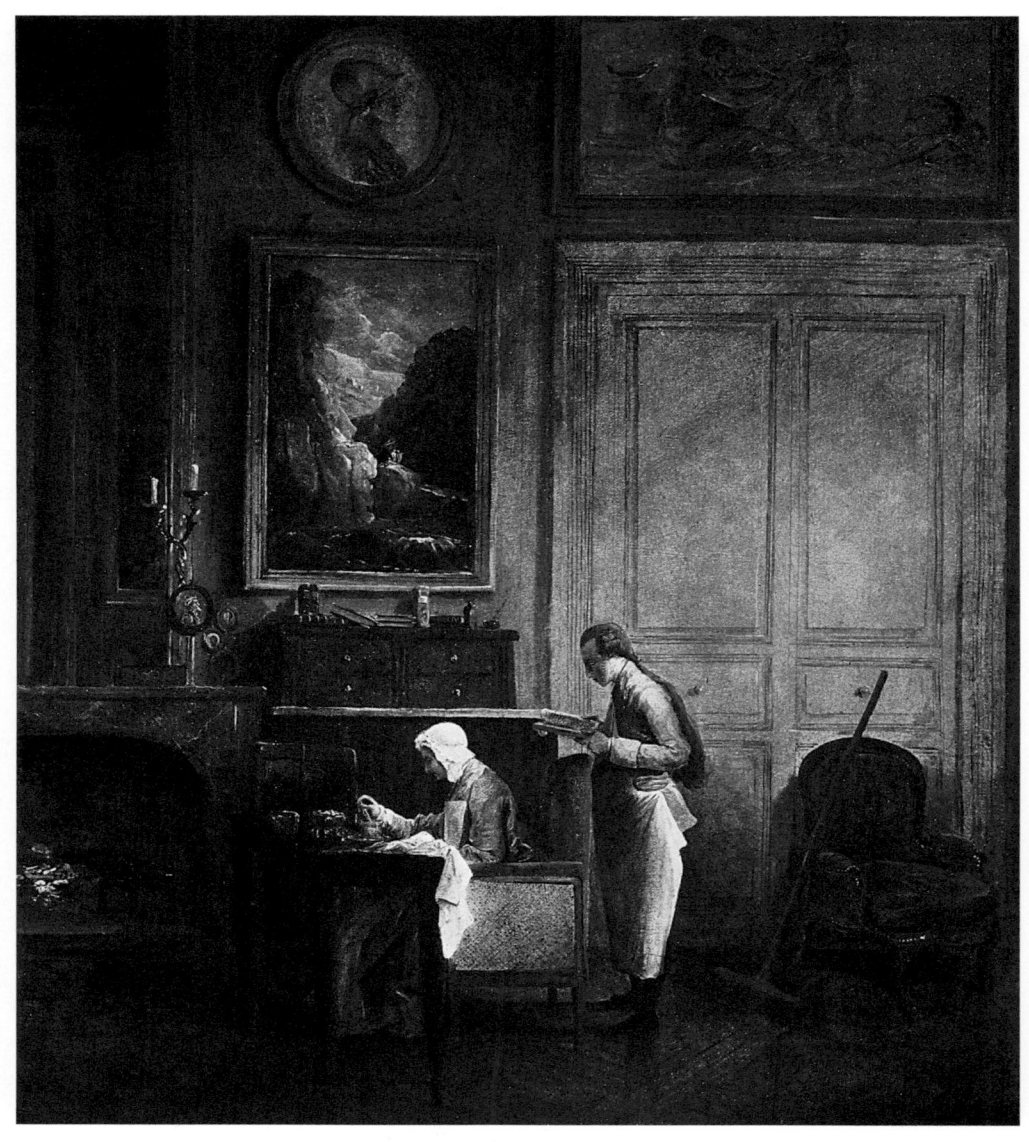

Fig. 2.18. Hubert Robert, *Le déjeuner de Madame Geoffrin*, ca. 1770–72.

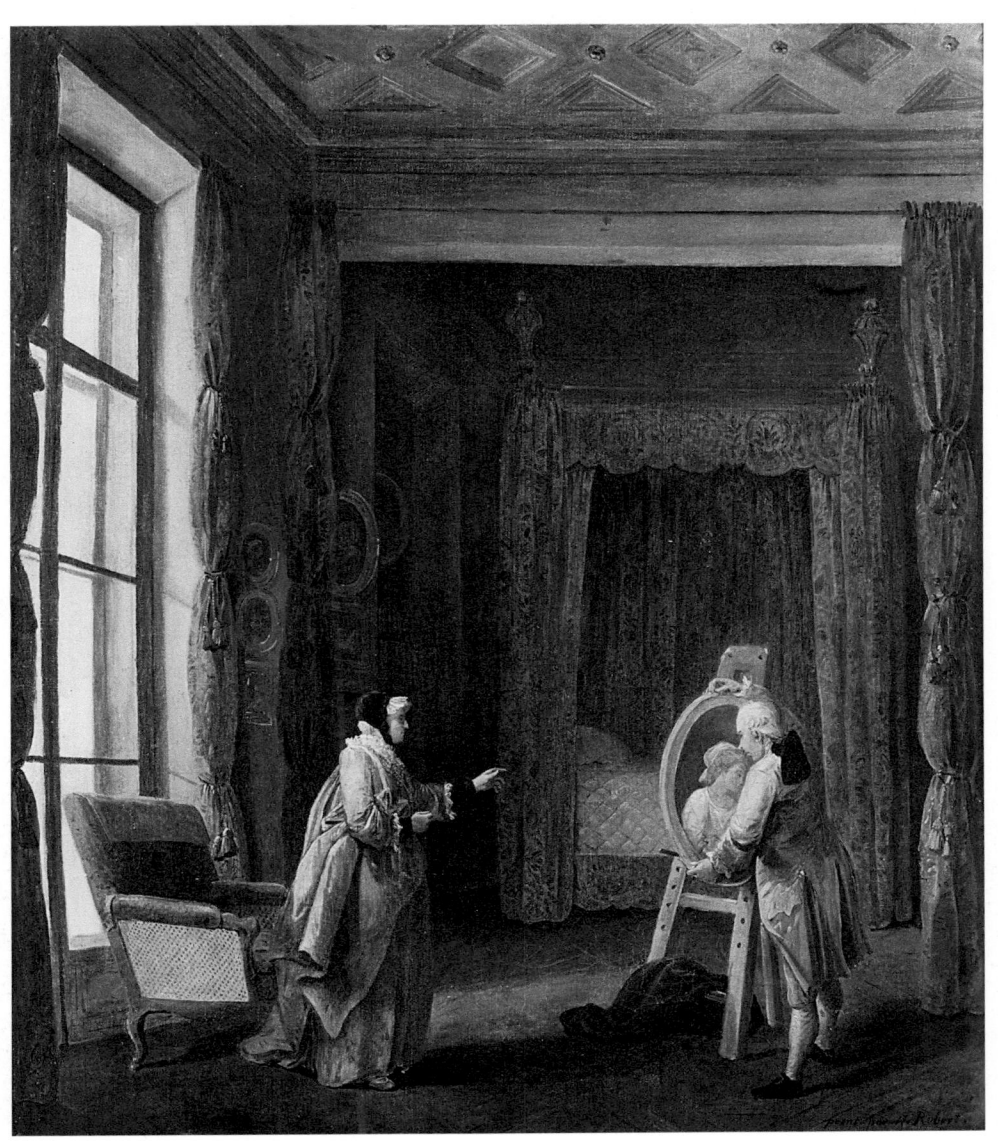

Fig. 2.19. Hubert Robert, *Présentation d'un tableau à Madame Geoffrin*, ca. 1770–72.

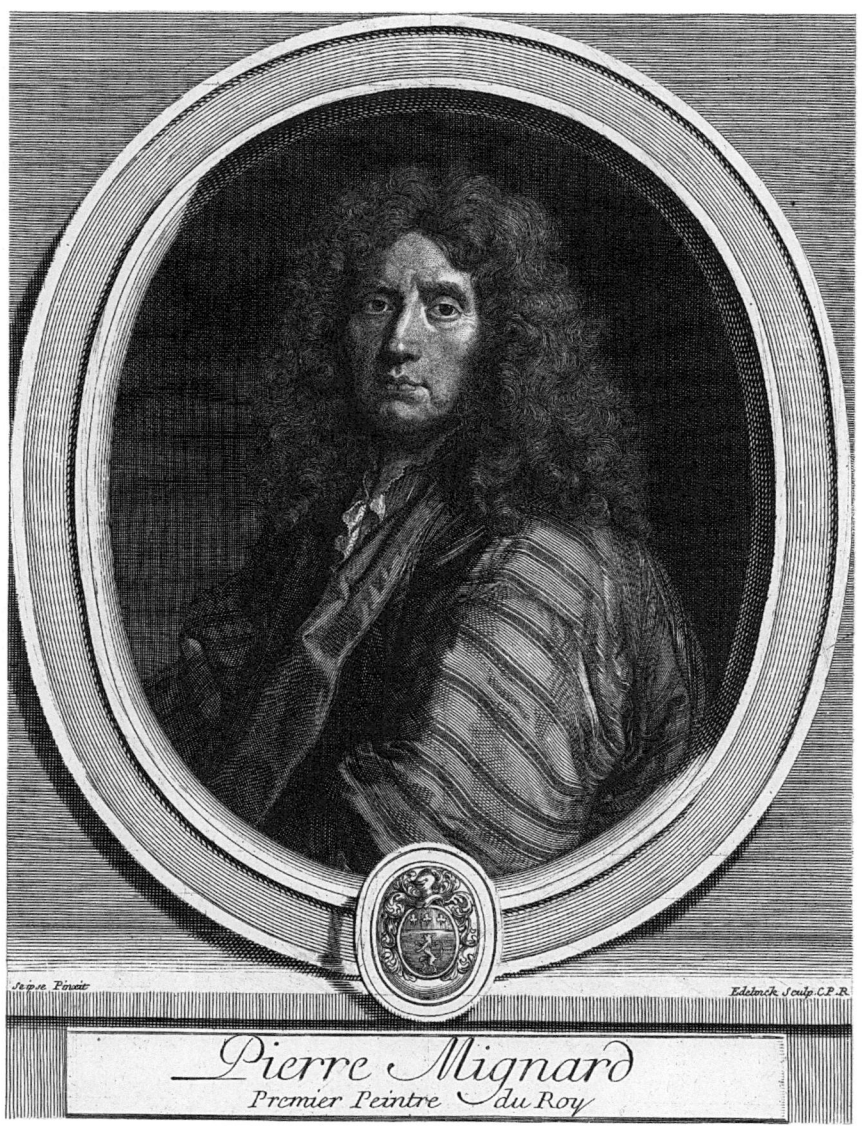

Fig. 2.20. Gerard Edelinck, *Pierre Mignard*, in Charles Perrault, *Les Hommes illustres qui ont paru en France pendant ce siècle, avec leurs portraits au naturel* (Paris: Antoine Dezallier, 1696–1700).

were created as the orders of society became less fixed.⁸⁵ Merit, not rank, became the basis for greatness, an idea that would have been emphasized in the mixed social environment of Geoffrin's salon from which Cochin's portrait project developed. Bell's analysis of these changes has similarly been addressed in the recent work of Lilti: the idea of the *grand homme* was one that shifted the idea of the "hero"—defined as an exemplary person, an incarnation of society's values, and someone to imitate—from emphasizing military prowess to focusing on an individual's intellectual talent.⁸⁶ It is perhaps not coincidental that a number of men that Cochin depicted and encountered during his lifetime, including Rousseau, David Hume, Denis Diderot, and Étienne Falconet, were involved in public discussions about what it meant to be famous.⁸⁷

The men whom Cochin represented were worth depicting because of the significance of their publications, their artworks, or other notable public displays of their greatness. But Cochin also knew a substantial number of them personally, and he could attest to displays of greatness that took place in the private realm that Enlightenment thinking emphasized. Cochin's personal connection to his sitters is apparent in the intimate format of his works, which was made possible by the fact that they were drawn from life. Perrault's illustrations, La Live de Jully's engravings, and those commissioned later by d'Angiviller were not the product of a close encounter with a sitter, as Cochin's drawings were; rather, they were copies of extant portraits of dead men. Cochin's use of pencil brought a sense of personal contact and immediacy to his portraits in a way that the burin could not. In Cochin's portrait of Chardin, for example, the artist did not shy away from capturing the sitter's prominent double chin and bulbous nose, similarly emphasized in La Tour's pastel. The copious shading of the subject's caterpillar-like eyebrows contrasts the arabesque line work used to delineate the curls of his powdered wig. Laurent Cars's engraving after Cochin's drawing changed the fluid pencil strokes into the strict cross-hatching inherent to intaglio work. Carefully rendered folds of flesh and fabric were reduced to a series of intersecting lines, giving the sitter's physiognomy a sculptural, frozen quality.

The acts of recording the participants in Geoffrin's salon in a visual form and displaying their portraits at the Salon, and critics' consistent use of the word *célèbre* or *célébrité* to describe these portraits, indicate a self-consciousness about the social importance and the historical interest of Geoffrin's circle. In other words, Cochin's medallion portraits created a visual and lasting record of Geoffrin's salon by representing its participants, who were some of the greatest intellectual talents of the day, and presenting them to the public.

One imagines that the sitters, with whom Cochin and Geoffrin were personally acquainted, hoped to attain the status of *grand homme* one day.

Critics claimed that Cochin had undertaken some sort of self-sacrifice when completing these drawings. Like the critics who claimed that La Tour was sacrificing earnings in order to depict France's illustrious men, La Font de Saint-Yenne suggested that Cochin sacrificed something else in order to present such an ambitious number of portraits at the Salon—in this case, time, which he could have been spending on his commissions from the court instead. While Joly described the drawn portraits as a form of "amusement," Salon critics were quick to point out that the man who worked for the *Menu plaisirs du roi* had displayed no engravings of royal festivals at the Salon. Notably, Cochin's inclusion of artists and amateurs in his series greatly pleased La Font de Saint-Yenne, who wrote:

I return to Sr. Cochin who has given us with his drawings exhibited at the Salon a public view not only of his singular esteem of all illustrious men, but also for the amateurs of the arts in forty-six small medallion portraits drawn in the best lines. I wish with all my heart and with the passion that I have for all those who can merit honor, that, despite the great works with which he is commissioned by the court with such distinction, he can steal some hours to incessantly execute a project that will immortalize the artist and the originals [sitters] and which will delight all who love to see the spirit and true physiognomy of the men whose works they admire.[88]

As a supposedly not-for-profit enterprise, Cochin demonstrated his appreciation for the important men of his time, and provided an opportunity for artists and amateurs to be immortalized as *hommes illustres*.

From the Salon to the Academy: A Failed Gift

Cochin's project, however, was not an act of self-sacrifice. He began creating engravings of his drawings in earnest in 1763, or had them engraved by amateurs who attended Geoffrin's salon. These print reproductions primarily depicted individuals who were of interest to the public so that Cochin could profit from the reproductions' sale, and often included men with whom he did not have personal contact.[89] Cochin was aware of how his portraits fit in with a growing desire for biographies and images of great men: prints after his own original drawings, made by other engravers, appeared in subsequent Salons, further extending and assuring their impact. The portrait project had begun as a form of documenting the illustrious members of Geoffrin's circle and had value for her in serving in that function, but Cochin appropriated the production of his portraits for his own professional gain.⁹⁰ Importantly, his plans for these portraits extended beyond both the private confines of Geoffrin's home and their public viewing at the Salon. The initial series of drawn portraits appears to have had value in a third arena: the Royal Academy.

We learn from a letter written by Cochin to the genre painter Jean-Baptiste Descamps that the portraits were supposed to have been left to Cochin in Geoffrin's will:

*I have retrieved your portrait from Madame de la Ferté-Imbault, daughter of Madame Geoffrin. I believe that I told you about the plan I had of bartering with her for the return of the portraits of our artists. Madame Geoffrin had promised to leave them to me in her last will and testament, but she forgot or did not manage to do it. Whatever the matter, I've gotten yours back. Perhaps you would like me to send it to you, but how do we settle this with my desire to give all these portraits to the Academy.*⁹¹

Cochin's letter gives us a sense of the personal nature of these objects. That Geoffrin had allegedly promised to leave them to Cochin suggests that these works were not commissioned, bought, and paid for by Geoffrin herself. The gesture of return situates the portrait drawings in a larger eighteenth-century tradition, in which it was customary to return evidence of personal relationships that had been exchanged between two parties—letters, portraits, gifts—at the end of their friendship or amorous affair, whether the end resulted from a rupture or death. Geoffrin followed this rule in her own life; she returned letters from the King of Poland after a rupture between them, explaining, "I could have burned [the letters], but I didn't have the strength: it seemed to me less cruel to put them back in the hands that wrote me these sacred letters."⁹² Geoffrin's similar promise to return Cochin's portraits suggests that these works of art were treated much like other eighteenth-century documents of intimate relationships.

Geoffrin's prolonged illness at the end of her life left this promise unfulfilled.⁹³ Cochin had to find another means to get his portraits back: bartering (*des trocs*), although with what or in what manner we do not know. Cochin's letter to Descamps points to a different and, in this case, conflicting destination for the works. Cochin claims that Descamps wanted his own portrait back, but Cochin informed him that he hoped to give the original drawings to the Academy. This donation, however, seems to have never been made, as there is no record of Cochin's drawings in the Academy's inventory, nor do we find a significant body of Cochin's medallion portraits in the collections of the École nationale supérieure des beaux-arts or the Louvre, where the majority of the Royal Academy's collection is held today.

Cochin's desire to donate his portraits to the Academy marks a shift in the role of those portraits, from being gifts offered to a patron responsible for a major site of extra-Academic and unofficial socializing to documenting artists' status in the official institution of artistic production of the period. In one sense, Cochin's intended gesture was not out of the ordinary. Artists often donated portraits to the Academy, and the Academy depended on such donations in order to increase its collection. Over the course of the eighteenth century, members of the Academy collectively donated twenty-six portraits.[94] Sometimes the portraits were representations of long-dead artists that were owned by members of the Academy. In other cases, the portraits were donated in memory of the artists who painted them. Alexandre Roslin offered a portrait of Jacques Dumont le Romain by his wife, Marie-Susanne Roslin (née Giroust), to the Academy after her death in 1772. Jean-Baptiste II Lemoyne donated his portrait of Charles Parrocel to the Academy in 1752. Lemoyne had given this portrait to Parrocel, who, in return, left the portrait to Lemoyne in his will after his death in 1752.[95] Chardin donated his portrait by Maurice Quentin de La Tour to the Academy in 1775.[96]

The donated portraits supplemented the official pictorial record created by the Academy's *morceaux de réception* portraits. As mentioned earlier in this chapter, artists seeking entry into the Academy as portraitists were required to complete two portraits, the subjects of which were assigned to them by the Academy. While not all the reception pieces created over the course of the Academy's history depicted artists, by the middle of the eighteenth century, the sitters were always chosen from among the Academy's members.[97] As Hannah Williams has demonstrated, the reception portraits served to visualize the Academy and its history, focusing on artists who had achieved the highest ranks of the Academy.[98] But, as she notes, portraitists, genre painters, and still-life painters were not allowed to be promoted to those positions, as the statutes of the Academy restricted promotion to history painters and sculptors.[99] Thus, artists working in the "minor" genres were excluded from the visual history of the Academy created by the *morceaux de réception* portraits, and had to find other ways to be included in the Academy's self-fashioned *galerie de grands hommes*. Cochin's desire to donate portraits of artists to the Academy can be read to correct the absence of non-history painters in the institution's visual record. Of the fifty-four artists drawn by Cochin and subsequently engraved by him or amateurs, only fourteen had been the subject of a *morceau de réception* portrait.[100]

The donated portraits also run counter to the *morceaux de réception* portraits in the types of relationships they display. Because the subjects of the reception portraits were in most cases assigned by the Academy, the artist and sitter were cast in relation to one another in a way that displayed the institution's internal hierarchy.[101] By being required to paint older, more established history painters, younger portraitists displayed their lower rank vis-à-vis the artist they represented.[102] Cochin's portraits, in contrast, bore witness to how artists socialized outside the Academy, in Geoffrin's salon and other spaces, where such hierarchies may have been downplayed.

Where are the Grandes Femmes*?*

The sheer number of portraits that Cochin and La Tour exhibited at the Salon of 1753 is anomalous in the history of the display of portraits at the Salon, and the reason that particular Salon included an unprecedented number of portraits. In the midst of a direct attack on the value of portraits in the context of a public exhibition, Cochin's elaborate portrait project was a means of representing extra-Academic associations that functioned in the semi-private sphere of Geoffrin's salon, and displaying them in the very public realm of the Salon. La Tour similarly displayed his engagement with Enlightenment culture at the Salon, which added to his own reputation as well as to that of his sitters. He also appears to have been involved in a wide network of portrait exchange with his fellow artists. At his death in 1788, La Tour bequeathed to an astounding number of artists "leurs portraits et miniatures" (their portraits and miniatures).[103] The vague description makes it difficult to determine who the authors of these portraits were. Were they portraits by La Tour? Were they self-portraits or perhaps even done by a third party? That the list of sitters includes people who were not artists suggests that the portraits were images of those people rather than works by them, but of course in the case of artists, those two categories might not be mutually exclusive. Even without the knowledge of the authors of these works, the list is a remarkable record of the most important artists of the period (Cochin, Vien, and Jean-Baptiste Pigalle), up-and-coming artists of the 1780s (François-André Vincent, Jacques-Louis David, and Jean-Simon Berthélemy), and two women artists, "Mme Guiart" (Adélaïde Labille-Guiard) and "Mme Lebrun" (Elisabeth Vigée-Lebrun).[104]

The appearance of two women artists in this list is noteworthy. The number of portraits of male artists at the Salon far outnumbered those of women artists, in part because women were in the minority in the official realm of artistic production. Even with this discrepancy taken into account, however, there were far more portraits of male artists by women artists than portraits of women artists by men. While Vigée-Lebrun, Labille-Guiard, and other women regularly represented their male colleagues, the favor was rarely returned. Similarly, it is striking that the vast majority of commentary on Cochin's and La Tour's portraits at the Salon of 1753 focused on depictions of men. We have no way of knowing if Cochin included any women in the forty-six drawings he displayed, although there may have been portraits of at least three.[105] In Salon criticism, the six portraits of women that La Tour displayed received far less discussion than those of the men. One of the rare comments on the women's portraits was a decidedly backhanded compliment from La Font de Saint-Yenne, who praised La Tour's ability to please women, who were "rarely satisfied with their portraits."[106]

La Tour's portraits of women were also listed in a very different way in the Salon *livret* than the others. In the information about the portraits, the men's names were all followed by their titles and academic associations. (Even the least decorated of the men, Rousseau, was listed with his self-styled title, "Citizen of Geneva.") With the exception of Silvestre, shown at his easel, and the Marquis de Voyer, depicted in armor, the men are shown without the attributes that speak to the roles listed for them in the *livret*. Their physiognomies, paired with their names and associations, were enough to demonstrate their celebrity; the viewing public did not need any more visual proof of their talent. The women, though, are not shown "being" but "doing": Madame Lecomte holds a piece of music; Mademoiselle Ferrand ponders Newton. The actions of these women are reflected in the descriptions of their portraits. Yet, we are given no other identifying information about them, not even the names of their husbands. The reversal of the relationship between text and image for the female sitters is notable in light of both the emphatic description of their male counterparts as illustrious men, and the dearth of criticism about these portraits.

The social and intellectual networks that Cochin and La Tour depicted were frequently formed within spaces run by women such as Madame Geoffrin and did not lack female participants. Indeed, it is likely that La Tour and Cochin met their female sitters in the same circles in which they were introduced to their male sitters. Yet, in the context of the Salon of 1753—and Cochin's and La Tour's engagement with changing categories of fame as a means of taking a stand against the growing antagonism against portraiture—the vastly different treatment of women has a certain logic to it. For example, one of La Font de Saint-Yenne's most quoted criticisms about the corrupting influence of portraiture was linked explicitly to the vanity of women.[107] With the emphasis placed on the importance of male sitters through the inclusion of their professional titles and affiliations, rather than through visible attributes or a public performance of achievement, celebrity as a form of greatness was the purview of the masculine: an inherent, intangible quality distinct from the superficial beauty that was emphasized in portraits driven by female vanity. The absence of discussion of women as famous or illustrious, and the relative scarcity of portraits of women artists at the Salon, raises important questions about the homosocial nature of the institutions of artistic production in eighteenth-century France, which will be addressed in the next chapter.

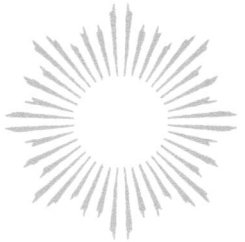

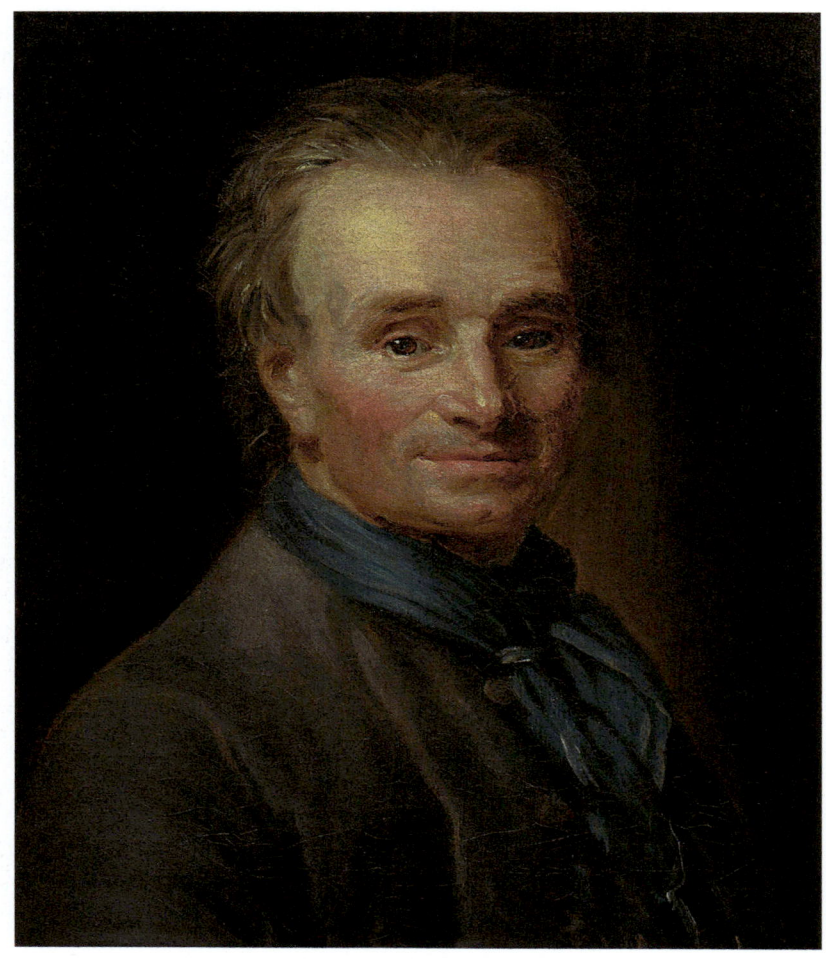

Fig. 3.1. Élisabeth-Vigée Lebrun, *Portrait of Jean-Baptiste II Lemoyne*, 1772.

Chapter 3

RE-EVALUATING RIVALRY

Vigée-Lebrun and Labille-Guiard at the Salons of the 1780s

"HERE YOU HAVE IT, a sad letter written to make celebrity disgusting, especially if one has the misfortune of being a woman."[1] So ends the seventh letter of Élisabeth Vigée-Lebrun's *Souvenirs*, which describes the slanderous rumors that circulated about her in the 1780s, specifically about her supposed love affairs with her patron, the Comte Charles-Alexandre de Calonne, and painter Guillaume Ménageot. Published in the 1830s, toward the end of Vigée-Lebrun's life, the letter suggests that although male artists used celebrity to advance their careers (as seen in the previous chapter), for women artists, the line between celebrity and infamy was dangerously thin.[2]

Male artists were able to take advantage of friendship because the Royal Academy depended heavily on a rhetoric of friendship that saw it as the purview of men, both in the institution itself and at its exhibitions. Yet, the Academy was not an exclusively masculine institution. While it consistently tried to forbid women from entering, or at least regulate how many were accepted, fourteen women were admitted into the Academy between its foundation in 1648 and its abolishment during the Revolution in 1793.[3] The apartments of the Louvre, where select Academicians lived and worked, were also home to members' wives and daughters, a number of whom were practicing artists, as well as male artists' female students and a select few women artists.[4] Away from the Louvre, heterosocial networks could be found in the neighborhood around the Palais Royal and in other areas where Academicians not housed in the Louvre established their residences.[5] During Revolutionary efforts to reform the Academy, prior to its dissolution, women's place in the institution was hotly debated. The Academy's successor, the

Institut de France (later the École des beaux-arts) completely excluded women artists, highlighting the relative openness of the Royal Academy to women artists when compared to nineteenth-century practices.[6]

Given the heterosocial makeup of the Academic community, an examination of amicability in the Academy and at the Salon is not complete without considering friendship between women, and between men and women. A particularly illuminating case study is found in the careers and lives of Adélaïde Labille-Guiard and Vigée-Lebrun. These two women were the most publicly discussed of the Academy's female members, in no small part because of their simultaneous acceptance into the Academy and because the four Salons they participated in were held during the decade that saw the largest amount of published Salon criticism.

Both Vigée-Lebrun and Labille-Guiard exhibited at venues that served as alternatives to the official Salon of the Academy, such as the Académie de Saint-Luc and Pahin de la Blancherie's Salon de la Correspondance. My focus here, as in the previous chapters, is on the criticism they received at the Academy's official Salon. What follows is not a holistic treatment of the œuvres of Vigée-Lebrun and Labille-Guiard, but rather a consideration of how the portraits they exhibited were interpreted by critics to encapsulate each woman's social network, with a particular eye to Enlightenment ideas about female friendship.[7]

From their debut in the official Parisian art scene, the two women were discussed as rivals. The author of *La véridique au Salon* noted in 1783, for example, that "[t]hese two rivals make great strides toward perfection."[8] References to rivalry, competition, and emulation appeared frequently in Academic discourse and Salon criticism, as was addressed in the first chapter, but these terms were as fluid as the word friendship was. Labille-Guiard and Vigée-Lebrun's rivalry differed from those among other artists because it was framed and discussed in gendered terms, most notably in the discussion of their approaches to painting. As Mary Sheriff and Laura Auricchio have discussed, Vigée-Lebrun was said to have a feminine "touch" in contrast to Labille-Guiard's more masculine painting style.[9] The rivalry of their styles was likely emphasized by the fact that, as Hannah Williams has shown, Vigée-Lebrun's and Labille-Guiard's displays of self-portraits in the same Academy Salons of the 1780s meant that the two more or less had a literal face-off, making it easy for Salon critics to compare them.[10]

Melissa Hyde notes in her review of the 2016 monographic exhibition on Vigée-Lebrun, organized by Joseph Baillio and Xavier Salmon, that the rivalry between the two women was largely a construction of Salon critics and the Academy itself.[11] Despite the copious critical commentary that positioned these women as "rivals," no evidence exists of specific social interactions between Labille-Guiard and Vigée-Lebrun. That Vigée-Lebrun did not mention Labille-Guiard's name among her copious references to professional and personal contacts in her *Souvenirs* suggests that the two had no particularly meaningful contact. Her only reference to Labille-Guiard was a veiled one couched in a discussion of her own interactions with Louis XVI's aunts in Rome after fleeing the Revolution in Paris: "I did not know that a woman artist, who has always been my enemy, I don't know why, tried, in all imaginable ways, to paint a bleak picture of me to these princesses."[12] This singular, oblique reference to Labille-Guiard is often taken as evidence of antagonism between the two artists.

Constructing Labille-Guiard's and Vigée-Lebrun's relationship as a rivalry, pure and simple, as Hyde notes, prevented them from ever being compared to their male counterparts, effectively excluding them from the male-dominated art historical narrative of eighteenth-century French painting.[13] This chapter seeks to look beyond the "catfight," to use Hyde's phrase, between the Academy's two arguably most famous *académiciennes*. Supposedly outsiders to the official Academic system by definition because of their gender, they were integrated into, and took advantage of, professional and patronage networks that intersected with the official Academic body that sought to exclude them. This resulted in the production, exchange, and display of portraiture that, like that of the male artists I have discussed previously, was meant to publicly promote their networks.

Salon critics' interpretations of these women's networks were influenced by debates about women's capacity for friendship, both with other women and with men. In the seventeenth and eighteenth centuries, the idea that women could be friends with one another, or even experience friendship at all, was hotly contested.[14] Michel de Montaigne, frequently quoted on the subject of friendship, dismissed outright women's potential for experiencing true friendship, claiming their souls were too weak.[15] Even female moralists doubted that women could experience true friendship. Anne-Thérèse de Marguenat de Courcelles, known as Madame de Lambert, concluded her *Traité de l'amitié* by lamenting that "women are unified by necessity, and never by choice."[16] Lambert, however, believed that friendship between men and women was possible, which she described in her *Avis d'une mère à sa fille*: "An honest woman (*honnête femme*) has the virtues of men: friendship, integrity, commitment to duty: a friendly woman has not only exterior graces, but a graceful heart and feelings."[17]

Anne Vincent-Buffault has argued that Lambert and other women like her in the late seventeenth and early eighteenth centuries, such as the Présidente Thiroux d'Arconville, championed mixed-sex friendship over female friendship as a means of justifying women's participation in the Republic of Letters.[18] By proving themselves capable of friendship with men, women could demonstrate that they possessed the masculine virtues required to participate in the semipublic world of the Republic of Letters. This has been likewise demonstrated in a number of scholars' examinations of correspondence between men and women in the Republic of Letters.[19] Notably, however, these examples of literary and intellectual friendship were enacted within the realm of correspondence. While a letter's audience was not necessarily limited only to its recipient, the written word did not have the kind of public audience that the visual display of friendship through portraiture—however defined—had at the Salon exhibition.

The separation of friendship between women, on the one hand, and mixed-sex friendship, on the other, is relevant in light of Vigée-Lebrun's comments about Labille-Guiard, the construction of the two women as rivals, and the reception of their portraits. Of particular note is Lambert's claim that women only formed friendships out of need, as Labille-Guiard and Vigée-Lebrun never needed each other. They had separate but overlapping social networks of men and women that assisted them on the path to becoming *académiciennes*. This is not to say that women artists did not support each other, because they certainly did. Marie-Thérèse Vien (née Reboul) presented Anne Vallayer-Coster for admission to the Academy in 1770. Vigée-Lebrun spoke warmly about women artists in her *Souvenirs*— notably, pastellist and painter Rosalie Filleul, Jeanne-Angélique Bocquet, and flower painter Marquise de Grollier, all in Paris, and Swiss painter Angelica Kauffman, whom she encountered in Rome. Labille-Guiard had at least nine female students, and, as will be discussed, created a self-portrait that celebrated both female friendship and female mentorship.

Despite the lived realities of the friendships between women artists, the construction of Labille-Guiard and Vigée-Lebrun as rivals demonstrates what Christine Roulston has identified as an eighteenth-century "discourse of separation *between* women." This discourse, which either claimed female friendship to be trivial and artificial, or sexual and therefore unnatural, allowed for a strategic delegitimization of female friendship and was part of a negative response to women's increasing participation in the public sphere.[20] Such a divide-and-conquer approach is apparent in the criticism of the portraits Labille-Guiard and Vigée-Lebrun displayed that publicized their social networks.

While Labille-Guiard was praised for her portraits of a well-established network of male Academicians that fit neatly within definitions of Academic (homo)sociability, Vigée-Lebrun's portraits of aristocratic women led to a consistent association with the false female friendship that was supposedly corrupting eighteenth-century sociability. Although both women exhibited portraits in subsequent Salons that showed the diversity of their friendship networks, the first impressions they created in 1783 proved hard to shake.

A Tale of Two Women

In order to best understand the role—both positive and negative—that friendship played in Labille-Guiard's and Vigée-Lebrun's careers, it is helpful to understand the women's different origin stories. The use of the word "story" here may seem to imply that what follows is fiction, which is not the case. On the contrary, we know much about both women's upbringing and training; their histories are often repeated, often in tandem. By considering the frequently recounted versions of their histories with a view to the portraits they displayed at the Academy's Salon, I aim to provide a more nuanced understanding of their integration into networks of artistic production and patronage.

The two women were born almost exactly six years apart—Labille-Guiard on April 11, 1749, and Vigée-Lebrun on April 16, 1755—on either side of the Place des Victoires in the parish of Saint Eustache, where they were both baptized. Labille-Guiard grew up on the rue Neuve des Petits Champs, between the Rue Richelieu and the Place des Victoires.[21] Vigée-Lebrun was born and lived for a short time on the nearby Rue de la Coquillère, before moving in with her stepfather on the Rue Saint-Honoré. This neighborhood was home to a number of artists who were members of the Royal Academy and of the Académie de Saint-Luc, because of its proximity to the Palais Royal and the Louvre. The contact the women had with artists in this neighborhood, both formally and informally, was an important part of their professional training.[22]

Then, the two artists' lives diverged. Labille-Guiard was the daughter of a *marchand mercier* who owned a shop called La Toilette and, according to Joachim Lebreton, "neglected [his daughter's] education."[23] As Clare Haru Crowston has demonstrated, the finances of the *marchands merciers* in Paris were dependent on carefully managed debt, and a large number of boutiques folded under that enormous weight.[24] This is perhaps why, in 1761, Labille-Guiard's father sold the contents of his shop to one Josephe Blondelu for the enormous sum of 8,550 livres, three years after becoming a *receveur* for the newly founded and highly profitable *lotérie de l'École militaire*.[25] *Receveurs*—or sellers of lottery tickets—made 5 percent of every ticket they sold, with little to no overhead involved.[26] The profit from the boutique's sale, coupled with the new, consistent income from her father's career change, may have factored into the start of Labille-Guiard's career. In 1763, when she was fourteen, she began her artistic training with a neighbor, miniaturist François-Élie Vincent.[27] She then became a student of Vincent's son, François-André Vincent, after he returned from Rome in 1775. As Laura Auricchio and Elizabeth Mansfield have demonstrated, the friendship between François-André Vincent and Labille-Guiard was lifelong, and the two would marry in 1800.[28] Vincent *fils* was a student of Joseph-Marie Vien, who was also close friends with Swedish portraitist Alexandre Roslin. Roslin lived on the Rue Feuillade from 1756 until 1764, probably less than a block from Labille-Guiard's childhood home, before relocating slightly farther down the Rue Neuve des Petits Champs. As Auricchio notes, both Roslin and Vien were supportive of women painters—both men were married to *académiciennes*—and Roslin presented Labille-Guiard for her admission into the Academy.[29]

Vigée-Lebrun was the daughter of Louis Vigée, a painter who was a member of the Académie de Saint-Luc and was her first teacher. In contrast to the neglect Labille-Guiard suffered during her upbringing, Vigée-Lebrun received a convent education.[30] After leaving the convent in 1766, she was quickly introduced to the artists and intellectuals whom her father regularly invited to both the family's Parisian residence and their country house in Neuilly.[31] When Louis Vigée died in 1767, his daughter was already well established in an impressive circle of artists and patrons, and frequented gatherings at the home of sculptor Jean-Baptiste Lemoyne the Younger, who lived in the Louvre, as well as those of others.[32] This introduction into society was central to her formation as an artist and to the cultivation of an important network of patrons, which eventually lead her to become one of Marie-Antoinette's preferred portraitists in 1778. Her understanding of the importance of networking in the world of the *mondaine* (high society) was made clear in her *Souvenirs*; they place far more emphasis on her social successes than on her successes within the Academy, as Bernadette Fort has noted.[33] Her nomination to the Academy was supported by the famed marine and landscape painter Joseph Vernet, whose portrait Vigée-Lebrun painted in 1774.

It is easy to place these two women in opposition to each other in terms of their upbringing and social networks. Labille-Guiard was part of a circle of Academicians centered around what might be called intersecting ateliers, groups of teachers and students who maintained close ties over the course of their careers. Vigée-Lebrun formed her network instead through her participation, from an early age, in aristocratic circles.[34] These different networks resulted in different routes to Academic acceptance, according to the extant written records. Vigée-Lebrun was accepted to the Academy by order of the king, in order to supersede her marriage to a man who sold paintings for a living, which conflicted with the Academy's proscription of its members' participation in the commerce of art.[35] Labille-Guiard was accepted through the Academy's usual voting procedure.[36]

Mary Sheriff has discussed at length the differences between the official Academic record in its minutes and Vigée-Lebrun's account of her acceptance, and between her acceptance and Labille-Guiard's.[37] The difference between how each woman's story was disseminated in the aftermath of the French Revolution also warrants consideration. In most of the literature, thanks largely to the story Vigée-Lebrun presented in her *Souvenirs*, written during the Bourbon Restoration, her career—her early involvement with aristocratic society and Marie-Antoinette—made her flight from Paris in 1789 a foregone conclusion.[38] Yet, we have no personal account from Labille-Guiard about her reception. According to *Nécrologie*, written by Lebreton, who was a member of the Institut National, created after the dissolution of the Academy, and subject of one Labille-Guiard's portraits (1795, Nelson-Atkins Museum of Art), Labille-Guiard had the option of calling upon Louis XVI's *surintendant des bâtiments*, the comte d'Angiviller, to assist her application, but instead "pushed forcefully against this oblique approach, declaring that she would be judged and not protected."[39] The comment, whether true or not, is easily read as a slight to Vigée-Lebrun's acceptance, and from 1803 forward, Labille-Guiard's acceptance was consistently described as uncorrupted by the intervention of the soon-to-be-deposed monarchy. The vast literature on male artists has demonstrated that there were many routes—protected or unprotected—to membership in the Academy, yet they are rarely compared against one another; furthermore, "oblique" paths to membership are often portrayed as triumphs.[40] As Elizabeth Mansfield has demonstrated in her work on François-André Vincent's supposed rivalry with Jacques-Louis David, we must take into account that rivalry is a product of historiography as much as of personal relationships.[41]

Despite Vigée-Lebrun's and Labille-Guiard's different upbringings and career tracks, their artistic networks overlapped. This is unsurprising given the limited number of Academicians that were in Paris at any given moment. An early overlapping member of their networks was Jean-Baptiste II Lemoyne. One of the most celebrated sculptors of his generation, he was also a renowned teacher. Both Vigée-Lebrun and Labille-Guiard painted portraits of him, both based on older artists' portraits of him. Their portraits had different audiences—one limited, the other that of the Salon—but those audiences were both distinctly tied to the friendships and social relationships that Vigée-Lebrun and Labille-Guiard utilized in their paths to becoming *académiciennes*.

In 1772, when she was seventeen, Vigée-Lebrun painted an oil portrait of Lemoyne (Fig. 3.1). It appears, on first glance, to be a reduced-size copy of Maurice Quentin de La Tour's pastel portrait of the sculptor that was displayed in the Salons of 1747 and 1763 (Fig. 2.2). Vigée-Lebrun, like La Tour, depicted Lemoyne without a wig, wearing a gray coat and blue neckerchief. Both artists captured the spirit of a man who, by all accounts, was very sociable, a well-loved teacher, with a direct yet kind gaze and a subtle smile. Yet, on closer inspection, it becomes evident that Vigée-Lebrun's portrait of Lemoyne is not a direct copy of La Tour's work, but rather was inspired by it, and demonstrates the personal contact the young female painter had with the sculptor. The most striking difference between her and La Tour's portraits is that Vigée-Lebrun aged her subject: his cheeks appear more sunken, his hairline further receded, and his hair thinner and less kempt than in La Tour's 1747 version. Her alterations suggest that she portrayed Lemoyne as he appeared at the age of sixty-eight rather than at forty-three.

Vigée-Lebrun's copy of La Tour's pastel remained in the Lemoyne family, probably as a gift to them from her. The work resonates with the purpose behind La Tour's pastel: he and Lemoyne had publicly acknowledged their friendship through the display of reciprocal portraits in the Salons in 1747 and 1763, as was discussed in Chapter 2. By copying La Tour's portrait and then giving it to the sitter, Vigée-Lebrun effectively inserted herself into a narrative of gift-giving. She simultaneously rendered an homage to her own friendship with Lemoyne and to that between Lemoyne and La Tour. Vigée-Lebrun had ample reason to offer such a gift to Lemoyne, whom she credited early on in her *Souvenirs* for her introduction to what became her clientele. She wrote at length about the time she spent at social gatherings at the sculptor's home in the Louvre, which included La Tour:

Lemoyne was of an extreme simplicity; but he had the good taste to assemble at his house a mass of famous and distinguished men; his two daughters did his home proud.... It is at Lemoyne's home that I met the famous lawyer Gerbier; his daughter, Mme de Roissy, very beautiful, and is one of the first women whose portrait I painted. Grétry [a famous composer of operas comiques], La Tour, the famous pastel painter, were often there; we laughed, we had fun.[42]

Lemoyne's gatherings offered an introduction into society, and especially to an important social network of patrons, that was crucial to Vigée-Lebrun's career as a portraitist.

Lemoyne also played an important role early in Labille-Guiard's career. Scholars are less certain about the type of contact she had with Lemoyne, who died in 1778, but she depicted one of the sculptor's most famous students, Augustin Pajou, in the act of making his teacher's portrait (Fig. 3.2). In her *Portrait of Pajou Modeling the Portrait of His Teacher, Lemoyne* (1783), Pajou is depicted as a rather disheveled half-length figure. He has no jacket, his sleeves are rolled back, and his necktie is missing, allowing his shirt to fall open. This unkempt appearance is explained by the fact that Labille-Guiard has represented him in the process of creation. His right hand gently cradles the clay bust he is modeling, while he holds a modeling knife in his left hand. He looks up at the viewer as if caught by surprise in a moment of inspiration.

This work, which was chosen as Labille-Guiard's *morceau de réception*, was exhibited publicly on two occasions in 1783—first, at Pahin de la Blancherie's Salon de la Correspondance, before her acceptance into the Academy, and then at the Academy's Salon after she became an *académicienne*. Both times, the portrait was well received. In the *Nouvelles de la République des lettres et des arts*, Pahin de la Blancherie wrote that the Pajou portrait was admired due to "the double interest it presents, in offering the traits of an artist who has been admired successively at past Salons for his statues of Bossuet, Descartes and Pascal and that of the famous Lemoine, of whom Pajou was a student and a friend, and whom he in fact emulates."[43] The "double interest" lay in the fact that this portrait is much more than a celebration of one artist. It is a celebration of *two* artists—student and teacher. The reiteration of the subject in the very title of the portrait calls the viewer's attention to that aspect of the portrait.[44]

Like that of Vigée-Lebrun, Labille-Guiard's portrait was inspired by an extant work. Pajou sculpted a bust of his teacher, not once, but twice. The first, a terracotta bust, was displayed at the Salon of 1759 (Fig. 3.3). This portrait was highly praised by critics; when it was shown again in 1763, Denis Diderot was particularly laudatory, without mentioning Pajou's name: "Oh, the beautiful bust of M. Lemoyne, he lives, he thinks, he looks, he sees, he listens, he is going to speak."[45] The bust appears to have been given to Lemoyne, as it stayed in the artist's family until it was given to the administrator of the Marine in Nantes in 1859 by the sculptor's grandson.

Pajou made a second version of his teacher's bust, without drapery, in a more classical vein, which was subsequently copied into marble and bronze

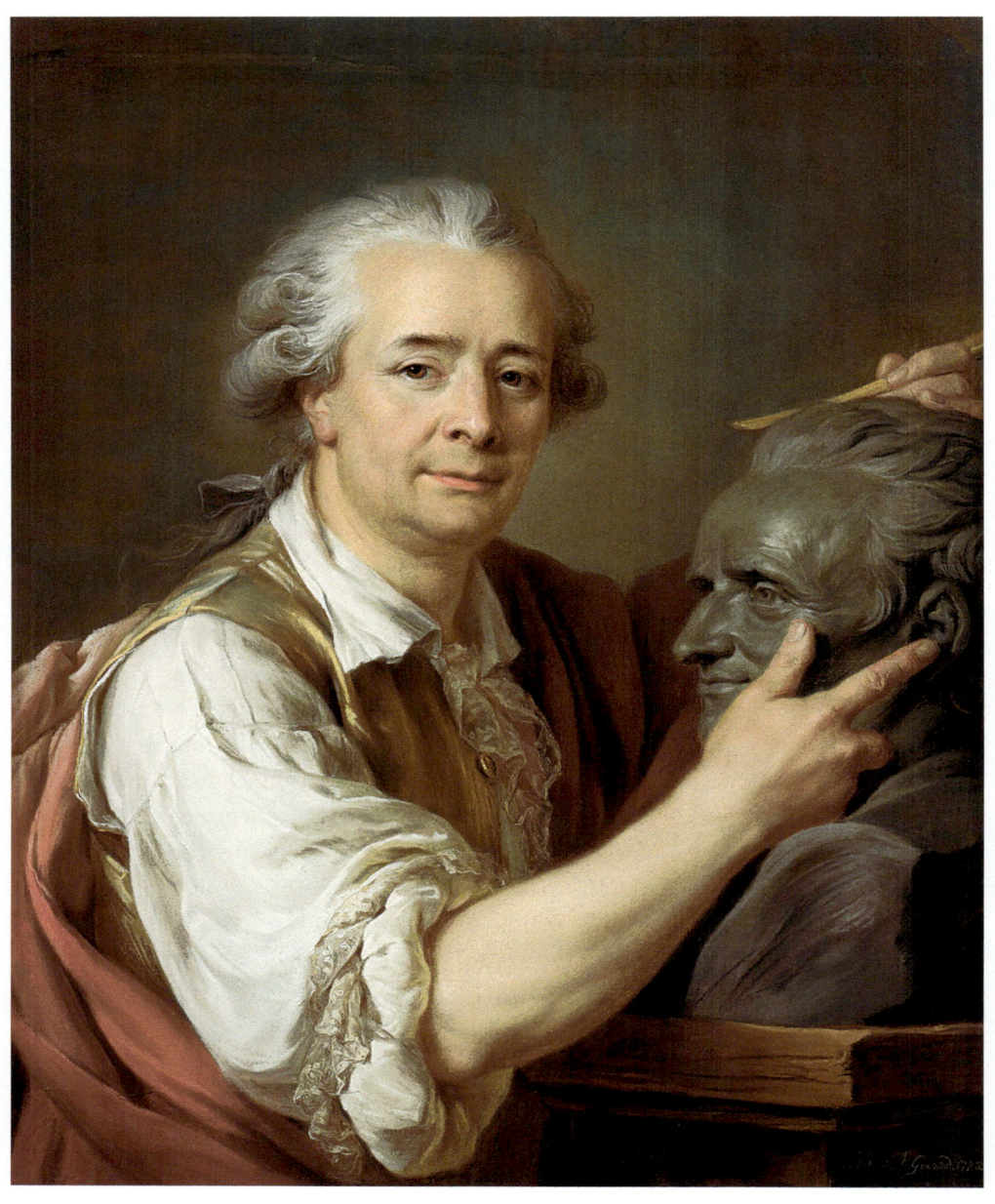

Fig. 3.2. Adélaïde Labille-Guiard, *Augustin Pajou Modeling the Bust of His Teacher, Lemoyne*, 1783.

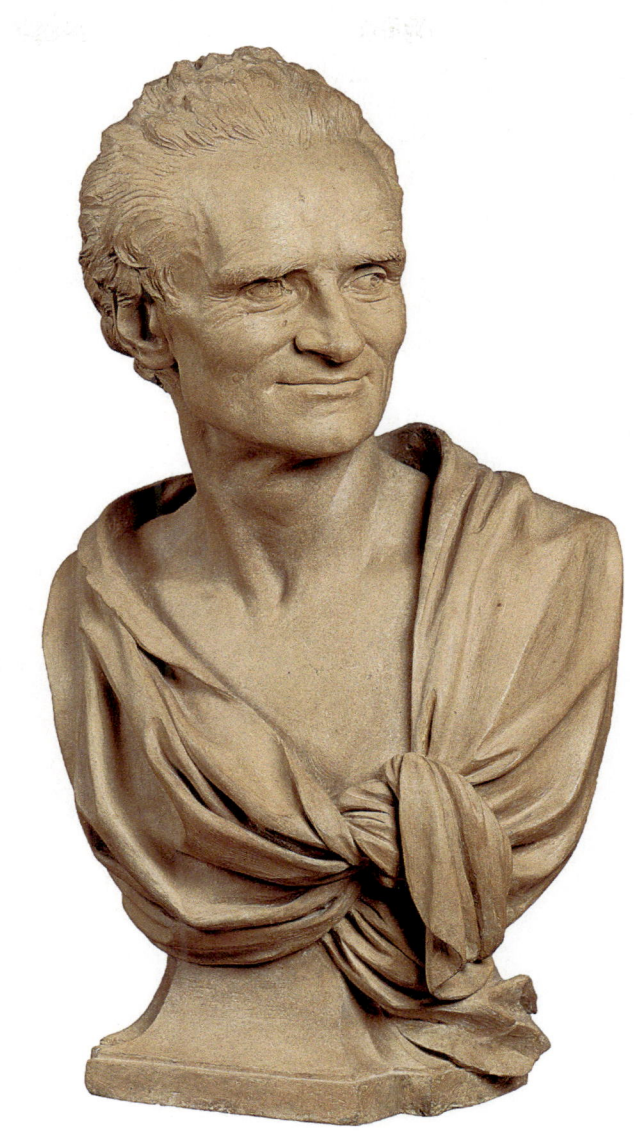

Fig. 3.3. Augustin Pajou,
Portrait bust of Jean-Baptiste II Lemoyne, 1759.

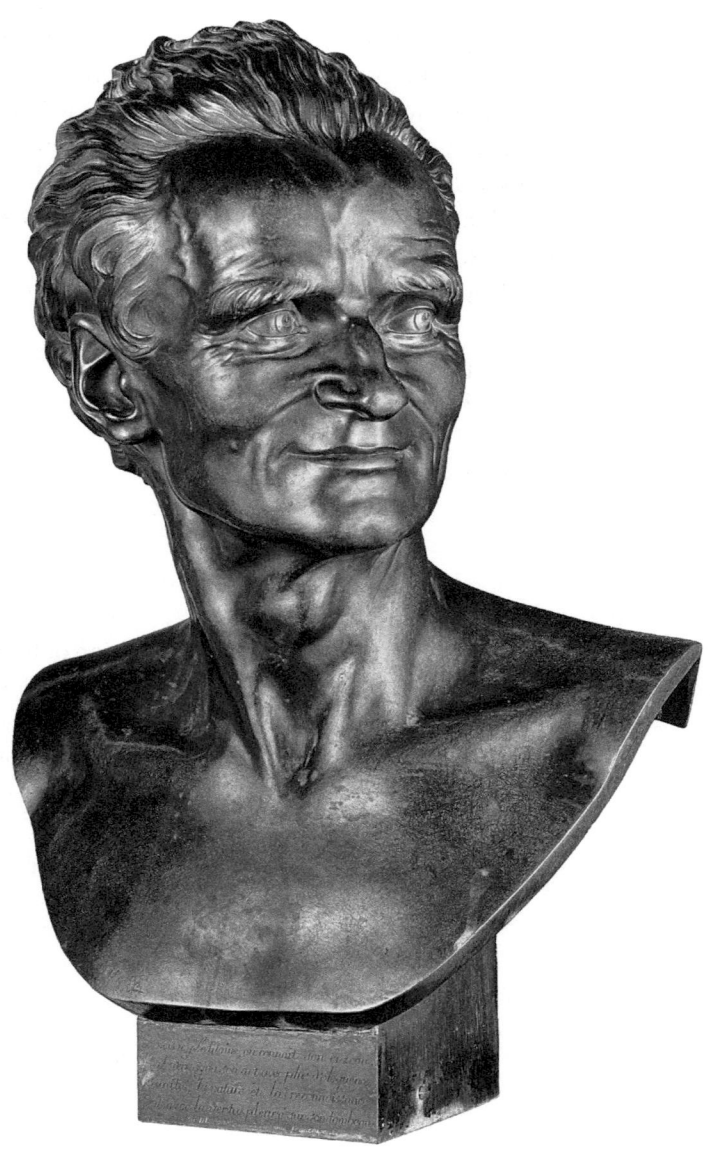

Fig. 3.4. Augustin Pajou, *Portrait Bust of Jean Baptiste II Lemoyne*, 1758.

(Fig. 3.4).[46] The removal of the drapery makes sense, as the work was destined to be copied into marble. Terracotta busts were preferred at the time because clay was thought to express the enthusiasm of the sculptor and gave a more ephemeral attitude to work that contrasted with the harder, more permanent feel of marble.[47] Removing the drapery classicized the bust, and the subsequent copying of the work into marble gave it a more eternal feel, which would have been appropriate to memorialize a highly regarded artist and teacher.[48] It is the second version of the bust that Labille-Guiard depicted Pajou modeling; the bust in her pastel portrait clearly lacks the drapery of the 1759 bust. Yet, her attention to detail in her rendering of the bust of Lemoyne implies that she had close contact with some version of the bust.

Both Vigée-Lebrun's and Labille-Guiard's portraits of Lemoyne make evident their broader networks of artists, but the portraits are neither copies nor citations of other works.[49] They are translations, and both women adapted the particular material qualities of pastel and terracotta into oil and pastel, respectively, while also engaging with the respective temporal differences between their portraits and those by elder men from which they worked. In La Tour's pastel portrait, the delicate powder of the pastel sits on the surface of the work, rendering Lemoyne a somewhat hazy figure, with an overall grayish-blue tone. Vigée-Lebrun took full advantage of the material qualities of oil paint to bring out Lemoyne's ruddy cheeks and lips and make his eyes seem to glisten, paying close attention to the reflection of light in his irises. Perhaps most notable is her treatment of the sculptor's right cheek and ear. Rather than rendering them with a sense of three-dimensional volume, she added a thick stroke of paint that suggests his ear cavity. These fluid brushstrokes, which vaguely portray rather than delineate the subject's features, give the painting a sense of immediacy as if it were completed quickly, reinforcing the idea that the painting is not a mere copy of an extant portrait, but one done from life.

Labille-Guiard worked in the opposite manner, translating wet clay to dry pastel. The art theorist Claude-Henri Watelet famously claimed in his discussion of pastel in *L'Art de peindre*, "Without [the] brush, the finger alone places and starts each shade."[50] In her portrait of Pajou sculpting Lemoyne's portrait, Labille-Guiard explicitly displayed her own touch as well as that of Pajou, creating a comparison of her use of pastel to her sitter's sculptural practice. Pajou's hand cradles the cheek of his master, an area where unblended marks of pastel are used to model the flesh, at times appearing like hatch marks. Short, strong strokes of black left unblended on the smooth surface of the flesh-toned pastel create the wrinkles of Lemoyne's eyes.

Pajou's thumb is placed as if it is pushing the soft clay to form the wrinkles, and the viewer can see the clay underneath his thumbnail. The emphasis on Pajou's hand resonates with Watelet's discussion of both clay and terracotta. His description of modeling in clay in the *Dictionnaire des arts* emphasizes the lack of tools used, highlighting the direct contact the ancient Greeks had with their material: "... they worked with a wooden modeling tool, like the moderns, but they also used their fingers and even their fingernails to model the finer parts... When [the Greeks] wanted to express that finishing a work is the most difficult operation, they would say it is when *clay gets under our nails*"[51] [emphasis mine]. Similarly, the unattributed article on "Modeling in Clay" in the *Encyclopédie* notes: "One doesn't need many tools, as one begins and makes the most progress on the work with the hands."[52] The understanding of the tactile connection between a sculptor's hand and the clay model was expressed by Diderot in the same terms as the understanding of the *touche* (artist's touch) in painting, as a direct index of the artist's genius and enthusiasm.[53] Writing to Falconet in 1768, Diderot stated: "Terracotta is the concern of genius; marble is the conclusion of the work."[54] In the portrait of Pajou, Labille-Guiard explicitly connected her touch in pastel to the enthusiasm of Lemoyne working in clay.

Vigée-Lebrun updated La Tour's portrait and gave it to the sitter. Labille-Guiard recreated the making of a portrait of a dead artist in the context of the portrait of a living one that thematized artistic networks and filiation, a theme that, we shall see, she continued to employ in her later works. Both women artists used their elder male colleagues' works to demonstrate their own social or educational connections to their friendship networks. That they translated those works into different media—and notably, not reproducible ones, such as etching or engraving—serves to distinguish them from their male counterparts.

As discussed in the previous chapter, the idea of an artist's touch was central to eighteenth-century discussions of artistic production. Ewa Lajer-Burcharth has explored the painter's touch as a means of expressing artistic individuation, arguing that the materiality of a particular medium was a tool for artists to negotiate their position in eighteenth-century artistic culture.[55] In Lajer-Burcharth's view, the act of copying is not about influence, but rather about developing one's own touch.[56] Most discussion on touch in this vein has been in regards to men copying other male artists' works or men painting women, for example in Melissa Hyde's and Lajer-Burcharth's analyses of François Boucher's portraits of Madame de Pompadour.[57] In these arguments, Pompadour emphasized her own touch—and her own agency—through Boucher's touch. Vigée-Lebrun and Labille-Guiard did not attempt to mimic the artists' touches that they were copying; given the change of medium, it would have been more or less impossible for them to do so. Instead, by translating the works that they did, they asserted their own agency and placed themselves within associated friendship circles through their own touch, providing a very direct comparison between each other and the male artists with which they interacted. Even when they had opportunities to make precisely this type of comparison, however, Salon critics woefully neglected to do so.

Feminine Displays/Masculine Testimonies

Critics in 1783 compared Labille-Guiard and Vigée-Lebrun to each other on the basis of their painting styles: Vigée-Lebrun was most often associated with an effeminate, soft touch, which corresponded to the ornate, decorative, and artificial, while Labille-Guiard's works were seen to have a hardy, virile, masculine—and therefore more "truthful"—handling of paint.[58] Mary Sheriff has demonstrated that the gendering of the two women's styles had particular ramifications for Vigée-Lebrun, given that she exhibited several history paintings, a genre that was supposedly the purview of men.[59] The gendering of their styles was also implicated in the types of social networks they displayed as their portraits were viewed by critics through a particular understanding of a woman's capacity for friendship.

Excluding their self-portraits and the portraits exhibited under the same number, in which the sitter is almost impossible to identify, there is a striking difference in the genders of the artists' typical sitters. Vigée-Lebrun's identified portraits included one of the Dauphin, and those of six women and girls: Queen Marie-Antoinette *en chemise*; the Marquise de la Guiche, daughter of the Duchesse de Polignac, dressed as a milkmaid; Catherine Grand (née Noël Catherine Verlée) (Fig. 3.5); a woman identified as Mme ✳✳✳; Vigée-Lebrun's own daughter, Julie; and the Dauphine. Labille-Guiard submitted eight portraits of men and one of a woman to the Salon. Seven of her sitters were male Academicians, one portrait depicted the actor Jean-Baptiste Brizard, and the only identified woman was Madame Mitoire, the granddaughter of well-known artist Carle Vanloo. The Academicians whose portraits Labille-Guiard displayed—Vien (Fig. 3.6), Jean-Jacques Bachelier (Fig. 3.7), Guillaume Voiriot, Jacques-Antoine Beaufort, Étienne-Pierre-Adrien Gois, Joseph-Benoît Suvée (Fig. 3.8), and Pajou—played a crucial role in her election to the Royal Academy.[60]

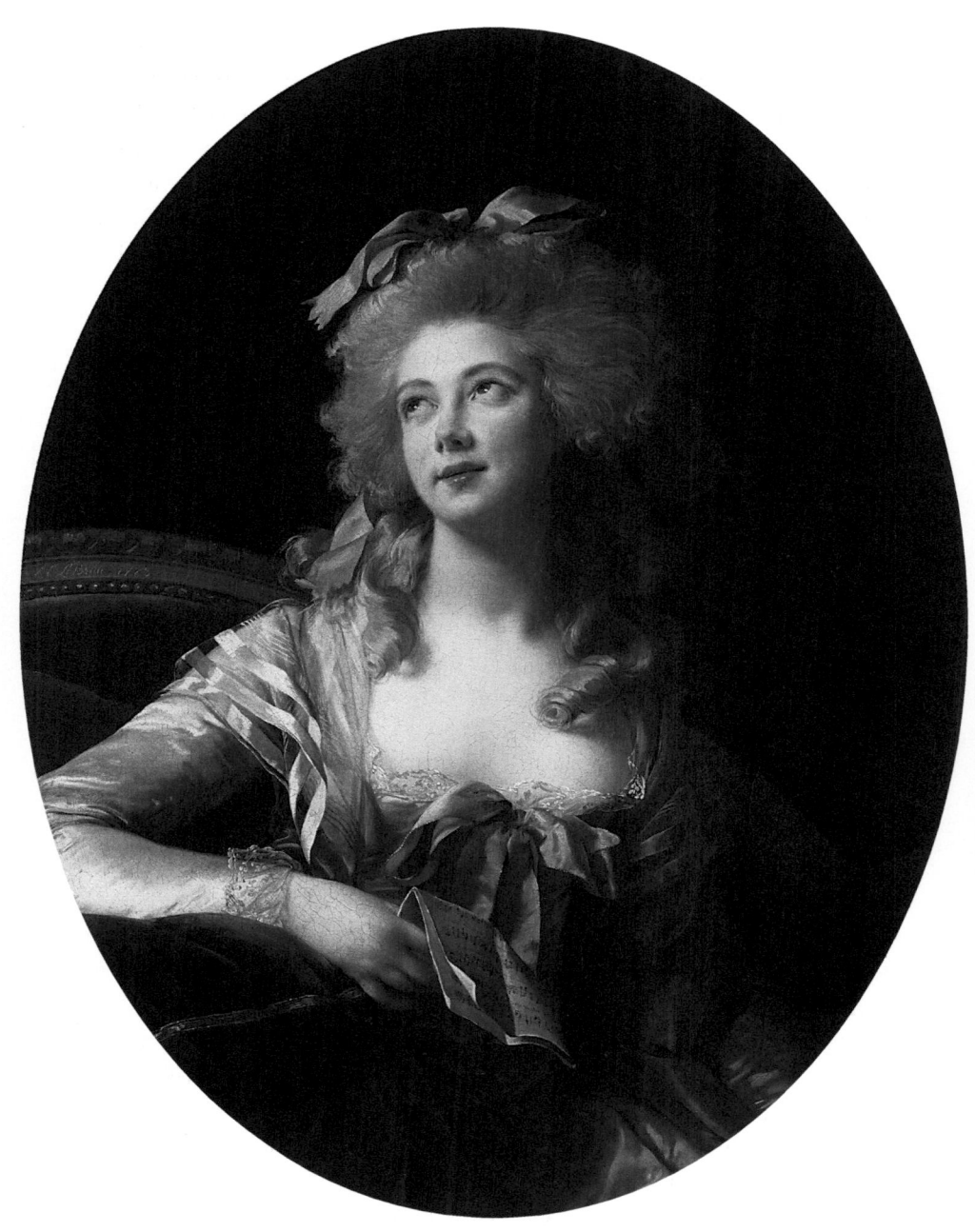
Fig. 3.5. Élisabeth Louise Vigée Le Brun, *Portrait of Madame Grand (Noël Catherine Vorlée)*, 1783.

While Vigée-Lebrun referenced many of her sitters in her *Souvenirs*, Labille-Guiard did not provide any firsthand testimony of her interaction with the subjects of her portraits. However, Labille-Guiard's portraits themselves and other archival documents demonstrate that her sitters belonged to an existing social circle of which she was undoubtedly a member, likely through her connection with the Vincent family.[61] She had been introduced to Vien by François-André Vincent, his student. Indeed, she had portrayed Vincent before she was accepted to the Academy, in a portrait that was displayed at the Salon de la Correspondance but not at her debut Salon (Fig. 3.9). The portrait, or a copy of it, ended up in Suvée's collection. Suvée's portrait was likewise destined for Vincent. Suvée and Vincent had become close during their stay at the Palais Mancini in Rome, during their time as Prix de Rome winners (their time in Rome will be addressed in the next chapter). Suvée was Bachelier's favorite student, and Suvée lived with Bachelier before winning the Prix de Rome in 1771.[62] It is possible that he later worked in Vien's studio.[63] It is also worth noting that the wedding contract of one of Labille-Guiard's students, Jeanne Bernard, was signed in Labille-Guiard's home on the Rue Richelieu by Vincent, Pajou, Suvée, and Charles-Nicolas Cochin, whose portrait Labille-Guiard displayed at the Salon of 1785.[64]

Given the stark contrast in the genders of Labille-Guiard and Vigée-Lebrun's sitters, Lambert's doubts about the possibility of female friendship in comparison to her belief in the virtuous nature of cross-gendered friendship, and the perception that friendship between women was always based on necessity and not choice, and thus could not be true friendship, need to be taken into account when examining critics' reactions to Vigée-Lebrun and Labille-Guiard's portraits. One of the most transparent commentaries on their work, *L'année littéraire*, noted that, unlike the "stiff, constrained" portraits that "announce the boredom of the sitter and the weariness of the artist," Labille-Guiard's portraits cause the viewer to "imagine they are conversing with the faithful image of the person she offers, by the easy manner and their noticeable facility: one can sense as it were the spirit and character of each of her models: the soul appears painted on their face." To this critic, at least, Labille-Guiard captured something deeper than the sitters' physical appearance. Her portraits presented the viewer with a subject to converse with rather than an object to look at. The same could not be said of Vigée-Lebrun's portraits of women, which were described in the same commentary with words that emphasized the external appearance of the sitters. They had "freshness" and "enchanting voluptuousness." In the case of Madame Grand, her portrait was deemed to

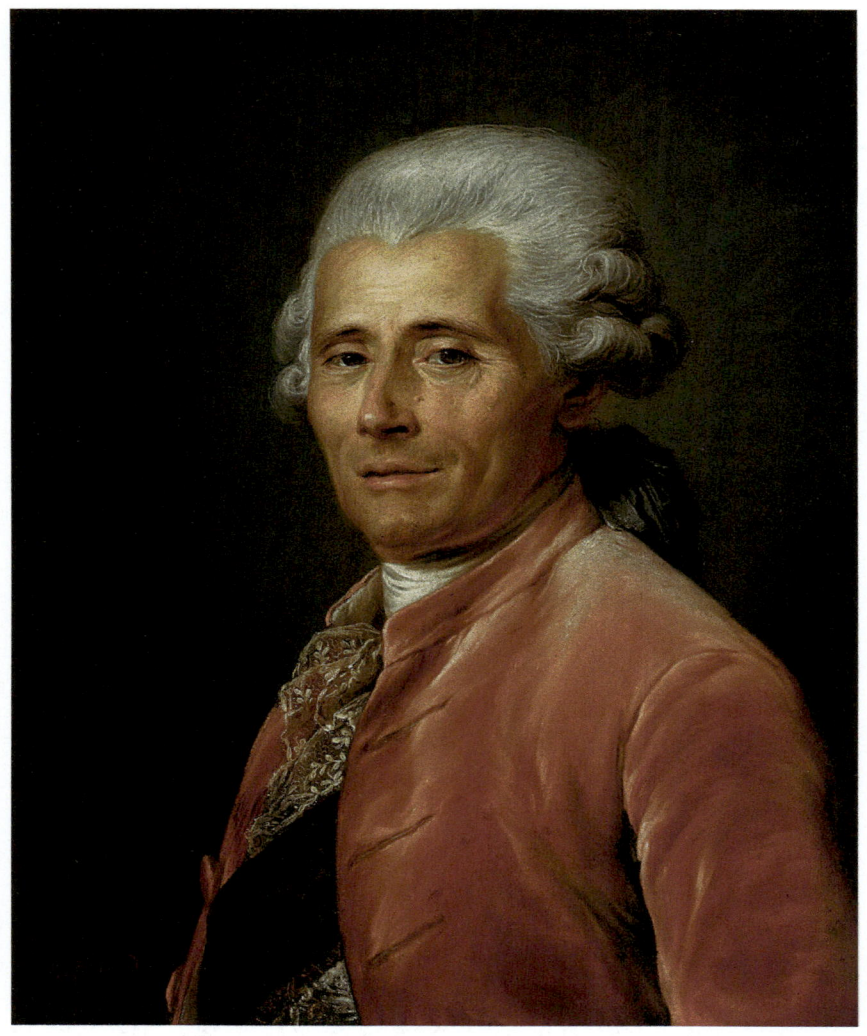

Fig. 3.6. Adélaïde Labille-Guiard, *Portrait of Joseph-Marie Vien*, 1783.

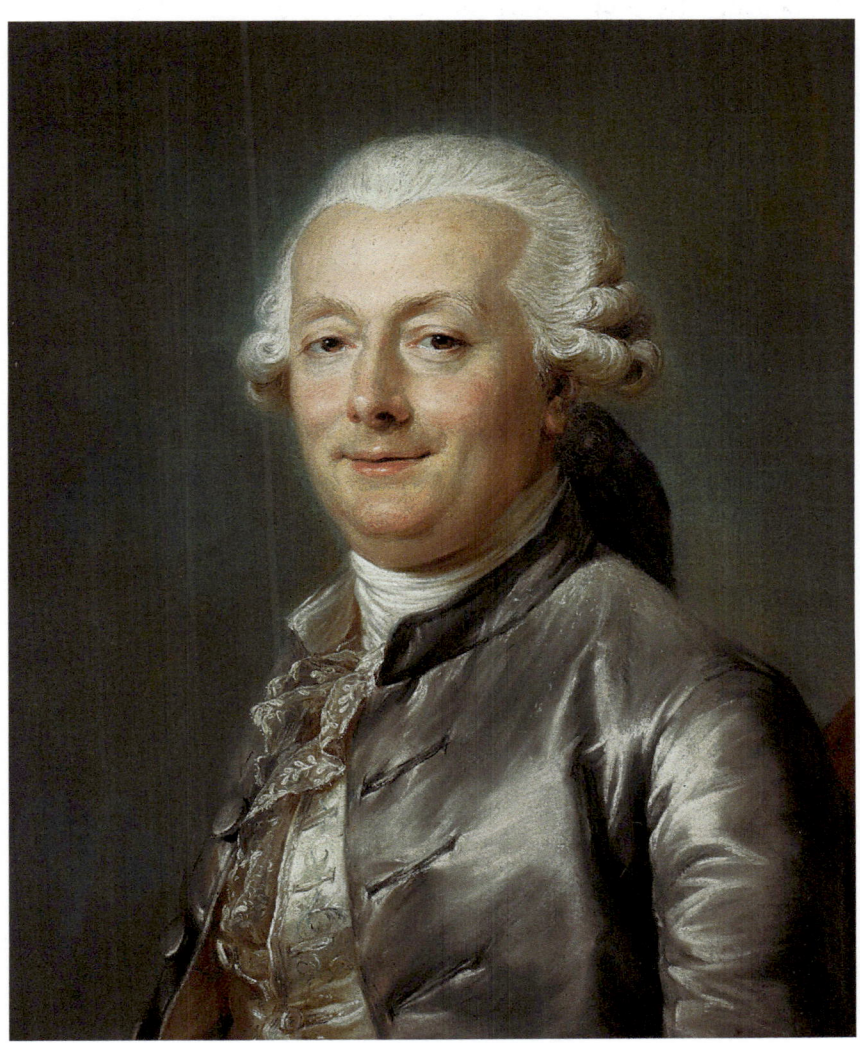

Fig. 3.7. Adélaïde Labille-Guiard, *Portrait of Jean-Jacques Bachelier*, 1782.

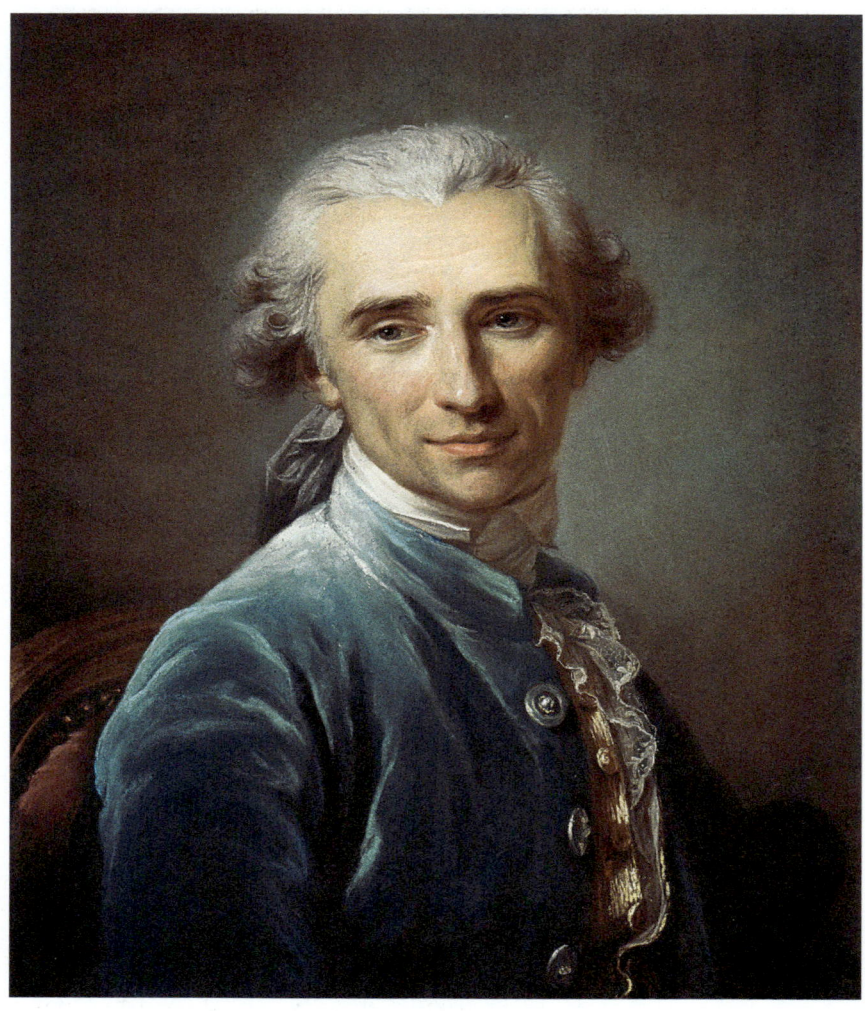

Fig. 3.8. Adélaïde Labille-Guiard, *Portrait of Joseph-Benoît Suvée*, 1783.

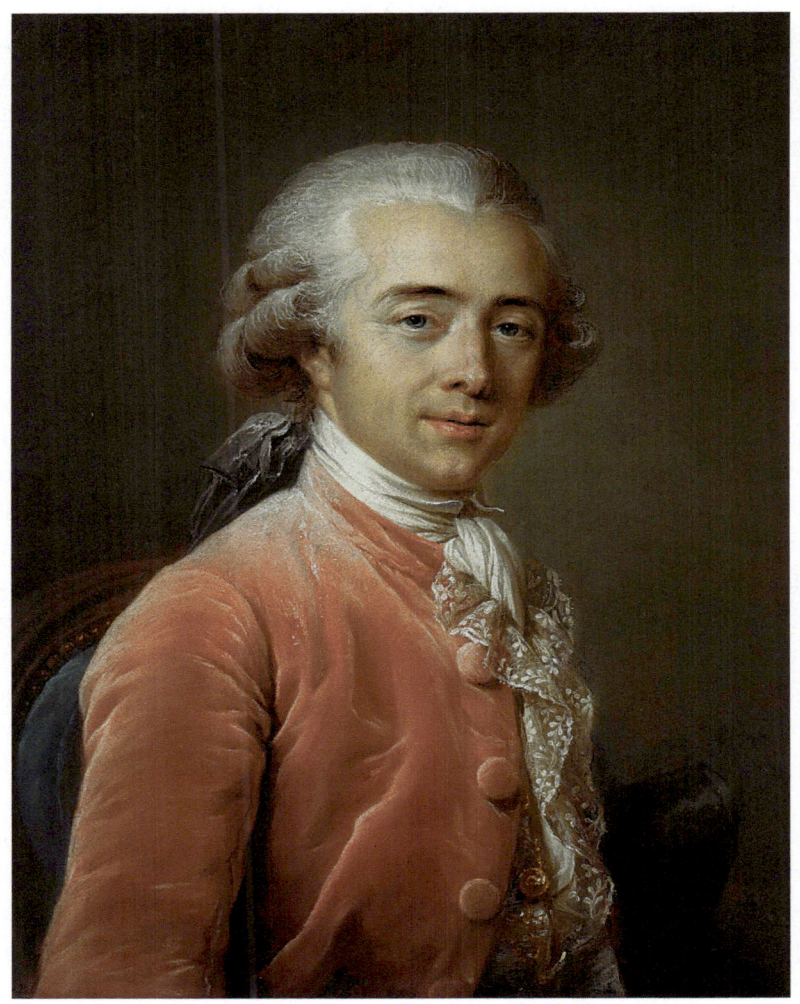

Fig. 3.9. Adélaïde Labille-Guiard, *Portrait of François-André Vincent*, 1782.

capture her "grace," but the portrait of the marquise de la Guiche dressed as a milkmaid was dismissed as "trivial."⁶⁵

Early in the eighteenth century, moralists such as the duc de La Rochefoucauld and Claude-Adrien Helvétius became increasingly concerned with the corrupting influence of self-interest on friendship. These fears were assuaged, in part, by an emphasis on sociability and by the codes that governed salon participation.⁶⁶ Yet the same codes that justified salon sociability were believed to create relationships between salon participants that were empty of affinity and sincerity, so the networks of elite *sociabilité* that Vigée-Lebrun participated in and displayed at the Salon were under attack in the 1780s. As Dena Goodman has argued, these criticisms were explicitly gendered: Rousseau, in his 1758 *Lettre à M. D'Alembert*, called out the women who ran weekly salon gatherings. His most insistent criticism of the corrupting nature of society is found in *Émile*, in which he claimed it was men's sensibility, not sociability, that allowed them to cultivate friendship.⁶⁷ Roulston has similarly noted the detrimental effect of Rousseau's and others' unease about the public role of women, their claims that friendship between aristocratic women was inauthentic, and their celebration of private, bourgeois—and more authentic—friendship between women.⁶⁸ Vigée-Lebrun's aristocratic clientele positioned her at the center of these criticisms. Not only did she represent women who participated in the salon gatherings that were believed to be inimical to true friendship, but she also hosted such events herself. Best known of them was her *souper à la grecque*, a dinner party in which all her guests dressed in costumes inspired by ancient Greece.⁶⁹ She commented in her *Souvenirs* on the rumors that it was an extravagant, expensive affair.⁷⁰

Vigée-Lebrun's friendship with a number of her sitters can, and should, be framed by eighteenth-century uses of the word "friendship" to mask patron-artist relationships. As seen in the previous chapter, men like Cochin and La Tour could rely on the blurry line between friend and patron to help them inoculate portraiture from accusations of greed and profiteering. But it appears that Salon critics were not willing to participate in such a suspension of disbelief when a woman was commissioned to represent an elite circle of women supposedly incapable of true (masculine) friendship. Vigée-Lebrun's association with female-dominated spaces was amplified due to her relationship with Marie-Antoinette, who became the center of rumors that reflected the suspicions of the erotic potential of female friendships, notably the queen's friendships with the duchesse de Polignac and Madame de Lamballe. Sheriff has noted how the combination of images of the queen *en chemise* and the marquise de la Guiche as a milkmaid easily reminded Salon viewers of the queen's feminine domain of the Petit Trianon, and the rumors of "unnatural" (i.e., sexual) relationships between women that followed the queen and her circle.[71]

Labille-Guiard's portraits of men instead represented a network formed in the official realm of Academic education, and demonstrated the homosocial nature of the Academy. The inclusion of her own self-portrait (now lost) among her network placed her within this circle. By displaying portraits of her male friends, Labille-Guiard presented herself as capable of sharing the more difficult but highly valued type of friendship between men and women. She was admitted into the Academy under the name of "Adélaïde des vertus," perhaps associating herself with the "honest woman (*honnête femme*) [who] has the virtues of men" that Lambert described as capable of experiencing mixed-sex friendship, and justifying her inclusion in the homosocial structure of the Academy.[72]

The different reception of Labille-Guiard's and Vigée-Lebrun's portraits in regard to friendship resonates with Louis de Jaucourt's discussion in the *Encyclopédie* of the "Display, testimony of friendship":

These two words are synonyms with this peculiar difference in usage: the former [display] says less than the latter [testimony]. Father Bouhours once pointed this out and time has not yet changed the improper application of these two terms. In fact, displays *of friendship relate more to the exterior: facial expressions and caresses. They designate manners, flattery, and obliging reception.* Testimonies, *on the other hand, focus more on the interior, on the soundness and duties of the relationship, and seem to apply to the heart. Thus a false friend makes* displays of friendship; *a true friend gives* testimonies *of it.* Displays *of friendship involve embracing those persons with whom one lives, obligingly welcoming, flattering, and caressing them.* Testimonies *of friendship entail serving others, looking after their interests, and meeting their needs. There is nothing more common at the court than* displays of friendship; *nothing is more rare than* testimonies. *In a word,* displays *of friendship are only vain signs of attachment, of affection;* testimonies *are the measure of it; but the union of hearts alone constitutes perfect friendship.*[73]

Jaucourt's description of the difference between superficial displays and true testimonies of friendship reiterates Rousseau's critiques of aristocratic (read: public) friendships. Vigée-Lebrun's portraits of pretty women dressed in the latest fashions or as milkmaids supposedly had no depth; they were superficial presentations of social connections, the thinking went, a "who's who" of aristocratic culture. Labille-Guiard depicted the public group of men who were bound together by student-teacher relationships and their shared status as Academicians. Her portraits acted as visual testimonies to deeper, masculine, emotional bonds.

Labille-Guiard's and Vigée-Lebrun's submissions to their first Salon and many of their critics' comments belie the fact that they both required the support of men *and* women from diverse social milieus to succeed. As Auricchio has shown, much was made in the public criticism of the fact that Labille-Guiard's portrait of Brizard belonged to the comtesse d'Angiviller, wife of the *surintendant de batîments*. It is to the comtesse that Labille-Guiard turned in response to slanderous rumors about her love affair with François-André Vincent, published in *Suite de Marlborough au Salon 1783*. Labille-Guiard wrote a letter to the comtesse, which ultimately led to the destruction of thirty-nine of the libelous pamphlets.[74] Vigée-Lebrun's network was made up of a number of male artists who offered her support. Her portrait of Joseph Vernet (1774) was hung in Pahin de la Blancherie's monographic show of Vernet at the Salon de la Correspondance in March and April of 1783.[75] Vernet presented Vigée-Lebrun for acceptance to the Academy a month later. In 1789, she displayed a portrait of Hubert Robert, which will be discussed at the end of this chapter. Both men feature prominently in her *Souvenirs*. Over the course of the 1780s, Labille-Guiard and Vigée-Lebrun expanded the types of friendship and patronage networks that they put on display at subsequent Salons. But their submissions to the Salon of 1783 created a precedent for how their works would subsequently be received as a result of the networks they displayed: Labille-Guiard would be associated with the realm of masculine friendship, and Vigée-Lebrun with the court and aristocratic society.

Friends and Family

In the Salon of 1785, Labille-Guiard exhibited six identified portraits, as well as a number of oil and pastel portraits, under the same number. While three of the portraits were of important aristocratic women, demonstrating her rising star at court, the rest of her exhibited works continued to highlight the synchronic and diachronic Academic networks that she emphasized in her 1783 offerings.[76] Among her works was the impressive *Self-Portrait with Two Pupils* (Fig. 3.10). Long considered her masterpiece, as well as the work that would earn her the place of painter to the aunts of Louis XVI, the almost 211-by-151-centimeter portrait depicts the artist at work, with two of her students, Marie Gabrielle Capet and Marie Marguerite Carreaux de Rosemond, behind her.

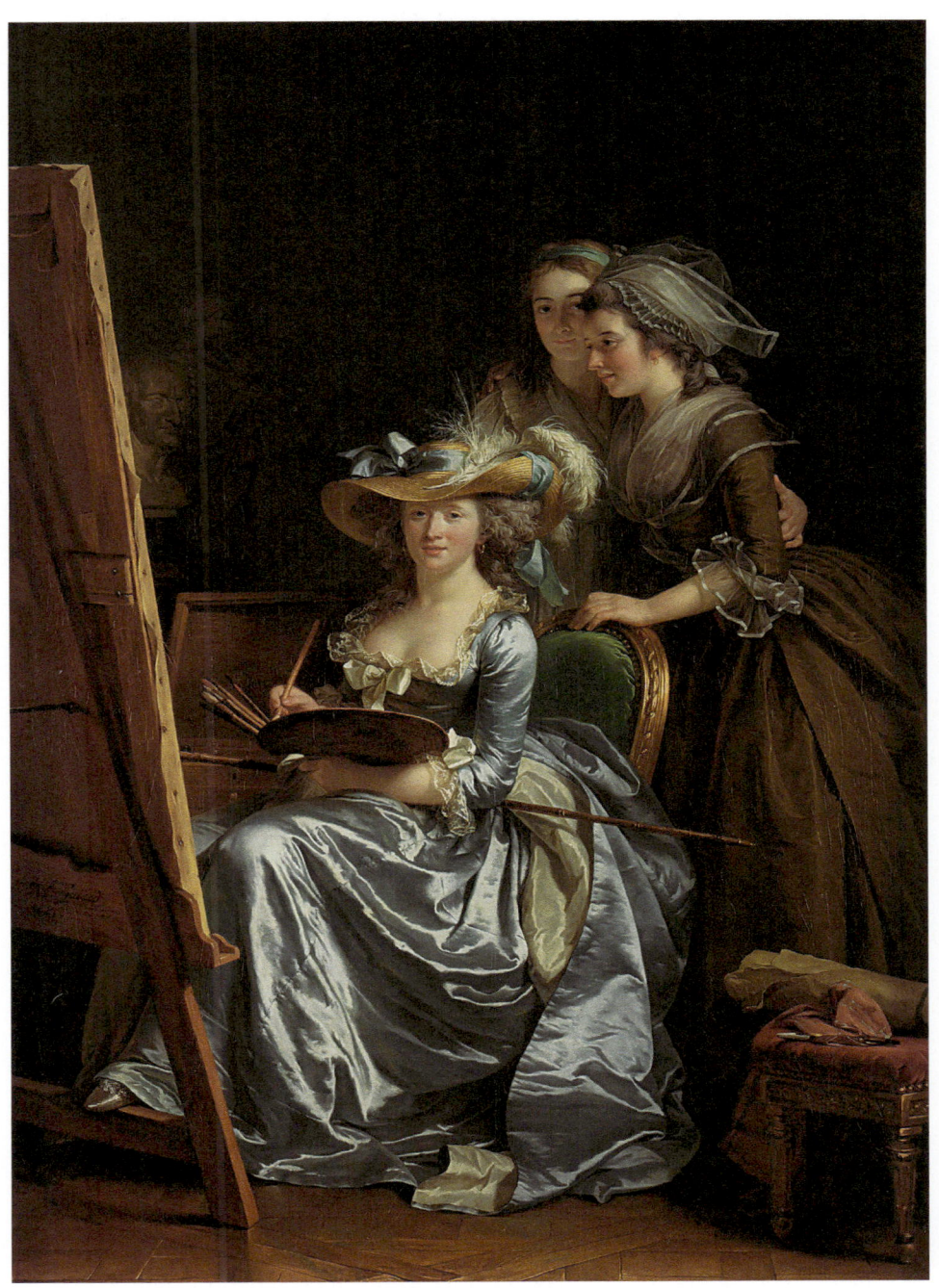

Fig. 3.10. Adélaïde Labille-Guiard, *Self-Portrait with Two Pupils*, 1785.

As in the previous Salon, critics were impressed with Labille-Guiard's "masculine" handling of paint. The pamphlet *Avis important d'une Femme, sur le Sallon de 1785: Par Madame E.A.R.T.L.A.D.C.S. Dédié aux femmes* stated, in feigned shock, that "the woman there is a man, I hear ceaselessly in my ear."[77] The *Observations critiques sur les Tableaux du Sallon* described the *Self-Portrait* as a "portrait composed in the genre of history, and in which one recognizes a vigorous touch, demonstrating the talent of the artist."[78]

With its large size and virtuoso treatment of silk, lace, and other luxurious materials, the work served as publicity for Labille-Guiard's talent as a portrait painter.[79] Thanks to the physical closeness of her students to her and to each other in the image, it also offered a demonstration of female friendship, and of Labille-Guiard's role as a teacher of a new generation of women artists. The depiction of Capet and Rosemond, their arms wrapped around each other, is a powerful alternative to the celebration of masculine friendship that has been the focus this study so far, one that at first might appear to contradict the criticisms of female friendship discussed above.

Labille-Guiard's portrait functioned within conceptions of appropriate female friendship. If Vigée-Lebrun's portraits of her sitters reminded critics of a corrupt, aristocratic, and public form of female friendship, then Labille-Guiard's students represented bourgeois, "private," and therefore acceptable, friendship. Both Capet and Rosemond were from modest backgrounds. Capet came from a bourgeois family in Lyon, while Rosemond was Swiss, and her unmarried parents came from farming families.[80] According to a critic of the Exposition de la Jeunesse, Labille-Guiard's nine students were "all of them pretty and likable, constituting an assembly of nine muses in the cradle of which Mme Guyard is the teacher."[81] The critic describes here a rather unusual situation—an atelier of (pretty and likable) women artists in training run by a professional woman artist—in domestic terms: the young women are compared to children in the cradle, and Labille-Guiard is framed as an *institutrice*, a woman hired to give lessons to young children.

The domestic quality of the *Self-Portrait with Two Pupils* may not have been a complete fiction, as Rosemond and Capet lived with Labille-Guiard at various points in their lives, and it reinforced the critic's description of Labille-Guiard's atelier not as a threatening place of inappropriate female friendship, but as a place of domestic harmony created by separating the sexes, as was promoted by authors such as Rousseau.[82] Paradoxically, this celebration of private female friendship took the form of a "portrait composed in the genre of history," displayed in perhaps the most public of venues that existed in eighteenth-century Paris. That this was a successful approach to representing young women's intimacy is demonstrated in Jean-Laurent Mosnier's strong reference to Labille-Guiard's work in his 1787 *Portrait of the Artist in His Studio*, which shows his two daughters admiring the work in progress, and that critics compared directly to Labille-Guiard's portrait.[83]

Labille-Guiard connected her strikingly feminocentric painting to the network of men she previously had put on display by depicting works by Pajou in the background. The theme of artistic lineage is brought together with biological lineage in the inclusion of Pajou's bust of Labille-Guiard's father, Claude-Edmé Labille. As with her portrait of Pajou, she included a reference to a sculpture that existed, and with which she would have been very familiar (Fig. 3.11).[84] Furthermore, Salon audiences would have had access to the bust, as it was also displayed in the Salon of 1785.

Salon critics missed (or ignored) the opportunity to compare Labille-Guiard's rendering of Pajou's bust to the original, with one exception. The radical anti-monarchist Antoine-Joseph Gorsas, writing under the pseudonym of Critès, wrote, "To your father, Guiard, I have thrown flowers," noting in a footnote that the comment referred to Pajou's bust of Labille: "(one was happy to pay homage to the father of an artist as amiable as he is understanding.) It shows that someone is looking after her."[85] Given Gorsas's political leanings, this was likely a backhanded compliment, but it demonstrates that, as Auricchio has argued, the inclusion of Pajou's bust, and of Jean-Antoine Houdon's sculpture of a vestal virgin next to it, was intended to counter the rumors about Labille-Guiard's affair with Vincent that circulated in 1783, and to demonstrate her propriety to Salon viewers.[86]

The bust was also a demonstration of the amicable connection between the Labille and Pajou families. It was modeled after a bust of Cicero (Fig. 3.12). As Guilhem Scherf has noted, this is unsurprising given the vogue for representing living people in the form of classical busts, possibly started by Houdon's 1771 portrait of Denis Diderot.[87] But the choice of model is striking. Cicero was one of the most-cited classical sources on friendship, and onward from at least 1782, Labille-Guiard and Pajou had a social, if not friendly, relationship. It is likely that Pajou's portrait of Labille was a gift in exchange for Labille-Guiard's portrait of Pajou and a portrait of his daughter Catherine-Flore Pajou.

That Labille-Guiard painted Pajou's daughter, and that Pajou sculpted Labille-Guiard's father, suggests another reference in the inclusion of Cicero, to the relationship between father and daughter. Cicero was the father of a single daughter and appears to have felt affection for her. In a letter to Atticus, he wrote: "I am delighted that your little daughter is bringing you such joy,

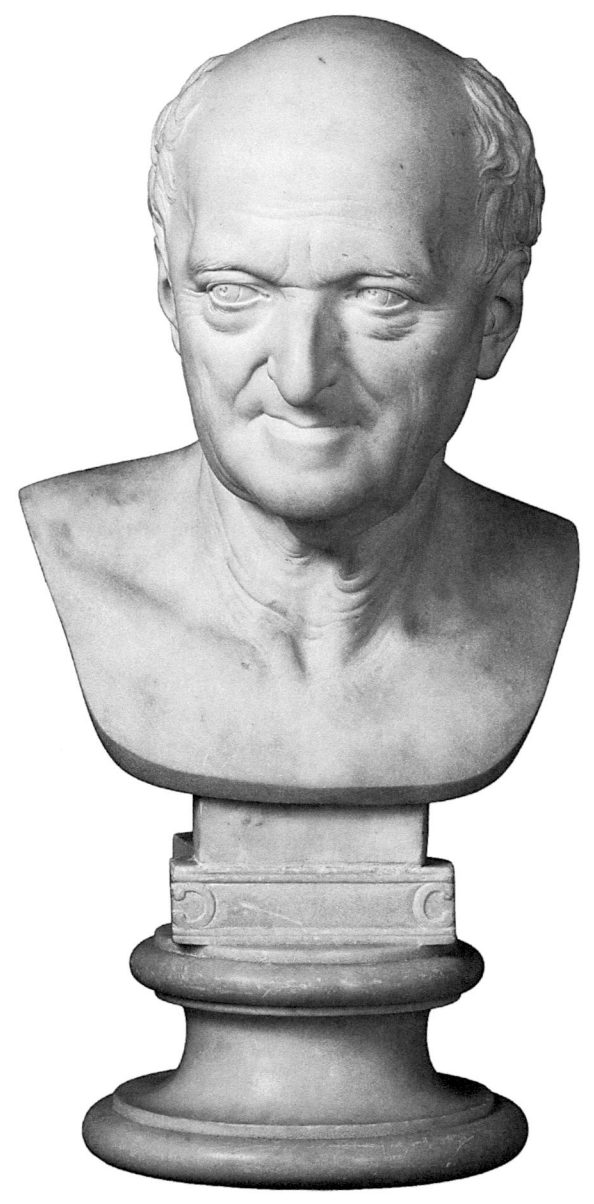

Fig. 3.11. Augustin Pajou,
Portrait Bust of Claude-Edmé Labille, 1785.

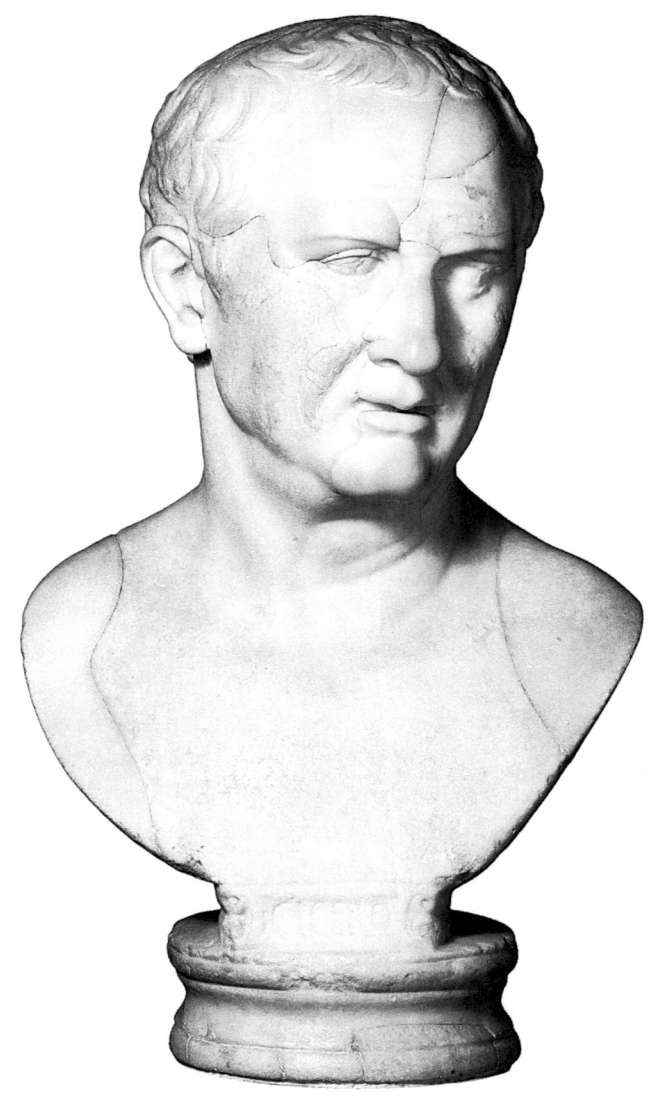

Fig. 3.12. *Marcus Tullius Cicero (106–43 B.C.)*.
Roman Greek Islands, 1st century B.C.

and that you agree with that Greek doctrine that 'it is natural to feel affection for children.' For if this is not that case then there can be no natural tie between one human being and another; if that is taken away. The whole essence of society is removed."[88]

Notably, Cicero's daughter Tullia divorced her husband, whose poor treatment of her Cicero had complained about. Labille and Pajou were both fathers of daughters who had ill-fated marriages. Labille-Guiard left her spouse shortly after their marriage in 1769, and starting in 1781, Pajou's daughter was in a problematic marriage with the sculptor Claude Michel, known as Clodion. She finally left Clodion in 1789 and returned to her father's household.[89] Labille-Guiard's inclusion of Pajou's bust of her father wove together a multitude of friendship types: an older association of friendship with kinship, the friendship between two fathers who shared concern about their daughters, the female friendship amongst Labille-Guiard's students that she fostered as their teacher, and, finally, the artist's own connection to a prominent network of male artists.

Along with the inclusion of Pajou's work in her self-portrait, Labille-Guiard demonstrated her continued participation in artistic friendship networks through portraits of three more *académiciens*: Charles-Amédée Vanloo (Fig. 3.13), Cochin (location unknown), and Vernet (Fig. 3.14). Her portrait of Vanloo is an outlier amongst her other portraits of artists. The portrait of Pajou was chosen as her *morceau de reception* when she was *agréé* (provisionally accepted) and *reçu* (fully accepted) into the Academy on the same day but, according to François-André Vincent, "her noble ambition was not satisfied," and she requested permission to complete a second reception piece in oil, with the subject chosen by the Academy.[90] The resulting portrait of Vanloo followed the formal conventions of previous reception portraits: the 130-by-98-centimeter canvas depicts him almost at full length, lavishly dressed, and sitting in a chair with brushes and palette in hand in front of a work in progress. At the same time that this portrait was destined for the Academy's collection, like all the *morceaux de réception*, it continued the theme of the 1783 series. Vanloo was the uncle of Madame Mitoire, who was the subject of a portrait in Labille-Guiard's first Salon.

The bust-length oil portraits of Cochin and Vernet—far more modest (56 × 46.5 cm)—were comparable in size and format to the 1783 pastels. These two paintings were also exchanged between the two sitters, and the works likely commemorated the men's collaboration on the engraving of Vernet's *Ports of France* series. Notably, the Salon catalogue mentioned specifically that the portraits of Cochin and Vernet were exchanged between them.[91]

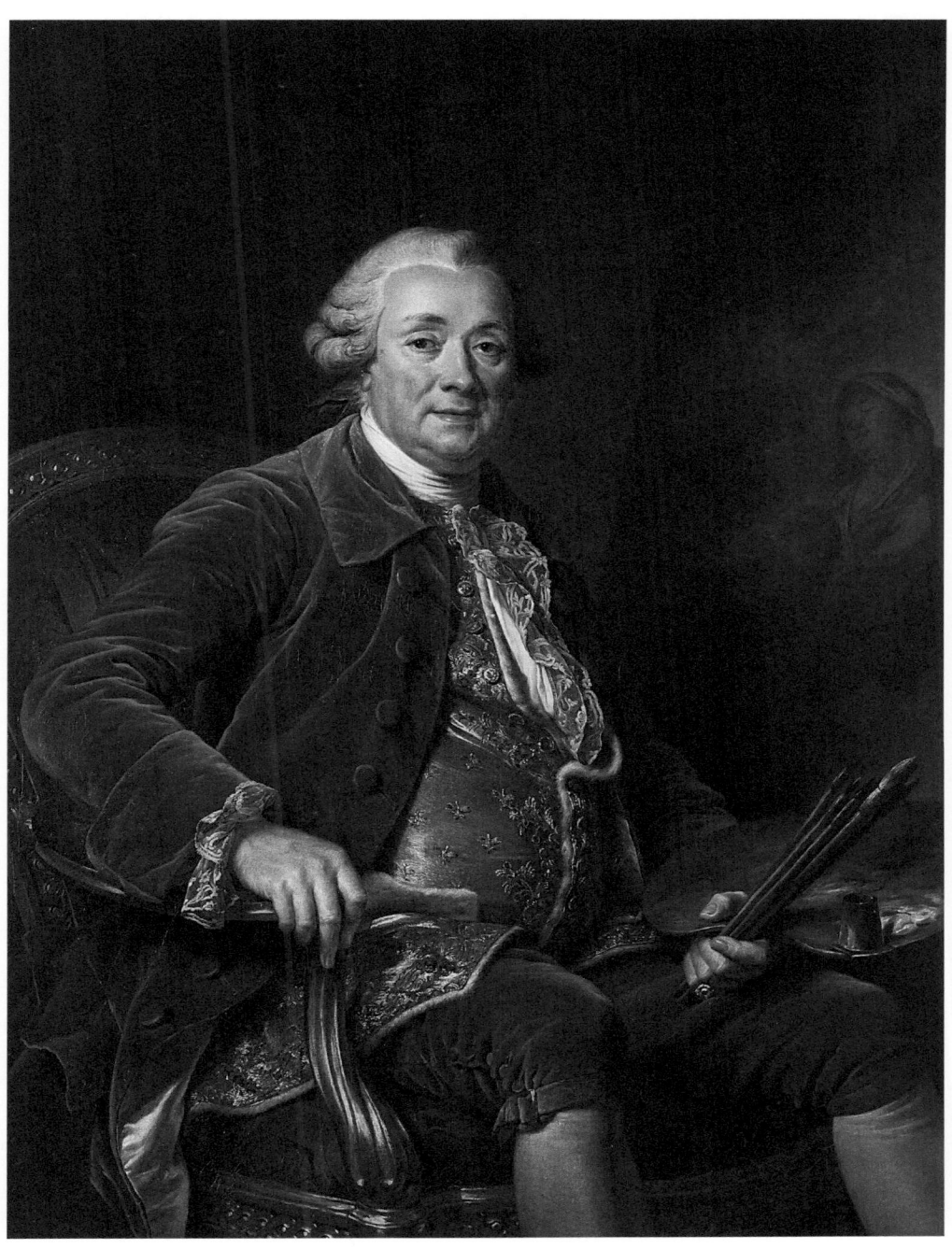

Fig. 3.13. Adélaïde Labille-Guiard, *Portrait of the Painter Charles-Amédée-Philippe Vanloo*, 1785.

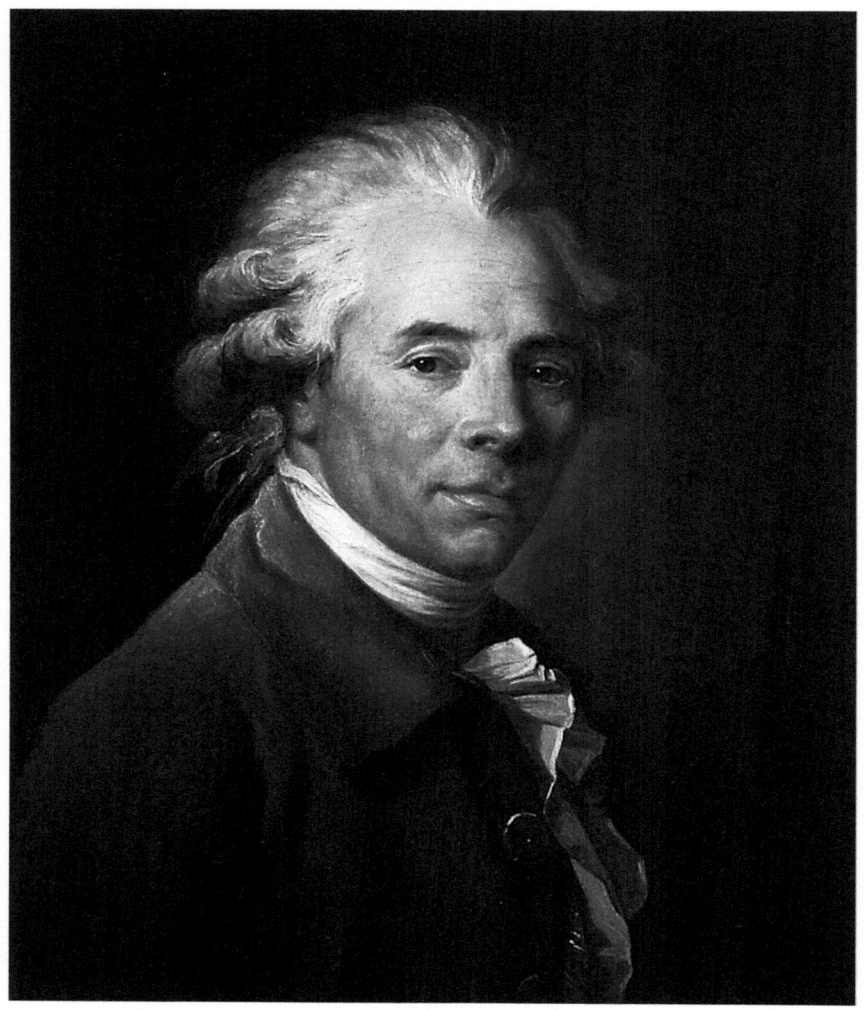

Fig. 3.14. Adélaïde Labille-Guiard, *Portrait of Joseph Vernet*, 1785.

All three of the portraits of artists received praise similar to those that Labille-Guiard had displayed in 1783, and critics again highlighted the appropriateness of her masculine touch to her Academician sitters.[92] The *Mémoires secrets*, in particular, claimed that of the three women artists exhibiting (the third being Anne Vallayer-Coster), it was Labille-Guiard who "triumphs and surrounds her works with cries of surprise and involuntary delight which is only roused by a real and brilliant merit."[93] After applauding her self-portrait, the critic then turned to her portraits of Vanloo, Vernet, and Cochin: "The other portraits made by this Academician are characterized by a severe brush, more appropriate to render hard-working and deeply occupied heads than the frivolous affections of the people of the world. She offers us an Amédée Vanloo, a Vernet, a Cochin, three artists who offer nothing less than thanks and kindness, but demand a thoughtful and vigorous touch."[94] Combined with the appearance of the portrait of her father in the large self-portrait, the portraits of Vanloo, Vernet, and Cochin again demonstrated her role in creating friendship portraits for a male homosocial network, and showed that she was actively engaged with the creation and exchange of portraits as a part of artistic friendship.

A Woman's Touch

Vigée-Lebrun's submissions in 1785 were similar in subject to her previous offerings: a selection of portraits of sitters from the upper echelons of French society, a portrait of the royal children, and a painting of a bacchante that straddled the line between *tête d'expression* and history painting. If Labille-Guiard's display of portraits of her male colleagues in 1785, painted in a manner that eschewed "frivolous affections," suggested to critics that she had the virtues of the *honnête femme* who, Lambert claimed, was capable of chaste cross-gendered friendship, then Vigée-Lebrun's society portraits did little to demonstrate that she was capable of creating work that went beyond merely "displaying" friendship. The same review in the *Mémoires secrets* that praised Labille-Guiard's self-portrait described Vigée-Lebrun's works in very different terms: "It is not the same with Madame le Brun, she dedicates herself to the prettiest women of the courts, the most *galantes*, and gives them all the pleasure of her brush."[95] Notable here is the description of her women as *femmes galantes*—which, along with its connotations of aristocratic pleasure, was also a term commonly used for prostitutes.[96] As a comment on an artist's style, "the pleasure of her brush" was an ambiguous statement. In a circle of aristocratic amateurs, it would have been a high compliment. In the context of growing suspicions about the public role of women and female friendships, it was decidedly less positive.

The critic Louis-Abel de Bonafous, abbé de Fontenay, noted in his discussion of Vigée-Lebrun's works, "There are even fewer who have the art of enchanting so much of the public by seductive productions." When shifting to discussion of Labille-Guiard's portraits, he compared the women artists to mythological figures: Labille-Guiard was akin to Diane, the chaste goddess of the hunt, while Vigée-Lebrun was Venus, goddess of love and seduction.[97] The association of Vigée-Lebrun with Venus is striking, considering the rumors that spread about her relationship with one of the two men whose portraits she displayed, Charles-Alexandre de Calonne, Louis XVI's minister of finance (Fig. 3.15). In the months following the 1785 Salon, the *Mémoires secrets* published numerous stories about Calonne and the artist, in which her patron supposedly offered her gifts that could only be interpreted as signs that a love affair existed between the two parties. The stories recounted the comte giving Vigée-Lebrun an extravagant gift of candy, which was actually gold *louis* (coins) wrapped in *billets de la caisse* (eighteenth-century bank notes), as well as a rumor that he was purchasing Watelet's country residence, Moulin Joly, for the artist.[98] Such stories were linked to Calonne's attempts as finance minister to redeem France's dire economic situation through tax reform. Despite his good intentions, he was accused of embezzling money from the state.[99] By supposedly accepting Calonne's gifts, Vigée-Lebrun became implicated in the minister's rumored disregard for the nation's financial security, as evidence of his willingness to use the state's money to please his preferred artist and lover. Such accusations linked her even more to her patroness, Marie-Antoinette, who was similarly plagued with rumors of exercising the capricious and dangerous female love of luxury, best exemplified in 1785's Diamond Necklace Affair.[100]

The anonymous author of the *Avis important d'une femme* wrote that Vigée-Lebrun's portrait of Calonne was the only work by her worth discussing because "it was on this occasion that she became fully the mistress (*maîtresse*) of her subject."[101] The undoubtedly politically motivated critic's use of the word *maîtresse* in reference to Vigée-Lebrun implied, as Sheriff has argued, that this portrait was the only decent one on view, that the artist had finally "mastered" her subject. Given the rumors of the affair between Vigée-Lebrun and Calonne that circulated after the Salon, the description of Vigée-Lebrun as a *maîtresse* may very well have been a double entendre. The portrait, in addition to putting her mastery on display, demonstrated that she had made herself Calonne's mistress.[102]

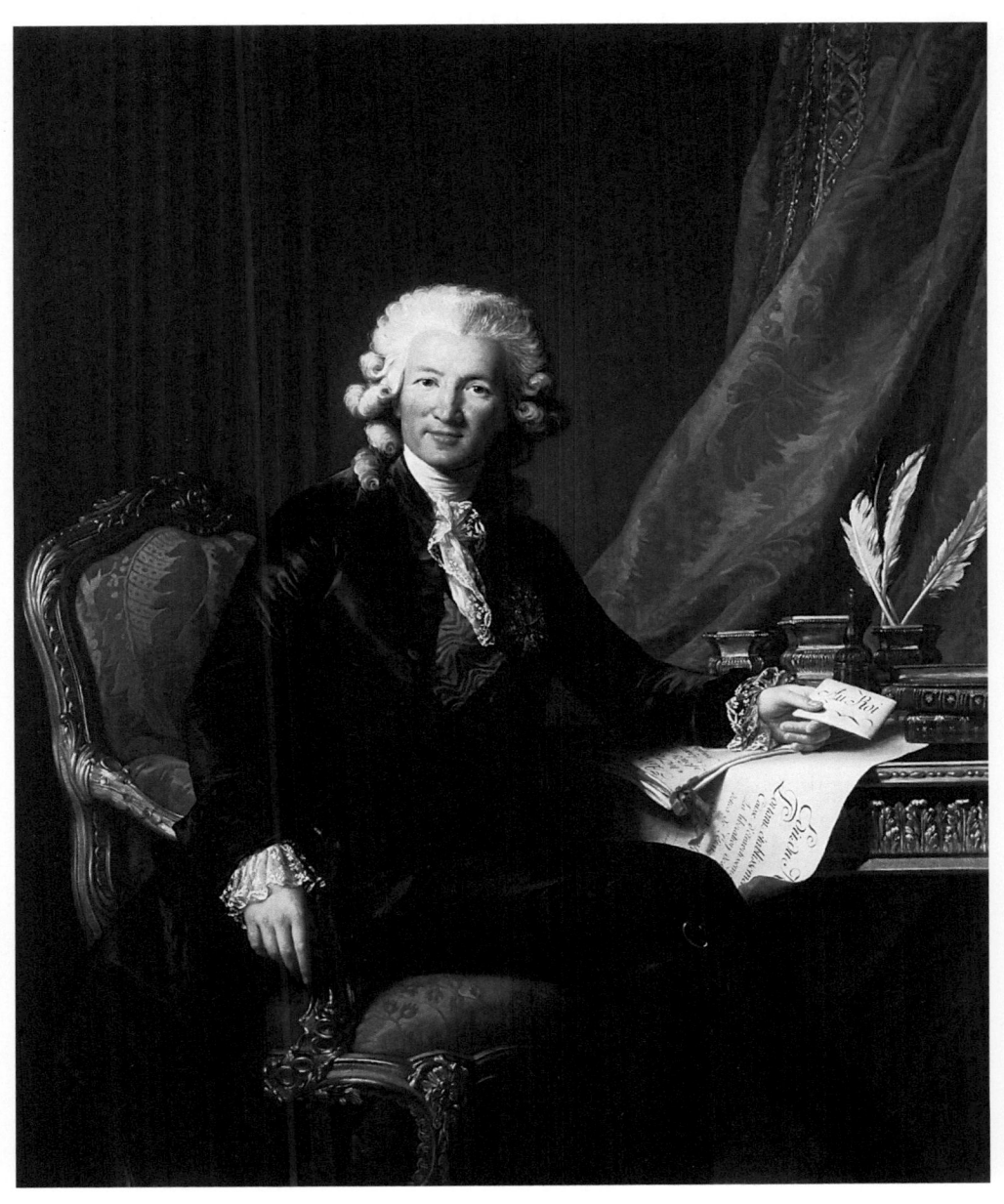
Fig. 3.15. Elisabeth-Louise Vigée-Lebrun, *Portrait of Charles-Alexandre de Calonne*, 1784.

The play on the word *maîtresse* in this quote calls attention to the uneasiness of women portraying men. The erotic potential of the painter's touch in eighteenth-century art has been a major point of discussion in the last decade. Many of these discussions often call upon the ancient myth of Pygmalion, in which the (male) sculptor's desire for the (female) object he has created brings Galatea to life.[103] Sheriff, for example, has used Pygmalion to demonstrate that, while it was believed that deviant desire-driven behavior in men could be cured through artistic creation, for similarly inspired women—Sheriff takes Heloïse as her female counterpoint—such resolution was impossible.[104] Others have looked at images of women's touch in regard to touching themselves, either in terms of autoerotic pleasure or women's use of makeup to literally "make up themselves."[105] But what about women touching men?

The representation of a woman's touch in cross-gendered situations drew attention to the anxiety about women touching men, specifically in the context of aristocratic gallantry. References to a seductive touch were certainly not lacking in the eighteenth century, frequently taking the form of representations of games such as blindman's buff by Nicolas Lancret and Jean-Honoré Fragonard, to name only two artists. Their pastoral scenes and *fête galantes* often switched up the gender roles of the blindfolded participant and the person who teased them with a shaft of wheat, a feather, or their hands. A particularly explicit representation of the specific dangers of a woman's touch is found in Abraham Bosse's print series of the five senses from the 1630s. While almost all the sensory scenes in Bosse's series depict men and women intermingling, the image of touch in one in particular gives a sense of agency to women that stands out among the other prints (Fig. 3.16). A man, a woman, and an old maid are depicted in a bedroom lavishly decorated with tapestries and paintings of Venus and Cupid. While there are two chairs in front of the fireplace, only one is occupied—by both the man and the woman. The woman is perched upon the man's lap, her leg boldly draped over his knee, exposing her knee and her stocking. She stares out at the viewer, aggressively holding the man's chin. His gaze is focused on her neck as he reaches toward her bosom, or possibly the pearl necklace adorning her neck. On the other side of the room, the old servant suggestively ties the bedcurtains into a shape reminiscent of a vulva. The text below it leaves no doubt of the role of *touche* in amorous behavior: "Although love is born from a beautiful object, the eye can't always be pleased by a (male) lover, because it searches for pleasure that can only arrive by touch."[106]

Unlike the example of Pygmalion and Galatea, in which a male artist creates the object of his desire that is then transformed from stone to flesh,

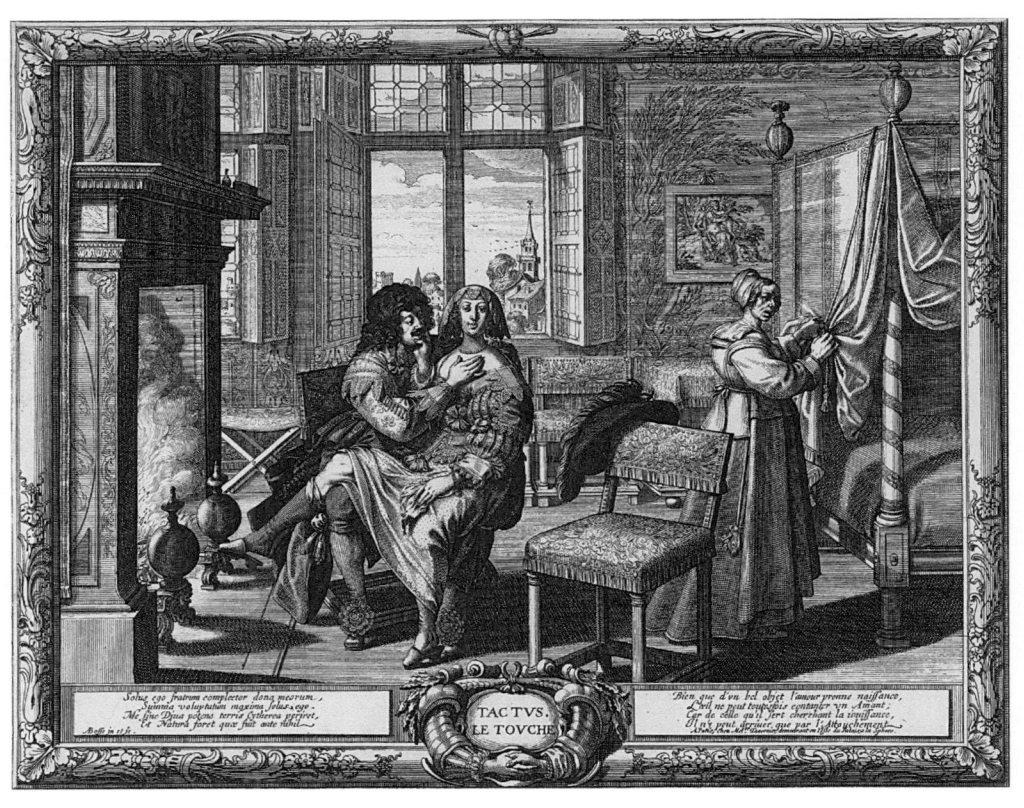

Fig. 3.16. Abraham Bosse, *Touch* from *The Five Senses*, ca. 1638.

in Bosse's image it is *la touche* that speaks, and its female personification is hardly passive. While she is sitting in her lover's lap, the woman's forceful hold of his face and her bold gaze suggest that it is her touch that controls the situation. Touch is explicitly linked to pleasure and, in this instance, it is the woman who is in charge. As in Bosse's print, the description in the *Avis important d'une femme* of Vigée-Lebrun as the "mistress" of her subject suggests both mutual physical pleasure between the woman painting and her sitter, but also positions the woman artist, and her touch, as firmly in control.

Women Interrupted

The Salon of 1789 opened in the wake of the first events of the French Revolution. Given the tumultuous political climate, the Academy's exhibition received far less critical attention than the Salons of the early 1780s had, and the political upheaval significantly disrupted the careers of Vigée-Lebrun and Labille-Guiard at a moment when they began to show different types of portraits at the Salon. Vigée-Lebrun displayed a number of portraits that spoke to an artistic, rather than aristocratic, community: a portrait of the wife of architect Pierre Rousseau, Marie-Andrienne Rousseau (née Potain); one of Alexandrine-Émilie Brongniart, the daughter of architect Alexandre-Théodore Brongniart; and a portrait of her longtime friend Hubert Robert (Fig. 3.17). Labille-Guiard displayed no portraits of male artists in 1787 or 1789, turning to portraits of aristocratic and royal women, as she was named painter of the aunts of Louis XVI—a position highlighted in the *livret* of the Salon of 1787—largely due to the critical acclaim of her *Self-Portrait with Two Students*.

Vigée-Lebrun's portrait of Robert is worth considering at length, as Pajou also displayed a portrait of Robert that year, a terracotta bust (Fig. 3.18). Pajou and Robert had been close friends since their time together in Rome at the Royal Academy's outpost at the Palais Mancini. Pajou displayed portraits of Vigée-Lebrun in terracotta and marble in 1783 and 1785, respectively. Robert was a participant in the same social gatherings as Vigée-Lebrun, and was the subject of a written "portrait" in Vigée-Lebrun's *Souvenirs*, in which she described him thus: "of all the artists I knew, Robert was the most popular in society."[107] All three artists had ties to the patron Jean-Joseph de Laborde. Robert was his artistic consultant and assisted with designing the gardens at Laborde's residence at Méréville, and acted as a go-between between Pajou and Laborde for sculptural commissions. Laborde purchased Vigée-Lebrun's portrait of Robert and one of her self-portraits in 1789.

Both Pajou's terracotta sculpture and Vigée-Lebrun's painting depict Robert with his head turned to the left, with a facial expression commonly linked to artistic inspiration, his eyebrows unkempt, and his clothing in a state of slight disarray. The formal similarities between Vigée-Lebrun's and Pajou's portraits of Robert have been noted, in passing, in many scholarly discussions.[108] It is more productive to think about these similarities within the framework of translation and the absence of comparisons of women artists to male artists in Salon criticism, with which this chapter began.

Vigée-Lebrun painted her portrait of Robert a year after Pajou completed his bust. Therefore (as in the case of her portrait of Lemoyne), she likely had access to both the bust and the sitter. And, as with her portrait of Lemoyne, she took Pajou's representation as her starting point, amplifying the expressiveness of Robert's bearing in it. She energized the bust by extending it to half-length and twisting Robert's torso. His right arm pushes on the ledge in front of him, his fingers curled around its edge, while his left arm, holding a palette and brushes, supports the weight of his leaning body. In both the bust and the painting, Robert is shown without a wig, but in Vigée-Lebrun's portrait, the elegant curls of the bust have come loose in an explosive tangle of powdered hair. The sheen of the subject's expansive forehead is implied by quick, messy brushstrokes where the artist added white to the paint to render his flesh. Most strikingly, she used the same method of applying paint to form his ear as she did in the portrait of Lemoyne she painted seventeen years earlier.

The dual display of the terracotta bust and the painted portrait suggests that Vigée-Lebrun's portrait of Robert has much in common with Labille-Guiard's translation of Pajou's terracotta portrait of Lemoyne into pastel. Recalling Diderot's claim that "terracotta is the concern of genius," Vigée-Lebrun's portrait ups the ante here, translating the enthusiasm of Pajou's sculpture to the medium of oil paint. This is not to say, however, that the 1789 portrait of Robert was a response, six years later, to Labille-Guiard's *morceau de réception*, because it certainly was not. Rather, it is yet one more example of a public display of artistic exchange and response made possible by the bonds of friendship formed between artists in Paris, whether within the walls of the Louvre, or in the communities of the social circles and neighborhoods that intersected with the Academic body, which was a theme of Vigée-Lebrun's other Salon offerings.

The Academy presented itself as a homosocial male community, as its reliance on classical ideals of "friendship" lent the institution a veneer of stability despite the personal and professional conflicts that existed within it.

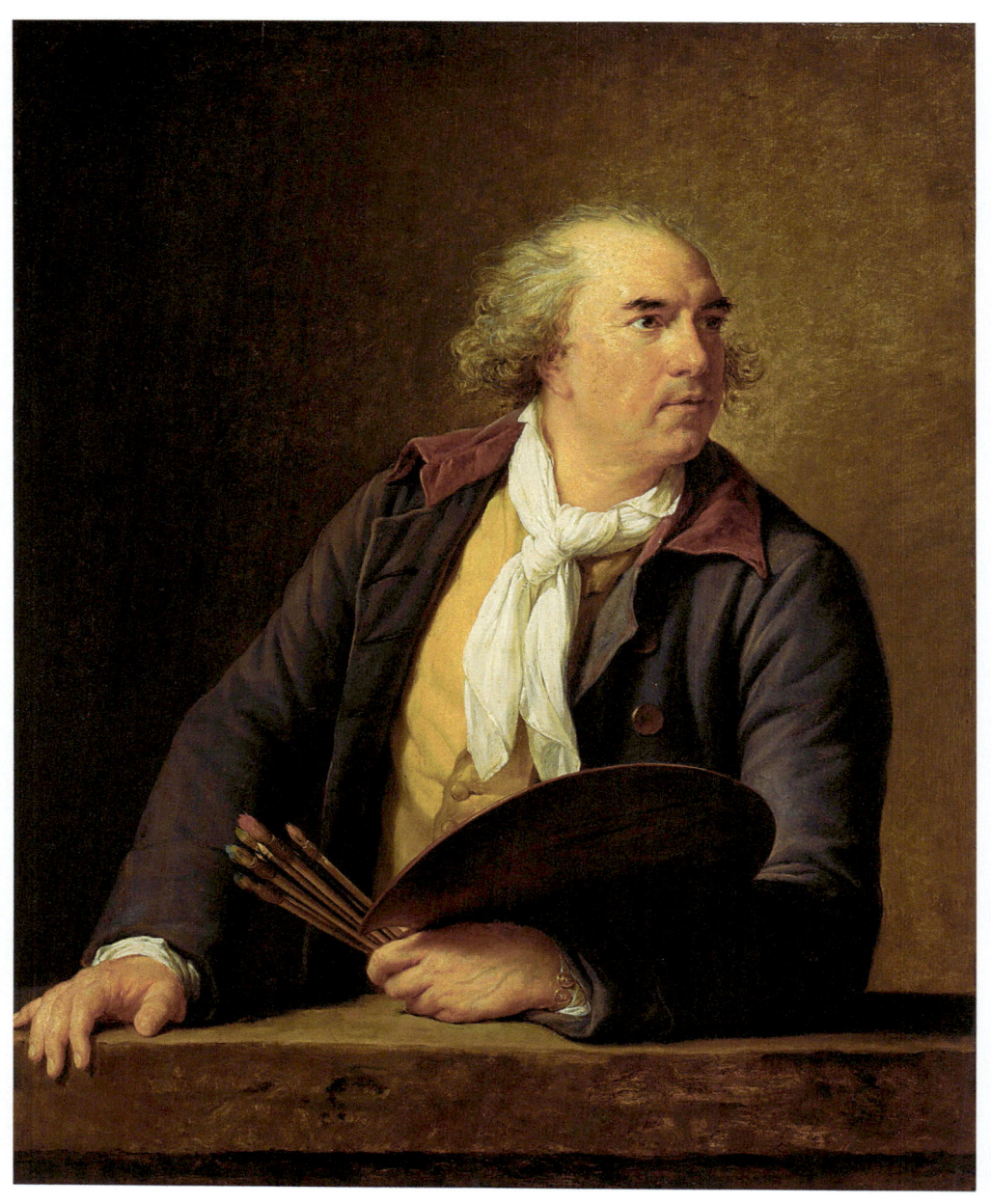
Fig. 3.17. Élisabeth Vigée-Lebrun, *Portrait of Hubert Robert*, 1788.

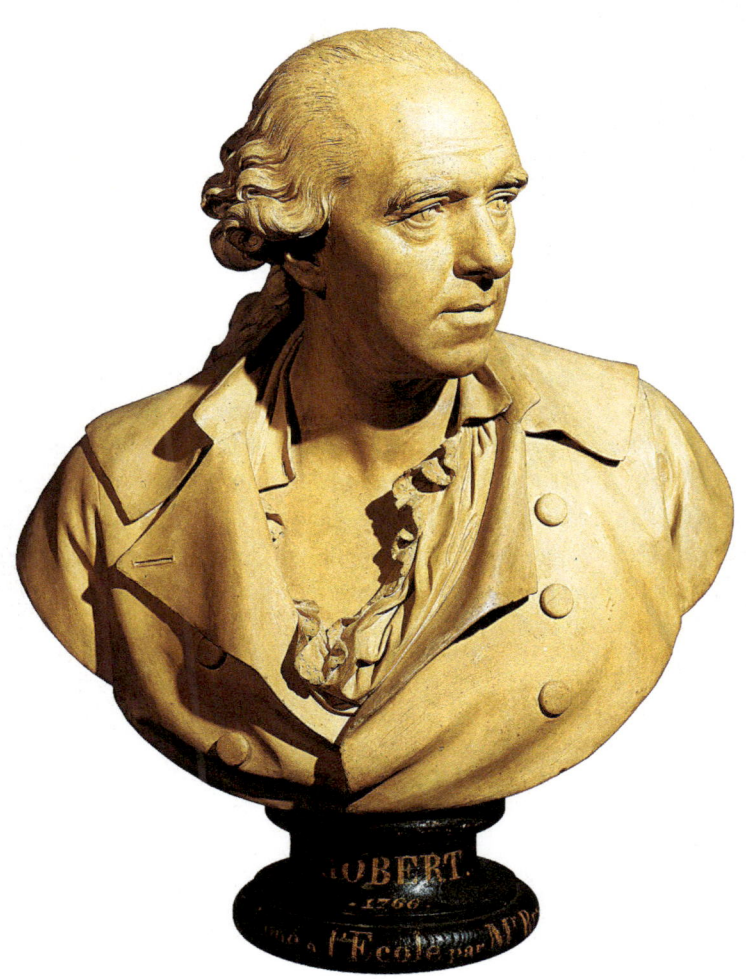

Fig. 3.18. Augustin Pajou, *Portrait Bust of Hubert Robert*, 1787.

Yet women were always present—as wives and daughters, and as students. Like those innumerable (and still to be discovered) women, Labille-Guiard and Vigée-Lebrun were well integrated into the masculine realm of the official art world from the start of their careers. They celebrated and promoted their friendships, with artists or patrons, through portraiture in the same way their male colleagues did. But as women, Labille-Guiard and Vigée-Lebrun's capacity for friendship was held to different standards.

The Academy was well aware of the dangers that mixed-gender sociability presented. In 1785, Labille-Guiard requested lodging in the Louvre, something that was well within her rights as an Academician. Her request, however, was denied, and that same year, the Academy banned women from participating in lessons in artists' studios in the Louvre.[109] While Anne Vallayer-Coster had been housed there since 1781, it seems that this regulation prevented Labille-Guiard from receiving lodging and studio space in the Louvre before the Revolution, as she had numerous female students. Jacques-Louis David and Joseph-Benoît Suvée were also reprimanded for allowing women students into their studios at the Louvre.[110] Alongside the fear of sexual impropriety lay a deep mistrust of female friendship. Academic discourse surrounding rivalry and competition insisted that these aspects of artistic education did not preclude friendship, but no such possibility was available for the handful of women the Academy accepted. Labille-Guiard and Vigée-Lebrun's treatment as "exceptional" women, unusually talented and ambitious for their sex, served to separate them from not only their male counterparts but also each other.

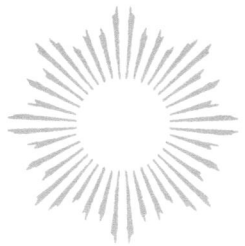

Chapter 4

FRIENDSHIP ABROAD

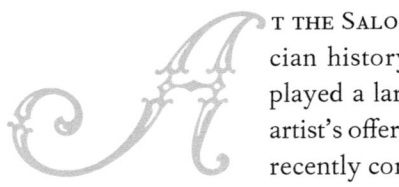T THE SALON OF 1777, the newly admitted Academician history painter François-André Vincent displayed a large group of fifteen works.¹ Many of the artist's offerings to his first Salon were inspired by his recently completed stay in Rome as a *pensionnaire du roi*, including several portraits of men with whom he had extensive contact during his stay there: his fellow pensioners painter Jean-Simon Berthélemy and architect Pierre Rousseau, as well as the collector Pierre-Jacques-Onésyme Bergeret de Grancourt. Critics appear to have been disappointed by the fact that Vincent's portraits outnumbered his history paintings, a reaction exemplified by one pundit's statement: "Destined to do great things, he is wasting his time making portraits, I fear."²

Traveling to Rome had long been the capstone of any aspiring artist's training, as it offered an unparalleled opportunity to study works by Renaissance and baroque masters as well as the antiquities in the ancient city and its environs. The trip was considered so important that, in 1664, only sixteen years after the Royal Academy of Painting and Sculpture in France was founded, the Academy created the Prix de Rome, a three-year funded trip to Rome for the institution's most promising young history painters and sculptors. In 1666, the Academy created an official satellite in Rome, the Palais Mancini, to house and support the young *pensionnaires*.³ By 1793, when it was briefly closed because of the French Revolution, 310 official pensioners had spent time at the Rome Academy, along with other artists who were housed there thanks to the support of patrons or other forms of private financing.⁴

Vincent's interest in portraiture did not go unnoticed during his time at the Palais Mancini. Charles-Joseph Natoire, the director of the French Academy in Rome at the time, commented in a letter to the *directeur-général des Bâtiments du Roi*, the Marquis de Marigny: "S. Vincent had recently made some very tasteful portraits; it seems this is the area in which he would like to work."[5] Natoire's compliment was undoubtedly disingenuous, given Vincent's own aspirations to be a history painter.[6] Like the Salon critics, Natoire looked down on Vincent's substantial portrait production. Yet, most likely unknown to Natoire, and certainly to Salon critics, Vincent's portrait production in Rome went well beyond those he displayed at the Salon. Most of his Rome portraits were anything but conventional and included a large number of caricatures and an enigmatic group portrait known as the *Portrait de trois hommes*. These unusual portraits had much to do with the specific social experience of a *pensionnaire*.

In Rome, student artists lived under the auspices of the Royal Academy but were physically separated from it. They were exclusively male; for the most part, they were unmarried, in their early twenties, and pursuing intense artistic study over extended periods of time in an exceptionally homosocial city.[7] The social context offered what historian and cultural anthropologist William M. Reddy has called an "emotional refuge." Such a context created connections between men that, even if temporary, were based not on kinship or rank, and fostered camaraderie and close relationships that were central to the formation of masculine identity.[8]

Several of the friendships discussed in previous chapters originated in Rome—for example, those between Hubert Robert and Augustin Pajou, and between Joseph-Marie Vien and Alexandre Roslin. Vincent and his cohort were no different, and, as seen in Chapter 3, Vincent remained close with Joseph-Benoît Suvée, François-Guillaume Ménageot, and Jean-Simon Berthélemy after their time in Rome together. While he displayed portraits of some of these men at the Salon—perhaps in an attempt to demonstrate the artistic and patronage networks he had formed in Rome, much like Maurice Quentin de La Tour and Charles Nicolas Cochin did (Chapter 2)—his Roman caricatures and paintings tell a story of artists' friendships that was not so concerned with the Salon public and the professional world of Paris. These works, which seem not to have been intended for large-scale public display, provide a view into how friendship was a motivation for experimentation with the genre of portraiture.

That Vincent's small circle of men developed an intimate bond is suggested by a letter Suvée wrote to Anicet-Charles-Gabriel Lemonnier in 1778.

Describing his voyage back to Paris, Suvée closed his letter with a message to fellow *pensionnaires*: "I would be too happy if everyone could be convinced of the sincerity of the feelings they have inspired in me.... Goodbye, my dear friend. I embrace you with all my heart, and I am your friend for life."[9] Later, Berthélemy's nephew, Charles-Nicolas Duchange, was struck by the frequency with which Vincent, Berthélemy, and Ménageot brought up their time in Rome late in life: "How many times I have seen them, old and all three of them together, like in Rome in their studios, or more often at a joyous dinner, bouts of laughter at stories of their thousand follies and even their loves."[10] Friendship was a frequent inspiration for Vincent's portraits, as evidenced in a large number of works he created during his stay in Rome, and his attraction to unusual forms of portraiture bears witness to the male bonding that studying abroad in Rome fostered. As a number of historians have noted, male bonding created camaraderie, which was often expressed through rituals of excess and misrule, frequently directed at patriarchal constructions of proper adult behavior.[11] These rituals, as Alexandra Shepard observes, were "deemed preferable to (and in some ways less dangerous than) intimate relationships between men, since they facilitated unacknowledged intimacy without surrendering a degree of competition and independence for the participants."[12] While the works under examination in this chapter did not enact the violent misrule that has been seen in other early modern contexts, such as those of the youth abbeys or of the journeymen analyzed in seminal works by Natalie Zemon Davis or Robert Darnton, they were a response to the masculine bonds of friendship made possible by the relative freedom pensioners were offered under the Academic directorship of Natoire.

Caricature and Camaraderie

Vincent's caricature and caricature-like drawings range from several series of handsomely finished, full-length figures and profile medallion portraits in black chalk or sanguine, to one-off images of people performing day-to-day activities, to small ink sketches that are perhaps best described as doodles.[13] One caricature of the history painter and fellow *pensionnaire* Pierre-Charles Jombert, for example, is a depiction of a rather spindly man stretched from the top to the bottom of two connected sheets of paper measuring an impressive 124 centimeters high (Fig. 4.1). Thick strokes of black chalk underscore the wrinkles of his rumpled, ill-fitting clothes. His legs appear like stilts, and his lanky arms hang loosely at his sides, weighed down by a pair of plump,

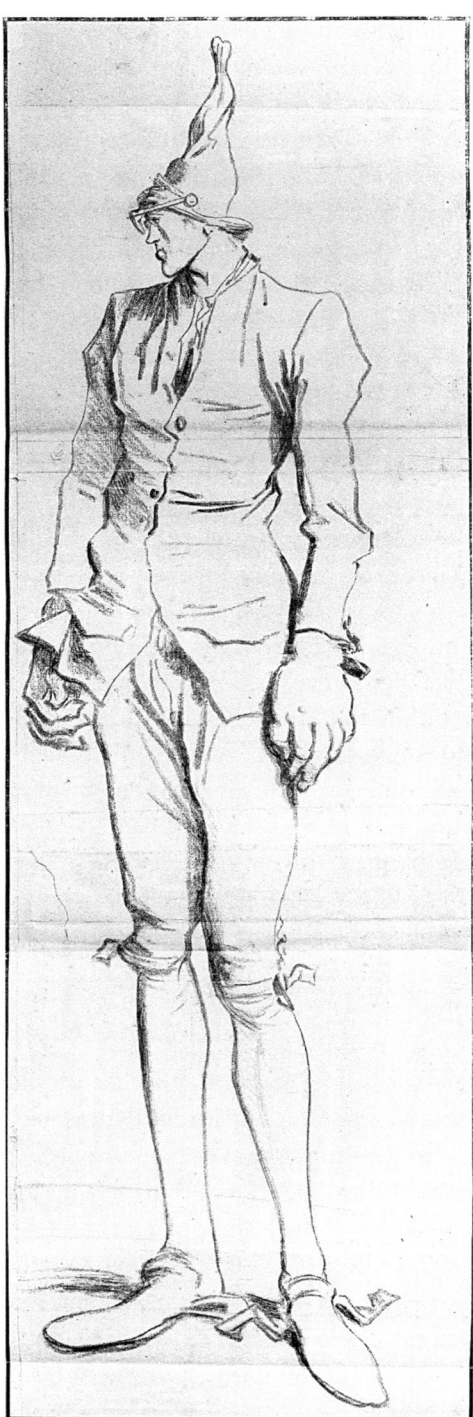

Fig. 4.1. François-André Vincent, *Caricature of the Painter Pierre-Charles Jombert*, 1774.

gargantuan hands. Covering his shrunken head is a tall *bonnet de coton* that spikes upward like a dunce cap, while a pair of spectacles dwarfs his thin, pointy face. Despite the imposing size of the drawing, the subject appears passive, almost oafish. Vincent seems to mock his colleague's striking physiognomy, but in this humorous and intimate representation, Jombert emerges as a gentle giant, seemingly unaware of his caricaturist's gaze.

Vincent was not the only pensioner at the Royal Academy in Rome to experiment with caricature. There is some evidence that caricature was an established practice among previous residents of the French Academy in Rome. Jacques Saly, for example, produced about seventeen caricatures during his stay in the 1740s. These were probably inspired by interactions with the Italian painter Pier Leone Ghezzi, who had established himself as a caricaturist of Italian tourists.[14] Among Vincent's cohort, a number of artists engaged with the practice of caricature. French sculptor Jean-Baptiste Stouf produced a series of caricature drawings (Fig. 4.2) that were etched by an amateur named Moricaud Franconville.[15] Jean-Simon Berthélemy caricatured Vincent in a state of surprise (Fig. 4.3), and Joseph-Barthélemy Le Bouteux manually copied Vincent's own full-length self-portrait in a sanguine drawing (Fig. 4.4). The large output of caricatures by this specific group, and their subsequent reproduction, strongly suggests that the creation of these works played an important role in these men's Roman experience.

Caricature's prominence in the visual culture of France in the long eighteenth and nineteenth centuries has recently gained the attention of art historians.[16] Their studies have tended to emphasize publicly circulated social and political caricature. When it comes to the *pensionnaires*' caricatures, however, their apparent lack of topical subject matter has relegated them to a lesser status as examples of mere artistic versatility and humorous formal experimentation versus more serious forms of artistic practice.[17] By focusing on graphic satire intended for a wide audience, scholars have overlooked other functions caricature may have served for artists in the eighteenth century that were inseparable from the sociable practices of drawing. The very particular environment of Rome offers a rich setting through which to consider the social lives of artists in the final stages of their training, and to examine Vincent's caricatures, and others like them produced by his fellow *pensionnaires*, as responses to shared Academic training and eighteenth-century drawing pedagogy.

In describing Vincent's caricatures as the artist's "other side," Jean-Pierre Cuzin has hinted that these drawings are a form of misrule.[18] This suggestion warrants further consideration, not only with regard to Vincent's

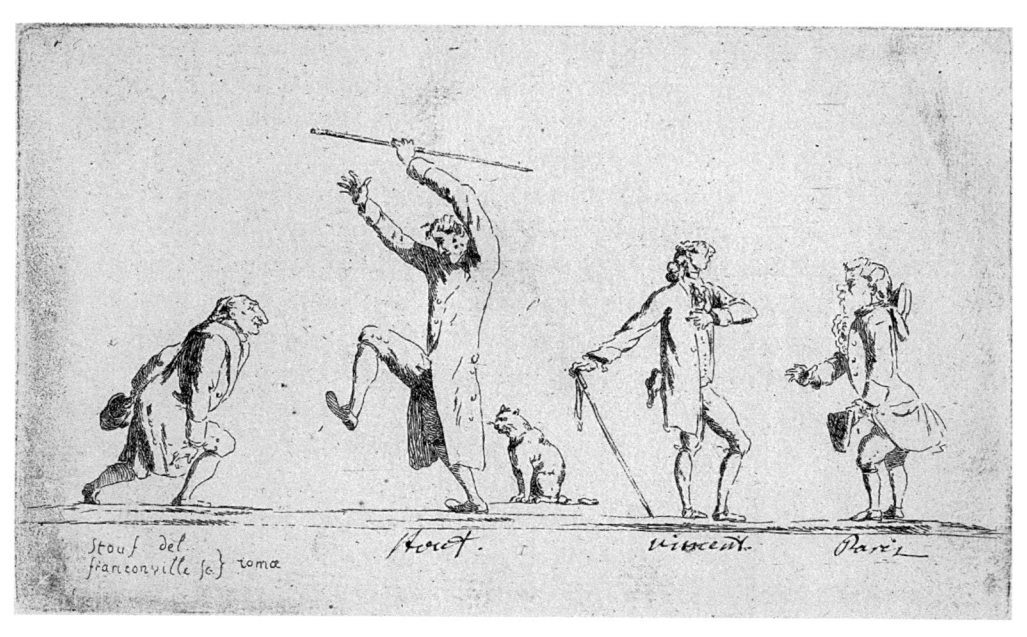

Fig. 4.2. Moricaud Franconville after Jean-Baptiste Stouf, *Caricatures*, early 1770s.

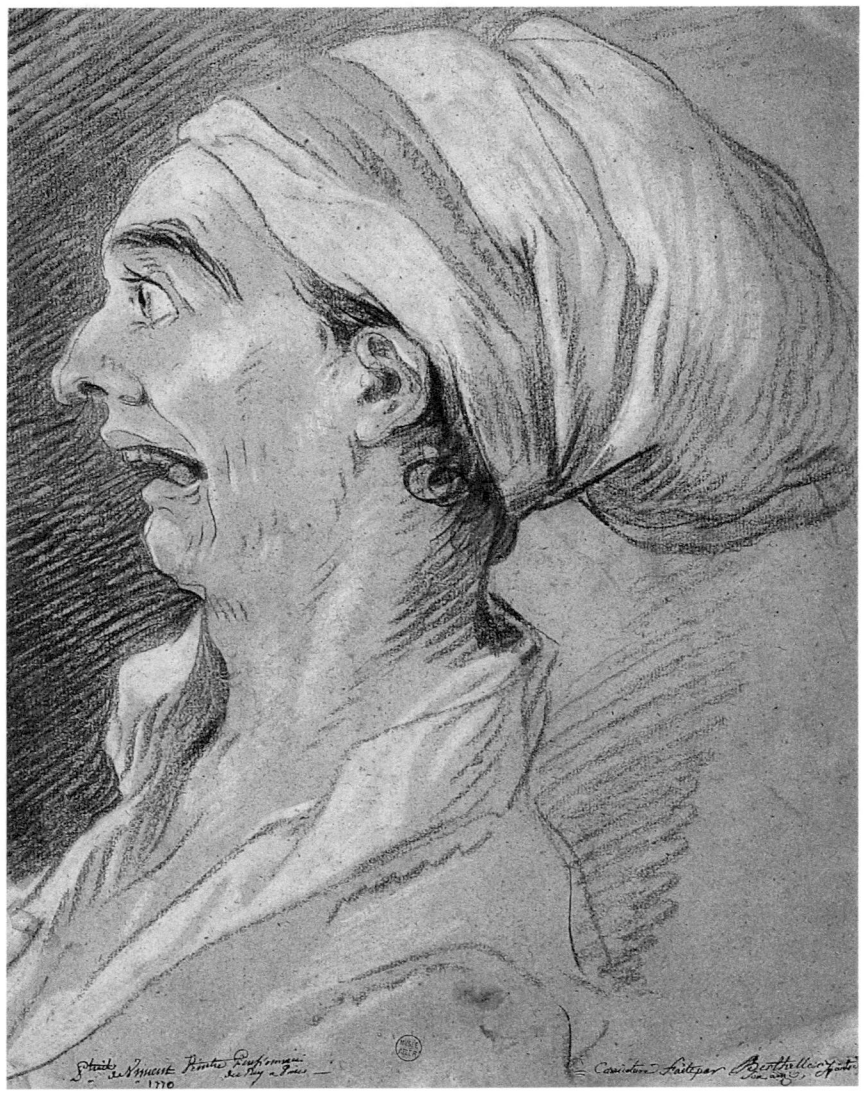

Fig. 4.3. Jean-Simon Berthélemy, *Caricature of François-André Vincent*, 1770.

personality but also as a means to better understand camaraderie between student artists. Caricature is, by definition, a form of excess. Drawn from the Italian word *caricare*, "to load," it depends on exaggeration for its effect. The particular form of disruption demonstrated in the practice of caricature did not exist in opposition to students' Academic upbringing; rather, it engaged with it. While Vincent's satirical drawings do represent people, they provide subtle visual evidence that the practice of drawing itself—in addition to the individuals at the Academy depicted in the drawings—may be read as an object of satire.

The practice of caricature by Vincent and his cohort was an excessive version of the daily practice of drawing in which these men participated as student artists. Before arriving in Rome, the *pensionnaires* had proved their talents in numerous Academic competitions, such as the Prix de quartier, the Prix Caylus, and the Prix de Rome. It is well known that the Academy relied on competitive emulation and that the ability to thrive in such an environment was necessary for an artist to win such contests.[19] The emphasis on competition, often discussed by scholars in the context of the atelier of Jacques-Louis David, created a direct connection between intense rivalry and the heady cultural politics of the French Revolution.[20] This narrative has a tendency to make the artistic production of the last decades of the eighteenth century seem emotionally and stylistically monotonous. As Elizabeth Mansfield highlights in her study of Vincent, social alliance played just as much of a role in artistic creation as did competition, and often led to surprising and delightful results.[21] Cuzin similarly draws attention to Vincent's sociable nature, claiming that the artist's caricatures demonstrate his "friendly confraternal spirit," and a "sense of group and even of privilege associated with winning competitions."[22] Vincent and his fellow *pensionnaires* were a group apart from the other students, distinguished by their talent and physically segregated from their Parisian colleagues during their study for three years or more at the Palais Mancini.

The drawings and etchings under examination here, created by a group of student artists, need to be situated in relation to drawing pedagogy.[23] This relationship finds support in Claude-Henri Watelet's discussion of caricature in the *Dictionnaire des arts de peinture, sculpture et gravure*. In his entry for "caricature," Watelet describes three types of the genre that have distinct purposes. The first type of caricature is that which is most studied in recent scholarship: published graphic satire with the goal of political or social critique. Watelet offers as an example the work of William Hogarth, who "in exaggerating the characters, customs and morals of his compatriots had,

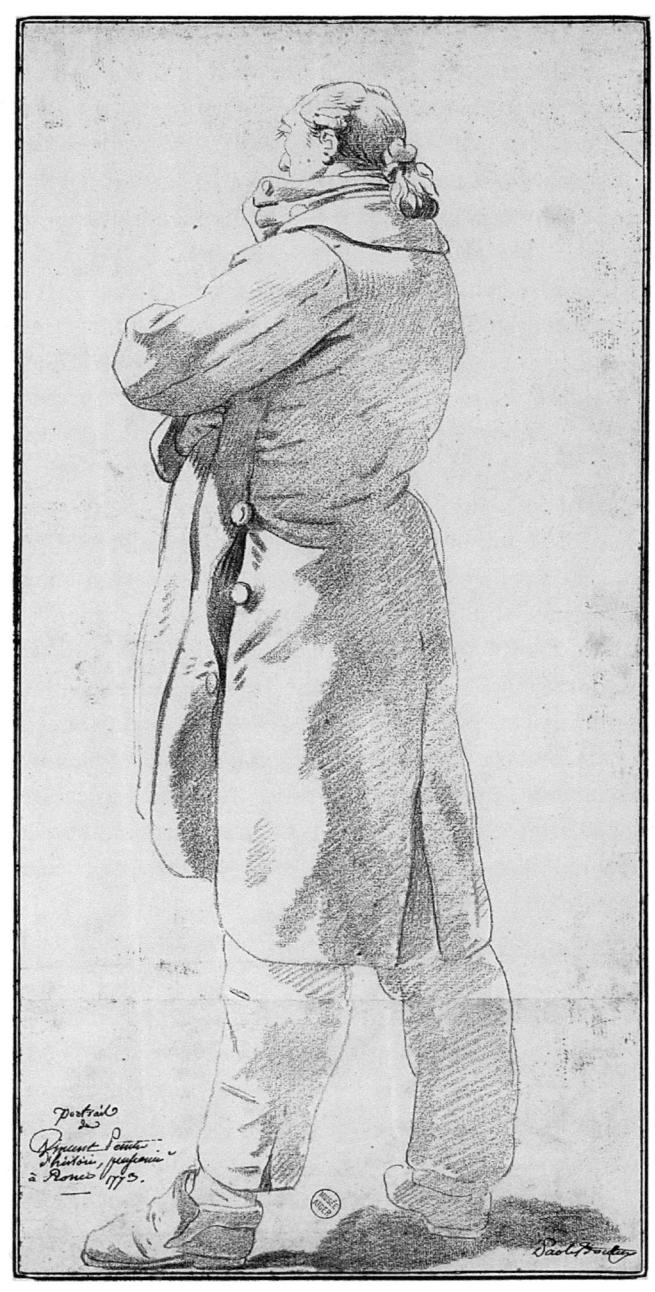

Fig. 4.4. Joseph-Barthélémy Le Bouteux, *Portrait-charge of Francois-André Vincent*, 1773.

no doubt, the intention of admonishing them."²⁴ The second form of caricature has very different intentions and is rooted in pleasure. Works of this type "mock the form rather than moral character" and are deemed less offensive than the first type because they poke fun at the physical form (for example, a trait such as size) rather than the spirit. They do not cross the line ("gardent ordinairement juste mesure") and are laughable (*risible*) rather than critical.²⁵

Finally, Watelet's description of a third type of caricature acknowledges that type's legitimate role in artistic practice: "Some masters . . . advise that painters always carry with them tablets or small notebooks, and sketch the physiognomic characters and expressions that strike them. It is natural, in these types of fleeting studies that take place in an instant, that an artist would more or less exaggerate, to better retain what he has observed. These types of caricatures are destined to be like secrets and of use only to the artist who made them."²⁶ Watelet's description of three types of caricatures—social commentary, sociable caricature, and exaggeration in mnemonic and educational contexts—created distinctions that did not exist in actual practice. Caricatures, in fact, often fulfilled more than one of the purposes he defined. For example, the *Livre de caricatures tant bonnes que mauvaises*, a volume of around four hundred satirical drawings by draftsman Charles-Germain Saint-Aubin and his circle of family and friends, includes numerous works directed at powerful patrons, connoisseurs, and political figures, and fits within Watelet's description of social or political critique.²⁷ Yet, as Colin Jones and Emily Richardson note, because of its vulgar and sometimes seditious content, it had a very limited audience. It engaged in a form of sociable caricature that went beyond Watelet's description of *juste mesure* in its bawdy humor and entered into the realm of political commentary in its personal attacks—but it served a private, rather than a public, audience.²⁸

Understanding the multivalence of caricature allows us to think more critically about the diversity of Vincent's drawings. Some of the caricatures he made fit comfortably within Watelet's description of caricature for educational purposes. His portrait of the painter Le Bouteux was quickly sketched in ink on reused paper, depicting the artist with an umbrella tucked under one arm and a cane in the opposite hand (Fig. 4.5). Le Bouteux's prominent, scruffy chin is delineated with frenetic lines; the outline of his boots, hat, and coattails is muddled by hasty, corrective strokes. The image is layered over and under other doodles, including a sketch of a human head and of geometric forms. The messiness of the drawing conjures Watelet's description of experimenting with exaggerated expression and character. Yet, Vincent's portrait of Jombert is too big to be secret (Fig. 4.1), too elaborate

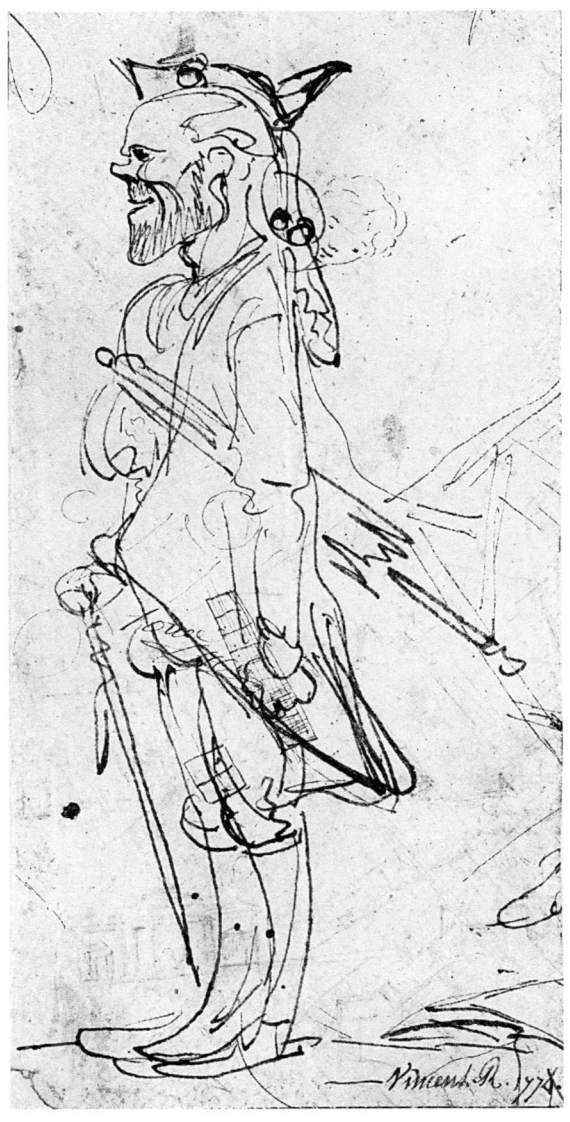

Fig. 4.5. François-André Vincent, *Portrait-charge of the painter Le Bouteux*, 1774.

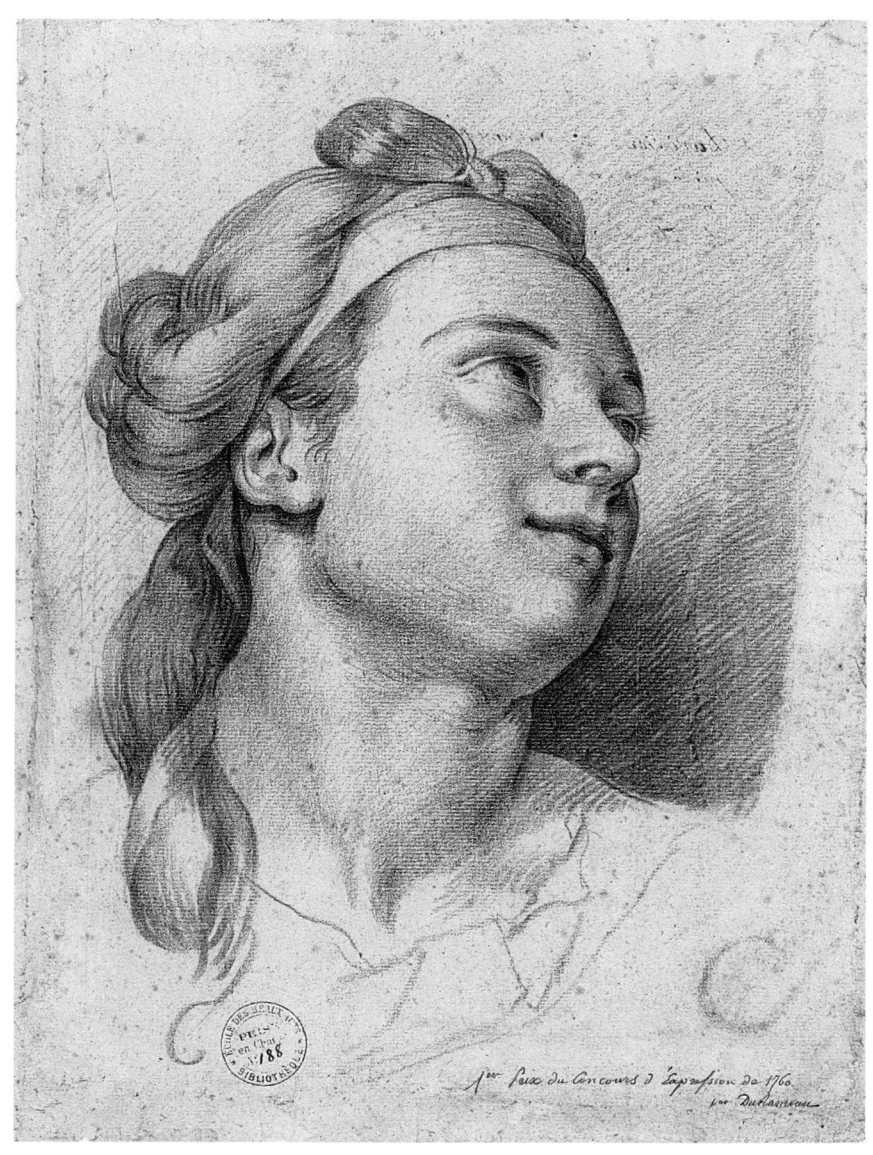

Fig. 4.6. Michel-Honoré Bounieu, *La Gaîté*, 1762.

in its execution to have been a study, and clearly mocks the subject's physical features, including his height, rather than making any social commentary.

The manner in which Vincent's caricatures cross Watelet's categories is seen in other *pensionnaires*' caricatures. History painter Berthélemy drew a caricature of Vincent during their time in the École des élèves protégés, a preparatory school that the winners of the Prix de Rome attended before their departure from Paris (Fig. 4.3).[29] Berthélemy depicted Vincent wearing a cotton nightcap. He is shown wide-eyed and slack-jawed, possibly reacting to one of the practical jokes commonly played among *pensionnaires*.[30] Berthélemy used this dramatic expression to distort Vincent's physiognomy. The deep lines around his chin and the bulging muscles in his neck suggest he is forcefully retracting his head, recoiling in horror or disgust. Like Vincent's portrait of Jombert, Berthélemy's work surpasses Watelet's discussion of quickly sketched caricature in its degree of finish. The portrait has been carefully rendered, including details such as the delicate eyelashes that frame Vincent's ogling eye. Berthélemy's deliberate placement of white chalk accentuates his comrade's cheekbones and the collar of his undone shirt. As the earliest known caricature created by a member of Vincent's cohort, this portrait provides the first suggestion that caricature was more closely related to Academic drawing than might initially be assumed. Its focus on the face of the sitter, and its highly finished quality, give the impression that the drawing is as much a study in expression as it is an occasion to poke fun at the sitter.

Parody and Pedagogy

Such close study from nature of expression was central to a young artist's training at the Royal Academy in Paris. Students participated in an annual competition, the Prix Caylus, in which they were required to create a large-scale drawing of a head, or a *tête d'expression*, enacting a particular emotion (Fig. 4.6). The chosen emotion, as Melissa Percival has discussed, was typically a mild passion, such as compassion or contentment (*douceur*), because—according to the prize's founder, the Comte de Caylus—such subtle expressions were unusually difficult for artists to capture and required close study of a live model.[31] These passions, Caylus claimed, were best conveyed by a woman's face; the model for the competition, therefore, was typically female.

Rendered in sanguine and white chalk, the traditional media used in Academic expression studies, Berthélemy's drawing of Vincent transplanted the practice of capturing expression into the realm of caricature by focusing not on a mild passion expressed by a woman, but on severe shock, an emotion categorized as "violent or terrible," expressed by a man.[32] Caylus excluded depictions of such extreme emotions from eligibility for the Prix Caylus precisely because he felt they lent themselves too easily to caricature, an idea that confirms what close bedfellows these two drawing practices, serious expression studies and caricature, were considered to be in Academic doctrine.[33] Denis Diderot noted the relationship between caricature and the close study of nature in his discussion of the portraits at the Salon of 1767. In his concluding remarks about the portraits of Gustaf Lundberg, he asked, "Why is it that history painters are usually poor portraitists? Why is it that a dauber on the Pont Notre-Dame will produce a better likeness than a dauber from the Academy?"[34] Diderot postulated that the amateur painter on the Pont Notre-Dame was more successful than the Academician because he stayed true to nature and was not beholden to Academic doctrine, social taste, or the study of antiquity. Both artists, however, used a certain amount of caricature in their work "because [the professor] produces a caricature favoring the beautiful, while the dauber, by contrast, produces a caricature favoring the ugly."[35] On one hand, the "dauber's" naive overdependence on nature is closer to the truth, but results in ugly exaggeration. On the other hand, the professor's portrait is aesthetically superior but hyperbolically beautiful due to Academic convention's emphasis on the ideal and the pressures of social taste.

As Percival has argued, Diderot's comment and Caylus's focus on mild emotion demonstrate that eighteenth-century artistic theory saw ideal beauty and caricature as "two sides of the same coin."[36] But Diderot's evocation of the word "caricature" in his discussion of these two extremes can be situated within broader Enlightenment discussions about vision. As Elizabeth Mansfield and Kelly Malone have argued, eighteenth-century satire was an extension of the Enlightenment belief in the primacy of sight in empirical reason.[37] The association of sight with reason and virtue made "seeing satirically," to borrow Mansfield and Malone's description, a means to cut through pretense and ignorance.[38] Furthermore, satire's ability to criticize convention relied frequently on parody, a means of calling attention to social and cultural norms by mimicking them.[39] The portrait by Diderot's dauber might be ugly, but it draws attention to the question of "truth" (with regard to likeness) in portraiture. As a parodic version of idealized portraiture, it must be taken seriously.

In his caricature of Vincent, Berthélemy appropriated an Academic format (the *tête d'expression*) and an Academic media (sanguine and white chalk) to depict an exaggerated facial expression that would have otherwise been excluded from the competition's repertoire. His caricature of Vincent is, in other words, a parodic form of the Prix Caylus. As such, it demonstrates that caricature was both a playful, and serious, form of drawing. Similarly, a group of impressive black chalk drawings by Vincent at the Musée Atger, which depict his fellow pensioners in full length, are a twist on another form of life drawing that was central to Academic pedagogy: the study of the male nude in the *école du modèle*. Drawing from the live male model was fundamental to the Academy's pedagogical program from its founding in 1648 until its dissolution in 1793.[40] It was included among the instructional activities listed in the Academy's founding statutes of 1666. The practice was also a key part of the curriculum at the Academy in Rome.[41] The consistency of the life drawing sessions in Rome and the frequency of sending *envoies*—examples of student work sent to Paris from Rome—varied under different Academy directors. Charles Natoire, the director during the period under consideration here, is credited with reinforcing pedagogical practices that had fallen by the wayside under his predecessor Jean-François de Troy.[42] By the end of his twenty-three-year directorship, however, Natoire seems to have stopped doing so, and the early 1770s coincided with a period during which the educational program, including the daily practice of life drawing, appears to have been neglected.[43]

There are few extant examples of Vincent's works that would have been the product of Academic "homework."[44] Artists in Rome were forbidden from copying after a nude model during Lent, and often turned to one another as models during this period. Using fellow students as models may have been a wider practice. In his essay on the Salon of 1767, Diderot mentioned, in a footnote: "At the school, once a week, the students assemble, one of them serving as a model. His comrade poses him and then wraps him in a piece of white fabric, draping it as best he can, and this is called drawing 'caricatures.'"[45] The dearth of opportunities for life drawing in Rome and the *pensionnaires*' recruitment of fellow students as models warrant attention with regard to the possible role that caricature played in drawing practice in Rome.

Like Berthélemy's drawing, Vincent's series is in the same media (black chalk) used in official student works. The high level of finish belies Watelet's description of caricature as a quick practice. Vincent's use of shading gives volume to the figures, with carefully rendered folds and wrinkles in the sitters' costumes, which include detailed buttons, buckles, and wigs. Vincent portrayed his fellow pensioners from behind or in profile, and their diverse poses and points of view resemble those that were created during life drawing sessions, where a professor posed a model and the distribution of students

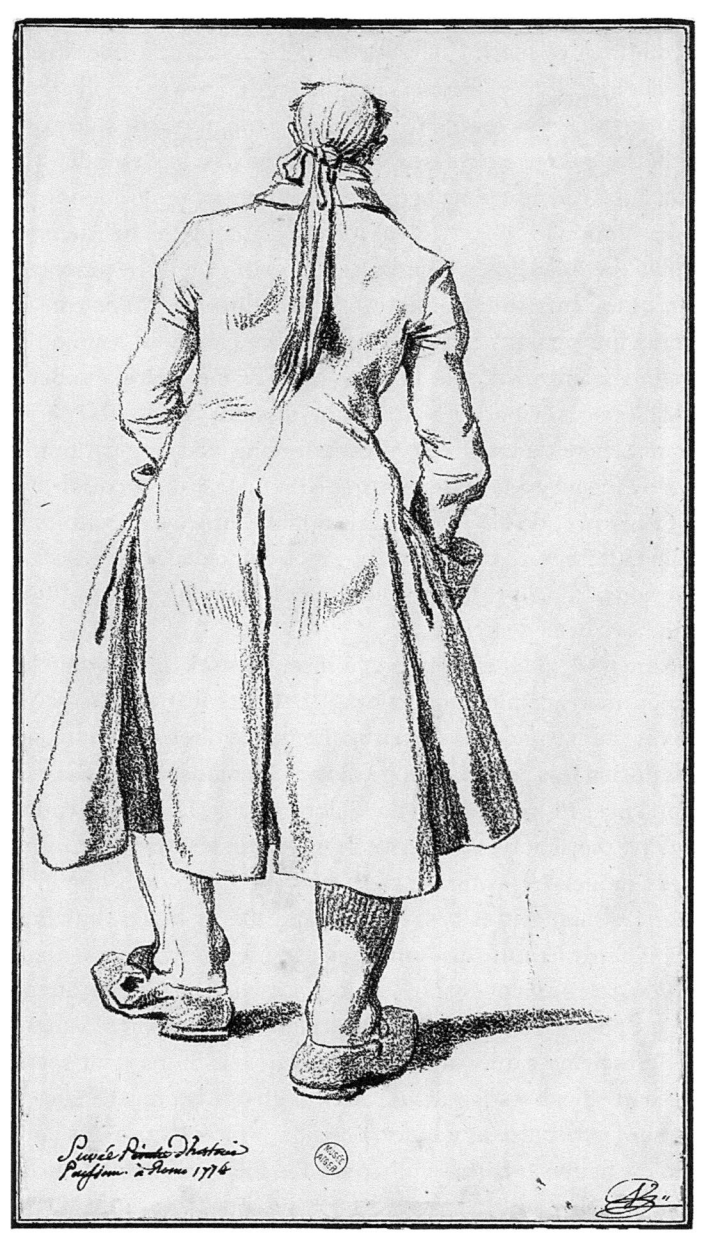

Fig. 4.7. François-André Vincent, *Portrait-charge of the Painter Suvée*, 1774.

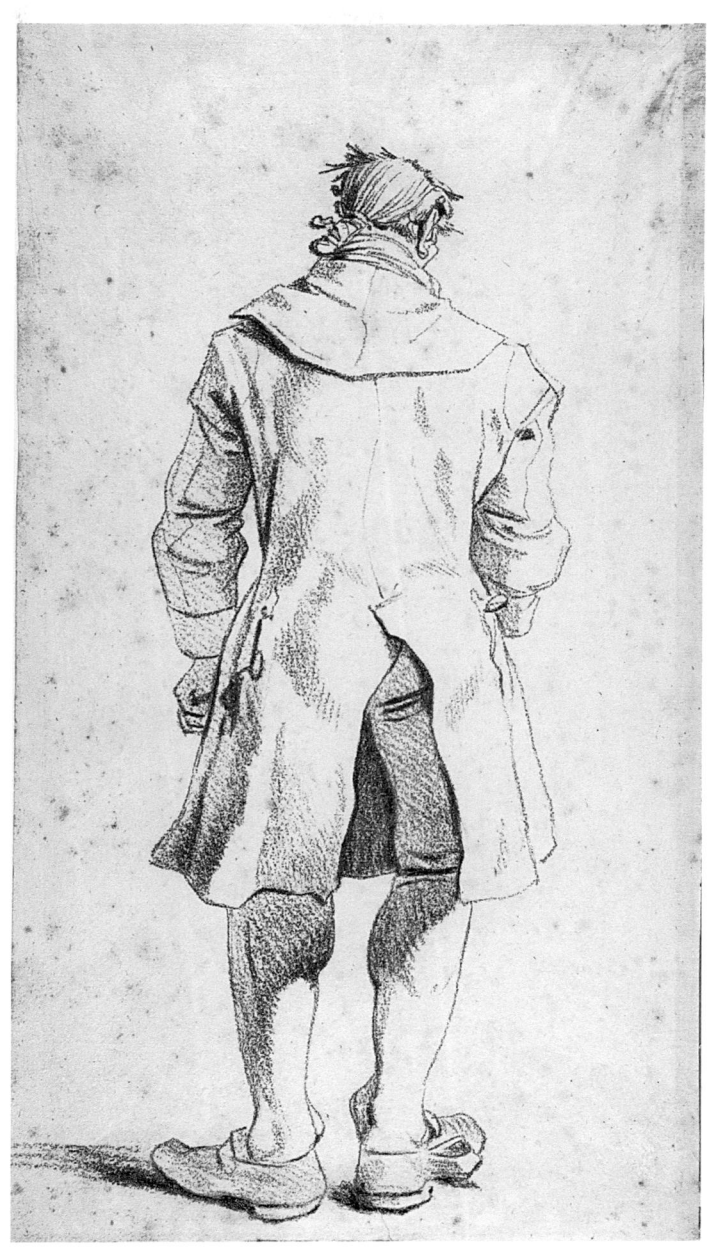

Fig. 4.8. François-André Vincent, *Portrait-charge of the Painter Suvée*, 1774.

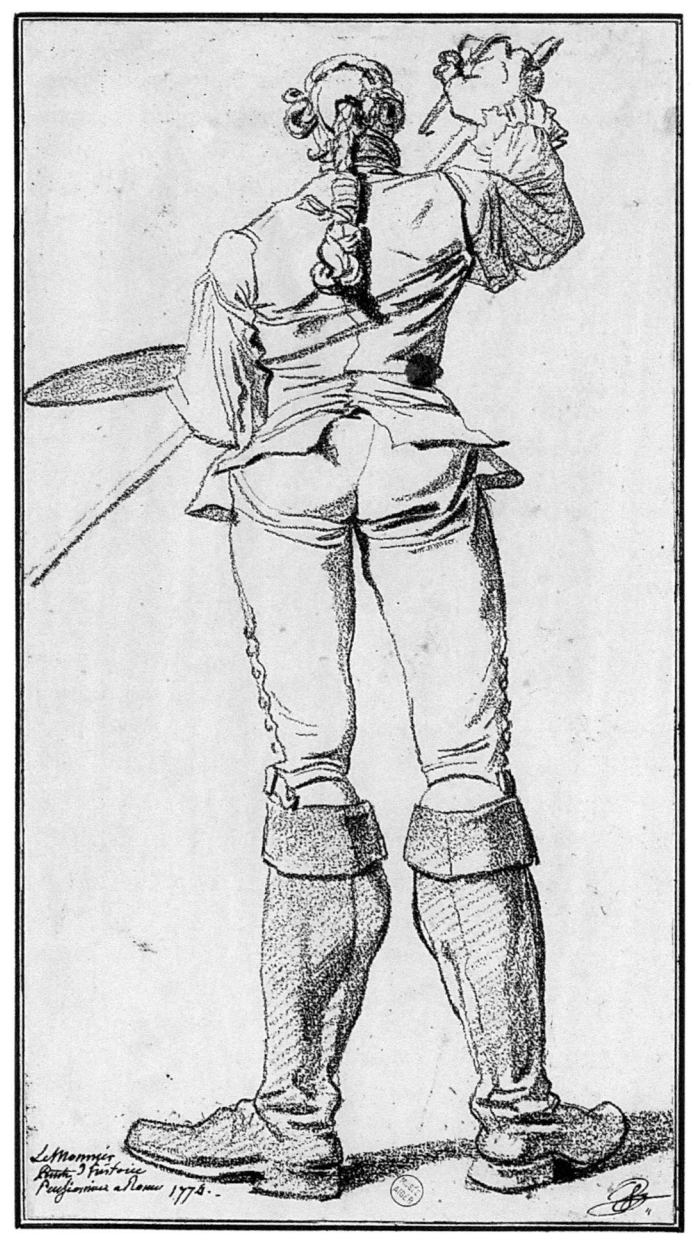

Fig. 4.9. François-André Vincent, *Portrait-charge of the Painter Lemonnier*, 1774.

around the room guaranteed that they would portray a variety of perspectives. For example, in two images of Suvée, Vincent slightly shifted the weight of his sitter. In one drawing, Suvée appears to step forward, allowing Vincent to accentuate the bend of his torso, and the use of foreshortening suggests that the figure is tipping forward (Fig. 4.7). In the other, Suvée seems more anchored, balanced on both feet, with a casual contrapposto curve highlighted by the seam of his coat (Fig. 4.8). These images of Vincent's companions from behind bear a striking resemblance to two life drawings, one by Suvée, and one by Vincent, now lost—but known from an engraving by Gilles Demarteau—which similarly use a rear view to highlight the S curve of the body created by an uneven distribution of weight.[46]

That Vincent's figures are clothed might seem to distance these drawings from the close study of human anatomy and musculature associated with studying the nude. Yet Vincent used clothed bodies precisely as the means through which to caricature his sitters. He exaggerated bizarre anatomies through their costumes and accessories, such as in his drawing of Lemonnier, whose short vest both frames and calls attention to his callipygian figure (Fig. 4.9). Absent, however, is the grotesque exaggeration of physiognomy that is typically associated with caricature, due to Vincent's use of the lost profile or his positioning of his sitters from behind. The drawings' lack of facial representation and their subtle level of exaggeration do not necessarily meet a typical expectation of "caricature," but in their appropriation of the models' poses and exaggerated anatomy, they can be reasonably read as a parody of life drawing.

Given the light-handed humor in these drawings, it is worth considering more seriously one of the other terms often used to describe them, the *portrait-charge*, which offers a means to understand the intersecting roles of exaggerated drawing practices in the *pensionnaires*' Academic training and the personal relationships they formed in Rome. *Charge* and *chargé* were the French words used to describe "loaded" or "charged" portraits. They predate the term *caricature*, which made its first appearance in Watelet's *Dictionnaire de l'Académie française* in 1762.[47] *Charge* and *chargé* implied exaggeration, usually to humorous effect, and Watelet's entry "charge et chargé" is closely tied to his definition of "caricature."[48] In comparing the two entries, we can see that sociable caricatures—those that focus on physiognomy and not on morals—belong to the subset of charged portraits. Watelet evoked the word "charge" early in the entry on "caricature" in his broad description of the genre's humor.[49] After this brief reference, he employed "charge" again only in his description of caricatures that are meant to please, not criticize, describing the *charge* as a "game of painting" that acts as a proof of talent and demonstrates an artist's ability to capture character and expression.[50] Furthermore, Watelet claimed in his entry "charge et chargé," as he did in his definition of "caricature," that both excess and exaggeration are an expected part of a student artist's development.[51] He referred specifically to their appearance in the process of drawing from the live model: "[W]hen one says that a line or contour is loaded, that a figure or expression is loaded, the point is but to criticize the artist's mistake, which is related only to his negligence or to some false idea that has misled him. Thus, the professor says very seriously to a student who is drawing after the model: Be more correct, more exact."[52] An artist's tendency to exaggerate, according to Watelet, is particularly apparent in anatomical drawing: "he exaggerates the muscles and their bulges, the articulations and the effects of their movements" ("il exagère les muscles et leurs renflements, les articulations et les effets de leurs mouvemens").[53]

Berthélemy and Vincent's interest in caricature is intriguing in that the two performed well in the Academic competitions that focused on perfecting drawing from the live model. Vincent won the Prix Caylus in 1767, the year before he entered the École des élèves protégés.[54] Both Berthélemy and Vincent won second-place medals for life drawing in the Prix de quartier in 1763.[55] The exaggeration in Vincent's full-length portraits comes from subtle errors, areas where Vincent could have been "more correct, more exact" in the anatomy of his figures, presenting skewed proportions: including massive calf muscles; tiny heads; long, spindly legs; or huge feet. Given the *pensionnaires'* successes in Academic life-drawing competitions, the cohorts' use of the "charged" portrait can be read as a form of bravado, a playful send-up of the very practices expected of student artists that they had mastered.

Watelet's definition of *charge* goes beyond the infelicities of students in ways that help us better understand caricature as a social practice at the Palais Mancini. He described exaggerated drawings as the "soul's first inspiration" ("première inspiration de l'âme") that allow an artist to "recall his idea and his intentions" ("se rappeler ses idées et ses intentions") when executing a complete work.[56] He concluded his discussion of the importance of exaggeration to memory by claiming: "This situation makes the *charge* not only excusable, but even necessary in some circumstances, up to a certain point."[57] Watelet was not the only writer who believed that exaggeration in drawing served an important purpose for painting. Pierre Mariette associated exaggeration with memory in his introduction to the Comte de Caylus's *Recueil de testes de caractère et de charges, dessinées par Léonard de Vinci*. In describing the role that Leonardo's close study of expression played in his practice, Mariette noted: "Sometimes he loaded them in the parts in which the ridicule was more sensitive, not so much for play but for committing them to memory with inalterable characters."[58]

Memory and Exchange

The emphasis on exaggeration as a memory device warrants particular attention because the circulation of the *pensionnaires*' caricatures suggests that they functioned as souvenirs of their artists' time in Rome. The series in the Musée Atger and other caricatures by Vincent exist as counterproofs, that is, as copies of drawings made by placing a damp, blank sheet of paper over an original and running it through a press, leaving a reverse image on the blank sheet. Original source drawings for these counterproofs occasionally survive. The large caricature of Jombert is a case in point, and the original is located in Metropolitan Museum's collection; this drawing has lost Jombert's feet. A drawing of Suvée, also in the Metropolitan Museum of Art, is the source of a counterproof drawing in the Musée Atger.[59] Vincent's counterproofs, as well as the portrait by Berthélemy, may have come from Vincent's collection, since the catalog of a posthumous 1816 sale of the artist's studio contents lists "thirty-three pieces of different subjects and caricatures" under the section "suite of drawings on individual sheets, sketches, studies, figure studies after nature and antique objects; expression studies, etc. by the deceased M. Vincent."[60] Toward the end of his life, Vincent annotated certain portraits with names and dates. The inscriptions correspond almost exactly to names listed in the student registry of the Royal Academy's records, and thus the group of caricatures acts as a sort of group portrait of the men who resided at the Palais Mancini during this period.[61]

Furthermore, the provenance history of some of the caricatures made by Vincent and other pensioners reveals that the original drawings had been intended for specific individuals. Vincent's portrait of Suvée and the profile of Jombert in the Metropolitan Museum can be traced back to the collection of Lemonnier, as can several caricatures of Lemonnier by Vincent now in private collections.[62] Berthélemy's nephew Jean-Charles-Nicolas Duchange mentioned in his biography of his uncle how "Vincent and Berthélemy either made remarkable portraits of each other, or *charges* sparkling with verve and spirit." He described "a charming caricature" by Vincent in the family's collection, "drawn in pen and sepia, in which Vincent exaggerated in the most amusing manner the great height and thinness of his friend."

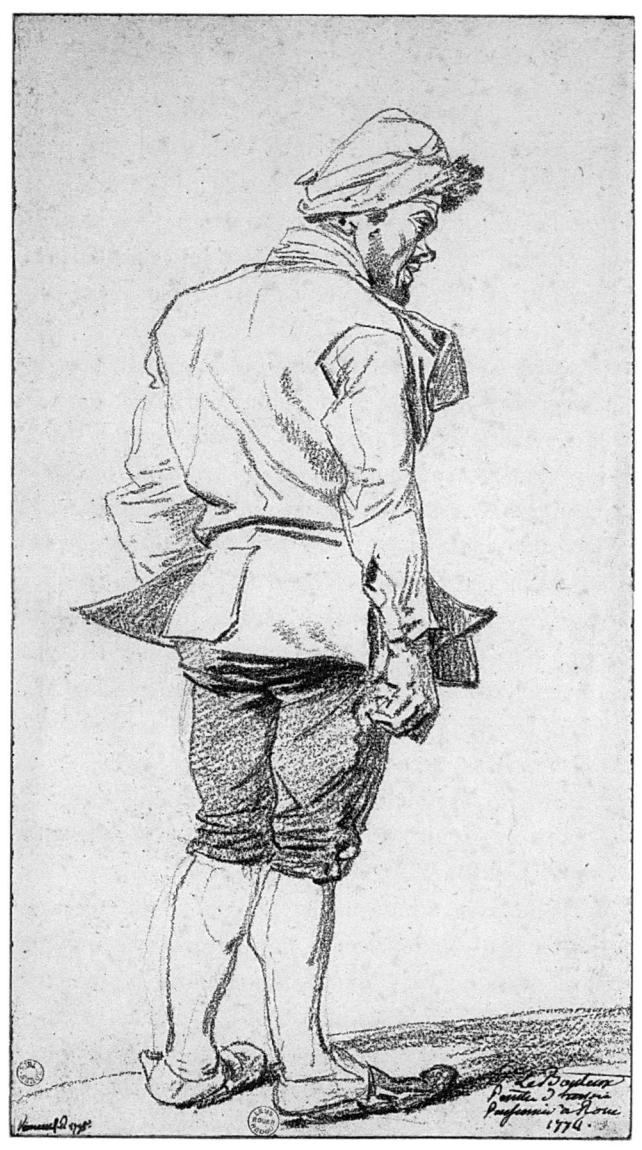

Fig. 4.10. François-André Vincent, *Portrait-charge of the Painter Le Bouteux*, 1774.

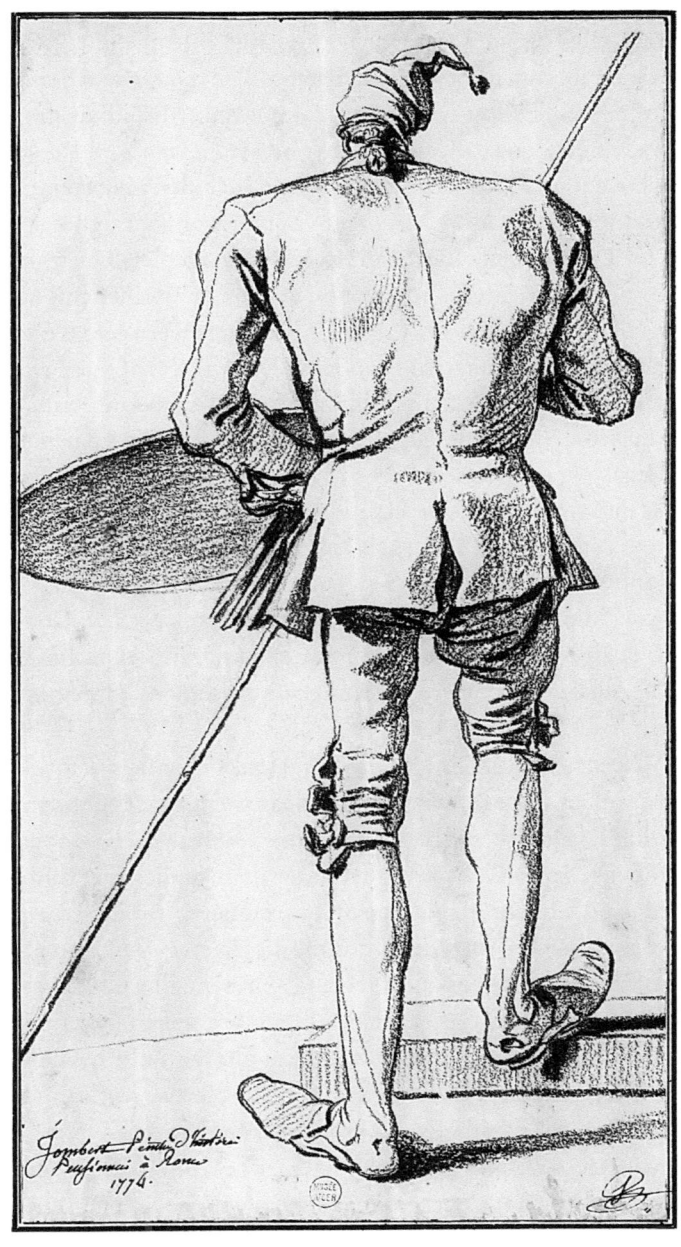

Fig. 4.11. François-André Vincent, *Portrait-charge of the Painter Jombert*, 1774.

Duchange also recalled seeing in Berthélemy's studio "another *charge*, also by Vincent, the pendant of that one."[63]

References to caricatures and *portraits-charges* also appeared in catalogues of the estate sales of many pensioners after their deaths in the early nineteenth century, though these are less specific. The *catalogue de vente* of Guillaume Moitte's collection from 1807, for instance, lists two drawings by Vincent, including "one caricature, figure of a seated man."[64] Suvée's collection, which went up for sale in the same year, included nine counterproofed caricatures by Vincent as well as other counterproofs of figure studies and sketches by Le Bouteux, Berthélemy, and Ménageot.[65] Cuzin has traced several now-lost caricatures to the inventories of Berthélemy and Ménageot.[66] As mentioned previously, Stouf's drawings were adapted to a reproducible medium by the amateur Franconville. Two sets of these etchings are in the public collections of the Bibliothèque nationale de France and the Nationalmuseum, Stockholm. The latter set is annotated with names inserted by the original owner of these works, the Swedish sculptor Johan Tobias Sergel. Sergel was in Rome at the same time as Vincent's cohort, is one of the figures represented in the etched series, and also appears in Vincent's drawings.[67] The reproduction and circulation of counterproofs and etchings was aided by the Palais Mancini housing its own printing press, which facilitated the exchange of drawings through counterproofing and experimentation in etching—techniques that were encouraged by Academy directors for pedagogical purposes.[68]

That Vincent and his fellow *pensionnaires* took advantage of the Academy's press to reproduce these drawings, exchanged them, and kept them throughout their lives strongly suggests that these *portraits-charges* operated as a memory device, more like souvenirs rather than studies for paintings to be completed later. The social function of the exaggeration of the *charge* is similarly discussed in Diderot's definition in the *Encyclopédie*. As in previous definitions, he emphasized excess: "It is the representation on canvas or paper, using colors, of a person, of an action, or more generally of a subject in which the exact truth and resemblance are altered only by the excess of ridicule."[69] Significantly, Diderot was quite concerned with the somewhat counterintuitive idea that the excess itself must not be excessive, as the subject must remain recognizable in order for the work to be effective: "[I]f you exaggerate, and it is not clear that that's what you had in mind, the being to which one compares your description no longer exists as the one you've taken for a model, your work will have no effect."[70] Diderot's emphasis on recognizability resonates with Vincent's treatment of his cohort in his drawings.

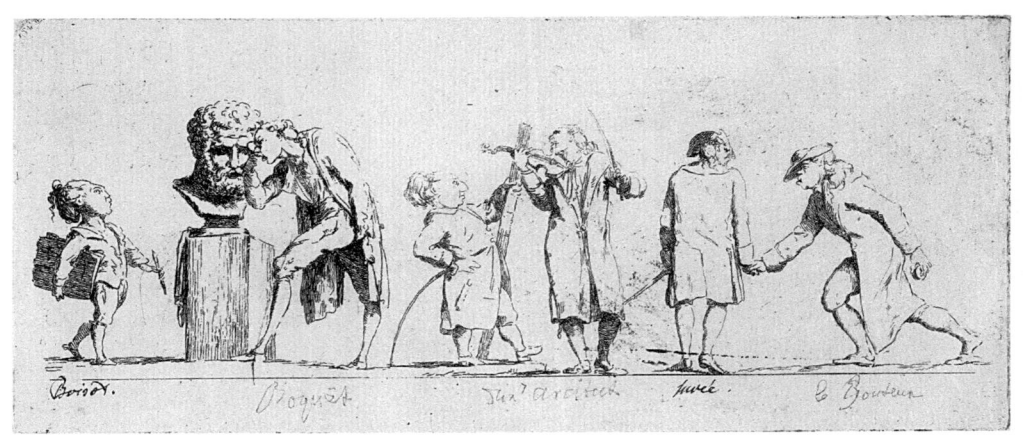

Fig. 4.12. Moricaud Franconville after Jean-Baptiste Stouf, *Caricatures*, early 1770s.

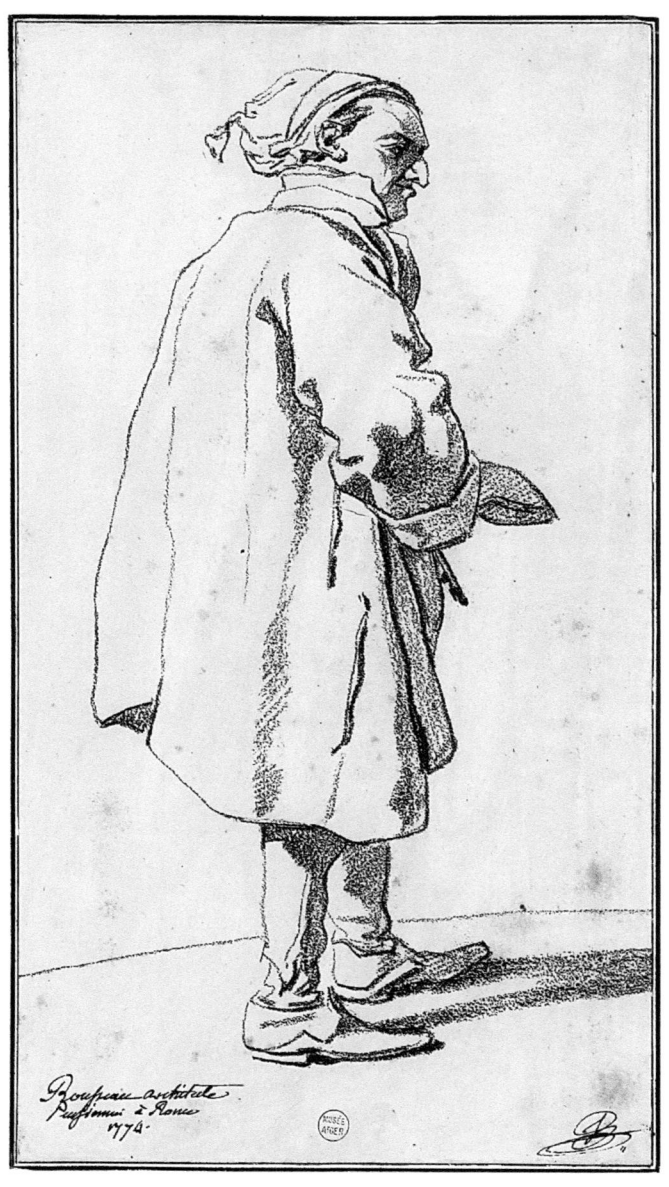

Fig. 4.13. François-André Vincent, *Portrait-charge of the Architect Rousseau*, 1774.

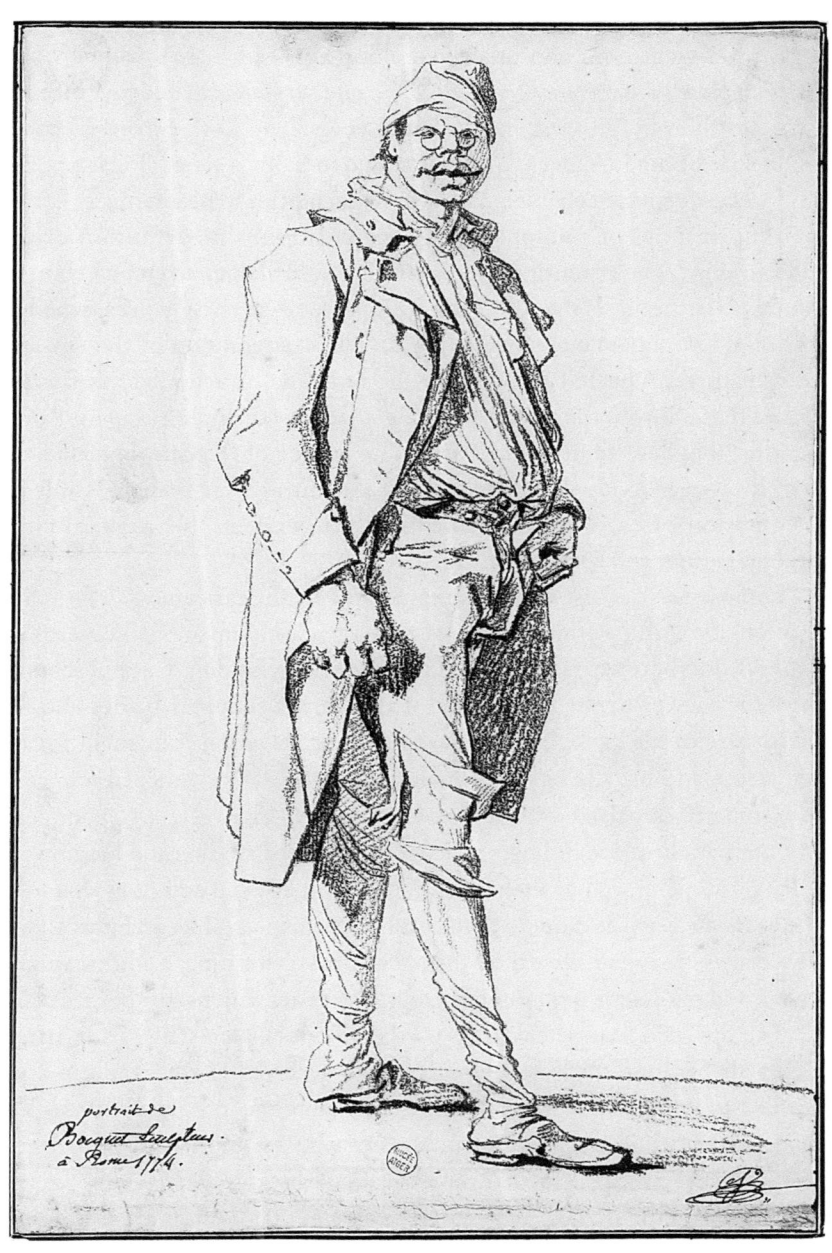

Fig. 4.14. François-André Vincent, *Portrait-charge of the Sculptor Boquet*, 1774.

Each individual has a "charged" aspect of their anatomy or costume, which becomes a leitmotif across Vincent's portraits of his colleagues. His portraits of Le Bouteux, both the quick sketch and parodic life drawing, focus on the artist's prominent nose and unshaven chin (Figs. 4.5, 4.10). Jombert was usually depicted wearing a *bonnet de coton*, and was identifiable in Vincent's portraits of him by his long, lanky figure (Figs. 4.1, 4.11). Suvée is shown from the back both in Vincent's drawings and in Stouf's series (Figs. 4.7, 4.8, 4.12).[71] These repeated characteristics allow each sitter to be identified, corresponding to Diderot's emphasis on recognition in his definition of the *portrait-charge*. The repetition of a particular nose shape, unshaven chin, or distinctive hat suggests that the humorous passages in these works, whether overt or subtle, operated as inside jokes. The exaggeration of the *pensionnaires'* features, repeated throughout the portraits, functioned as an *aide-mémoire* that allowed the artists, with a glance, to recall their time in Rome long after they had returned to Paris. The humor of the drawings and the recognition of individuals by their physical features were made possible by the condition of close and sustained contact between the artists: living, working, eating, and socializing together.

The closeness of these men is demonstrated by the caricatures. The sitters are often shown in various states of disarray, sometimes on the verge of *déshabille*. Jombert wears disheveled and ill-fitting clothing. Careful shading allows the viewer to see the outline of the artist's shoulder blades and the musculature of his back, making it appear that his coat is too small for his large frame and his slippers too small for his feet. His oversized *bonnet de coton*, sometimes paired with a set of spectacles (Figs. 4.1, 4.11), suggests encounters in the more intimate spaces of the artists' studios and lodgings of the Palais Mancini, rather than at the more formal social activities that took place in Rome, such as dinners or musical performances. The architect Pierre Rousseau is likewise shown in informal dress, donning a nightcap and banyan; and sculptor Simon Boquet proudly appears with beady, bespectacled eyes, fish lips, and a large tear in his partially undone pants (Figs. 4.13, 4.14).

Not all of these men maintained the same level of camaraderie after returning to Paris, where they would be thrust into the internal politics of the Royal Academy and, eventually, into the French Revolution. But in the early 1770s, as winners of the Prix de Rome, the men caricatured in these series had effectively won the highest accolades possible at that point in their training. Vincent's portraits suggest that Rome offered both a temporary reprieve from the continuous cycle of competition they had experienced as students in Paris, and the freedom to socialize, to play, and, importantly, to become friends.

Travel Companions: The Portrait de trois hommes

The sheer quantity of caricatures, their reproduction, their circulation among the pensioners, and their appearance in inventories and estate sales confirm that, for the residents of the Palais Mancini, portraiture was an important social practice. Caricature—due to its ease of execution, reproduction, and exchange—was the most prevalent material demonstration of the sociability shared among the *pensionnaires*, but it was not the only means by which Vincent made visible the camaraderie he experienced abroad.

Vincent made his way back to Paris from Rome in October 1775. Like many artists, he did not make this voyage alone, traveling with a fellow pensioner, Rousseau.[72] The two men stopped in Marseille, a common resting point for travelers who chose to travel by sea back to Paris. There, Vincent and Rousseau were reunited with Philippe-Henri Coclers van Wyck, a Belgian painter whom they had met in Rome.[73] While in Marseille, Vincent painted the *Portrait de trois hommes* to commemorate this reunion (Fig. 4.15). The canvas, almost three feet by two-and-a-half feet, shows Vincent in costume, standing in a nondescript space with Rousseau and Coclers van Wyck. A large blank canvas fills the majority of the background. Vincent and Coclers van Wyck clasp their hands around a set of paintbrushes while Rousseau holds a compass angled awkwardly toward his body.

The subject of the *Trois hommes* is made clear through its composition: the proximity of the men to each other, the central position of Vincent's and Coclers van Wyck's clasped hands, Rousseau's compass, and the blank canvas suggest that it is about friendship and artistic practice. The work appears to have stayed in Marseille with Coclers van Wyck when Vincent and Rousseau continued their journey, but Vincent made a drawn copy of the painting, as a souvenir of sorts, to take with him. An inscription on the back of the canvas, "entrusted to citizen Beaussier by Van Wyck" ("confie à cit[oyen] Beaussier par Van Wyck"), suggests that Coclers van Wyck retained possession of the work until the French Revolution, when he handed it over to Monsieur Beaussier.[74] The history of the painting suggests that the portrait took a passing moment—the brief reunion of the men in Marseille—and transformed it into something permanent.

The men depicted were themselves in a moment of professional transformation. After the completion of this portrait, all three went on to establish themselves within the official realms of artistic production in France.

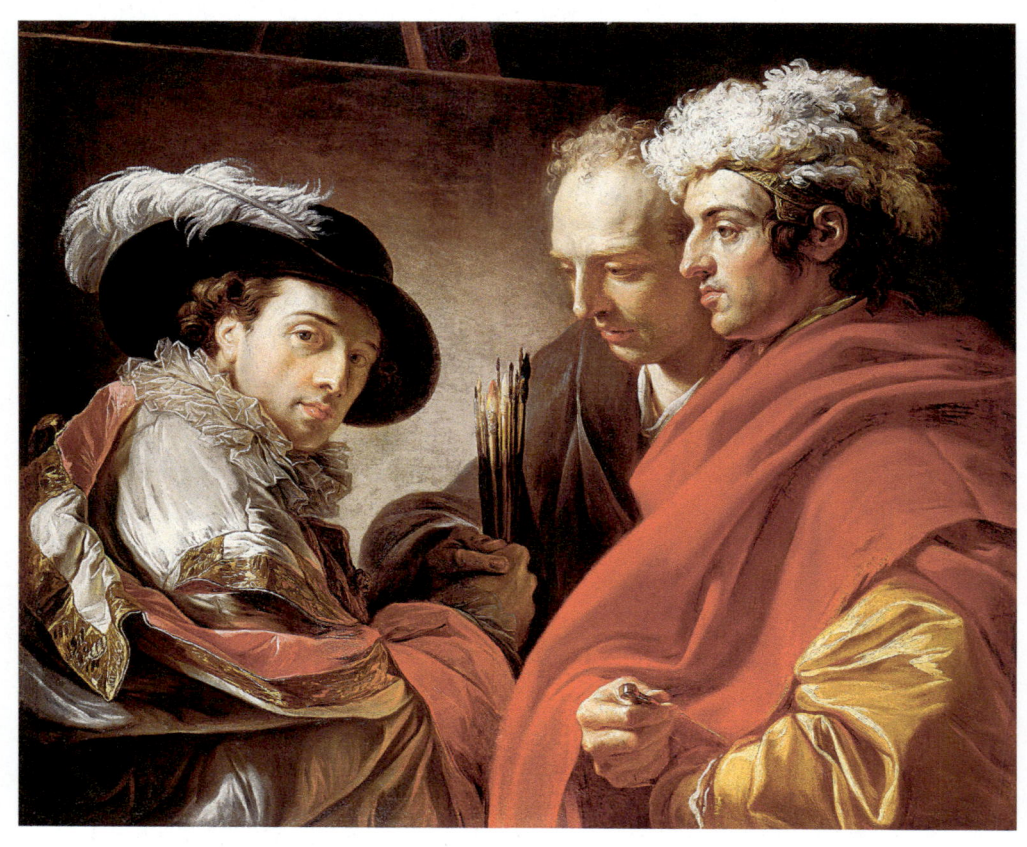

Fig. 4.15. François-André Vincent, *Portrait de trois hommes*, 1774.

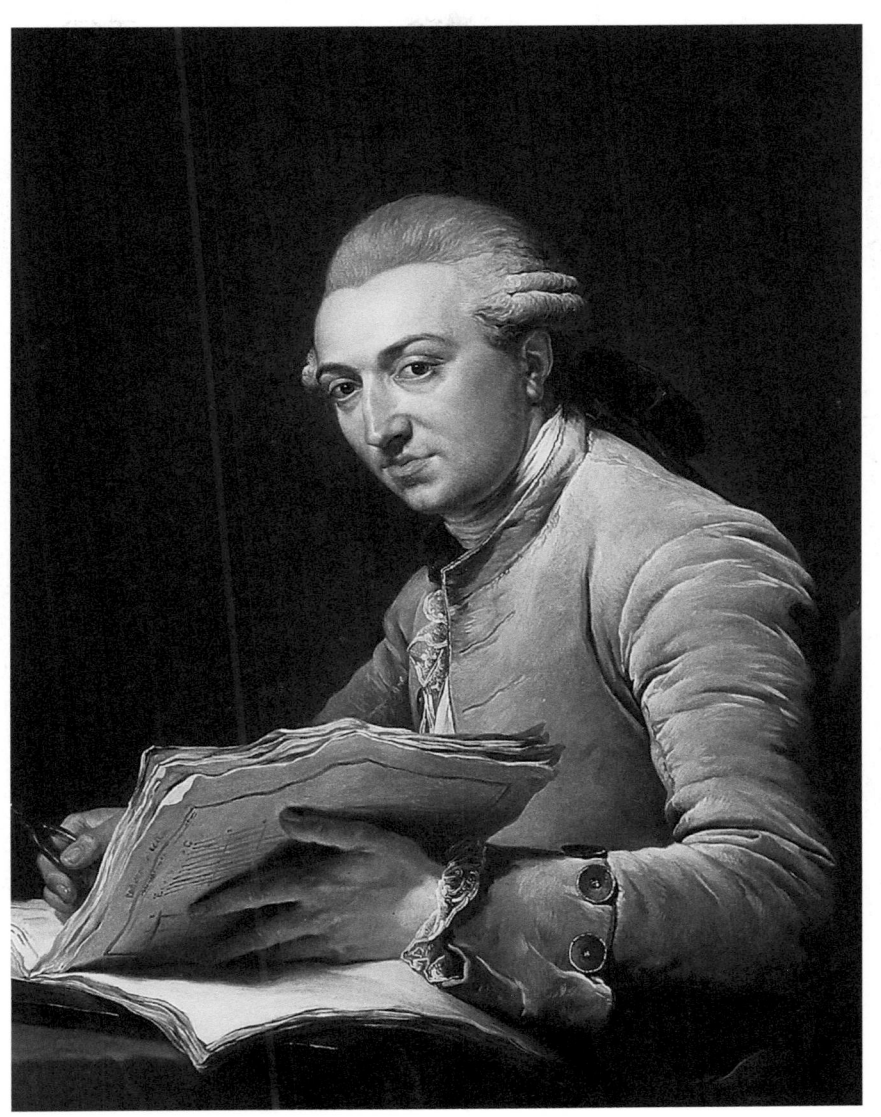

Fig. 4.16. François-André Vincent, *Portrait of Pierre Rousseau*, 1774.

Vincent and Rousseau were accepted into academies of painting and sculpture and of architecture, respectively, shortly after returning to Paris. Coclers van Wyck became a member of the Royal Academy of Marseille (in either 1776 or 1786) and, eventually, in the institution's final years, its director.[75] As Mansfield has noted, this self-actualization may have been prefigured in Rousseau's awkward handling of the compass.[76] Unlike Vincent's more straightforward portrait of the architect exhibited in 1777, which shows him at work, in the *Trois hommes*, Rousseau points this instrument at himself, a gesture that seems to proclaim, "I am an architect" (Fig. 4.16).

A number of fascinating group scenes emerged after the 1789 Revolution, from Louis-Léopold Boilly's *A Gathering of Artists in the Studio of Isabey* (1798) to Henri Fantin-Latour's *Studio in Batignolles* (1870). The handful of group portraits by and of French artists created before that time, however, represented artists' families, usually emphasizing artistic genealogy. In Louis-Michel Vanloo's portrait of his uncle Carle Vanloo and his family, for example, Carle Vanloo is shown sketching his daughter while his son looks on, holding a drawing portfolio (Fig. 4.17). The blank canvas leaning against the wall in the background, and a small still life vignette of brushes, paints, and rags in the lower right remind us of the elder Vanloo's work as painter. Behind the group, Carle's wife Christine (née Soumis), a renowned singer, holds sheets of music; a guitar lies on the floor. While Louis-Michel Vanloo paid tribute to the visual and musical artistry of his family, his portrait also fit within a growing trend of representing family life in more intimate interior scenes, which was associated with changing views about love and parenting that were part of the rise of the bourgeois family over the course of the century.[77] The portrait presents a happy family depicted in a domestic space, grouped together in a believable manner that gives the scene a relaxed and intimate quality. At the same time, this work is concerned with the continuation of an artistic dynasty. The family's talents lay both in the visual and musical arts, and the work celebrates the gifts that were passed down from both the paternal and maternal lines of the family.[78] Similar themes are found in Jean-Marc Nattier's family portrait, in which Nattier holds a palette and brushes while his wife, Marie-Madeleine Delaroche, sits at her harpsichord (Fig. 4.18). Their eldest daughter, Marie-Catherine Pauline, studies a musical score while their son, Jean-Frédéric-Marc, presents a *porte-crayon*, a tool used to hold chalk.[79]

Vincent's group portrait stands out among the few eighteenth-century group portraits that were produced by French artists. It has more in common with triple portraits made in the last half of the eighteenth century that commemorated travel to Italy. In 1751, Italian painter Giuseppe Baldrighi painted a triple portrait of himself with two other men in pastel (Fig. 4.19).[80] The man in the center has been identified as Swedish painter Alexandre Roslin; the man on the right may be the French sculptor Jean-Baptiste Boulard.[81] Baldrighi, a court painter in Parma, became acquainted with Roslin and Boulard during their stay in Parma, where they were working for the court. Baldrighi and Roslin both moved to Paris—Roslin permanently, Baldrighi for a shorter stay—the year after the completion of this painting. And while there is no record of Roslin and Baldrighi's interaction in Paris, Roslin referred to Baldrighi as "one of his oldest friends" in a letter to his cousin, Adolph Ulrich Wertmüller, in 1779.[82] Like Vincent's portrait, Baldrighi's work shows a meeting between three men in a nondescript space. The foreigners are depicted in full dress with proper wigs, while the Italian, on the left, is represented with an air of informality in a fine blue silk house robe embroidered with a gold flower pattern, as well as a blue silk cap. Roslin's forward gaze implies that we are interrupting an intense conversation. The active gestures of the men make it apparent that a lively, friendly debate is taking place. Boulard's arm is around Roslin's shoulder; all three men's hands are in demonstrative positions, and Baldrighi's slightly parted lips imply speech.

A second group portrait of international friendship is found in the self-portrait of British painter James Barry alongside English architect James Paine and French painter Dominique Lefèvre, produced in 1767 (Fig. 4.20). Barry looks over his shoulder at the viewer, while the ghostly figures of Paine and Lefèvre behind him are copying the Belvedere torso, one of the most famous classical statues in the Vatican, itself a phantomlike apparition in the upper right corner of the canvas. If Baldrighi's work is a conversation piece, Barry's painting is more focused on artistic life in Rome. Barry prominently depicted the palette and brushes of one of his companions. The strong horizontal line in the lower third of the painting, which creates a division between the gray tonalities of Barry's companions and the deeper brown tones of his own coat, makes the painting read as an ambiguous *mise en abyme*. Also, the Italian-born French painter Jean-François Rigaud made a triple portrait of three Italian artists living in London in 1777: Francesco Bartolozzi, Agostino Carlini, and Giovanni Battista Cipriani (Fig. 4.21). The expatriate status of the artists, all of whom were founding members of the Royal Academy of Painting in London, further underscores the relationship between the triple portrait and travel. It is unclear—and unlikely—that Vincent would have been familiar with these specific paintings. It is notable, however, that all the works have as common themes travel, amicability, and artistic practice.

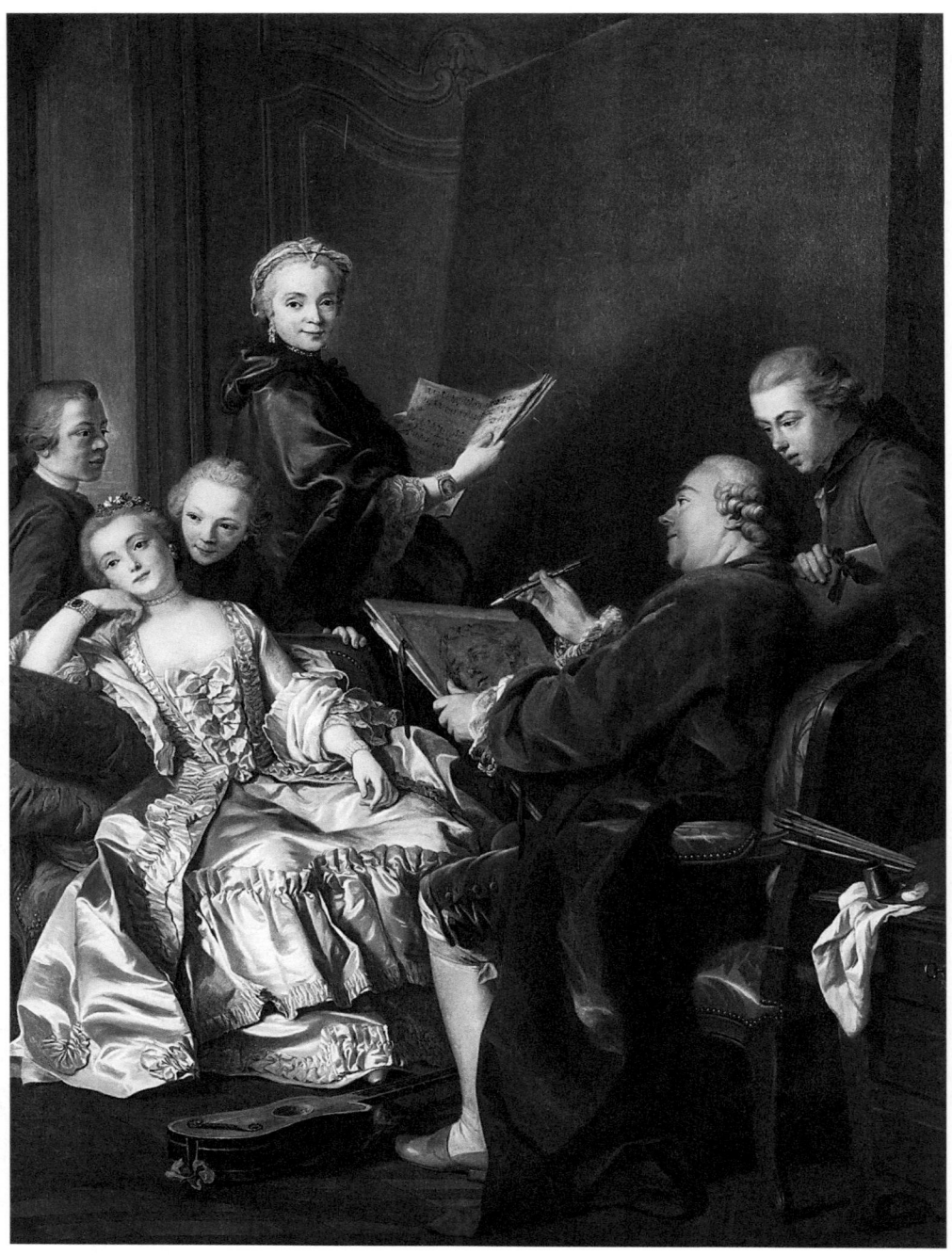

Fig. 4.17. Louis-Michel Vanloo, *Portrait of Carle Vanloo and His Family*, 1757.

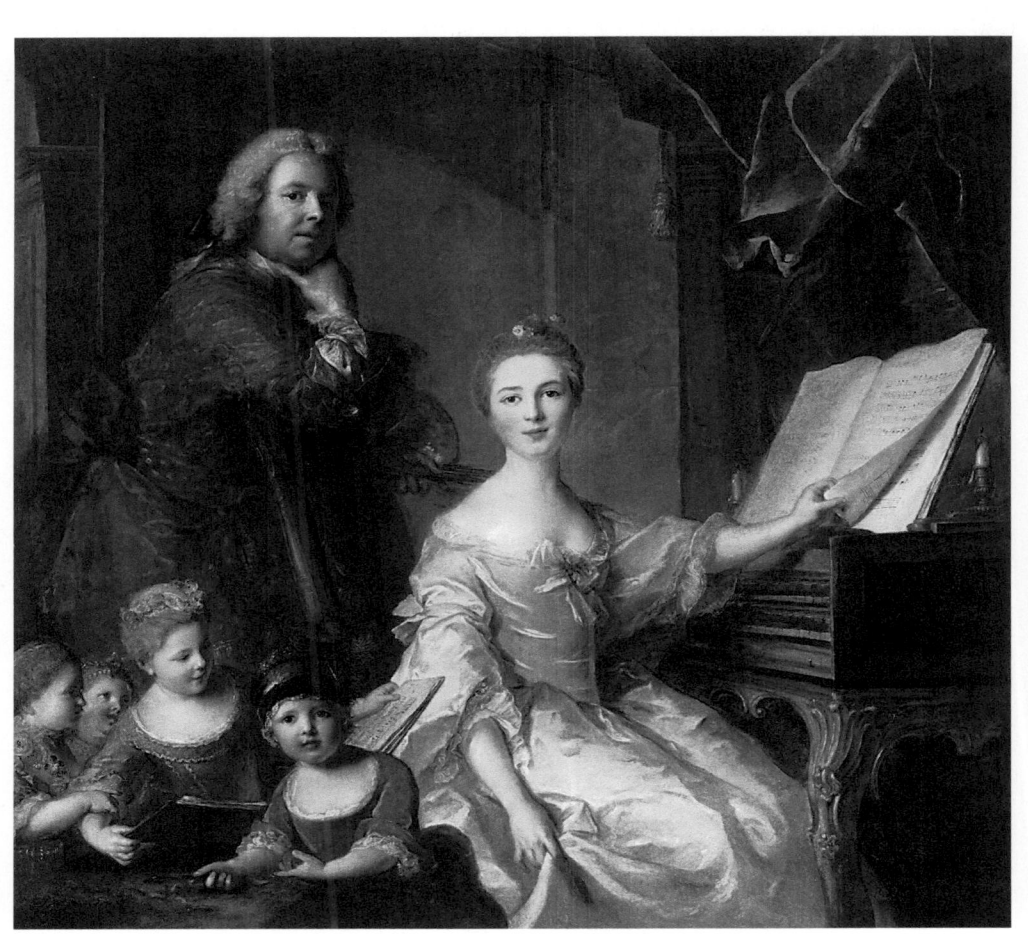

Fig. 4.18. Jean-Marc Nattier, *Portrait of the Artist and His Family*, 1732–62.

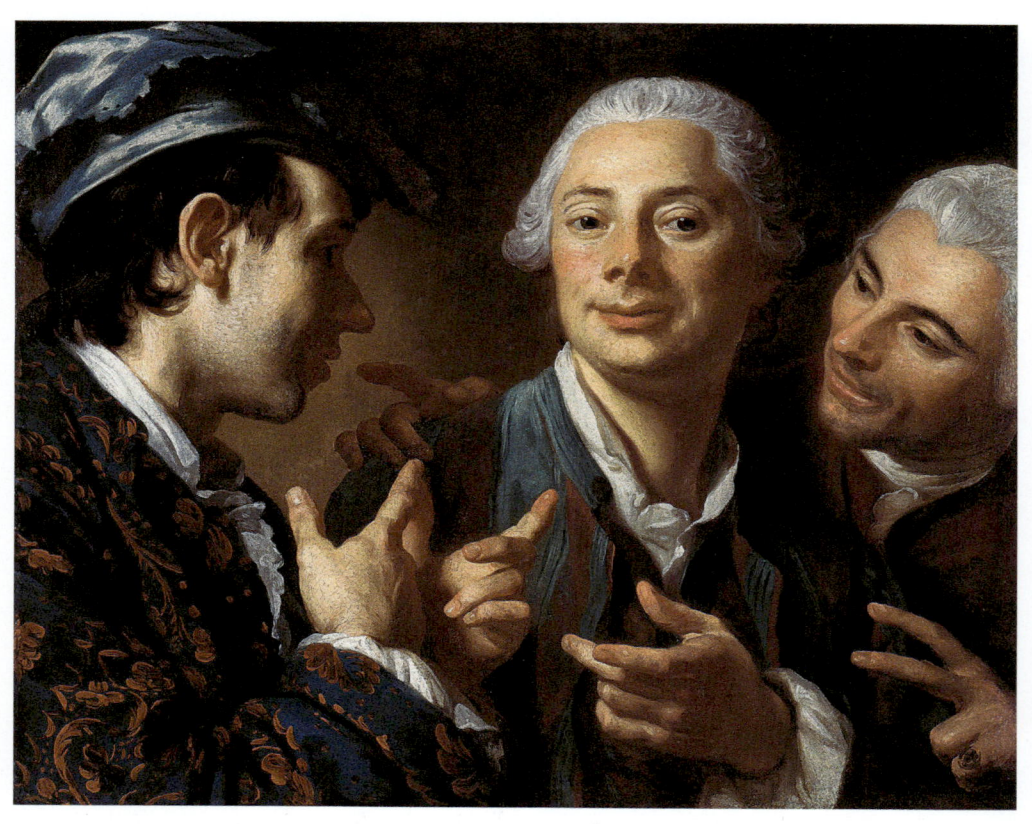

Fig. 4.19. Giuseppe Baldrighi, *Triple Portrait of Artists*, 1751.

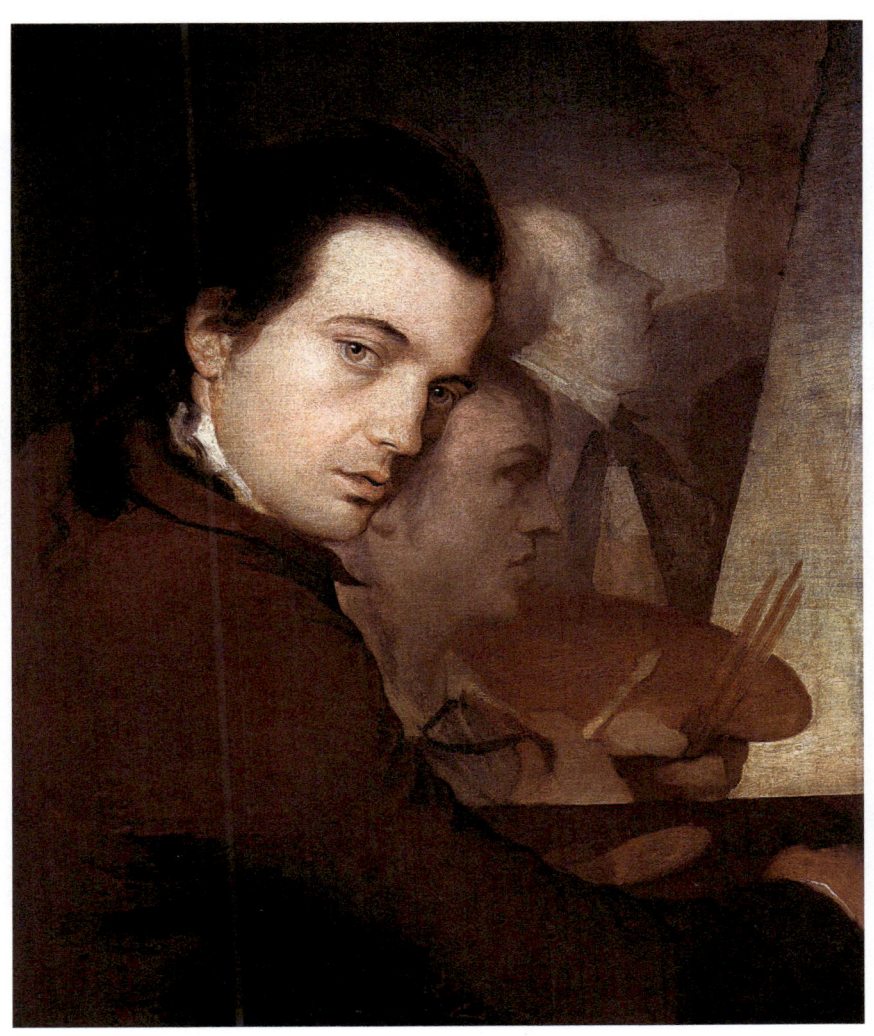

Fig. 4.20. James Barry, *Self-Portrait with James Paine and Dominique Lefèvre*, 1767.

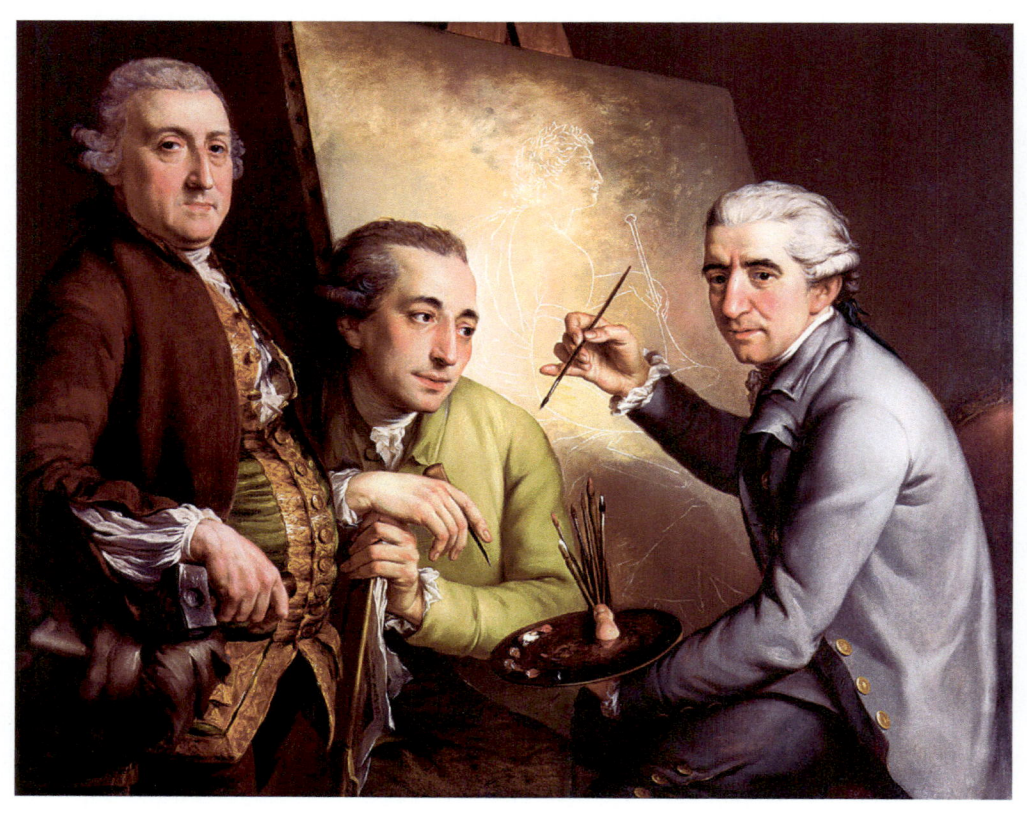

Fig. 4.21. Jean-François Rigaud, *Portrait of Francesco Bartolozzi, Agostino Carlini, and Giovanni Battista Cipriani*, 1777.

In contrast to the representations of familial passage of talent, these works avoided a full-length representation of their figures, preferring a certain intimacy to their work. The full-length figures in the family portraits, however, put substantial distance between themselves and the viewer. Thus, although the viewer is looking at intimate, domestic moments, (s)he is still kept from having the sense of fully participating in these scenes. Vincent's, Baldrighi's, Barry's, and Rigaud's tightly cropped works instead push the figures toward the viewer. The direct gaze of one figure in each painting invites the viewer to feel as if she or he is engaged in the scene at hand. The employment of the closely cropped triple portrait in Italy suggests that the format was appropriated specifically to represent the common bond of friendship formed during travel. It prefigured the Freundschaftsbild created by the Nazarenes, a genre taken up by young artists in Rome without Academic sponsorship. These men banded together in a Romantic revival of medieval fraternity, frequently incorporating Christian iconography in their representations of friendship.

The eighteenth-century paintings also looked backward to the friendship portrait, which developed in the Italian Renaissance and the seventeenth century. Often discussed with regard to the rise of the humanist portrait during the period, the friendship portrait drew much of its iconography from the philosophical writings of Cicero, Pliny the Elder, and Aristotle.[83] These discussions centered on the notion of the true friend being a person's "double": true friends shared one soul between two bodies. In order to be true friends, two individuals had to have the same qualities, come from the same social class, and share a love of goodness. Most Renaissance examples of the friendship portrait focus on two individuals, frequently representing them in the same pictorial space, overlapping each other or touching, as seen in Pontormo's *Portrait of Two Friends* (c. 1522) (Fig. 4.22), which explicitly references friendship through the inclusion of a sheet of paper held by one of the figures that contains texts from Cicero's *De Amicitia*.[84]

The interaction of the figures with the viewer in Renaissance friendship paintings implies that the works may have been oriented toward a third or even fourth party.[85] In the seventeenth century, the implied third party was a friend of the artist and/or sitter, who was incorporated into the painting itself. The triple portrait of artists may have had its origins in Caravaggesque art of the first few decades of the seventeenth century, drawing from the half-length figures found in genre scenes by Caravaggio and his followers, such as *The Fortune Teller* (c. 1594) and *The Cardsharps* (c. 1594).[86] Artists on the move appear to have adopted this format for memorializing meetings and reunions

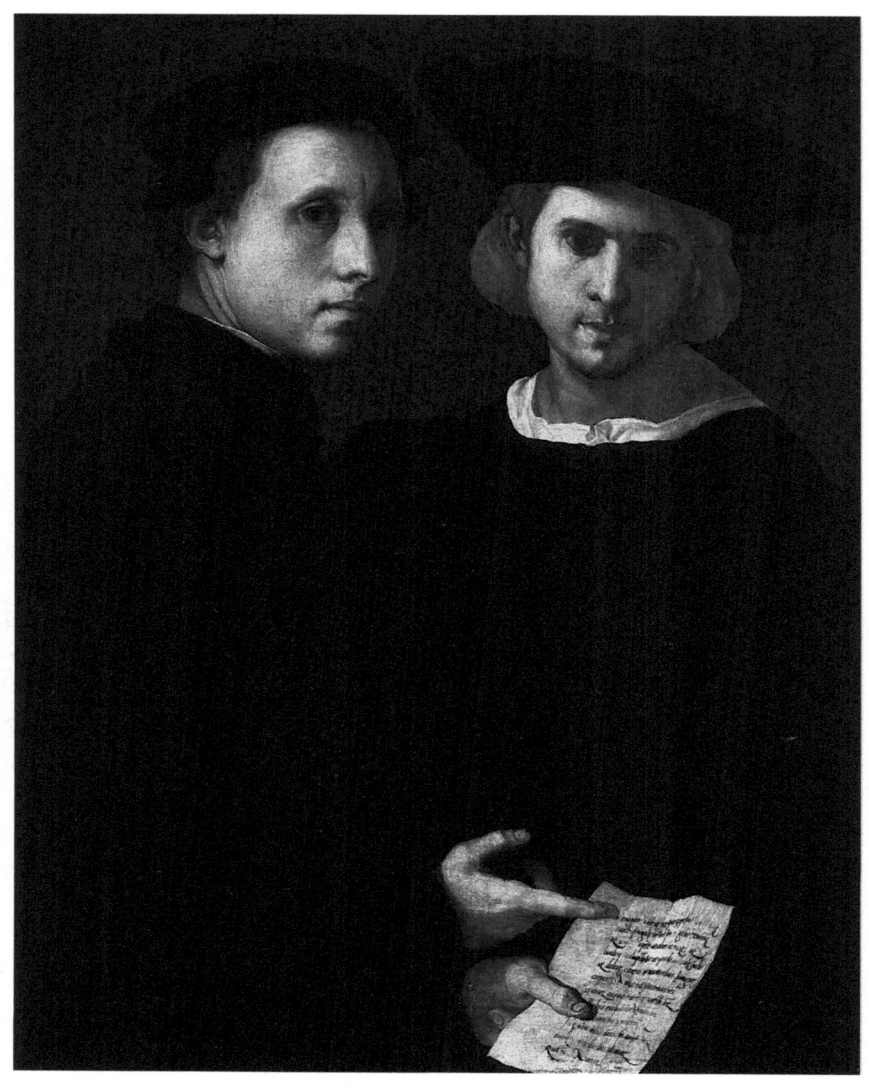

Fig. 4.22. Jacopo Pontormo, *Portrait of Two Friends*, ca. 1521–24.

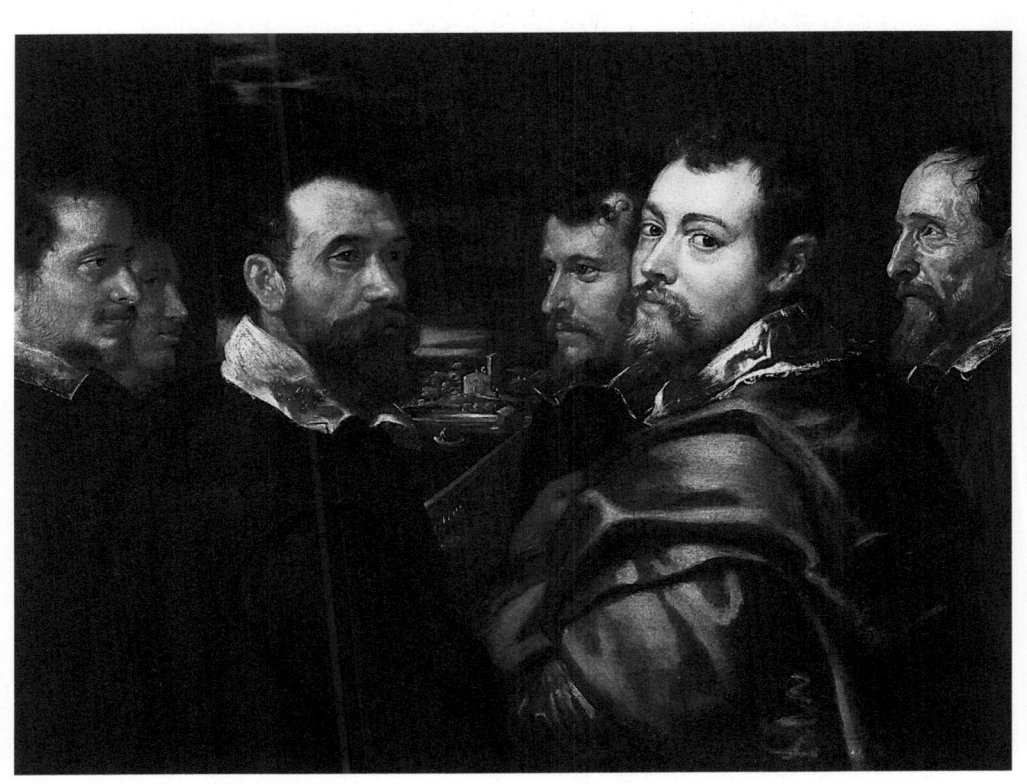

Fig. 4.23. Peter Paul Rubens, *Self-Portrait in a Circle of Friends from Mantua*, ca. 1602–5.

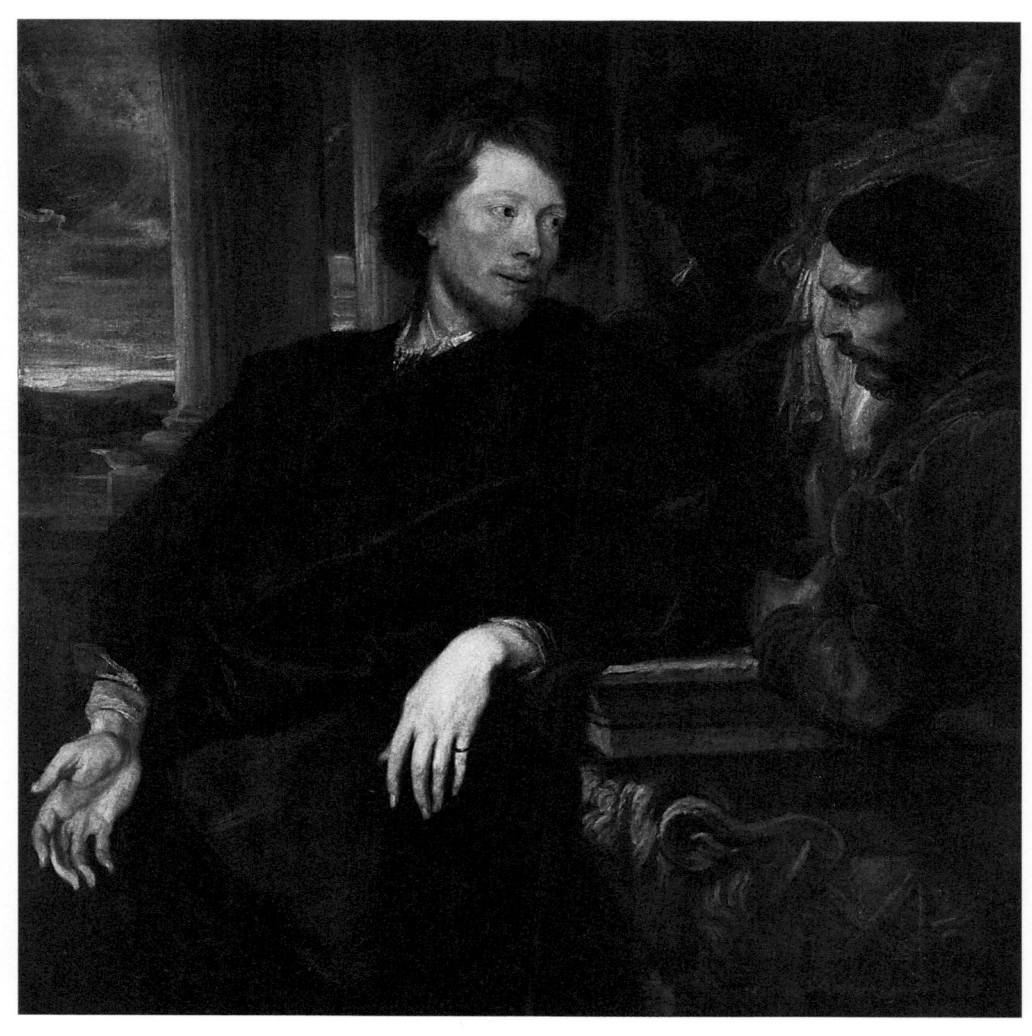

Fig. 4.24. Anthony van Dyck, *Portrait of George Gage with Two Servants*, 1622–23.

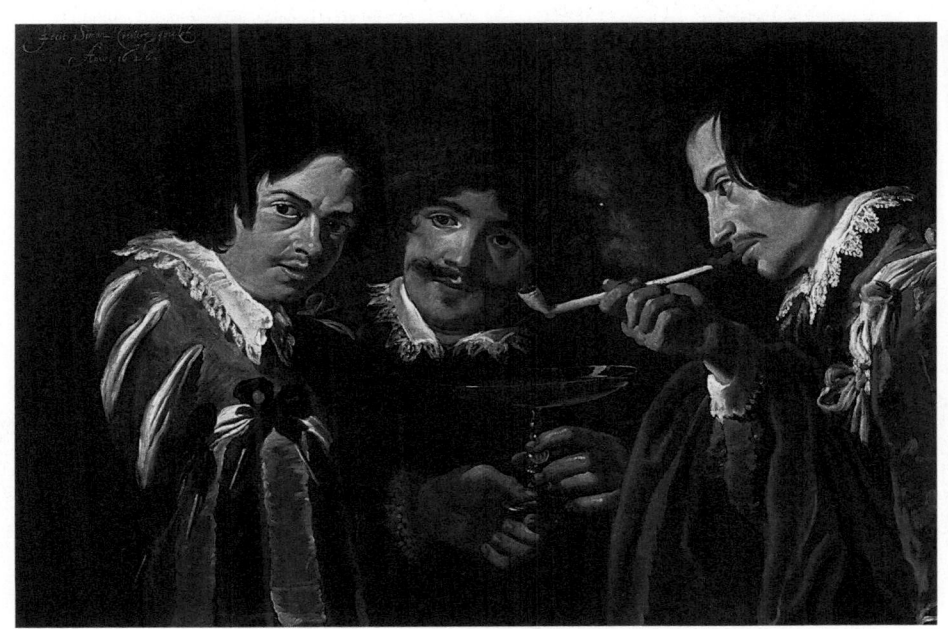

Fig. 4.25. Simon de Vos, *Artists' Portraits as Smokers and Drinkers*, 1626.

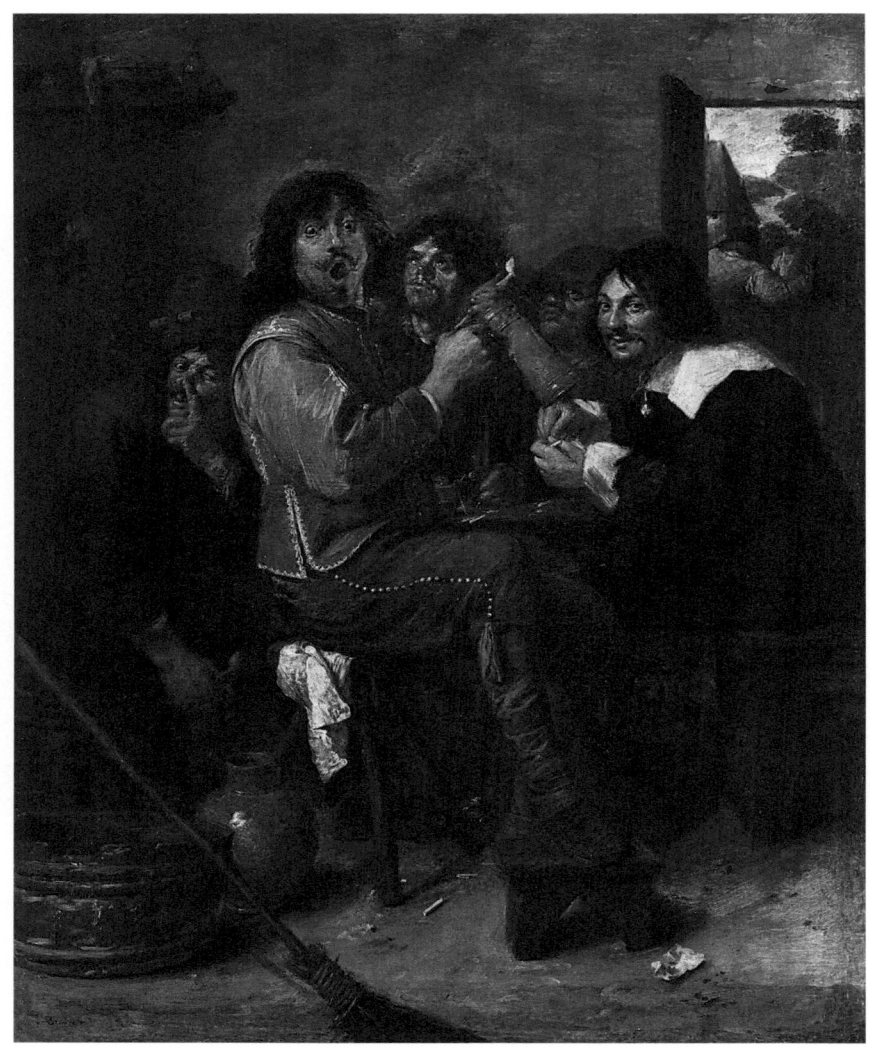

Fig. 4.26. Adrien Brouwer, *The Smokers*, ca. 1636.

in foreign locales. Peter Paul Rubens painted his half-length *Self-Portrait with Circle of Friends in Mantua* (1602–5) during a stay in Italy (Fig. 4.23). The triple portrait type was sufficiently associated with friendship among artists that Anthony van Dyck's depiction of three men grouped around a sculpture, painted while he was in Italy, was once believed to be a portrait of Rubens with two other artists (Fig. 4.24).[87]

The eighteenth-century artists' works also bear some resemblance to Dutch and Flemish group portraits of artists in undignified settings that cross the boundary between portraiture and genre painting. For example, the bawdy behavior in Simon de Vos's *Artists' Portraits as Smokers and Drinkers* (1626), now considered to be a triple portrait, commemorated his meeting in Aix-en-Provence with Jan Cossiers and Johan Geerloff (Fig. 4.25). Adrien Brouwer depicted himself with Cossiers and Jan Davidsz de Heem in a work known as *The Smokers* (c. 1636), which shows the artists smoking and drinking in a tavern (Fig. 4.26).[88] In contrast to the lowlife, ribald humor of both of these images of friends smoking and imbibing, Vincent's *Portrait de trois hommes* declares its interest in serious artistic practice by placing its men in a studio environment (if a nondescript one). Yet, the triple portrait was established as a fitting format for representing friendly encounters and constituted a prototype for the *Trois hommes*.

Friendship, Fantasy, and Fancy Dress

Vincent's painting stands out from the other images of traveling artists discussed in his use of enigmatic costume, a technique that can be traced to the previous century and is shown most prominently in Eustache Le Sueur's *Réunion d'amis* (c. 1640) (Fig. 4.27). Commissioned by Anne de Chambré, a war treasurer, patron, and amateur lutenist, the work depicts the individuals who regularly gathered at Chambré's home to discuss and listen to music. Alain Mérot has described the men in the painting as an "academy," or "group of friends, noble or bourgeois, lay people or ecclesiastics, who gather regularly at a rich person's house."[89] Most of the identities of the sitters remain a mystery, with the exception of Le Sueur himself, pictured in front of a canvas and holding a drawing, and the lutenist Denis Gaultier, who poses with his instrument. But the mixture of the costumes (both allegorical and contemporary) and attributes of the sitters endow the painting with multilayered meaning: it records the members of the group and their professions, but may also operate as an allegory of the five senses or the temperaments.[90] Importantly, the unusual subject matter and esoteric iconography of the work

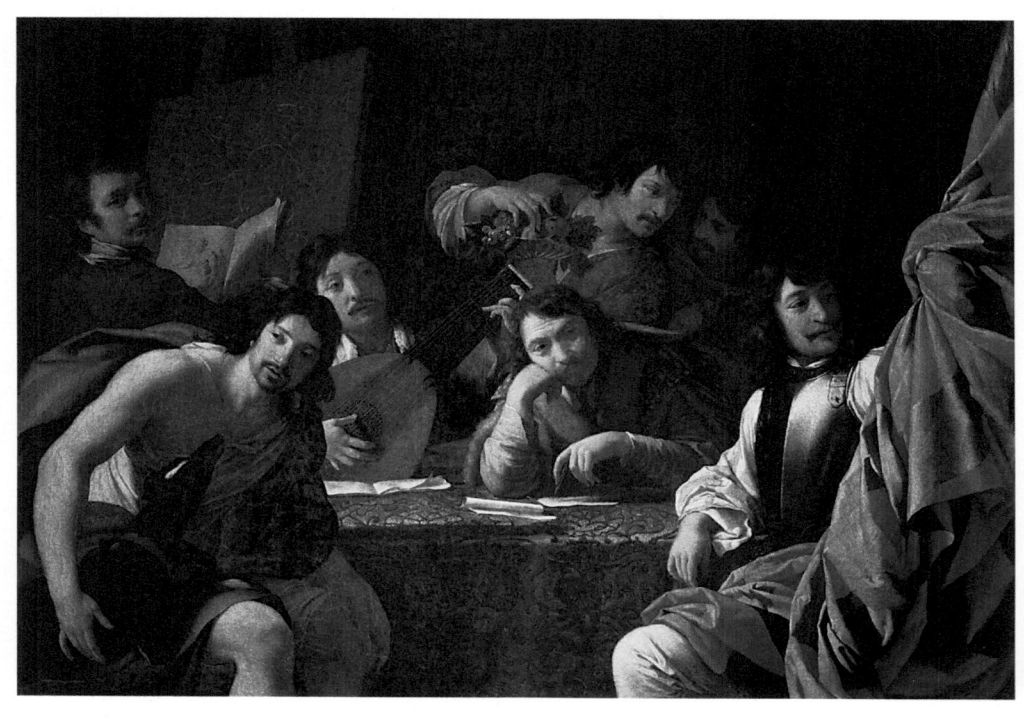

Fig. 4.27. Eustache Le Sueur, *Réunion d'amis*, 1640–44.

would have been inspired by the bonds created by the voluntary association between the men depicted, and would have reinforced those bonds—only those participating in the painting would understand how to read it. Such secret iconography appears similarly in Joshua Reynolds's group portraits of the Society of Dilettanti, demonstrating that portrayals of voluntary association, friendship, and secret visual languages lasted well into the eighteenth century (Figs. 4.28, 4.29). The common thread that connects Le Sueur's, Reynolds's, and Vincent's portraits, separated by about 140 years, is their creation in a context of exclusive male homosociability, whether it be Chambré's "academy," the circle of Dilettantis who had participated in the Grand Tour, or the milieu of student-artists in Rome.

Like Le Sueur's portrait, Vincent's *Trois hommes* leaves much to be desired with regard to how we should interpret the sitters' dress. Rousseau's profile and classicizing dress bears some resemblance to Roman medallion or coin portraits. (It is worth noting that the profile is one that was used to represent humanist architects of the Italian Renaissance, although it is difficult to clearly identify Rousseau as any particular individual.)[91] Coclers van Wyck's dress appears contemporary, perhaps a modest house robe or painter's smock. Vincent's costume is the most readily identifiable—a *costume espagnole*, a form of seventeenth-century dress that had been popular in the Netherlands under Spanish rule. In France, the dress was a reference to the golden age of Henri IV, which became a popular subject for history paintings as well as the theme for royal masked balls during the reign of Louis XVI.[92]

The *Portrait de trois hommes* was not the first time Vincent had depicted himself in this type of dress. He also wears the *costume espagnole* in a self-portrait from around 1766 (Fig. 4.30). Vincent made this early self-portrait, once thought to be by Jean-Honoré Fragonard, before he departed for Rome. The painting lacks the boldness and confidence of his self-portrait in the later *Trois hommes*. In the earlier self-portrait, he appears younger, almost naive, and less self-assured than the jaunty fellow in the triple portrait with his hat tilted at a raking angle. The self-portrait's romantic, dreamlike feel and focus on a singular individual, however, has much in common with Fragonard's *portraits de fantaisie*, sometimes called fantasy figures, a group of approximately sixteen portraits painted by Fragonard around 1769 (Fig. 4.31). These enigmatic paintings blend the genres of portraiture and expression study, and act as a display of painterly bravado. The identities of Fragonard's sitters, mostly depicted in *costume espagnol*, have been long debated, as have the paintings' status as "portraits," although the emergence of a sketch in Fragonard's hand has secured the identities of the majority of the sitters.[93]

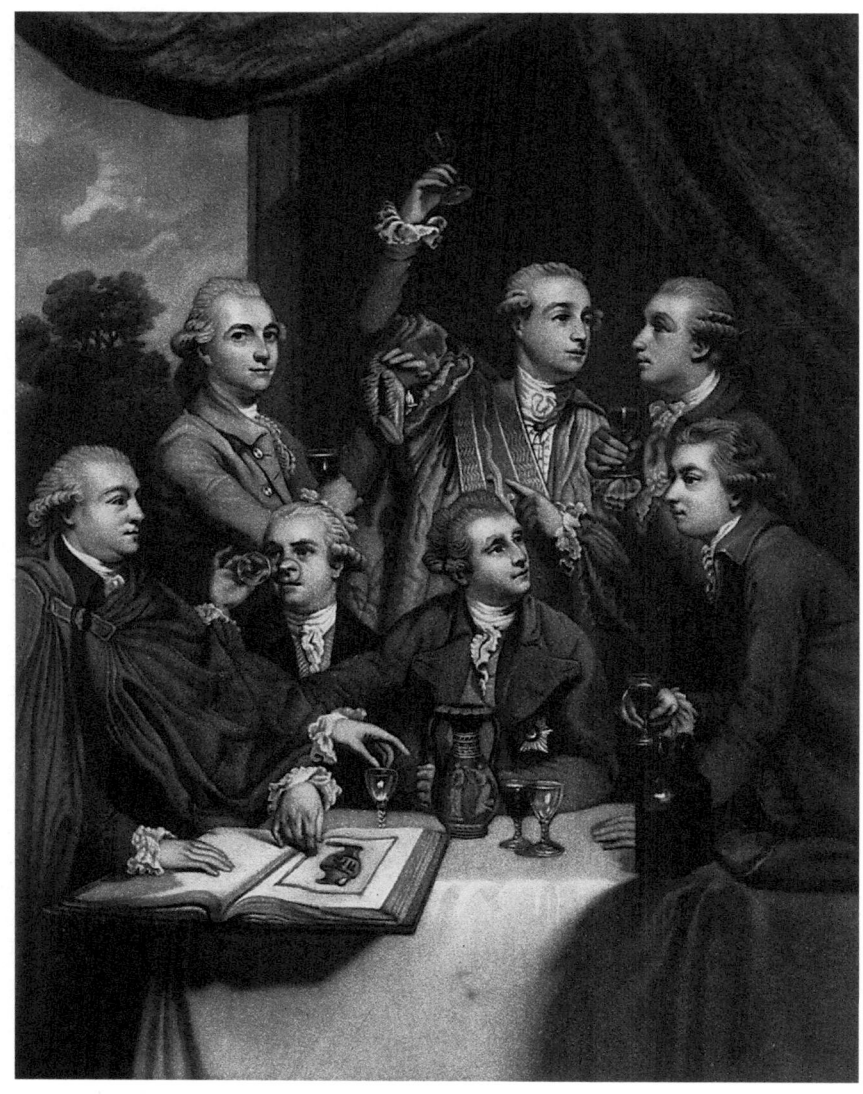

Fig. 4.28. Charles Algernon Tomkins, after Joshua Reynolds, *Members of the Society of Dilettanti*, mid-nineteenth century.

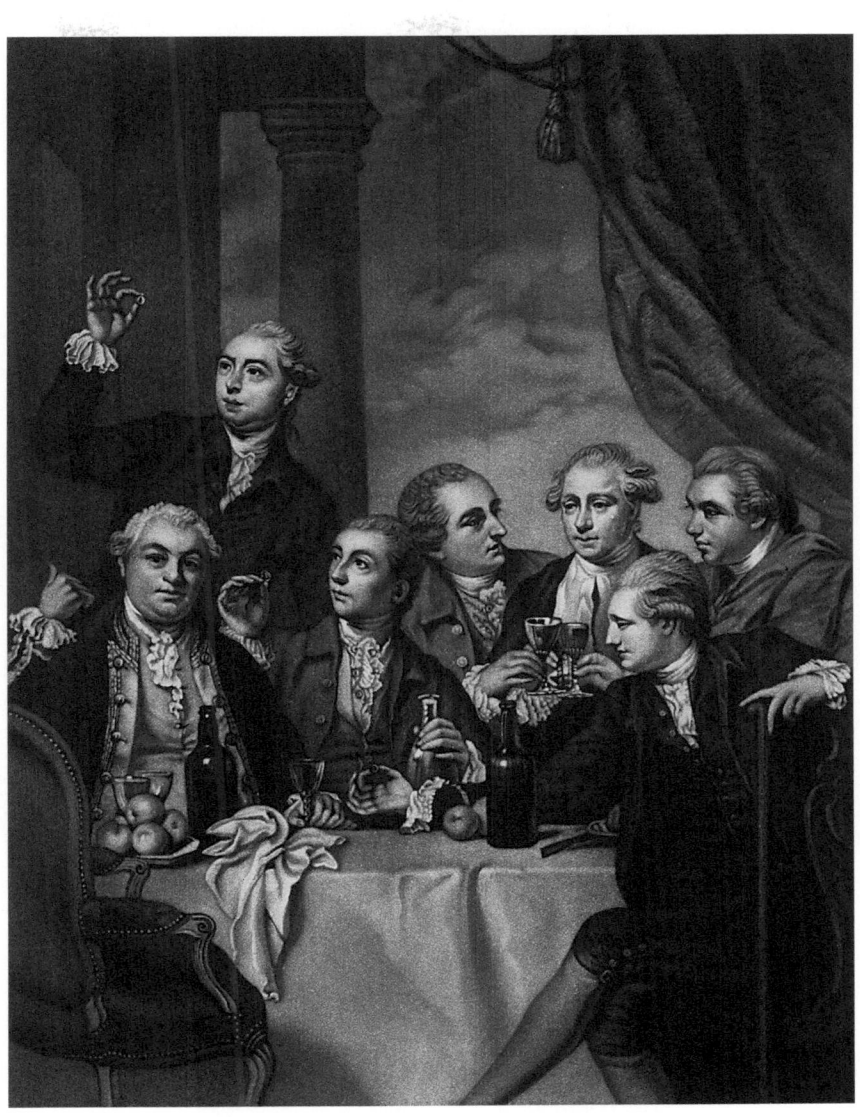

Fig. 4.29. Charles Algernon Tomkins, after Joshua Reynolds, *Members of the Society of Dilettanti*, mid-nineteenth century.

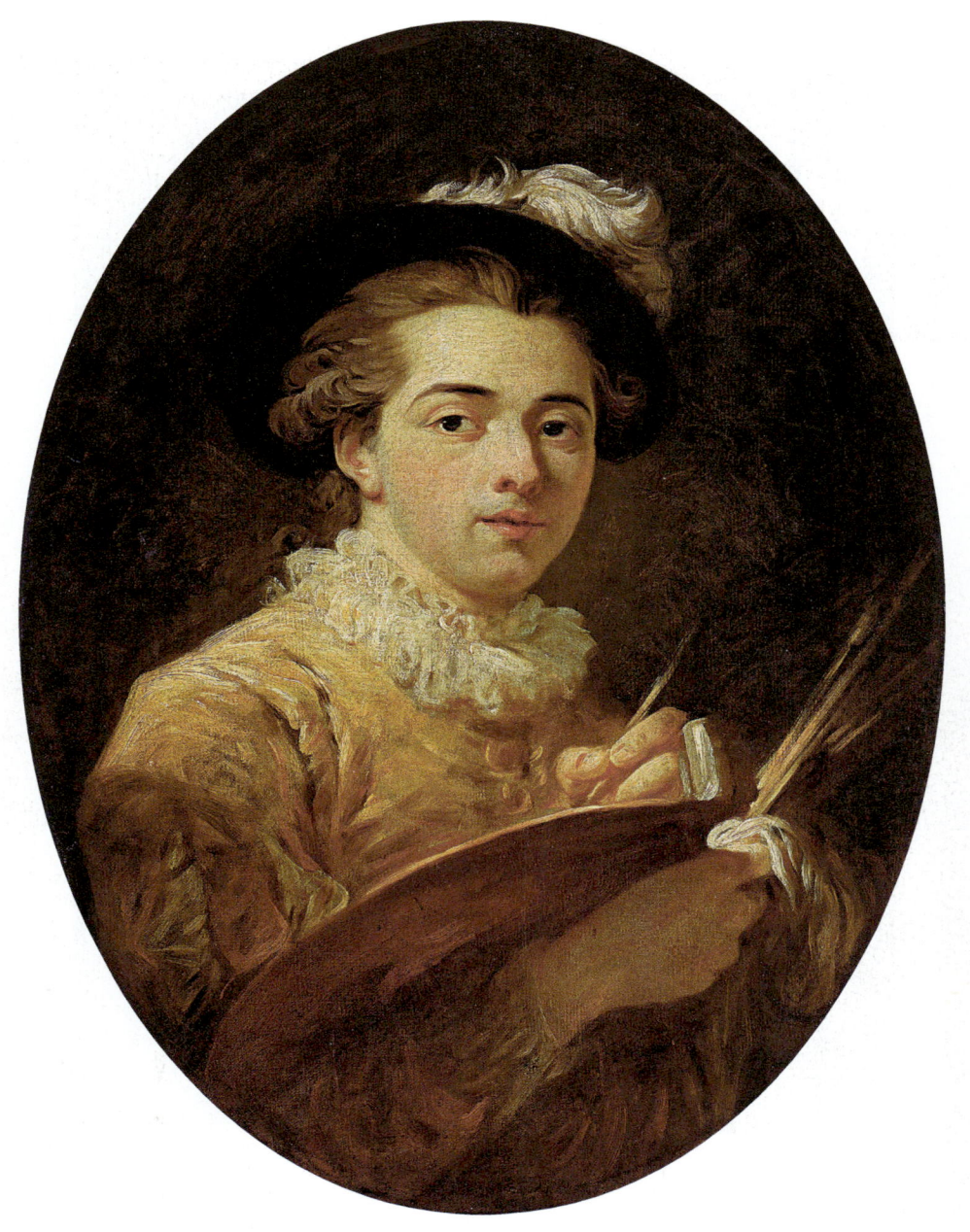

Fig. 4.30. François-André Vincent, *Self-Portrait*, 1766.

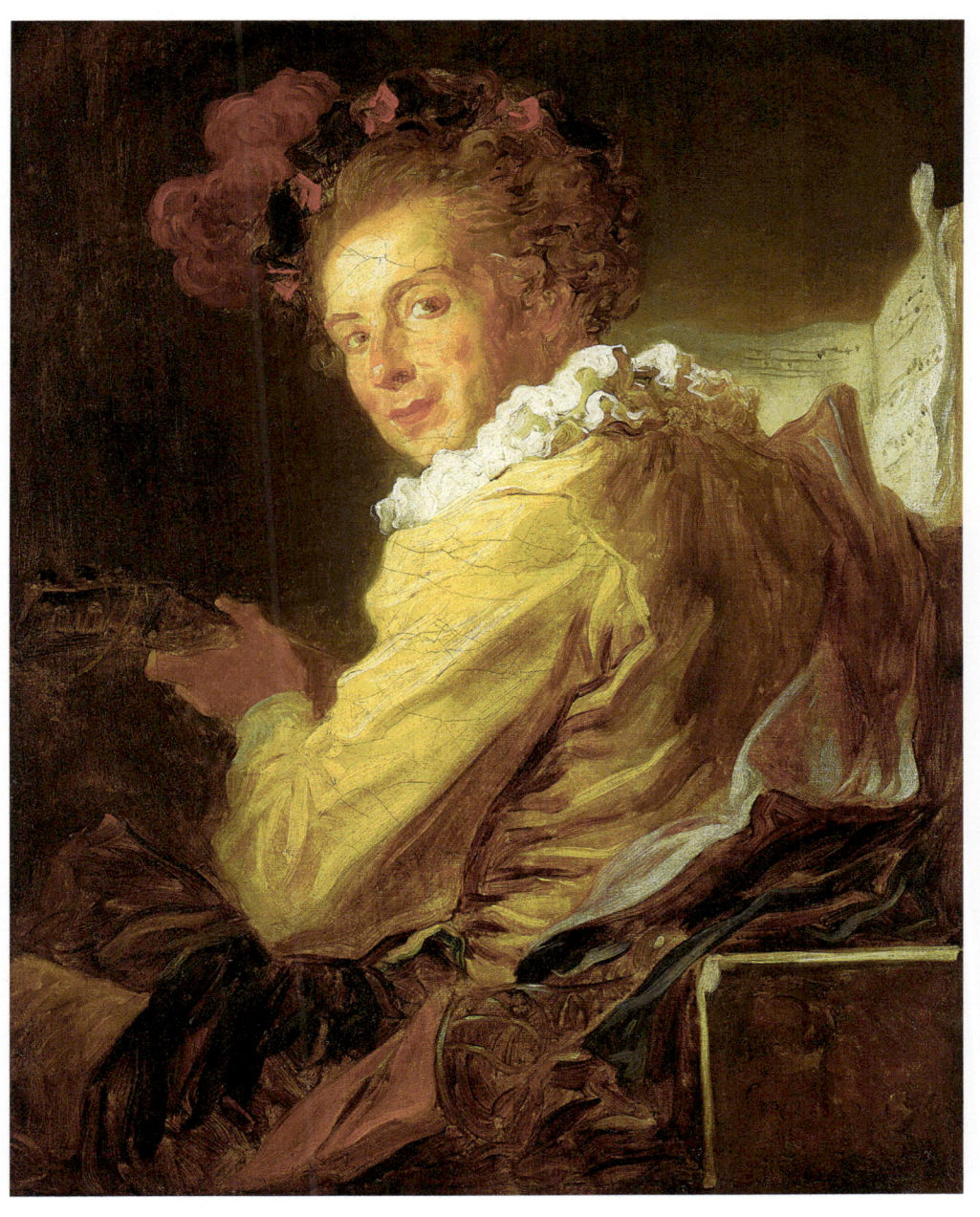

Fig. 4.31. Jean-Honoré Fragonard, *Portrait of Louis Richard de La Bretèche*, ca. 1769.

They represent a circle of patrons and acquaintances; in other words, specific segments of Fragonard's social network. While Vincent's self-portrait was once thought to be inspired by Fragonard's series, Cuzin's recent redating of the portrait places it before Fragonard's, and thus it is likely that Vincent was thinking of other artists known for their fantasy portraits, such as Alexis Grimou.[94] The reference to the Fragonard series in the *Trois hommes* is perhaps more overt, as Vincent employed the same three-quarter turn over the shoulder seen, for example, in Fragonard's portrait of M. de la Bretèche. By 1774, Vincent knew Fragonard well, as he had accompanied Fragonard and his patron, Pierre-Jacques-Onésyme Bergeret de Grancourt, in their travels in Italy.

The fantasy figure had a much longer history predating Fragonard's works, as has been demonstrated by Melissa Percival, with the *costume espagnole* appearing frequently in works that mixed fantasy and sociability, most notably those by Carle Vanloo: *A Pasha Having a Mistress's Portrait Painted* (1737), the *Conversation espagnole* (1754), and the *Lecture espagnole* (1755) (Figs. 4.32–4.34).[95] All three works contain figures in versions of seventeenth-century dress in scenes of shared sociable practices of reading, music, and artistic production. Notably, at least two of the three works—*A Pasha Having a Mistress's Portrait Painted* and the *Lecture espagnole*—include portraits. Vanloo depicted himself, shown painting his wife, Christine Soumis, in the *Pasha*; Soumis appears as the governess in the *Lecture espagnole*. Vincent's *costume espagnol* is not the only reference to *portraits de fantaisie* in the *Trois hommes*. Rousseau's and Coclers van Wyck's ambiguous costumed identities and expressions are also characteristic of the genre.[96] In Percival's work on fantasy portraits, she considers how donning a costume in this context is a form of *travestissement*, or fancy dress. Unlike *déguisement* (disguise), which implied being unrecognizable, *travestissement* in the eighteenth century suggested a temporary transformation into someone or something else. In their performative nature, Fragonard's fantasy portraits, Percival claims, "embody an eighteenth-century culture of leisure and spectacle which did not distinguish between participants and observers."[97] With the popularity of costume balls in both France and England, eighteenth-century life provided many opportunities to engage in such moments of temporary transformation, both as participant and observer.

Artists in Rome were well versed in *travestissement*. Carnival was celebrated in Italy during an extended period of parades and balls that offered opportunities for artists to wear masks and costumes. The pensioners of the Academy frequently took part in carnival festivals and organized themed parades.

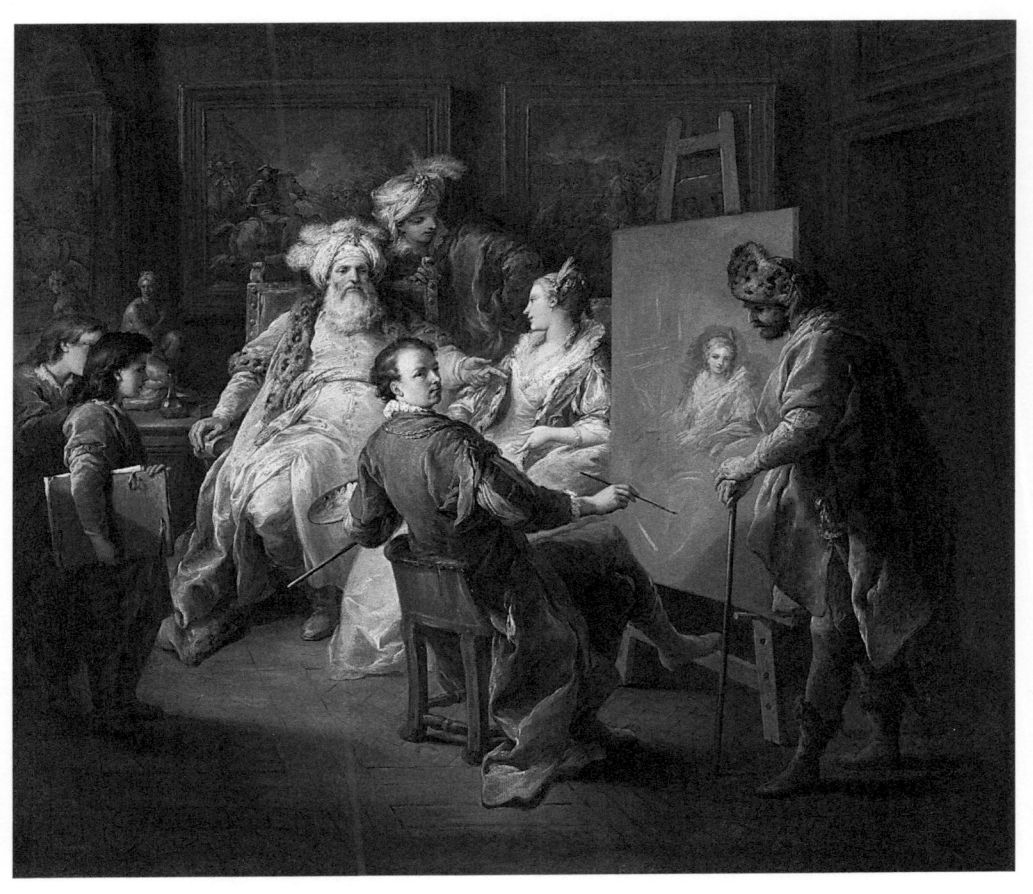

Fig. 4.32. Carle Vanloo, *A Pasha Having a Mistress's Portrait Painted*, 1737.

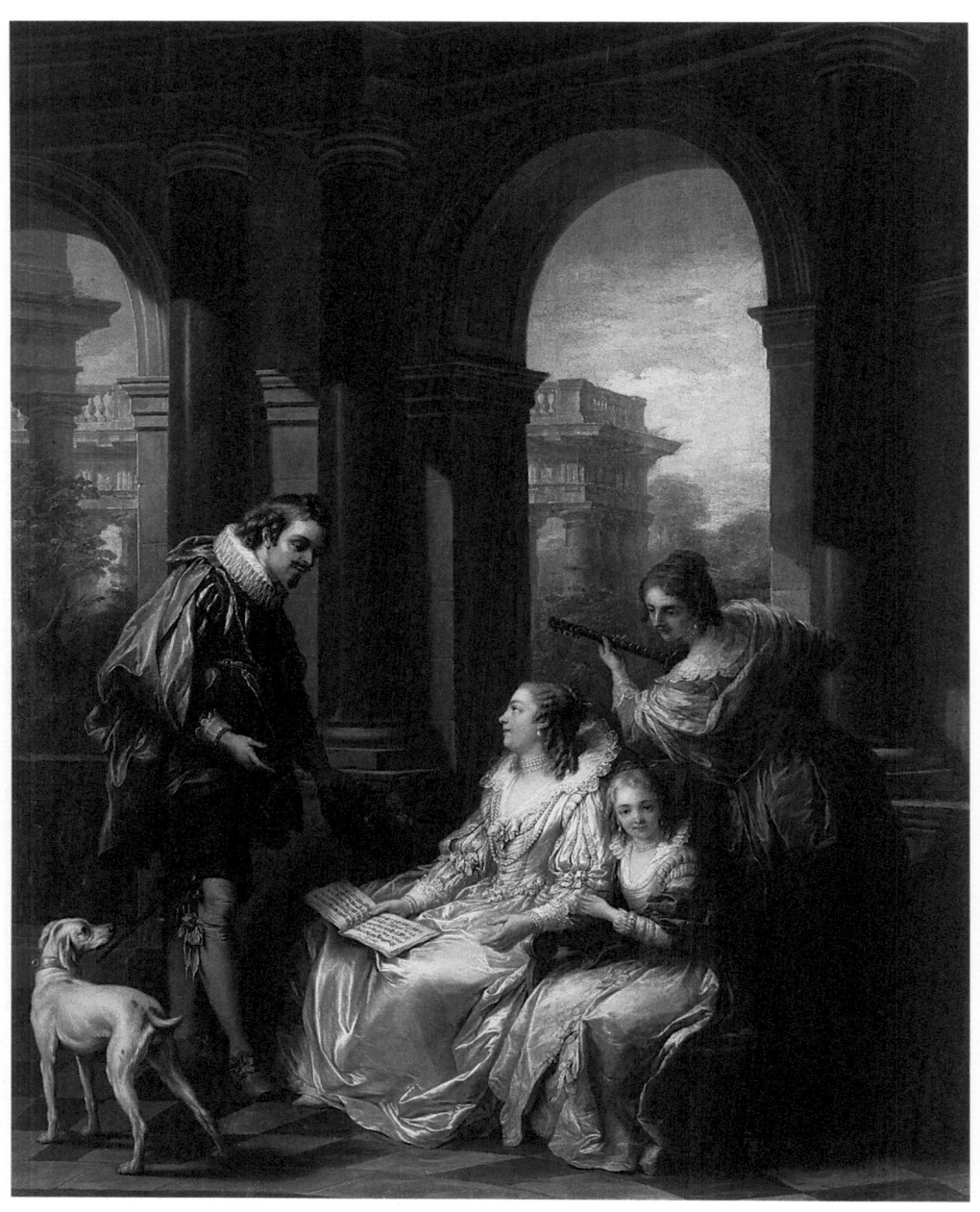

Fig. 4.33. Carle Vanloo, *La conversation espagnole*, 1754.

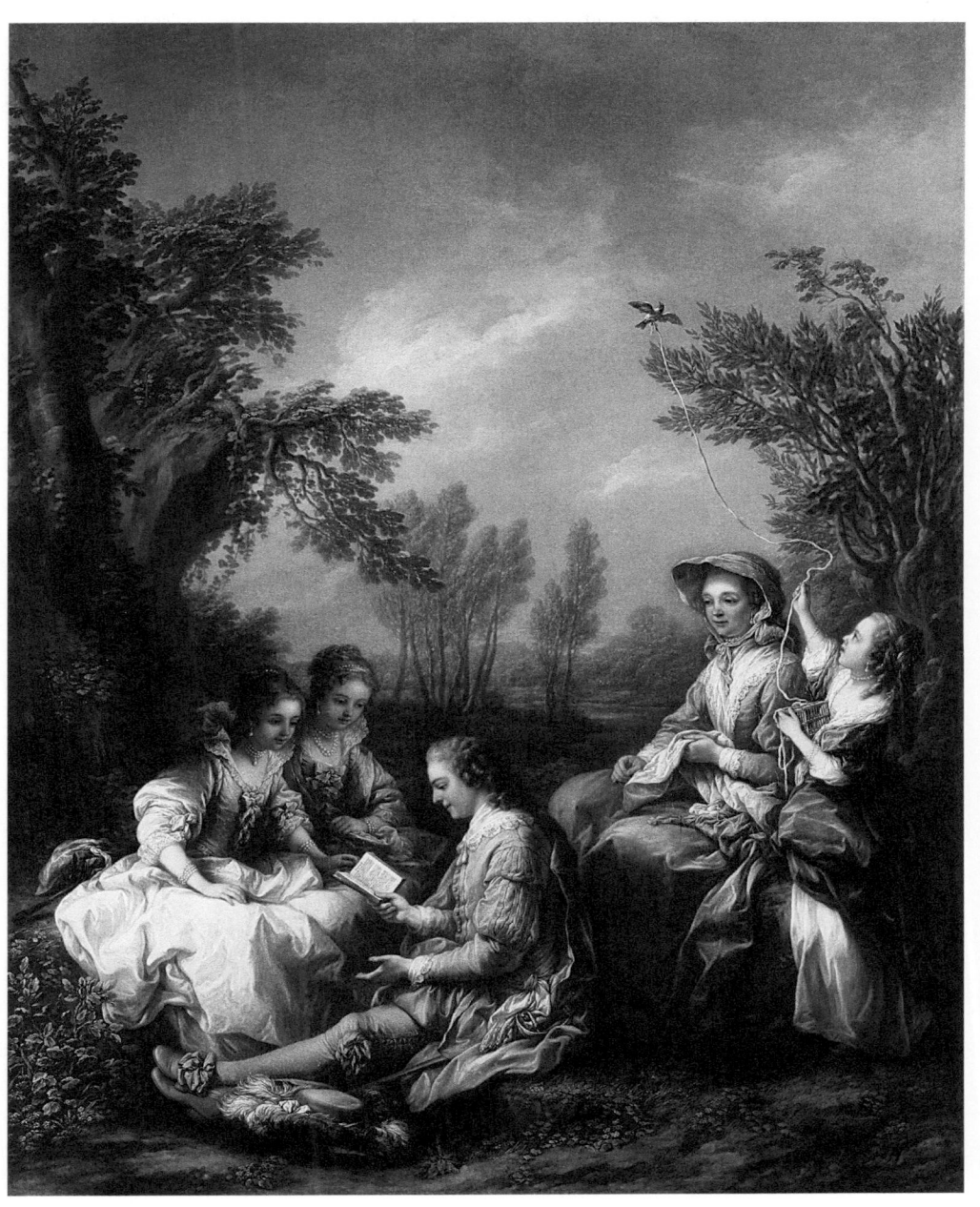

Fig. 4.34. Carle Vanloo, *La lecture espagnole*, salon of 1761.

These parades provided a forum for the artists to exhibit their talent, from designing costumes to fabricating garments and building the elaborate vehicles that pensioners rode upon. The skills that the pensioners displayed in designing their carnival costumes mirrored those that they possessed as artists. Much as painters used paint on canvas to mimic satin and gold, the pensioners painted cloths to mimic luxurious textiles, which, according to the director of the Academy in Rome at the time, Jean-François de Troy, "could not have better resembled magnificent fabrics and embroideries."[98] Artists' transformation of cheap items into expensive-seeming ones demonstrated their artistic skills, and the artworks created to commemorate these carnivals document the ease with which fancy dress slid into fantasy. Joseph-Marie Vien created elaborate drawings (Petit Palais, Paris) recording the costumes for 1748's *Caravane du sultan à La Mecque* (1748) (Fig. 4.35).[99] His drawings were subsequently etched and published in a book dedicated to de Troy.[100] While supposedly "portraits" of the participants in the parade, none of Vien's figures are recognizable in their physiognomy; rather, the emphasis is on portraying the *pensionnaires*' elaborate costumes and capturing their visual trickery of turning cloth into luxurious embroidered fabrics. Jean Barbault also painted works based on the pensioners' *caravane*, and recorded 1751's *Mascarade des quatre parties du monde* in a series of paintings (Musée des Beaux-Arts et d'Archéologie de Besançon).

There is no evidence that the costumes worn by Vincent, Coclers van Wyck, and Rousseau in the triple portrait were used in a specific carnival parade, or that this painting referred to such a specific event. Nonetheless, the *Trois hommes* reflected the inventive spirit of the festivals with which the artists in the portrait would have been familiar. The mix of transfiguration and spectacle, and of play between artist, performer, and observer, is obvious. Vincent fashioned himself as the subject of a fantasy portrait by positioning himself in front of a blank canvas, and directly referenced his role as the producer of this portrait by displaying the brushes that he used to paint it. The tips of the painted brushes are loaded with the colors of the painting in which they are presented: the large brush's tip is covered in red paint that matches the hue of Rousseau's cloak; next to it is a brush coated in silver; and the rest of the brushes correspond to the browns and blacks of Vincent's hat, Coclers van Wyck's coat, and the background of the painting. Vincent presented himself as both artist and the spectacle being painted.

Rousseau's seemingly unfinished costume, however, is at odds with the polish of Vincent's *costume espagnole*. While Vincent has dramatically rendered the sheen of the golden sleeves and voluminous red drapery, the headpiece

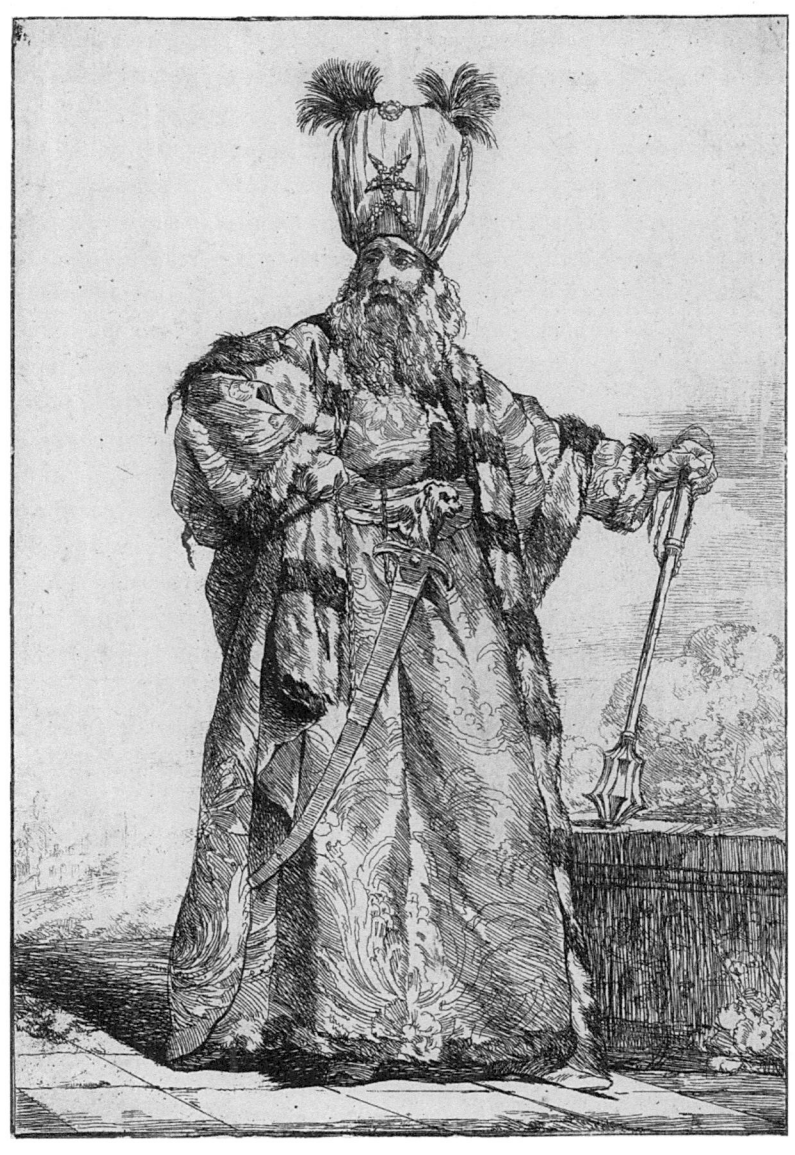

Fig. 4.35. Joseph Marie Vien, *Le Grand Visir (The Grand Vizir)*, from the series *Caravane du Sultan à la Mecque*, 1748.

remains an unidentifiable mass of white material, rendered in quickly applied white impasto, atop a golden fabric that is tied at the back of the architect's head. A drawing by Vincent's fellow *pensionnaire* Lemonnier, said to be of his brother in "fancy dress," shows a man in a tantalizingly similar costume, with voluminous sleeves, dramatic drapery, and a headdress that appears to be made of feather-like material tied around his head (Fig. 4.36). As in Vincent's portrait of Rousseau, Lemonnier appears to concentrate more on capturing the physiognomy of his brother than on exaggerating the polish of his costume. Both of these works are opposite in focus to Vien's drawings of the *caravane du Sultane*, which forgo capturing the likeness of the sitters in favor of elaborating their costumes into something fantastic, yet believable.

The publication of Vien's drawings, as Perrin Stein has noted, was meant to promote the camaraderie and collaboration of the *pensionnaires*, to further the reputation of the French Academy in Rome.[101] Vincent's portrayal of Coclers van Wyck, between Vincent and Rousseau, in his triple portrait, similarly highlights the collaborative aspect of artistic *travestissement*. The intimacy of the central gesture—with Coclers van Wyck's hand clasped around Vincent's, holding the brushes—could imply a shared ownership over the portrait's creation, even if it did not represent physically placing paint on the canvas. While no evidence exists to suggest that the physical painting was the product of anyone but Vincent, there is nonetheless an important suggestion of verbal collaboration that could have played a role in the process of making the group portrait.

The works under examination here differ from those in previous chapters in that both the caricatures and the triple portrait do not seem to have been intended for public display to a broad audience, such as those of the Academy's Salon. We do not know how widely the artists' caricatures circulated outside their coterie. The lack of any mention of them in the *Correspondance des directeurs* suggests that these images were never shown at any exhibition open to a large viewing public. The large size of some of the drawings, however—particularly those by Vincent—seems at odds with the idea that they were exclusively for private circulation. Cuzin has suggested that Vincent's sheets were hung, poster-style, in someone's studio in Rome, possibly Vincent's own.[102] If this were the case, then the more intimate exhibition of the drawings and prints in the artists' studios at the Academy in Rome could be read as evidence that this group of artists shared a connection that ran deeper than their similar *métiers*. Similarly, the size and composition of the triple portrait is perhaps evidence of an intended engagement with an audience; its enigmatic subject, however, suggests that its viewership would

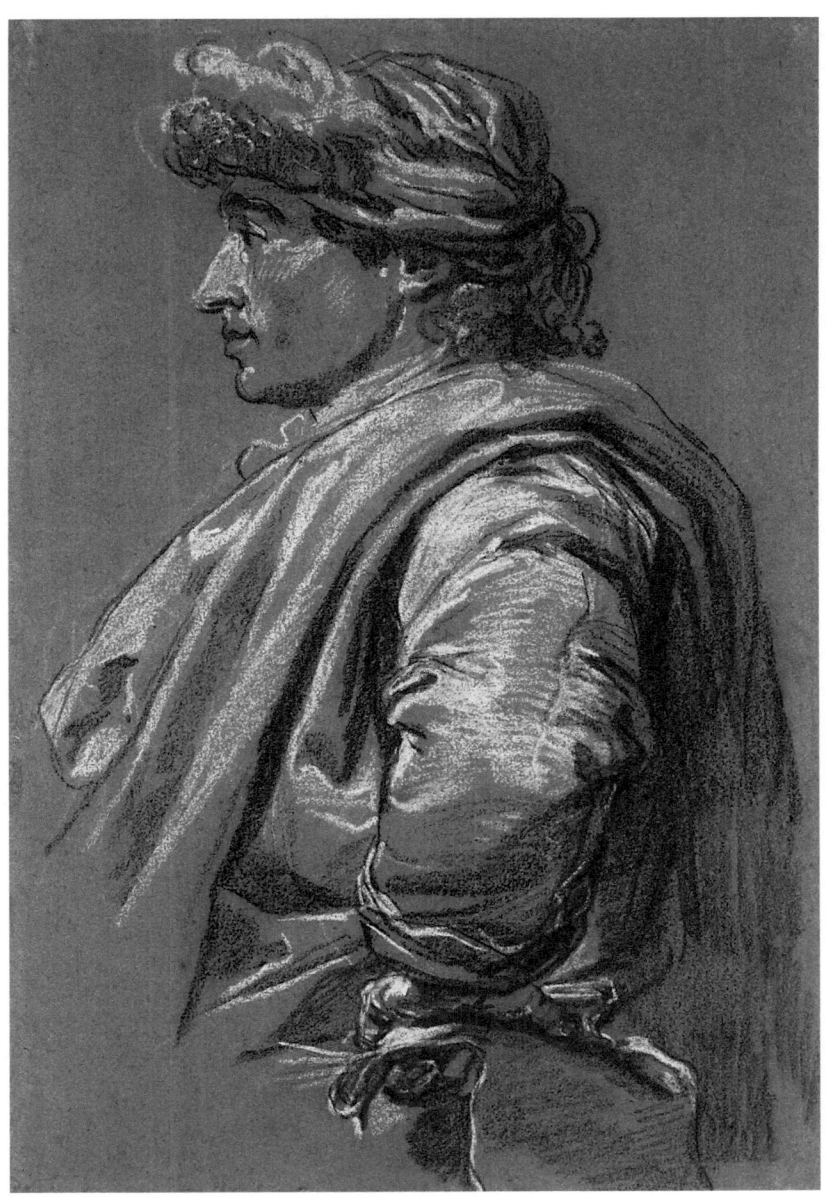

Fig. 4.36. Anicet-Charles-Gabriel Lemonnier, *Portrait of the Artist's Brother in Fancy Dress*, n.d.

be limited, perhaps only to those invited into the home or workshop space of its owner(s).

Caricature operated as an excessive version of the Academic drawing promoted by competitions as a means for artists to demonstrate their talent. Importantly, the practice of caricature was by no means in opposition to these artists' training, but rather existed in dialogue with it—the drawings and etchings that resulted were extensions of the competitions that led the artists to Rome. Through their reproduction by counterproofing and etching, and subsequent circulation among the *pensionnaires*, caricatures functioned as meaningful souvenirs of the camaraderie the artists shared as students, even if it was fleeting. In many ways, the *Trois hommes* is a continuation of those caricatures that surpasses them in scale and ambition. It thematizes the ideas of friendship and artistic practice that helped give rise to the triple portrait typology and comments self-consciously on the history of that typology. The work oscillates between depiction of friendship and professional portrait, between reality and fantasy. Vincent's *Portrait de trois hommes* and his caricatures both demonstrate that the emotional refuge of friendship was liberating for him, for it allowed him to explore and push the boundaries of portraiture.

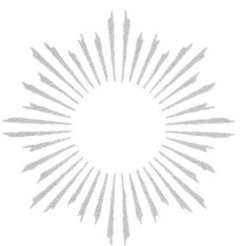

EPILOGUE

In 1765, Charles Mathon de la Cour claimed that the friendship shared by the members of the Royal Academy of Painting and Sculpture was necessary to push French art to its highest level.[1] His description was idealized, gendered masculine, and in line with the Royal Academy's dependence on classical ideals of friendship to present itself as a stable, self-governing, homosocial institution. However, artists' friendships were formed and cultivated in a variety of spaces—neighborhoods, artists' homes, gatherings hosted by Parisian society, and circles established abroad—and these spaces cultivated relationships that fell outside the Academy's ideal of friendship.

The creation, exchange, and display of portraits offers a view into artists' varied social networks and relationships, and demonstrates that artists reacted to evolving definitions of friendship that were generated by Enlightenment thinking. Maurice Quentin de La Tour and Charles-Nicolas Cochin took advantage of new conceptions of friendship and celebrity, exhibiting portraits at the Salon that garnered acclaim and added to the public recognition of their sitters. Adélaïde Labille-Guiard and Élisabeth Vigée-Lebrun followed their example, only to find that their own gender—and the genders of their sitters—caused their capacity for friendship and their propriety to be called into question. François-André Vincent's portraits show, in contrast, that when shielded from the public eye, friendship could foster an intimacy that encouraged experimentation with portraiture.

The definition of friendship was hardly fixed before 1789, and Revolutionary politics did little to help settle the questions on it raised in the previous decades. Marisa Linton has argued that the Jacobins considered friendship an

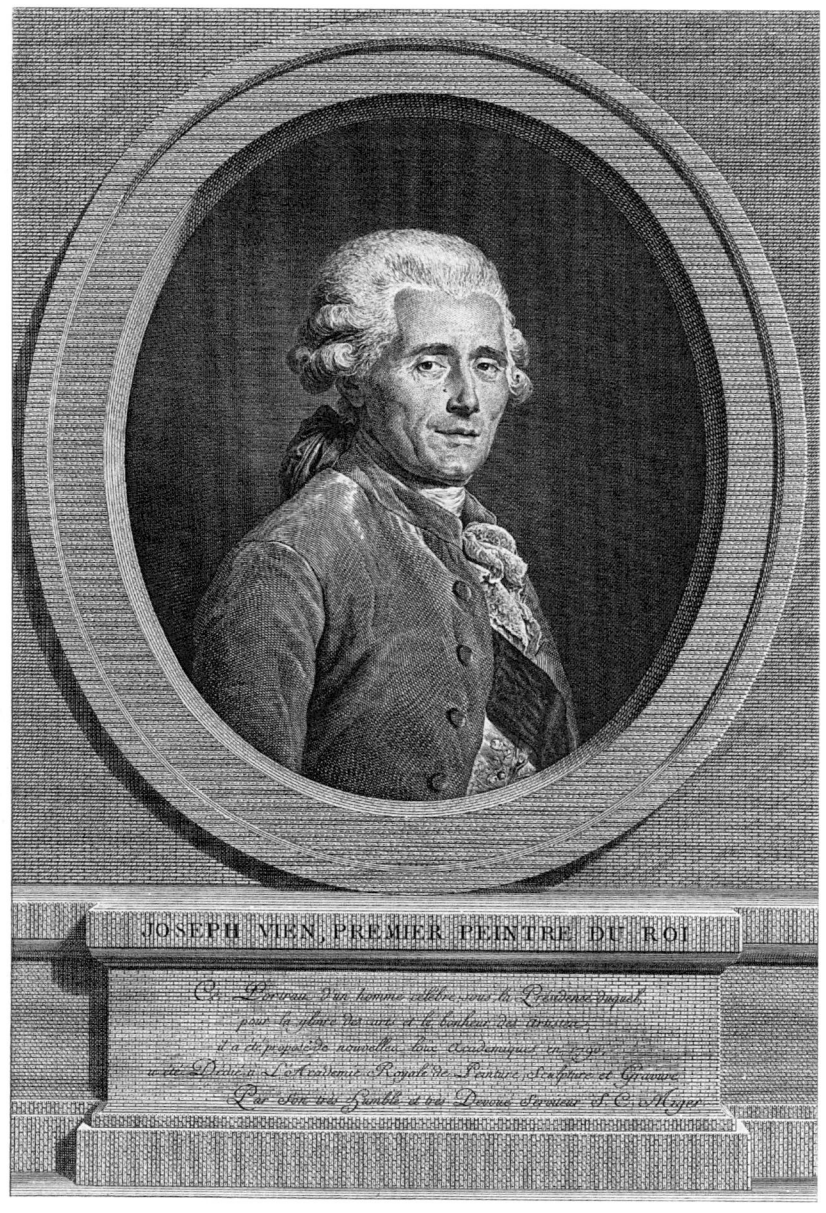

Fig. 5.1. Simon-Charles Miger after Adélaïde Labille-Guiard, *Joseph Vien*, in or after 1790.

ideal form of association, as it had been viewed in the early modern period, but friendship was also highly suspect. If it appeared to be disconnected from the Enlightenment ideals of *sociabilité*, then friendship could be seen as a remnant of royal patronage and self-serving social advancement.[2] Furthermore, the private nature of friendship that some definitions prioritized contradicted Revolutionary ideals: individuals were expected to put the *patrie* above all personal ties including friendship. Most damning of all, the privacy that friendship networks offered was seen as a potential space for political conspiracy and counterrevolutionary activity.[3] Many of these concerns about private friendship had already been made manifest in the criticism of the Academy's Salon exhibitions in the 1780s, as critics appropriated the word "friend" to legitimize their opinions and lay claim to a public role for friendship in line with emerging Republican ideals.

Some of the Revolutionary concerns about friendship had, somewhat ironically, already been discussed in the Royal Academy. In the first half of the century, Antoine and Charles Coypel warned of the negative effects of friendship, addressing specifically that it could encourage the formation of cabals that divided, rather than unified, a group. Their fears seem particularly prescient in light of the heated debate about the future of the Royal Academy that the Revolution created. Differences in opinion fractured the Academy's body into three distinct camps, loosely based on the social networks described in the chapters of this book. Vincent, joined by several members of his cohort in Rome, was part of a progressive party working to align the Academy with Revolutionary ideals. This group also included Labille-Guiard, who fought for greater inclusion of women in a reformed Academy.[4] Joseph-Marie Vien, by this time director of the Academy, led a group of officers who hoped to preserve the rights and privileges of the Academy's members. Finally, Jacques-Louis David and his circle constituted a group of dissidents seeking to dissolve the Academy entirely.[5]

Portraiture played a role in the battle over what the Academy would become. With Vien increasingly at odds with the proposed Central Academy recommended by Vincent and his circle, Simon-Charles Miger, a member of Vincent's group, secretly engraved Labille-Guiard's portrait of Vien that had been displayed at the Salon of 1783 (Fig. 5.1). The engraved portrait was intended as a gesture of reconciliation between the reformers and the director.[6] A framed copy was presented to Vien at the meeting of the Royal Academy on December 31, 1790. Copies were distributed to each member of the Academy, and several artists requested that the copperplate be purchased so that it could be added to the Academy's collection of portraits of artists.

As Elisabeth Mansfield has argued, the choice of Labille-Guiard's portrait was intentional and pointed.[7] Initially shown at the Salon of 1783 to display her place in a network of friends and colleagues, its reappearance in the midst of the reform of the Academy was an attempt to remind Vien of his own personal and professional bonds with the reformers. While warmly received, it did not have the desired effect of softening Vien to their recommendations.[8] Ultimately, David's dissidents won out and the Royal Academy of Painting and Sculpture was dissolved in 1793.[9]

The French Revolution also had a dramatic effect on the public display of portraits.[10] While the Salon, now open to all artists, offered an important form of publicity for artists whose aristocratic patrons had fled the country or met with the guillotine, the increased visibility of portraits at the Salon created increased criticism.[11] Promoting social networks carried more risk than it did for artists like Cochin and La Tour in 1753. As Amy Freund has argued in her study of portraiture during the Revolution, the new political regime's rhetoric of transparency, and the increased consumption of portraiture by the public— at the Salon, through private commissions, and through the purchase of reproductive prints—encouraged greater scrutiny of both a portrait's artist and its subject.[12] The social connections documented by a portrait, when interpreted as political allegiances, were potential sources for criticism or worse for artists. Labille-Guiard exhibited fourteen well-received portraits of deputies serving in the National Assembly at the Salon of 1791, but was highly criticized for her portrait of Charles-Roger, Prince de Bauffremont, a member of the Estates-General who did not join the National Assembly, which was displayed along with them.[13] Vigée-Lebrun fled France because of her royal connections; the pastellist Anne-Rosalie Bocquet Filleul was guillotined for hers.[14] The rapidly changing political situation and guilt by association that accompanied the Revolution turned one of portraiture's greatest strengths, its ability to make friendship publicly visible, into a liability.

Private friendships between artists, of course, did not go away, and in certain cases the Revolution forced artists into situations that fostered particularly close relationships between those who faced or fled the guillotine. Joseph-Benoît Suvée painted his fellow prisoners in the prison of Saint-Lazare.[15] Marie-Gabrielle Capet, one of Labille-Guiard's students portrayed in her large self-portrait, spent the years between 1792 and 1795 in a house in Pontault-en-Brie, a town about thirteen miles outside of Paris, with Vincent and Labille-Guiard.[16] By the end of the Terror, they had become a sort of family.[17] Capet is a particularly apt artist to conclude with, as the portraits she exhibited after the Revolution engaged with friendship in many of the same ways that have been discussed in this book: she exhibited portraits of artists that demonstrated her participation in a known social network; she inserted herself into an artistic lineage; and specifically, she created an ambitious and inventive portrait that was inspired by her private relationship with Labille-Guiard and Vincent.

In 1798, Capet exhibited several miniature portraits of Vincent, one of Labille-Guiard, and one of a student of Vincent's, Étienne Pallière. In 1799, she exhibited a pastel and a miniature portrait of Suvée, and a pastel and a miniature of another one of Vincent's students, Charles Meynier. In 1800, she presented a miniature of the sculptor Jean-Antoine Houdon.[18] These portraits of well-known artists did garner attention. An official report to Emperor Napoleon on the arts written in 1808 singled her out among women painters for her portraits of artists: "From the exhibition of 1796, we have seen good portraits in miniature, pastel and oil by Mlle Capet. She has since surpassed herself in the portraits of Monsieurs Suvée, Meyner, de Vandœuvre, and Madame Vincent [Labille-Guiard], of whom she is the most distinguished student."[19]

The same year as this report was issued, Capet presented the most ambitious painting of her career at the Salon: a modest group portrait in oil that was described in the *livret* as *A Painting representing the late Madame Vincent (student of her husband). She is busy making a portrait of M. Senator Vien, comte de l'Empire and member of the Institute of France, regenerator of the French school, and Vincent's teacher. The artist, who is represented charging her palette, has put the principle students of M. Vincent into this painting* (Fig. 5.2).[20] The painting shows Labille-Guiard at her easel in a well-appointed, crowded studio, *porte-crayon* in hand. Capet herself is seated at a miniature desk in the foreground, a reference to the medium for which she was best known. She looks at the viewer, momentarily distracted from her task at hand of preparing Labille-Guiard's palette with color in anticipation of her teacher finishing the underdrawing for the portrait and switching to work in oil paint. Vincent stands behind his wife, gesturing to something on her canvas, which is turned away from the viewer. Vien, the subject of the work in progress, sits in his senatorial costume, with his son and daughter-in-law behind him. The rest of the crowd is made up of nine of Vincent's students: Jacques-Augustin Pajou, Jean Alaux, Etienne and Léon Pallière, Jean-Joseph Ansiaux, Jean-François-Leonor Mérimée, Charles Thévenin, Charles Meynier, and François-Édouard Picot.[21]

Capet's packed studio scene was likely inspired by the success of Louis-Léopold Boilly's *A Gathering of Artists in the Studio of Isabey*, exhibited ten years

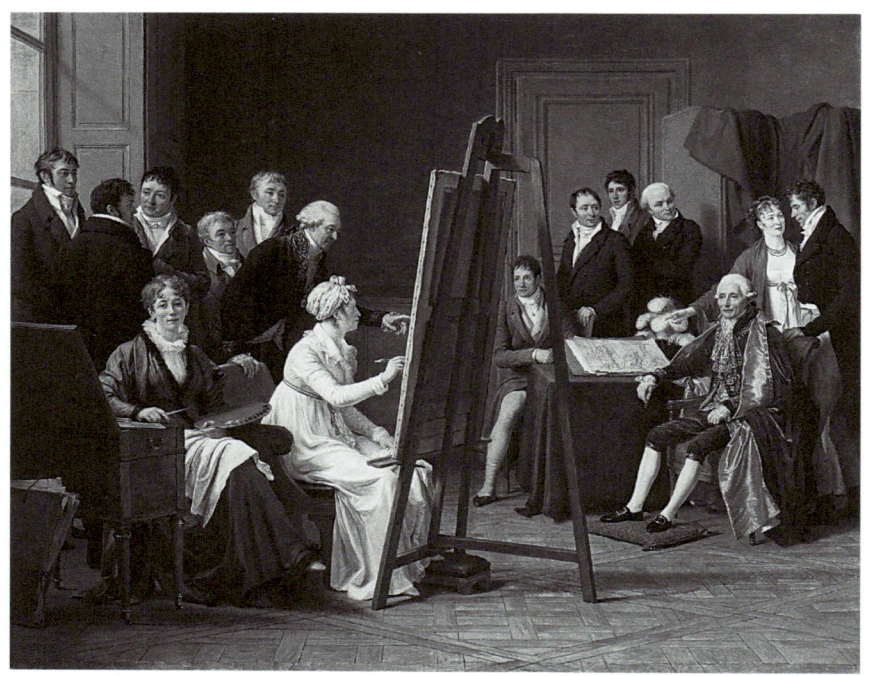

Fig. 5.2. Marie-Gabrielle Capet,
Studio Scene: Adélaïde Labille-Guiard Painting the Portrait of Joseph-Marie Vien, 1808.

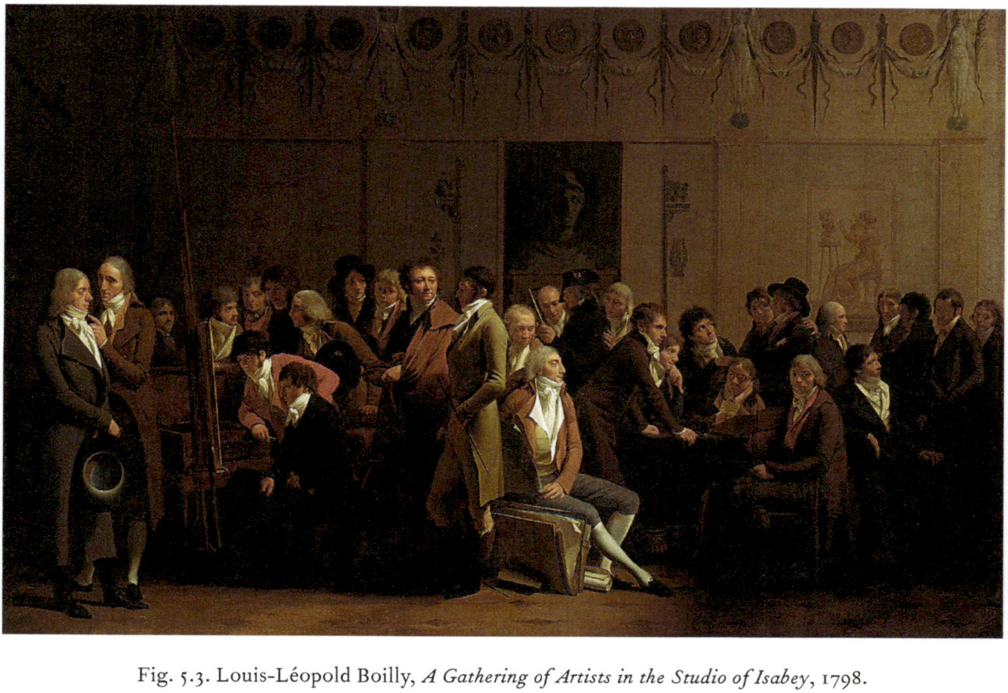

Fig. 5.3. Louis-Léopold Boilly, *A Gathering of Artists in the Studio of Isabey*, 1798.

earlier in 1798 (Fig. 5.3). As Susan Siegfried has argued, Boilly's painting represents "professional or personal allegiances that [the artists] themselves declared," exemplifying the need to redefine artistic networks that had been previously made obvious by the centralized institution of the Royal Academy.[22] Much as Boilly's painting sought to define artistic community in the wake of the Revolution, Capet's group portrait sought to define her own artistic community by representing the circle of artists she met through Labille-Guiard and Vincent.

Capet's painting included a telescoping of history, however. Labille-Guiard had created a portrait of Vien in 1782, long before he was made a senator of the Empire. The portrait was a modest pastel, not like the large-scale oil portrait on which Labille-Guiard works in Capet's depiction. This anachronism, read in conjunction with the *livret* description, suggests that Capet's work was more than a public homage to Labille-Guiard. The painting engaged with contemporary cultural politics and the ongoing redefinition of French art in the wake of the Revolution, first highlighted by Thomas Gaehtgens.[23]

The report to Napoleon in 1808 that spoke so highly of Capet also celebrated Vien as a symbol of Academic tradition and the founder of the modern French school. The former director of the Academy and *premier peintre du roi* had indeed been fêted throughout Napoleon's regime. He received more honors than any other artist during the period. In 1795, Vien was one of only six painters to be named to the *beaux-arts* section of the newly created Institut de France. He was made a senator in 1799, was the first artist to win the Legion of Honor in 1803, and was appointed a comte de l'Empire in 1808.[24] The *livret* description for Capet's painting plainly reminded viewers of these achievements. The catalogue also included another pointed reference to Vien, describing him as the *régénérateur* (regenerator) of the French school, the exact words that Joachim Lebreton used to describe him in his introduction to the 1808 report.[25] By moving Vien's portrait sitting with Labille-Guiard forward almost twenty years, Capet effectively made the historical event of the painting of Vien's portrait contemporary, linking her now-deceased teacher not to the *ancien régime* but to the current Empire.

As Séverine Sofio has argued, Capet's focus on Vincent and his students was likely a move to position them as the true inheritors of Vien's artistic legacy in the face of David's claims to that legacy during a period when the future of French art was still under debate.[26] Furthermore, Vien was not only the grand patriarch of the French school, but he was also Capet's artistic "great-grandfather," so to speak. Vien had trained Vincent, who trained Labille-Guiard, who, in turn, taught Capet. Capet's painting displayed her own social connections to the Empire's most illustrious artist and asserted her place as one of his descendants. The work is a celebration of her paternal lineage, and a tribute to her friendship network and to the greatness of the French school. As Heather Belnap Jensen has demonstrated, Capet's ode to Vien tapped into a new interest in paternalism and the role of fathers in their daughters' educations, seen in other post-Revolutionary paintings such as Constance Mayer's *Self-Portrait with Artist's Father* (1801, Wadsworth Atheneum), and Louis-Léopold Boilly's *A Sculptor's Studio: Picture of a Family* (1804, Musée des arts décoratifs).[27] Such imagery, Jensen argues, positioned women as key players in the regeneration of France after the Revolution.[28] Capet's painting, which places the artist and Labille-Guiard in the foreground of a room filled with male artists of different generations, can be read as a bold, but unrealized, vision that the future of the French school was female.[29]

By successfully weaving together artistic lineage, friendship, cultural politics, and self-promotion, Capet's work aptly demonstrates that embracing emerging ideas about friendship helped artists to negotiate the changing politics of the post-Revolutionary period. Sarah Horowitz has shown that friendship and ideology in the nineteenth century were closely intertwined, and friendship was central to healing the wounds created by the fractious politics of the French Revolution, and to rebuilding trust and social cohesion.[30] While the nineteenth century is often seen as a period when public and private life were divided from each other, friendship continued to straddle that divide. Friendship, thanks to its malleability, continued to be, as it had been in the eighteenth century, a social bond that had both political and personal significance.

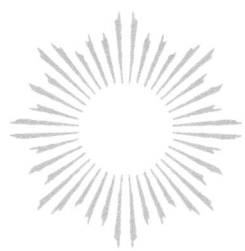

Endnotes

INTRODUCTION

1 "Un suédois me demandoit avant-hier monsieur, si toutes les Académies du Royaume rendoient compte au Public de leur travail, comme celle de Peinture." Charles Mathon de La Cour, *Lettres à Monsieur *** sur les peintures, les sculptures, et les gravures, exposées au Sallon du Louvre en 1765. Seconde Lettre* ([Paris]: De l'Imprimerie de d'Houry, Imprimeur de Mgr. le Duc d'Orléans, [1765]), 3, https://catalogue.bnf.fr/ark:/12148/cb42334340x.
2 After becoming full *académiciens*, members of the Academy could be promoted to higher positions, including (in order from lowest to highest) *conseiller, adjoint à professeur, professeur, adjoint à recteur*, and *recteur*. History painters were the only members of the Academy who could achieve ranks higher than *conseillers*. On the Academy's structure, see Reed Benhamou, *Regulating the Académie: Art, Rules and Power in Ancien Régime France* (Oxford: Voltaire Foundation, 2009), and Hannah Williams, *Académie Royale: A History in Portraits* (Burlington, VT: Ashgate, 2015), Chapter 2.
3 "... est merveilleuse pour exciter l'émulation ..." Mathon de La Cour, *Lettres à Monsieur ****, 4.
4 "Il me semble voir une coquette habile qui dispute le terrain à ses Amans: A force de gradations et d'adresse, elle irrite les désirs, et porte les passions à leur comble." Ibid.
5 "Malgré cela rien ne trouble leur union. Ils se soutiennent les uns les autres. Ils vantent avec plaisir les bons ouvrages de leurs Confrères. Enfin ils sont amis, quoique rivaux, avantage rare et bien plus précieux que tous les talents." Ibid., 5–6.
6 "When an author writes a book, nothing prevents others from writing; but when a sculptor is commissioned to make a Masoluem, others are often left without a job." ("Quand un Auteur fait un livre, rien n'empêche les autres d'écrire; mais lorsqu'un Sculpteur est chargé d'un Mausolée, il arrive souvent que les autres restent sans occupation.") Ibid., 5.
7 "The education and communal life in the time of the Spartans made them one family. You see the same with the men who were raised from a young age in the breast of the Academy. They go to Rome, they reside under the direction of the same Master, and under the same roof. Upon returning to Paris, they get workshops and housing in the Louvre." ("L'éducation et la vie communes ne faisoient autre-fois de tous les Spartiates qu'une seule famille. Vous voyez de même ici des hommes qui sont élevés dès leur bas âge dans le sein de l'Académie. Ils vont à Rome, et ils y demeurent sous la direction d'un

même Maître, et sous le même toît. De retour dans leur Patrie, ils obtiennent des ateliers et des logemens au Louvre.") Ibid., 6–7.

8   "Ils se voyent sans cesse, ils se consultent sur leurs Ouvrages, il se délassent ensemble de leurs travaux. Par-là des hommes que le hazard avoit rassemblés, viennent à s'aimer comme des frères. Si des raisons d'intérêt causent entr'eux quelque contestation, c'est un nuage qui se dissipe dans un moment, et l'amitié triomphe toujours." Ibid., 7.

9   For an overview of classical definitions of friendship, see Daniel Lochman and Maritere López, "Introduction: The Emergence of Discourse: Early Modern Friendship," in *Discourses and Representations of Friendship in Early Modern Europe, 1500–1700*, eds. Daniel Lochman and Maritere López (Burlington, VT: Ashgate, 2011), 1–28.

10 Mathon de La Cour, *Lettres à Monsieur ***,* 7.

11 Article XIII of the *Status et Règlements* of the Academy stated: "No person in the future will be accepted and named Professor who has not be named Adjoint, and no one will be named Adjoint who does not demonstrate his ability in life drawing and in History, either in painting or sculpture, and has not given the Academy a history painting or bas-relief which was prescribed." ("Que nulle personne à l'avenir, ne sera reçeue [sic] et ladite charge de Professeur qu'il n'ayt esté nommé Adjoint, et nul sera nommé Adjoint qu'il n'ayt fait connoistre sa capacité en la figure et en l'Histoire, soit en Peinture ou en Sculpture, et qu'il n'ayt mis dans l'Académie le tableau d'histoire, ou bas-relief, qui luy aura este ordonné.") Benhamou, *Regulating the Académie*, 124.

12 For a broad overview of friendship in the early modern period, see Maurice Aymard, "Friends and Neighbors," in *A History of Private Life III: Passions of the Renaissance*, eds. Philippe Ariès and Georges Duby, trans. Arthur Goldhammer (Cambridge, MA: Harvard University Press, 1989), 403–46; Reginald Hyatte, *The Arts of Friendship: The Idealization of Friendship in Medieval and Early Renaissance Literature* (Leiden: Brill, 1994); David Garrioch, "From Christian Friendship to Secular Sentimentality: Enlightenment Re-Evaluations," in *Friendship: A History*, ed. Barbara Caine (London: Equinox, 2009), 166–67; Daniel T. Lochman, Maritere López, and Lorna Hutson, eds., *Discourses and Representations of Friendship in Early Modern Europe, 1500–1700* (Burlington, VT: Ashgate, 2011).

13 "Affection mutuelle, réciproque entre deux personnes à peu près d'égale condition." "Amitié" in *Dictionnaire de l'Académie française, 1st Edition (1694)* in *Dictionnaires d'autrefois*, University of Chicago, The Project for American and French Research on the Treasury of the French Language (ARTFL), http://artfl-project.uchicago.edu/.

14 Denis Diderot and Claude Yvon, "Friendship," The Encyclopedia of Diderot & d'Alembert Collaborative Translation Project, trans. Jeffrey Merrick (Ann Arbor: MPublishing, University of Michigan Library, 2003), http://hdl.handle.net/2027/spo.did2222.0000.182. Accessed March 25, 2012. Originally published as "Amitié," *Encyclopédie ou Dictionnaire raisonné des sciences, des arts et des métiers* (Paris, 1751), 1:361–62. On Enlightenment sociability, see Dena Goodman, *The Republic of Letters: A Cultural History of the French Enlightenment* (Ithaca, NY: Cornell University Press, 1994), 4–8; Daniel Gordon, *Citizens without Sovereignty: Equality and Sociability in French Thought, 1670–1789* (Princeton, NJ: Princeton University Press, 1994), Chapter 1; Jessica L. Fripp, et al., "Introduction," in *Artistes, savants et amateurs: art et sociabilité au XVIIIe siècle (1715–1815)*, eds. Jessica L. Fripp, et al. (Paris: Mare & Martin, 2016), 13–28.

15 A notable exception is Williams, *Académie Royale*, which has a chapter devoted to friendship. Charlotte Guichard has addressed friendship as defined by artist-patron relationships in *Les amateurs d'art à Paris au XVIIIe siècle* (Seyssel: Champ-Vallon, 2008).
16 *Eighteenth-Century Studies* dedicated a special issue to eighteenth-century friendship: "The Politics of Friendship," vol. 32, no. 2 (Winter 1998/1999). Other notable studies include Janet M. Todd, *Women's Friendship in Literature* (New York: Columbia University Press, 1980); Anne Vincent-Buffault, *L'exercice de l'amitié: pour une histoire des pratiques amicales aux XVIIIe et XIXe siècles* (Paris: Editions du Seuil, 1995); Emrys Jones, *Friendship and Allegiance in Eighteenth-Century Literature: The Politics of Private Virtue in the Age of Walpole* (Basingstoke, UK: Palgrave Macmillan, 2013); Kenneth Loiselle, *Brotherly Love: Freemasonry and Male Friendship in Enlightenment France* (Ithaca, NY: Cornell University Press, 2014). On friendship and commercial society, see Allan Silver, "Friendship in Commercial Society: Eighteenth-Century Social Theory and Modern Sociology," *American Journal of Sociology* 95, no. 6 (1990): 1474–1504. On gender and friendship, see Katherine O'Donnell and Michael O'Rourke, eds., *Love, Sex, Intimacy, and Friendship Between Men, 1550–1800* (Basingstoke, UK: Palgrave MacMillan, 2007); and Lewis C. Seifert, and Rebecca May Wilkin, eds., *Men and Women Making Friends in Early Modern France* (Burlington, VT: Ashgate, 2015).
17 See, for example, Ronald Sharp, "Friendship as Gift Exchange," in *Friendship and Literature: Spirit and Form* (Durham, NC: Duke University Press, 1986), 82–117.
18 On this point, see Bryan Mangano, *Fictions of Friendship in the Eighteenth-Century Novel* (Cham, Switzerland: Palgrave Macmillan, 2017).
19 Marisa Linton, "Fatal Friendships: The Politics of Jacobin Friendship," *French Historical Studies* 31, no. 1 (2008): 51–76; Loiselle, *Brotherly Love*, 201–43.
20 Adam Sutcliffe, "Friendship and Materialism in the French Enlightenment," in *Representing Private Lives of the Enlightenment*, ed. Andrew Kahn (Oxford: Voltaire Foundation, 2010), 251–68.
21 On this point, see "The Band of Brothers," in Lynn Hunt, *The Family Romance of the French Revolution* (Berkeley: University of California Press, 1992), 53–88.
22 Naomi Tadmor, *Family and Friends in Eighteenth-Century England: Household, Kinship and Patronage* (Cambridge: Cambridge University Press, 2011), and Jones, *Friendship and Allegiance in Eighteenth-Century Literature*. See also Eva Österberg, "Challenging the Private-Public Dichotomy: Friendship in Mediaeval and Early Modern Society," in *Friendship and Love, Ethics and Politics: Studies in Mediaeval and Early Modern History* (Budapest: Central European University Press, 2010), 23–90.
23 Colin Bailey, *Patriotic Taste: Collecting Modern Art in Pre-Revolutionary Paris* (New Haven, CT: Yale University Press, 2002); Guichard, *Les amateurs d'art*; Perrin Stein, ed., *Artists and Amateurs: Etching in Eighteenth-Century France* (New Haven, CT: Metropolitan Museum of Art, distributed by Yale University Press, 2013).
24 Guichard, *Les amateurs d'art*, 72–80.
25 Jean Locquin, "La lutte des critiques d'art contre les portraitistes au XVIIIe siècle," *Archives de l'art français, nouvelle période* II (1913): 309–20. For more on the slow decline of respect for portraiture over the course of the century, see also Chapter 1 of Tony Halliday,

Facing the Public: Portraiture in the Aftermath of the French Revolution (Manchester: Manchester University Press, 1999).

26 The promotion of *grands hommes* was tied to the Royal Academy's campaign to promote history paintings. For example, D'Angiviller's *grand hommes* series started in the 1770s. Jean Locquin, *La peinture d'histoire en France de 1747 à 1785* (Paris: Arthena, 1978); Andrew McClellan, "D'Angiviller's 'Great Men' of France and the Politics of the Parlements," *Art History* 13, no. 2 (June 1990): 175–92; Jean-Claude Bonnet, *Naissance du Panthéon, Essai sur le cultes des grands hommes* (Paris: Fayard, 1998). For more on the popularity of the *grands hommes*, see Thomas Gaehtgens, "Du Parnasse au Panthéon: la représentation des *hommes illustres* et des *grands hommes* dans la France du XVIIIe siècle," in *Le culte des grands hommes, 1750–1850*, eds. Thomas Gaehtgens and Gregor Wedekind (Paris: Maison des sciences de l'homme, 2009), 135–71.

27 On portraiture during the Revolution, see Amy Freund, *Portraiture and Politics in Revolutionary France* (University Park: The Pennsylvania State University Press, 2014).

28 Thomas E. Crow, *Painters and Public Life in Eighteenth-Century Paris* (New Haven, CT: Yale University Press, 1985).

29 Halliday, *Facing the Public*, 6.

30 Ewa Lajer-Burcharth, "Psyche in the Boudoir," in *Necklines* (New Haven, CT: Yale University Press, 1999), 236–306; Melissa Hyde, "The Makeup of the Marquise," in *Making Up the Rococo: François Boucher and His Critics* (Los Angeles: Getty Publications, 2006), 107–44; Ewa Lajer-Burcharth, "Pompadour's Touch: Difference in Representation," *Representations* 73, no. 1 (2001): 54–88; Melissa Hyde, "Under the Sign of Minerva: Adélaïde Labille-Guiard's Portrait of Madame Adélaïde," in *Women, Art and the Politics of Identity in Eighteenth-Century Europe*, eds. Melissa Hyde and Jennifer Milam (Aldershot, UK: Ashgate Publishing Limited, 2003), 139–63; Laura Auricchio, "Self-Promotion in Adelaide Labille-Guiard's 1785 *Self-Portrait with Two Students*," *The Art Bulletin* 89, no. 1 (2007): 45–62. For more general discussions of the performance of the self in portraiture, see also Richard Brilliant, *Portraiture* (London: Reaktion Books, 1991); Harry Berger, Jr., *Fictions of the Pose: Rembrandt Against the Italian Renaissance* (Stanford, CA: Stanford University Press, 2000); Shearer West, *Portraiture* (Oxford: Oxford University Press, 2004).

31 Many of these monographs take the form of exhibition catalogues, such as those focused on the careers of artists such as Jean-Marc Nattier, Alexandre Roslin, and Maurice Quentin de la Tour. Portraits by history painters have been more thoroughly examined—for example, Hyde's and Lajer-Burcharth's work on artists such as François Boucher and Jacques-Louis David address their portrait production—although most frequently focus on members of the royal family, the king's mistresses, and men who would have been considered *grands hommes* during the period.

32 Marcia Pointon, *Hanging the Head: Portraiture and Social Formation in Eighteenth-Century England* (New Haven, CT: Yale University Press, 1998); Freund, *Portraiture and Politics*, 15–48.

33 Williams, *Académie Royale*.

34 Dena Goodman, "Public Sphere and Private Life: Toward a Synthesis of Current Historiographical Approaches to the Old Regime," *History and Theory* 31, no. 1 (1992): 1–20.

35 Vincent-Buffault, *L'exercice de l'amitié*, 185–249; Christine Roulston, "Separating the

Inseparables: Female Friendship and Its Discontents in Eighteenth-Century France," *Eighteenth-Century Studies* 32, no. 2 (Winter 1998/1999): 215–31; Stuart Curran, "Dynamics of Female Friendship in the Later Eighteenth Century," *Nineteenth-Century Contexts* 23 (2001): 221–39; Crawford, Seifert, and Wilkin, *Men and Women Making Friends*; Anthony J. La Volpa, *The Labor of the Mind: Intellect and Gender in Enlightenment Cultures* (Philadelphia: University of Pennsylvania Press, 2017).

Chapter 1
FRIENDSHIP IN THE ACADEMY

1 "Il y aura une estroite union et bonne correspondance entre ceux de l'Académie, n'y ayant rien de plus contraire à la vertu que l'envie, la mesdisance et la discorde, et, si, quelqu'un y estoit enclin et qu'il ne s'en voulust corriger, après la réprimende que l'Ancien luy en fera, l'entrée de l'Académie luy sera défendue." Reed Benhamou, *Regulating the Académie: Art, Rules and Power in Ancien Régime France* (Oxford: Voltaire Foundation, 2009), 97.
2 See Article VII in the statutes of 1664, and Article 35 in the statutes of 1777. Ibid., 122, 153.
3 In 1765, a letter from the Imperial Academy in St. Petersburg, Russia, read aloud during one of the Academy's meetings, described the relationship between the two thusly: "[The Russian Academy] adds that, desiring to maintain an esteemed correspondence and friendly reciprocity with the [French] Academy, they ask us to return their sincere sentiments." ("Elle ajoute que, desirant entretenir avec l'Académie une correspondance d'estime et d'amitié réciproques, elle la prie de lui accorder le retour de ses sentiments sincères.") Anatole de Montaiglon, *Procès-verbaux de l'Académie royale de peinture et de sculpture (1648–1792)*, 10 vol. (Paris: J. Baur, 1875), 7:312. On loyalty and friendships in international intellectual networks, see Anne Goldgar, *Impolite Learning: Conduct and Community in the Republic of Letters, 1680–1750* (New Haven, CT: Yale University Press, 1995); April Shelford, *Transforming the Republic of Letters: Pierre-Daniel Huet and European Intellectual Life, 1650–1720* (Rochester, NY: University of Rochester Press, 2007); Kenneth Loiselle, "Friendship and Loyalty in Early Modern Europe," in *Face of Communities: Social Ties between Trust, Loyalty and Conflict*, eds. Anna Feickert, Anna Haut, and Kathrin Sharaf (Göttingen: Vandenhoeck & Ruprecht University Press, 2014), 121–36.
4 As Daniel Roche has demonstrated, friendship was often a topic of the *éloges* of academies outside of Paris. Roche, *Le Siècle des Lumières en Province: Académies et académiciens provinciaux, 1680–1789*, 2nd ed. (Paris: Éditions de l'École des hautes études en sciences sociales, 1989), 2:376.
5 The idea of the *conférences* appeared in the founding statutes written in 1648, although the practice was not regularized until 1653. Between 1708 and 1736, it was the directors of the Academy who were most frequently tasked with reading the monthly lectures, although later the lectures were given by other members of the Academy, and by some *amateurs associés*. Jacqueline Lichtenstein and Christian Michel, eds., *Les Conférences de l'Académie Royale de Peinture et de Sculpture* (Paris: École nationale supérieure des beaux-arts, 2006), 1:1, 42–43, 4:1, 15.
6 Ibid., 1:25–26.

7 Daniel Lochman and Maritere López, "Introduction: The Emergence of Discourse: Early Modern Friendship," in *Discourses and Representations of Friendship in Early Modern Europe, 1500–1700*, eds. Daniel Lochman and Maritere López (Burlington, VT: Ashgate, 2011), 4–5.

8 Loiselle, "Friendship and Loyalty in Early Modern Europe," 131.

9 Jonathan Dewald, *Aristocratic Experience and the Origins of Modern Culture, 1570–1715* (Berkeley: University of California Press, 1993), 106.

10 On virtue and social prestige, see Marisa Linton, *The Politics of Virtue in Enlightenment France* (New York: Palgrave, 2001), 31–37.

11 For a broad overview of changes to friendship, see Anne Vincent-Buffault, *L'exercice de l'amitié: pour une histoire des pratiques amicales aux XVIIIe et XIXe siècles* (Paris: Éditions du Seuil, 1995), 75–134; David Garrioch, "From Christian Friendship to Secular Sentimentality: Enlightenment Re-Evaluations," in *Friendship: A History*, ed. Barbara Caine (London: Equinox, 2009), 165–214; Adam Sutcliffe, "Friendship in the European Enlightenment: The Rationalization of Intimacy?," in *Conceptualizing Friendship in Time and Place*, eds. Carla Risseeuw and Marlein van Raalte (Leiden: Brill, 2017), 143–66.

12 Thomas E. Crow, *Painters and Public Life in Eighteenth-Century Paris* (New Haven, CT: Yale University Press, 1985), 1–5. See also Bernadette Fort, "Voice of the Public: The Carnivalization of Salon Art in Prerevolutionary Pamphlets," *Eighteenth-Century Studies* 22, no. 3 (1989): 368–94; Richard Wrigley, *The Origins of French Art Criticism: From the Ancien Régime to the Restoration* (Oxford: Oxford University Press, 1993).

13 On the role of amateurs in the Academy, see Charlotte Guichard, "Taste Communities: The Rise of the Amateur in Eighteenth-Century Paris," *Eighteenth-Century Studies* 45, no. 4 (2012): 519–47.

14 Lichtenstein and Michel, *Conférences*, 4:1, 29. Antoine Coypel was the main lecturer for the Academy between 1708 and his death in 1722, and his conferences were the most reread ones in the institution's history.

15 "... unanimement a prié Monsieur Coypel de continuer le commentaire qu'il a commencé sur l'Épitre en vers à son fils, et d'en vouloir faire la lecture à Compagnie les jours de conférences." Ibid., 4:1, 40.

16 Coypel began his lecture on May 7, 1712, breaking it up into nineteen different lectures, giving six in 1712, four in 1713, three in 1714, two in 1718, two in 1719, and the final two in 1720. Coypel's lectures did not follow the order of the commentary published in 1721, or the original order of the verses of the poem. The collected lectures were published under the title *Discours prononcez dans les conférences de l'Académie Royale de peinture et de sculpture: par M. Coypel ecuyer, Premier peintre du Roy, de Monseigneur le Duc d'Orléans Régent* (Paris: J. Collombat, 1721). Parts of the series—although we do not know which specific sections—were reread over the course of the Academy's history, in 1738, 1744–45, 1748, 1757–59, 1773, 1784, 1786, 1790, and 1791. Lichtenstein and Michel, *Conférences*, 4:1, 29, 32–33.

17 Lichtenstein and Michel, *Conférences*, 3: 260.

18 Ibid., 4:1, 17.

19 Ibid., 4:1, 43–44

20 Jean-Baptiste Brissaud, *Manuel d'histoire du droit français* (Paris: A. Fontemoing, 1908),

1821. Originally cited in Dewald, *Aristocratic Experience*, 105; Jean-Louis Flandrin, *Families in Former Times: Kinship, Household and Sexuality*, trans. Richard Southern (Cambridge: Cambridge University Press, 1979), 159. Maurice Daumas has also noted the use of the language of friendship within the structure of kinship in eighteenth-century Besançon. Daumas, *L'affaire d'Esclans: Les conflits familiaux au XVIIIe siècle* (Paris: Seuil, 1988), 116–20.

21 Christian Michel, *The Académie Royale de Peinture et de Sculpture: The Birth of the French School, 1648–1793*, trans. Chris Miller (Los Angeles: Getty Publications, 2018), 88.

22 As Lichtenstein and Michel note, Charles Coypel claimed in his *Vie d'Antoine Coypel* that men of letters attended Antoine's *conférences* as frequently as did *amateurs de peinture*. Lichtenstein and Michel, *Conférences*, 4:1, 17. On the creation of the amateur, and on patron-artist friendship, see also Charlotte Guichard, *Les amateurs d'art à Paris au XVIIIe siècle* (Paris: Champ Vallon, 2008), 24–41.

23 See Dewald, *Aristocratic Experience*, 105.

24 See Antoine Lilti, *Le monde des salons: sociabilité et mondanité à Paris au XVIIIe siècle* (Paris: Fayard, 2005); Guichard, *Les amateurs d'art*.

25 "Les conseils qui nous sont donnés par des personnes dont l'amitié nous est connue nous sont assurément plus d'impression que les autres. Car il entre souvent beaucoup d'amour-propre dans la démangeaison de donner des avis. Combien des gens se persuadent mériter tout l'honneur d'un ouvrage sur lequel ils auront fait une critique heureuse, dont l'auteur même aurait profiter!" Lichtenstein and Michel, *Conférences*, 4:1, 43.

26 "Ce hasard leur donne la liberté de critiquer toujours, de l'établir dans le monde pour les seuls connaisseurs et les seuls arbitres du bon goût. Alors les décisions ne leur coûtent plus; ils les font même sans voir ce qu'ils critiquent et sans l'examiner; les simples les écoutent; les ignorants les admirent et les auteurs révoltés en sont toujours les victimes." Ibid.

27 "So advice is tiring; the best seem suspect: the artist, realizing that they are only given to him by pretension, gives in to his own vanity; he perseveres, persists, and often hardens against the very truth he discerns." ("Alors les conseils fatiguent; les meilleurs paroissent suspects: l'auteur, s'apercevant que l'on ne les lui donne que par ostentation, s'abandonne lui-même à sa propre vanité; il s'obstine, il s'opiniâtre et se roidit souvent contre la vérité même qu'il entrevoit.") Ibid.

28 "Qu'il est aisé cependant de distinguer ce que l'amitié fait conseiller de ce que décide le vain orgueil! Le véritable ami loue en public ce qui peut être loué et critique en particulier ce qui lui paroît foible ou défectueux. L'homme vain et fastueux loue dans le tête-à-tête et devient froid ou censeur impitoyable quand il est entouré." Ibid.

29 "... un ami fidèle, équitable censeur, qui nous marque sincèrement le défectueux de nos ouvrages, qui sache nous éclaircir dans nos doutes et réchauffer nos idées." Ibid., 4:1, 44.

30 According to Aristotle, lesser friendships not rooted in disinterestedness actually push men toward vice and excess. Linton, *The Politics of Virtue*, 37–46; Lochman and López, "Introduction," 3–6.

31 Linton, *The Politics of Virtue*, 31–37.

32 Reed Benhamou, "Discipline and Punishment in the Académie Royale de Peinture et de

Sculpture," in *Institutional Culture in Early Modern Society*, eds. Anne Goldgar and Robert I. Frost (Bedfordshire, UK: Brill, 2004), 249–50.

33 Hannah Williams, *Académie Royale: A History in Portraits* (Burlington, VT: Ashgate, 2015), 162–66.

34 "Les avis que l'on donne en public, ne peuvent avoir qu'un mauvais effet. Ils irritent celui qui les reçoit. Le dépit lui ôte la confiance et la docilité: outre que la honte le force à l'apologie, pour ne pas demeurer livré à la malignité de ceux qui sont présents. Ainsi on ne remporte d'autre fruit d'un avis si mal placé, que d'avoir chagriné son ami, et souvent d'avoir réjoüi ses ennemis." Louis de Sacy, *Traité de l'amitié* (Paris: Chez Jean Moreau, 1704), 102–3.

35 Cicero, *On Friendship*, trans. W. A. Falconer (Cambridge, MA: Harvard University Press, 1923), 209.

36 Daniel Roche, *France in the Enlightenment*, trans. Arthur Goldhammer (Cambridge, MA: Harvard University Press, 1998), 435. On the role of friendship in the Republic of Letters, see Shelford, *Transforming the Republic of Letters*.

37 Lochman and López, "Introduction," 4.

38 Lichtenstein and Michel, *Conférences*, 4:1, 43.

39 Sharon Kettering, *Patronage in Sixteenth- and Seventeenth-Century France* (Burlington, VT: Ashgate, 2002).

40 See Donald Furber, "The Myth of *amour-propre* in La Rochefoucauld," *The French Review* 43, no. 2 (December 1969): 227–39; Charles-Olivier Stiker-Métral, *Narcisse contrarié: l'amour-propre dans le discours moral en France, 1650–1715* (Paris: Honoré Champion, 2007).

41 "Ce que les hommes ont nommé amitié, n'est qu'une société, qu'un ménagement réciproque d'intérêts . . ." La Rochefoucauld defined *amour-propre* as "l'Amour de soi-même et de toutes chose pour soi" ("the love of oneself and of all other things for one's own sake") and said it was also inherent to man. François de La Rochefoucauld, *Réflexions, sentences et maximes morales* (Paris: E. Ganeau, 1714), 40, 52.

42 De Sacy, *Traité de l'amitié*, 289–90.

43 Ibid., 290. For more on the moralists' debates about friendship in the eighteenth century, see Frédérick Gerson, *L'Amitié au XVIIIe siècle* (Paris: la Pensée universelle, 1974), 31–70.

44 "C'est le défaut de l'amour-propre qui arrête ordinairement le progrès de nos études. Comme on s'aime toujours trop, on se flatte toujours trop aisément, et l'on est souvent satisfait de soi-même quand on est fort éloignée de contenter les autres." Lichtenstein and Michel, *Conférences*, 4:1, 66.

45 ". . . travaillé à m'humilier moi-même." Ibid., 4.1, 71.

46 Ibid.

47 ". . . les flatteurs sont bien plus émus que les amis sincères." Ibid.

48 "Elle vient aussi sans qu'on s'en aperçoive de l'amitié personnelle que l'on a pour les auteurs et de l'amour-propre que l'on a pour soi-même, car beaucoup de gens, ne pouvant se distinguer par leurs propres talents, cherchent à se donner un relief dans le monde par la réputation de leurs amis. Alors pour se flatter eux-mêmes, ils embrassent avec tant de chaleur le parti de ceux qu'ils affectionnent, qu'ils cherchent à détruire tout ce qu'ils croient qui peut s'oppose à leur gloire; ceux même qui la peuvent partager leur

deviennent odieux. Ainsi se forment les cabales. On se cantonne dans le parterre, on y place des admirateurs pour ses amis et des censeurs contre les autres, et l'injustice audacieuse usurpe avec empire la place même de la raison." Ibid., 4.1, 48.

49 Ibid., 4.1, 48–49.
50 Pierre Rosenberg, "Le Concours de Peinture de 1727," *Revue de l'art*, no. 37 (1977): 29–42; Candace Clements, "The Duc d'Antin, the Royal Administration of Pictures, and the Painting Competition of 1727," *The Art Bulletin* 78, no. 4 (1996): 647–62.
51 On the *concours* in French Academies, see Jeremy L. Caradonna, *The Enlightenment in Practice: Academic Prize Contests and Intellectual Culture in France, 1670–1794* (Ithaca, NY: Cornell University Press, 2012).
52 These competitions were central to the Academy's conception of an artistic education that was built around emulation. From the very beginning of their training, aspiring student-artists were introduced to a system that was driven by competition. Emulation has been well addressed in discussions of eighteenth-century artistic education. See Thomas Crow, *Emulation: Making Artists for Revolutionary France* (New Haven, CT: Yale University Press, 1995); Nicholas Mirzoeff, "Revolution, Representation, Equality: Gender, Genre and Emulation in the Académie Royale de Peinture et Sculpture, 1785–1793," *Eighteenth-Century Studies* 31, no. 2 (Winter 1997–98): 153–74. For a discussion of emulation and gender, see Laura Auricchio, "The Laws of Bienséance and the Gendering of Emulation in Eighteenth-Century French Art Education," *Eighteenth-Century Studies* 36, no. 2 (2003): 231–40. For a more general discussion of emulation in the last half of the eighteenth century, see John Iverson, "Emulation in France, 1750–1800," *Eighteenth-Century Studies* 36, no. 2 (2003): 217–30.
53 On the results of the *concours* in relationship to public opinion, see Rosenberg, "Le Concours de Peinture de 1727," 79–80; Clements, "The Duc d'Antin, the Royal Administration of Pictures, and the Painting Competition of 1727."
54 Lichtenstein and Michel, *Conférences*, 4.2, 406; Clements, "The Duc d'Antin, the Royal Administration of Pictures, and the Painting Competition of 1727."
55 On Lemoyne's ambitions to be the director of the Academy, see Hannah Williams, "The Mysterious Suicide of François Lemoyne," *Oxford Art Journal* 38, no. 2 (June 2015): 239.
56 Rosenberg, "Le Concours de Peinture de 1727," 30; Michel, *Charles-Nicolas Cochin et l'art des lumières* (Rome: École française de Rome, 1993), 46; Christophe Leribault, *Jean-François de Troy, 1679–1752* (Paris: Arthena, 2002), 88–89. For details on Lemoyne's suicide, see Hannah Williams, "The Mysterious Suicide of François Lemoyne."
57 Jules-Hippolyte Le Marie Chevalier de Valory, "Jean-François de Troy," in *Mémoires inédits sur les membres de l'Académie royale de peinture et de sculpture*, eds. Louis Dussieux, et al. (Paris: J. B. DuMoulin, 1854), 2:265.
58 Jacqueline Lichtenstein, "L'ignorant ou le spectateur désintéressé," in *Les raisons de l'art. Essai sur les limites de l'esthétique* (Paris: Editions Gallimard, 2014), 91–92.
59 "Malheureusement cela nous devient plus difficile; nous avons peine à convenir qu'il se trouve de notre temps des personnes qui possèdent dans notre art des perfections que nous n'avons pu acquérir: nous le pardonnons aux anciens, ils semblent avoir expié cette offense en cessant de vivre." Lichtenstein and Michel, *Conférences*, 4:2, 409.

60 "Ne nous y trompons pas: l'orgueil qui nous cause divers mouvements, perce même dans les discours qui nous paraissent le plus modestes. Nous louons les autres quelquefois, mais nous ne parlons pas longtemps d'eux, si ceux qui nous écoutent n'ont pas la politesse de nous contraire." Ibid., 4:2, 409–10.
61 Ibid., 4:2, 410.
62 "Le public eut longtemps peine à comprendre qu'ils puissent conserver ces nobles sentiments, possédant tous trois des parties si éminentes dans le même talent: mais enfin, ayant jamais couru chez l'un sans lui entendre faire l'éloge des productions des autres, ce redoutable public, dont les suffrages se partagent presque toujours, se vit contraint de les réunir en leur faveur et de convenir que tous trois se faisaient autant révérer par une façon de penser si élevée, qu'ils exitaient d'admiration par l'excellence de leur pinceau." Ibid., 4:2, 410–11.
63 Charles Coypel, *Discours sur la peinture, prononcez dans les conférences de l'Académie Royale de peinture et sculpture* (Paris: Chez P. J. Mariette, 1732).
64 Lichtenstein and Michel, *Conférences*, 5:1, 42.
65 Ibid., 5:1, 50–51.
66 "Renouveler en faveur des arts le beau siècle du Grand Colbert, c'est son projet." ("To renew the arts to the great century of the Grand Colbert, that is its intention.") Ibid., 5:1, 51.
67 Jacqueline Lichtenstein, in her essay "L'ignorant ou le spectateur désintéressé," has examined the exchange between Charles Coypel and La Font, convincingly arguing that it was a pivotal moment in the debate over art criticism, the formation of good taste, and the idea of a public audience for art. Though she is largely interested in the changing idea of the art critic, the rise of the amateur (or "vrai connaisseur"), and arguments about taste, she also discusses the "disinterested spectator," which equally calls attention to the shifting conceptions of friendship—conceptions that the Academy would be forced to confront over the next four decades.
68 "Ce n'est donc que dans la bouche de ces hommes fermes et équitables qui composent le Public, et qui ne tiennent aux Auteurs, ni par le sang, ni par l'amitié, ni par la profession, que l'on peut trouver le langage de la vérité." In the *Réflexions*, La Font wrote: "to propose critical, but modest, reflections, without passion and without any personal gain, could make artistes realize their mistakes, and encourage them to greater perfection." ("de proposer des réflexions critiques, mais modestes, sans passion et sans aucun intérêt personnel, qui pussent faire apercevoir aux Auteurs leur défaut, et les encourager à une plus grande perfection.") Étienne La Font de Saint-Yenne, *Réflexions sur quelques causes de l'état présent de la peinture en France avec un examen des principaux Ouvrages exposés au Louvre le mois d'Août 1746* (La Haye: Chez Jean Neaulme, 1747), 2; Étienne La Font de Saint-Yenne, *Lettre de l'auteur des réflexions sur la peinture et de l'examen des ouvrages exposés au Louvre en 1746* (1747), 6, http://catalogue.bnf.fr/ark:/12148/cb307154065.
69 Lichtenstein, "L'ignorant ou le spectateur désintéressé," 108.
70 On the changing perception of friendship, see Linton, *The Politics of Virtue*; Marisa Linton, *Choosing Terror: Virtue, Friendship, and Authenticity in the French Revolution* (Oxford: Oxford University Press, 2015); Loiselle, "Friendship and Loyalty in Early Modern Europe."
71 Even though they were listed in the official *livret* as "plusieurs portrait sous le même

numero," Leblanc listed them all by name: "Madame la Comtesse de Lovendal, Monsieur le Maréchal de Saxe, de l'autre Monsieur le Duc de Yorck, Madame de Montmartel; plus bas, au milieu Monsieur le Comte de Clermont, à sa droite Monsieur le Moine sculpteur, Monsieur Binet, Monsieur l'Abbé Le Blanc, à sa gauche Monsieur Gabriel, premier Architecte du Roi, Monsieur Cupis, Monsieur Mondonville." Jean-Bernard Le Blanc, *Lettre sur l'exposition des ouvrages de peinture, sculpture, etc. de l'année 1747* (1747), 83–84, http://catalogue.bnf.fr/ark:/12148/cb30760089d.

72 "... de méchantes langues ont osé avancer que cet ouvrage avoit été fait pour M. de La Tour et lui avoir été donné en payement du portrait de M. l'abbé Le Blanc: d'autres ont dit que si cela étoit, ils le trouvoient bien mal payé." Ibid.

73 "I believe to have glimpsed in him a friend of Monsieur Vien; but in this circumstance the laws of friendship should give way to those of justice and truth." ("Je crois appercevoir en lui un ami de Monsieur Vien; mais dans cette circonstance les droits de l'amitié doivent céder à ceux de la justice et de la vérité.") *Lettre critique, à un ami, sur les ouvrages de Messieurs de l'Academie, exposés au Sallon du Louvre* (1759), 18, https://catalogue.bnf.fr/ark:/12148/cb423292112.

74 See Wrigley, *The Origins of French Art Criticism*, 165–76.

75 On the rise of the amateur and their role as critics, see Guichard, *Les amateurs d'art*; Mary D. Sheriff, *Fragonard: Art and Eroticism* (Chicago: University of Chicago Press, 1999), 132–38. On the politicization of Salon criticism, see Crow, *Painters and Public Life*; Wrigley, *The Origins of French Art Criticism*.

76 The use of this sort of literary mode has been discussed by Bernadette Fort, who argues that using "minority" writers, such as women, children, and blind men, or adopting the form of popular genres such as vaudeville, were means of representing public opinion and wresting authority away from the Academy and its supporters. See Fort, "Voice of the Public."

77 "I regret to not be enough of a connoisseur to be aware of their beauty, nor knowledgeable enough to see their faults." ("Je regrettois de n'être pas assez connoisseur pour en sentir les beautés, ni assez éclairé pour en voir les défauts.") *Le visionnaire, ou Lettres sur les ouvrages exposés au Sallon; par un ami des arts* (Amsterdam: n.p., 1779), 5, http://catalogue.bnf.fr/ark:/12148/cb33646333w.

78 "Vous y êtes très-redoutée." Ibid., 7.

79 Ibid., 8.

80 "Il est bien mon ami aussi ... je me joins, de tout mon cœur, aux éloges que vous en faites." Ibid., 9.

81 "Ma sœur ... cet Artiste a du merité, il ne faut pas le décourager par votre sévérité." Ibid., 12–13.

82 Ibid., 13.

83 "Je sais combien vous l'aimez." Ibid., 23.

84 "Vous souffrez, mon frère ... mais soyez assuré que je suis autant son amie que vous: à la vérité, je suis plus difficile à l'égard de mes amis, que je ne le suis pour les autres; c'est pourquoi je continue." Ibid., 26.

85 "... un ami fidèle, équitable censeur, qui nous marque sincèrement le défectueux de nos ouvrages, qui sache nous éclaircir dans nos doutes et réchauffer nos idées." Lichtenstein and Michel, *Conférences*, 4.1, 44.

86 Guichard, "Taste Communities," 531.
87 Ibid., 531–32.
88 In defending François-André Vincent's *President Molé and the Insurgents*, he says, "... I was next to him when he painted it." ("... j'étois à côté de lui lorsqu'il les peignoit.") *Le visionnaire*, 16.
89 "... vous voyez comme elle traite un de mes meilleurs amis." Ibid., 28.
90 "[L]es femmes sont cruellement exigeantes ... mais souvent on se trouve bien de suivre leurs conseils." Ibid.
91 "Celui qui examine des ouvrages d' esprit, pour en porter son jugement, les expliquer, les éclaircir, &c. Il signifie encore Censeur, celui qui trouve à redire à tout." "Critique," in *Dictionnaire de l'Académie française*, 4th ed. (Paris: Chez la Vve B. Brunet, 1762), 444. *Dictionnaire Vivant de la Langue Française*, accessed August 8, 2018, https://dvlf.uchicago.edu/mot/critique.
92 "Critique s.f. L'art, la faculté de juger d'un ouvrage d'esprit." Ibid.
93 Ibid.
94 *Le visionnaire*, 19–20.
95 Jennifer M. Jones, *Sexing La Mode: Gender, Fashion and Commercial Culture in Old Regime France* (Oxford: Berg, 2004), 117.
96 On the language of taste and employment of these words, see Sheriff, *Fragonard*, 117–42.
97 On Rousseau's criticism of the Salons, see Dena Goodman, *The Republic of Letters: A Cultural History of the French Enlightenment* (Ithaca, NY: Cornell University Press, 1996), 53–73.
98 Jean-Jacques Rousseau, "Discourse on the Arts and Sciences," in *The Basic Political Writings (Second Edition)*, trans. and ed. Donald A. Cress (Indianapolis, IN: Hackett Publishing Company, 2011), 17.
99 Paul, *Sur la peinture* (The Hague: Chez Hardouin, 1782), 74, http://catalogue.bnf.fr/ark:/12148/cb310675793. "[E]n général n'aiment aucun Art, ne se connoissent à aucun, et n'ont aucun génie." Jean-Jacques Rousseau, *Politics and the Arts: Letter to M. D'Alembert on the Theatre*, trans. Allan Bloom (Ithaca, NY: Cornell University Press, 1968), 103.
100 "... nous vîmes avec la plus grande satisfaction plusieurs tableaux de mademoiselle Vallayer. Ils sont peints avec vérité, avec gout et avec facilité. La critique ne put nous dissimuler combien elle était flattée de voir dans ce Sallon des ouvrages d'une personne de son sexe. Elle s'entendit sur l'utilité d'encourager par cet honneur, celles qui ont assez de vertu pour sacrifier les plaisirs qui s'offrent de toutes parts dans leur jeune âge, a celui de se livrer au travail assidu qu'exige l'étude d'arts aussi difficiles. Elle temoigna le plus vif deplaisir de ne lui voir dans ce lieu aucune compagne et cependant, ajout-a-elle, d'autres encore en tout dignes: et si je fais bien compter, il en est jus qu'a trois que je pourrois citer ... elle s'arrêta, et je n'osai demander qu'elle s'expliquât plus clairement, car elle parut n'en vouloir pas dire davantage." *Le visionnaire*, second letter, 8–9, https://catalogue.bnf.fr/ark:/12148/cb423440947.
101 Anatole de Montaiglon, *Procès-verbaux*, 8:53. The three women Criticism references are the last three women accepted to the Academy: Anna Dorothea Therbusch, Marie-Thérèse Vien (née Reboul), and Marie-Suzanne Roslin (née Giroust). However, Criticism's

mention of the three ignores that Mme Roslin died in 1772. The last two women accepted to the Academy before the Revolution, Adélaïde Labille-Guiard and Élisabeth Vigée-Lebrun, were accepted in 1783.

102 See Mary D. Sheriff, *The Exceptional Woman: Elisabeth Vigée-Lebrun and the Cultural Politics of Art* (Chicago: University of Chicago Press, 1997), 78–79; Laura Auricchio, *Adélaïde Labille-Guiard: Artist in the Age of Revolution* (Los Angeles: J. Paul Getty Museum, 2009), 29; Séverine Sofio, *Artistes femmes. Parenthèse enchantée XVIII–XIXe siècle: La parenthèse enchantée XVIIIe–XIXe siècles* (Paris: CNRS Éditions, 2016); Paris Amanda Spies-Gans, "Exceptional, but Not Exceptions: Public Exhibitions and the Rise of the Woman Artist in London and Paris, 1760–1830," *Eighteenth-Century Studies* 51, no. 4 (2018): 404–6. Hannah Williams provides a particularly detailed discussion of artistic families in *Académie Royale*, Chapter 4.

103 "[L]es femmes sont cruellement exigeantes ... mais souvent on se trouve bien de suivre leurs conseils." *Le visionnaire*, 28.

104 On this point, see Katharine J. Hamerton, "Rousseau and the New Domestic Art of Women's Taste," *Proceedings of the Western Society for French History* 37 (2009): 99–115. See also Genevieve Lloyd, *The Man of Reason: "Male" and "Female" in Western Philosophy* (New York: Routledge, 2002), 58–64.

105 Jean-Jacques Rousseau, *A Discourse on Inequality*, trans. Maurice Cranston (London: Penguin Books, 1984), 65.

106 Ibid.

107 "Gardez-vous de conclure de ce que vous avez entendu, que les Ouvrages sur lesquels la Critique a développé ses sentiments, ne soient pas néanmoins dignes d'estime, sans cela elle ne s'y seroit pas arrêté; ainsi, ne diminuez rien de la considération que vous devez aux Artistes qui les ont produits. La Peinture est un Art extrêment difficile; il embrasse une grande quantité de parties, qu'il faudroit réunir pour échapper à la Critique. Aussi ne doit-elle pas avoit pour but de déprimer l'Artiste, mais de l'avertir." *Le visionnaire*, 39.

108 "L'Amateur qui, parce qu'il paie des Tableaux (dont le plus souvent il ne sent pas le mérite), se croit en droit de juger les Artistes ... Ce sera encore un ou deux anciens Artistes, qui, respectant ceux qui, comme eux, ont blanchi dans les Arts, exercent leur bile sur leur jeunes Confreres, auxquels ils croient pouvoir donner des préceptes, et le font avec tant de confiance en leurs lumières, qu'ils semblent dire à ceux à qui ils parlent: Imitez-moi." *Le Pourquoi ou L'ami des artistes* (Geneva, 1781), 6, http://catalogue.bnf.fr/ark:/12148/cb33545178w.

109 Ibid., 6–7.

110 "[J]e laisse aux Artistes à qui je soumets mes observations, à juger si les Critiques sont plus utiles que dangereuses." Jean-Baptiste-Claude Robin, *L'Ami des artistes au Sallon. Par M. l'A. R.* (Paris: Chez L'Esclapart, 1787), 6–7, http://catalogue.bnf.fr/ark:/12148/cb36120422б.

111 "Combien de ces Ecrits ne doivent leur existence qu'au besoin que leur Auteur avoit de quelques louis! Alors il faut être spirituel, plaisant; sacrifier la raison et la justice à un bon mot; ou bien faire une Critique froide, qui ne seroit lue que par les Artistes qu'elles intéressoient." Ibid., 7–8.

112 "L'Epigraphe que j'ai choisie rend tous me sentimens. Amis des Arts, je ne viens point

les désoler, ni d'une main malignement perfide, leur faire de mortelles blessures. Je ne viens pas non plus, par une lâche complaisance, pallier les défauts ni les ériger en beautés. L'excès par-tout est un défaut. Mais comme un ami vrai, en louant les vertus, tonne sans faiblesse sur les vices de son ami; de même en louant les nombreuses beautés du Sallon, je serai impitoyable sur les productions défectueuses qui figurent à côté des chef-d'œuvres du génie." *Messieurs, ami de tout le monde!*, (1783), 5, http://catalogue.bnf.fr/ark:/12148/cb33484482c.

113 Lochman and López, "Introduction," 4.

114 "... ce nouveau Jupiter promet ensuite *de tonner sans foiblesse sur les vices de ses Amis*, et il tient parole. Presque toujours sa foudre mal dirigée frappe à tort et à travers." *L'impartialité Au Sallon, Dédiée à Messieurs Les Critiques Présens et à Venir* (Boston, 1783), 5, https://catalogue.bnf.fr/ark:/12148/cb33428424x.

Chapter 2
CELEBRATING CELEBRITY

1 The best biography on Cochin is Christian Michel's *Charles-Nicolas Cochin et l'art des lumières* (Rome: École française de Rome, 1993).

2 Per Michel, this group's central figure was Charles Parrocel. Also included were French and foreign artists, such as John-Martin Preisler, Jean Restout, Jean-Siméon Chardin, Jacques-Philippe Le Bas, Étienne Jeaurat, François Boucher, Jean-Baptiste Massé, Michel-Ange Slodtz, and George-Frederick Schmidt. Ibid., 48–51.

3 Ibid., 51.

4 Christine Debrie and Xavier Salmon, *Maurice-Quentin de La Tour: prince des pastellistes* (Paris: Somogy, 2001), 44.

5 On the genesis and reproduction of this portrait, see Hervé Cabezas, "Voltaire, ses portraits, par Maurice-Quentin de La Tour et Joseph Rosset, et leur reproduction, au Musée Antoine Lécuyer de Saint Quentin," *Bulletin de la société de l'histoire de l'art français*, année 2009 (2011): 175–202.

6 It is difficult to get an exact count of the number of portraits displayed, as the salon *livret* frequently describes an artist's offerings as "several portraits under the same number." In all likelihood, the number of portraits is higher than the table demonstrates. Whenever possible, I have used annotated versions of the Salon catalogue and mentions of unlisted portraits in Salon criticism to take into account the number of actual portraits displayed. Along with the "several works" issues, until midcentury, engravings and drawings were not included in the numbered count in the catalogue. The total number of works in this table reflects my own incorporation of these unnumbered works.

7 Michel, *Charles-Nicolas Cochin*, 50.

8 On the history of the cult of "great men" in France, see David Bell, *The Cult of the Nation in France: Inventing Nationalism, 1680–1800* (Cambridge, MA: Harvard University Press, 2003), 107–39.

9 "[Q]ui y gagne de quoi bien faire boüillir son pot, parce qu'il n'y point de bourgeoise un peu coquette et un peu à son aise qui ne veuille avoir son portrait." Pierre Richelet, "Portrait," in Pierre Richelet, *Dictionnaire de la langue françoise ancienne et moderne. Tome 2, I–Z, vol. 2* (Amsterdam: aux dépens de la Compagnie, 1732), 453. For more on

the criticism of the genre of portraiture, see Jean Locquin, "La lutte des critiques d'art contre les portraitistes au XVIIIe siècle," *Archives de l'art français* 7 (1913): 309–20; Michael Müller, "Sans nom, sans place et sans mérite'? Réflexions sur l'utilisation du portrait en France au XVIIIe siècle," in *L'art et les normes sociales au XVIIIe siècle*, eds. Thomas W. Gaehtgens, Christian Michel, and Martin Schieder (Paris: Éditions de la Maison des sciences de l'homme, 2001), 383–402.

10 The crisis of history painting in the 1730s and 1740s has been well discussed. See Jean Locquin, *La peinture d'histoire en France de 1747 à 1785: étude sur l'évolution des idées artistiques dans la seconde moitié du XVIIIe siècle* (Paris: Arthéna, 1978), 1–13; Thomas E. Crow, *Painters and Public Life in Eighteenth-Century Paris* (New Haven, CT: Yale University Press, 1985).

11 La Font describes portraiture as "the most lucrative genre of [painting]" ("genre le plus lucratif dans cet art"). Étienne La Font de Saint-Yenne, *Reflexions sur quelques causes de l'état présent de la peinture en France. Avec un examen des principaux ouvrages exposés au Louvre le mois d'août 1746* (La Haye: Chez Jean Neaulme, 1747), 20–21.

12 "Soyez doux, liants parlez peu, écoutez beaucoup, recherchez l'amitié de ceux qui joignent le grand usage du monde à la pureté de mœurs. Acquérez avec eux ce ton noble si nécessaire pour être admis dans la bonne compagnie. La bonne compagnie seule peut nous mettre en état d'exprimer vivement, noblement et avec délicatesse les passions de l'âme si difficiles à bien rendre en peinture." Louis Tocqué, *Le Discours de Tocqué sur le genre du portrait*, ed. Arnauld Doria (Paris: J. Schemit, 1930), 18.

13 "Je vais encore plus loin, et je dis, que ce n'est qu'a ses portraits que M. Mignard premier peintre du Roy fut redevable de son élévation. Il les traitoit superieurement, et c'est etoit pour lui un moien sûr de gagne de bien et des se faire des amis." Donat Nonnotte, *6e discours de M. Nonnotte les avantages du portrait et la manière de le traiter*, Ms 193, folio 59–69, Académie des sciences, belles-lettres et arts de Lyon.

14 The use of friendship to equal the playing field between artist and patron has a long history. For example, this was a strategy used by Giorgio Vasari in his *Lives of the Artists* in describing patron-artist relationships. On the rhetoric of friendship in patronage during the Renaissance, see Guy Fitch Lytle, "Friendship and Patronage in Renaissance Europe," in *Patronage, Art and Society in Renaissance Italy*, eds. F. W. Kent and Patricia Simons (Oxford: Clarendon Press, 1987), 47–62; Jill Burke, "Patronage and the Art of Friendship: Piero del Pugliese's Patronage of Filippino Lippi," in *Changing Patrons: Social Identity and the Visual Arts in Renaissance Florence* (University Park: The Pennsylvania State University Press, 2004), 85–101; Sharon Kettering, *Patronage in Sixteenth- and Seventeenth-Century France* (Burlington, VT: Ashgate, 2002).

15 "Cet art de sa naissance excita un empressement universelle. Parvenu peu à peu à sa perfection, on l'emploi a représenter tout ce qui pouvoit toucher le cœur et plaire à l'esprit. L'amitié, le respect, la reconnoissance élèvent des monuments à la mémoire des parens, des amis, des grands hommes. Le sublime talent de faire des ressemblances vives et spirituelles, fit éclore des prodiges qui étonnèrent. Les grands Princes, les Philosophes, les chefs de familles, les hommes vertueux, la Beauté et les Grâces, devinrent des modèles, dont on crut devoir laisser des images à la postérité." Nonnotte, *6e discours*.

16 "Par celui de M. La Tour, M. le Moine a voulu acquitter la dette de son portrait au pastel, exposé par celui-ci au Sallon [sic] précédent et reçu avec applaudissement de tout le Public. Que M. le Moine l'a bien acquittée et qu'il est peu dans le monde d'aussi bon payeurs!" Guillaume Baillet de Saint-Julien, *Reflexions sur quelques circonstances presentes. Contenant deux lettres sur l'exposition des tableaux au Louvre cette année 1748 à M. le Comte de R***. et une autre lettre à Monsieur de Voltaire au sujet de la Tragédie de Semiramis*. (n.p., 1748), 9, http://catalogue.bnf.fr/ark:/12148/cb30047462j.

17 As Paul Albert Besnard notes, the display of Parrocel's portrait was mentioned in a handwritten annotation in the *livret* in the Collection Deloynes. Besnard, *La Tour: La Vie et l'oeuvre de l'artiste* (Paris: Les Beaux-arts, 1928), 35.

18 A further analysis of the significance of the inequality of this exchange is found in Hannah Williams, *Académie Royale: A History in Portraits* (Burlington, VT: Ashgate, 2015), 209–14.

19 Xavier Salmon, *Pastels du Musée du Louvre XVIIe–XVIIIe siècles* (Paris: Éditions Hazan, 2018), 172; Xavier Salmon, *Maurice Quentin de La Tour: le voleur d'âmes*, exh. cat. (Versailles: Artlys, 2004), 60.

20 "Cette dépendance réciproque des hommes, par la variété des denrées qu'ils peuvent se fournir, s'étend sur des besoins réels ou sur des besoins d'opinion." "Commerce," in *Encyclopédie, ou dictionnaire raisonné des sciences, des arts et des métiers, etc.*, eds. Denis Diderot and Jean le Rond d'Alembert. University of Chicago, ARTFL Encyclopédie Project, eds. Robert Morrissey and Glenn Roe (Autumn 2017 Edition), http://encyclopedie.uchicago.edu/.

21 Dena Goodman, *The Republic of Letters: A Cultural History of the French Enlightenment* (Ithaca, NY: Cornell University Press, 1996), 140.

22 Daniel Gordon, *Citizens without Sovereignty: Equality and Sociability in French Thought, 1670–1789* (Princeton, NJ: Princeton University Press, 1994), 52.

23 Ibid.

24 Ibid., 72.

25 On May 27, 1751, La Tour achieved the rank of *conseiller* in the Royal Academy, the highest office a portraitist could attain. He also received lodgings at the Louvre, an annual pension of one thousand livres, and he benefited from commissions from the royal family. Besnard, *La Tour*, 52.

26 *Explication des peintures, sculptures, et autres ouvrages de Messieurs de l'Académie Royale* (Paris: l'Imprimerie de J. J. E. Collombat, 1753), entries 74–91.

27 Jean-François Marmontel, Jean-Pierre Mariette, and others described La Tour's efforts to integrate himself into social circles. On this point, see Rena M. Hoisington, "Maurice-Quentin de La Tour and the Triumph of Pastel Painting in Eighteenth-Century France" (PhD diss., New York University, 2006), 183–201; Thomas W. Gaehtgens, "Du Parnasse Au Panthéon?: La Représentation des hommes illustres et des grands hommes dans la France du XVIIIe siècle," in *Le Culte des grands hommes, 1750–1850*, eds. Thomas W. Gaehtgens and Gergor Wedekin (Paris: Maison des sciences de l'homme, 2009), 145–50.

28 "[C]ette foule d'hommes obscurs, sans nom, sans talens, sans réputation, même sans phisionomie." Étienne La Font de Saint-Yenne, *Sentimens sur quelques ouvrages de Peinture, Sculpture et Gravure, Écrits à un Particulier en Province* (n.p., 1754), 140, http://

catalogue.bnf.fr/ark:/12148/cb30715417t. These are almost the exact same words he used in 1747: "des êtres obscurs sans caractère, sans nom, sans places, et sans mérite." La Font de Saint-Yenne, *Reflexions*, 22.

29 "... portraits have become a necessary spectacle to each Frenchman ..." ("... les Portraits sont devenus un spectacle nécessaire à chaque François...") La Font de Saint-Yenne, *Sentimens*, 233.

30 "Tels sont ceux des bons Rois, des Reines vertueuses, et de tous nos Souverains humains et bienfaisans"; "ministres ... qui zélés pour l'honneur de la nation, et plus encore pour la tranquillité, l'abondance et l'aisance des peoples ..."; "héros de valeur et d'humanité ..."; "Magistrats intègres et irréprochables ..."; "Ambassadeurs des Cours étrangères et les nôtres ..."; "Nos excellens auteurs, dont les mœurs, le génie, les vastes et utiles connoissances illustrent leur patrie soit dans les sciences, les Belle-lettres, ou les Beaux arts." Ibid., 134–39.

31 Antoine Lilti, *Figures publiques: l'invention de la célébrité, 1750–1850* (Paris: Fayard, 2014), 12–13.

32 Ibid., 13–14.

33 "La célébrité est l'avantage d'être connu de ceux que vous ne connaissez pas." Quoted in ibid., 148.

34 Ibid., 144–47.

35 By the 1780s, the *Dictionnaire de l'Académie française* had added an important set of distinctions to the definition of *célèbre* in order to delineate it from its synonyms famousness (*fameux*) or illustriousness (*illustre*): "It says less than illustrious, and is more noble that famous." ("Il dit moins qu'*illustre*, et il est plus noble que *fameux*.") "Célèbre," Jean-François Féraud, *Dictionnaire critique de la langue française (1787–88)* in *Dictionnaires d'autrefois*, University of Chicago, The Project for American and French Research on the Treasury of the French Language (ARTFL), http://artfl-project.uchicago.edu/.

36 Along with Lilti's work, see also Leo Braudy, *The Frenzy of Renown: Fame and Its History* (Oxford: Oxford University Press, 1986); Joseph Roach, *It* (Ann Arbor: University of Michigan Press, 2007); Chris Rojek, *Celebrity* (London: Reaktion, 2010).

37 Chris Rojek has referred to this process as "celebrification." See Rojek, *Celebrity*, 181–99. See also Roach, *It*, 17–21. On the collection of celebrity heads, see Marcia Pointon, *Hanging the Head: Portraiture and Social Formation in Eighteenth-Century England* (New Haven, CT: Yale University Press, 1997).

38 Lilti, *Figures publiques*, 31.

39 Ibid., 17. Jürgen Habermas, *The Structural Transformation of the Public Sphere: An Inquiry into a Category of Bourgeois Society*, trans. Thomas Burger and Frederick Lawrence (Cambridge, MA: MIT Press, 1991).

40 Gill Perry, *Spectacular Flirtations: Viewing the Actress in British Art and Theatre, 1768–1820* (New Haven, CT: Yale University Press, 2007). See especially Chapter 2, "Spectacular Appearances: Exhibiting the Actress and 'Divine Excess.'" See also Heather McPherson, *Art and Celebrity in the Age of Reynolds and Siddons* (University Park: The Pennsylvania University Press, 2017).

41 "[I]l préfère la consolation de faire le portrait des homme illustres, à l'avantage de faire celui des gens opulens." *Mercure de France* (October 1753), 162.

42 Hoisington, "Maurice-Quentin de La Tour," 182.
43 "[A] pleasure to paint those as he knew them to make them famous in the Arts or in the Sciences." ("[U]n plaisir de peindre ceux comme lui ont sçu se rendre célébres dans les Arts ou dans les Sciences.") Jean-Bernard Le Blanc, *Observations sur les ouvrages de MM. de l'Académie de peinture et de sculpture, exposés au Sallon du Louvre, en l'Année 1753, et sur quelques Ecrits qui ont rapport à la peinture. A monsieur le Président de B*** (1753), 37, https://catalogue.bnf.fr/ark:/12148/cb307600095b.
44 "C'est son amour et son zèle pour honneur de la nation, qui lui fait ajouter à l'immortalité des écrits de nos auteurs illustres, celle de leurs Portraits, qui transmettront à la posterité l'esprit de leurs phisionomies et la vie de leurs traits graves d'après lui à la tête de leurs ouvrages." La Font de Saint-Yenne, *Sentimens*, 160.
45 "Cet Artiste célèbre a exposé au *Salon* plusieurs de ces Chefs-d'œuvres de l'Art qu'on ne peut se lasser d'admirer. Il semble avoir voulu donner un double prix à ses Ouvrages; les curieux les rechercheront un jour, parce qu'ils sont de M. de La Tour et parce qu'ils représentent des Hommes Illustres de notre siècle." Jacques Lacombe, *Le salon* (1753), 27, http://catalogue.bnf.fr/ark:/12148/cb307088043.
46 As Hoisington notes, Manelli's inclusion was perhaps La Tour's attempt to demonstrate his participation in the *querelle des Bouffons*. Hoisington, "Maurice-Quentin de La Tour," 191–96.
47 Jeanne Charpentier and Michel Charpentier, eds. *L'Encyclopédie* (Paris: Éditions Bordas, 1967), 3–10.
48 "Il nous cite *l'Esprit des lois, la Henriade, l'Histoire naturelle*, les *Plaidoyers* de Cochin, les *Sermons* de Massilon, les *Opéras* de Rameau, les Portraits de La Tour, l'*Encyclopédie* enfin ouvrages qui seront sans doute immortels." Friedrich Melchior Grimm and Denis Diderot, *Correspondance littéraire, philosophique et critique de Grimm et de Diderot depuis 1753 jusqu'en 1790*, vol. 1 (Paris: Furne, 1829), 86.
49 Jean Le Rond d'Alembert, *Preliminary Discourse to the Encyclopedia of Diderot*, trans. Richard N. Schwab with the collaboration of Walter E. Rex (Chicago: University of Chicago Press, 1995), ix–lii.
50 I thank Dena Goodman for this insight.
51 "A ces traits par le zèle et l'amitié tracés, / Sages arrêtez-vous; gens du monde passez." A number of critics mentioned the verses, as did the *Correspondance littéraire* of September of 1753. See Grimm and Diderot, *Correspondance littéraire*, 1:61. The verses were not added to subsequent copies of Rousseau's portrait. It is important to note that, in 1753, Rousseau was still on good terms with d'Alembert and Marmontel.
52 "Quelque temps après mon retour à Mont-Louis, La Tour, le peintre, vint m'y voir, et m'apporta mon portrait en pastel, qu'il avait exposé au salon, il y avait quelques années. Il avait voulu me donner ce portrait, que je n'avais pas accepté. Mais madame d'Épinay, qui m'avait donné le sien et qui voulait avoir celui-là, m'avait engagé à le lui redemander. Il avait pris du temps pour le retoucher. Dans cet intervalle vint ma rupture avec madame d'Épinay; je lui rendis son portrait; et n'étant plus question de lui donner le mien, je le mis dans ma chambre au petit château." Jean-Jacques Rousseau, *Les confessions de J. J. Rousseau, citoyen de Genève*, vol. 4 (Lyon: Chez J. S. Grabit, 1793), 128.
53 His hesitation to accept the portrait is found in a letter dated January 9, 1763, to Toussaint-Pierre Lenieps. See Besnard, *La Tour*, 63.

54 "Oui Monsieur, j'accepte encore mon second portrait. Vous savez que j'ai fait du premier un usage aussi honorable à vous qu'à moi, et bien précieux à mon cœur. Monsieur le Maréchal de Luxembourg daigna l'accepter: Madame la Maréchal a daigné le recueillir. Ce monument de votre amitié, de votre générosité, de vos rares talents, occupe une place digne de la main dont il est sorti ... il sera sous mes yeux chaque jour de ma vie; il parlera sans cesse à mon cœur; il sera transmis à ma famille, et ce qui me flatte le plus dans cette idée est qu'on s'y souviendra toujours de notre amitié." Rousseau to La Tour, 14 October 1764, quoted in Besnard, *La Tour*, 68–69.

55 Braudy, *The Frenzy of Renown*, 371–80; Lilti, *Figures publiques*, Chapter 5, "Solitude de l'homme célèbre."

56 "On compte dans le Sallon [*sic*] jusqu'à dix-huit portraits de M. de La Tour. Parmi ce grand nombre, il n'y a que celui de M. Bachaumont qui soit fait dans le goût de ce que vous avez déjà vû de cet Artiste. Tous les autres portraits sont d'une nouvelle manière. Les couleurs y sont moins fonduës, et on ne doit pas les regarder de près. Malgré ce reproche, on ne peut se défendre de reconnoître dans le pastel de ce Maître une fraîcheur qui efface tout ce qui est à l'huile." Pierre Estève, *Lettre a un ami, sur l'exposition des tableaux faite dans le grand Sallon du Louvre, le 25 août 1753* (n.p., 1753), 14–15, http://catalogue.bnf.fr/ark:/12148/cb320842700.

57 "Ceux de M. le Marquis de Voyer et de M. Silvestre ne sont pas moins parfaits chacun dans son genre. Comme ce dernier est un Portrait de Peintre, on pourroit dire que M. de La Tour l'a fait pour les Peintres, et qu'en effet ce sont ceux qui connoissent le mieux les difficultés de l'Art qui l'admireront le plus. Il y a dans cette tête des passages imperceptibles, des clairs dans les ombres, et des ombres dans les clairs, qui lui donnent tout le relief et toute la rondeur de la nature." Leblanc, *Observations*, 35.

58 For an overview of the change in status of the artist in Europe, see Vivien Greene, "Un espace d'expérimentations: le portrait d'artiste," in *Portraits publics, portraits privés, 1770–1830*, exh. cat., ed. Sébastien Allard (Paris: Réunion des Musées nationaux, 2006), 180–203.

59 "Nos excellens auteurs, dont les mœurs, le genie, les vastes et utiles connoissances illustrent leur patrie soit dans les sciences, les Belle-lettres, ou les Beaux arts." La Font de Saint-Yenne, *Sentimens*, 139.

60 Portraits were often listed together in the *livret* as "several portraits under the same number" ("plusieurs portraits sous le même numéro").

61 Estève, *Lettre a un ami*, 15. For a full analysis of critical discussions of La Tour's multiple styles, see Hoisington, "Maurice-Quentin de La Tour," 145–70.

62 Estève, *Lettre a un ami*, 15.

63 "Sans pinceau, le doigt seul place & fond chaque teinte." Claude-Henri Watelet, *L'art de peindre, poëme avec des Réflexions sur les différentes parties de la peinture* (Paris: H.-L. Guérin et L.-F. Delatour, 1760), 52.

64 See especially Mary D. Sheriff, *Fragonard: Art and Eroticism* (Chicago: University of Chicago Press, 1990), 140–41; Melissa Hyde, "The Make-Up of the Marquise," *Making Up the Rococo: François Boucher and His Critics* (Los Angeles: Getty Publications, 2006); Ewa Lajer-Burcharth, "Pompadour's Touch: Difference in Representation," *Representations* 73, no. 1 (2001): 54–88; Mary D. Sheriff, *Moved by Love: Inspired Artists and Deviant Women in Eighteenth-Century France* (Chicago: University of Chicago Press,

65 Roach, *It*, 49.
66 Joseph Roach, "Celebrity Erotics: Pepys, Performance, and Painted Ladies," *The Yale Journal of Criticism* 16, no. 1 (2003): 214–15.
67 On the development of the *morceau de réception* portrait, see Williams, *Académie Royale*, 27–42.
68 "Quarante-six petits Portraits en Médaillons dessinés par M. Cochin le fils," listed under number 179 in the *Explication des peintures, sculptures, et autres ouvrages*.
69 Using Michel's appendix, one can identify drawings that date to 1753 or earlier, and works that were engraved by 1754. Possible inclusions are: the Marquis de Marigny (engraved by Watelet, 1752); Bouchardon (listed in critics' commentary); Boucher (engraved by Cars, 1754); Jean-François de Troy, 1750 (listed in critics' commentary); Parrocel (engraved by Cochin, 1753); Pierre (engraved by Watelet, 1754); Silvestre, 1753; Vanloo (engraved by Daullé, 1754); Breteuil, 1752; Caylus (engraved by Cochin, 1752); La Live (engraved by La Live de Jully, 1754); Marquis de Voyer (engraved by Watelet, 1754); Watelet (engraved by Watelet, 1753); d'Alembert (engraved by Watelet, 1754); Leblanc, 1750, Marguerite Lecomte (engraved by Watelet, 1753); Benaglio, 1750; Cochin (engraved by Daullé, 1754); Jacquier, 1750 (mentioned by critics); Le Seur, 1750; Copette, 1753; Boutin (engraved by Watelet, 1752); Regny, 1751; Lady Hervey, 1752; and Mme Favart, 1753. See Michel, *Charles-Nicolas Cochin*, 617–26.
70 "[A] renfermé dans deux grands cadres les portraits de beaucoup de nos plus célèbres Maîtres et de plusieurs hommes illustres d'Italie." Antoine-Joseph Garrigues de Froment, *Sentimens d'un amateur sur l'exposition des tableaux du Louvre, & la critique qui en a été faite* (n.p., 1753), 42, http://catalogue.bnf.fr/ark:/12148/cb33601209q.
71 "[L]es Hommes illustres Modernes parmi lesquels sont avec justice ceux de presque tous les artistes dont on voit des ouvrages au Salon." Jacques-Gabriel Huquier, *Lettre sur l'exposition des tableaux au Louvre, avec des notes historiques*, 1753, 49, http://catalogue.bnf.fr/ark:/12148/cb30629516r.
72 "[L]es gens de lettres, les peintres, les sculpteurs et les amateurs des arts." Leblanc, *Observations*, 45.
73 Michel notes, "It is impossible today to indentify the models of a larger number of the non-engraved portraits, without doubt often little known friends or relations." ("Il est aujourd'hui impossible d'identifier les modèles d'une large partie des portraits non-gravés, sans doute souvent ceux des amis ou de relations de Cochin peu connus.") He limits his list of models, therefore, to those whose drawings were engraved. See Michel, *Charles-Nicolas Cochin*, 617. It is worth noting that Jombert explained it was necessary to separate the portrait medallions from the rest of Cochin's work in his introduction to them in his catalogue of Cochin's work. Jombert listed only 121 engravings; however, his catalogue is not complete, as Cochin lived and was quite productive after 1770. Jombert, *Catalogue de l'oeuvre de Ch. Nic. Cochin fils; écuyer, chevalier de l'Ordre du Roy* (Paris: Prault, 1770), 122–31.
74 R. Claude Catroux, "Hubert Robert et Mme Geoffrin," *Revue de l'art ancien et moderne* 40, no. 227 (1921): 40.

75 "Le Sr. Cochin pendant que les amateurs et les artistes s'assemblent chez Mad. Geoffrin un jour de la semaine les a dessinés de profil dans une forme de médaillon. Il s'est promis de les graver tous et de nous les donner pour mettre à la tête de ce Recueil de M. le Comte de Caylus. Le S. Cochin a dessiné plusieurs amateurs et plusieurs artistes qui sont reçus et très bien accueillis tous les Lundi. Madame Geoffrin donne chez elle un dîné appelé le dîné des Arts, et tandis que les uns sont à la conversation, le S. Cochin se recrée à dessiner ou ses confrères ou des amateurs, en sorte que son intention serait de les faire graver tous pour en faire une suite de portraits." Quoted in Charlotte Guichard, *Les amateurs d'art à Paris au XVIIIe siècle* (Paris: Champ Vallon, 2008), 220.

76 A list of the portraits owned by Geoffrin is found in the sale catalogue, R. Claude Catroux, *Catalogue de huit tableaux par Hubert Robert; quarante-trois dessins par Cochin, portraits du XVIIIe siècle provenant du salon de Madame Geoffrin et appartenant au comte de la Bedoyère* (Paris: Henri Baudoin et Jules Féral, 1921).

77 "[A]utant de têtes dignes en effet d'être frappées en Médailles, soit à cause de la célébrité des personnes qu'elles représentent, soit à cause de l'art avec lequel leur ressemblance y est rendu." Leblanc, *Observations*, 45–46.

78 Lilti, *Figures publiques*, 126.

79 "[P]ortraits au crayon de plusieurs hommes célèbres, la plûpart très-ressemblans, tous parfaitement dessinés." Lacombe, *Le salon*, 29.

80 "Cet habile Artiste ne brillera jamais mieux que dans ses Ouvrages ... La postérité ne peut manquer d'applaudir à l'entreprise noble et généreuse qu'il a formée de nous donner en Médaillon les Portraits de nos plus illustres Artistes ou Concitoyens. Elle pourra les contempler un jour dans ces monumens célèbres qui les rendront immortels, quand ils ne le seroient pas déja par leurs Ouvrages, et s'assûrer de les y trouver aussi vrais, aussi ressemblans que s'ils se montroient eux-mêmes à ses yeux." Guillaume Baillet de Saint-Julien, "Lettre de M. des R. à M. le Comte de ***," in *Lettre à Mr Chardin sur les caractères en peinture* (Geneva: n.p., 1753), 22, http://catalogue.bnf.fr/ark:/12148/cb30047451w.

81 For a list of these works, see Bell, *The Cult of the Nation in France*, 113.

82 La Live's portraits for this project can be found in Rés Ef 34 no. 51–101, Bibliothèque nationale de France, Département des estampes et de la photographie, Paris. He was assisted by Augustin de Saint-Aubin.

83 Bell, *The Cult of the Nation in France*, 116–17.

84 Ibid., 124.

85 Braudy, *The Frenzy of Renown*, 7.

86 See Chapter 4 of Lilti, *Figures publiques*.

87 Diderot and Falconet debated at length in the correspondence about whether it was better to be famous when alive or dead. Hume and Rousseau's falling out was greatly publicized, and Rousseau commented on his own issues with celebrity in the *Confessions*. Braudy, *The Frenzy of Renown*, 371–80.

88 "Je reviens au Sr. Cochin qui nous a donné dans ses crayons exposés au salon une prévue publique non seulement de son estime singulière pour tous hommes illustres, mais encore pour les amateurs des beaux arts dans quarante-six petits portraits en médaillons dessinés au premier trait. Je souhaite de tout mon cœur, et avec passion que j'ai pour tout ce qui peut honorer le mérite, que, malgré les grands ouvrages dont il est

chargé par la Cour avec tant de distinction, il puisse dérober quelques heures pour exécuter incessamment un projet qui immortalisera le peintre et les originaux, et qui sera délices de tous qui aiment à voir l'esprit et la vraie phisionomie des hommes dont ils admirent les ouvrages." La Font de Saint-Yenne, *Sentimens*, 176.

89 Michel, *Charles-Nicolas Cochin*, 617.

90 Twenty of the forty-three portraits Geoffrin owned were engraved. Ibid.

91 "J'ai retiré votre portrait de chez Mme de la Ferté-Imbault, fille de Mme Geoffrin. Je crois que je vous avais communiqué le projet que j'avais de lui proposer des trocs pour ravoir ces portraits de nos artistes. Mme Geoffrin m'avait promis de me les laisser par son testament, mais elle l'a oublié ou on le lui a fait obtenir. Quoi qu'il en soit, j'ai retiré le vôtre. Vous auriez peut-être envie que je vous le renvoyasse, mais comment arranger cela avec le désir que j'ai de donner tous ces portraits à l'Académie." Cochin to Descamps, 9 March 1778. Quoted in ibid., 121. According to Michel, forty-three of Cochin's medallion portraits were in Geoffrin's collection, including the portraits of Boucher, Chardin, Pierre, Vien, and Guay.

92 "J'aurais pu brûler [les lettres], mais je n'en ai pas eu la force: il m'est moins cruel de les remettres entre les mains qui m'ont tracé ces sacrés caractères." Mme Geoffrin to the King of Poland, 1768. Published in Stanislas Auguste Poniotowski and Marie-Thérèse Rodet Geoffrin, *Correspondance inédite du roi Stanislas-Auguste Poniatowski et de Madame Geoffrin (1764–1777)*, ed. Charles Moüy (Geneva: Slatkine Reprints, 1970), 347. Geoffrin and Stanislas had a close relationship that seems to have been broken during her visit to see him in Poland, perhaps because she was meddling in court affairs. Maurice Hamon, *Madame Geoffrin: femme d'influence, femme d'affaires au temps des Lumières* (Paris: Fayard, 2011), 442–88.

93 Geoffrin suffered an attack of erysipelas on August 28, 1776, that left her paralyzed for the final year of her life.

94 André Fontaine noted that these types of gifts were the driving force behind the growth of the Academy's collection. Over the course the eighteenth century, fewer artists were accepted to the Academy—and therefore there were fewer reception pieces—but donations grew. See Fontaine, *Les collections de l'Académie royale de peinture et de sculpture* (Paris: H. Laurens, 1910), 55–85.

95 Ibid., 70. In the same séance, Michel-François Dandré-Bardon offered his portrait by Alexandre Roslin (Salon of 1756).

96 Ibid.

97 See Williams, *Académie Royale*, appendix 1.

98 Ibid., Chapter 1.

99 Ibid., 103. For a visualization of the Academic hierarchy, see Table 2.1 in Williams's work.

100 As an engraver, Cochin was himself never the subject of a reception portrait, despite his relatively high position in the Royal Academy as *secrétaire perpetuel*, a position he attained in 1755. See Michel, *Charles-Nicolas Cochin*, 81–91.

101 Exceptions to this process were made for artists who were *agrée* and *reçu* on the same day, as in the example of Élisabeth Vigée-Lebrun and Adélaïde Labille-Guiard. In these cases, the reception piece was chosen from among the works the applicant had brought to the assembly.

102 On the *morceaux de réception* as a rite of passage, see Williams, *Académie Royale*, 92–112.

103 "[À] Messieurs et dames: Houdon; Casanova; Berthélemy, Callet, Ducreux; Rigaud; Bailly; Faujas de Saint-Fond; Soulavie; Baral; Mongoldier; Charles et Robert, frères; l'abbé Regley; Monjoie, peintre; Cochin; Pierre, premier peintre; Vien; Demours, sa femme et son fils; Vincent; Boizot; Nelson; Brérion, au Louvre; Gois; Brenet; Bachelier; Tardieu; Lépicié; Pajou; Belle; Monot, architecte; Doyen; Bridan; Pasquier; Greuze; Mme Guiart; Mme Lebrun; David; M. Piscatory; Voiriot; Wille; Lagrenée; Lagrenée le jeune, Renou, ——part; Guérin; Robert; Pigalle et son épouse; Sorbier; Fayol; Boulanger; Mouchy; Durameau; Roslin; Duplessis; Loir; Beaufort; Rouillé de l'Étang; Marigny; leurs portraits et miniatures." La Tour also left portraits to the actress Mlle Clairon and the economist and *encyclopédiste* François Véron Duverger de Forbonnais. Besnard, *La Tour*, 117.

104 On Vigée-Lebrun, see Mary D. Sheriff, *The Exceptional Woman: Elisabeth Vigée-Lebrun and the Cultural Politics of Art* (Chicago: University of Chicago Press, 1997); Joseph Baillio and Xavier Salmon, eds., *Élisabeth-Louise Vigée-Lebrun*, exh. cat. (Paris: Réunion des musées nationaux, 2015). On Labille-Guiard, see Anne-Marie Passez, *Adélaïde Labille-Guiard, 1749–1803: biographie et catalogue raisonné de son œuvre* (Paris: Arts et métiers graphiques, 1973); Melissa Hyde, "Under the Sign of Minerva: Adélaïde Labille-Guiard's Portrait of Madame Adélaïde," in *Women, Art and the Politics of Identity in Eighteenth Century Europe*, eds. Melissa Hyde and Jennifer Milam (Burlington, VT: Ashgate Publishing, 2003), 139–63; Laura Auricchio, *Adélaïde Labille-Guiard: Artist in the Age of Revolution* (Los Angeles: J. Paul Getty Museum, 2009).

105 Likely candidates include: Lady Hervey, 1752; Mme Favart, 1753; and Marguerite Lecomte (engraved by Watelet, 1753); see Michel, *Charles-Nicolas Cochin*, 617–26.

106 "[R]arement satisfaites d'elles dans leurs portraits," La Font de Saint-Yenne, *Sentimens*, 161. This was the portrait of Mme de Geli, who wrote to La Tour in September of 1753: "Receive, I ask, my very dear Monsieur, the most sincere compliment that has ever been given to you, about the beauty and success of your works ... you have raised my portrait to the height of perfection, it is the admiration and pleasure of Paris; the noise reverberates to my mountain. I will leave it one of these days, to go to the Louvre and appear, in public, to join my acclaim to theirs, and convince them that they have never been so right in their life." ("Recevez, je vous prie, mon très cher Monsieur, le plus sincère compliment qui vous ait jamais étté [sic] fait, sur la beauté et les succès de vos ouvrages ... vous avez éleves [sic] mon portrait au comble de la perfection, c'est l'admiration et le plaisir de tout Paris; le bruit en a retantit jusque sur ma montagne, ausy vai-je la quitter un de ses jours, pour aller au Louvre montrer ma figure, au public, joinder mes acclamation au leurs, et les convaincre, que de leur vie, ils ont jamais eut tant de raison.") Quoted in Charles Desmaze, *Le Reliquaire de M. Q. de La Tour, peintre du roi Louis XV, sa correspondance et son oeuvre* (Paris: Ernest Leroux, 1874), 22–23. Given the lack of discussion of her portrait in Salon criticism, she may have felt obligated to demonstrate her personal appreciation of the work.

107 La Font de Saint-Yenne, *Reflexions*, 23–24.

Chapter 3
RE-EVALUATING RIVALRY

1. "Voilà vraiment une triste lettre, faite pour dégoûter de la célébrité, surtout lorsqu'on a le malheur d'être femme." Louise-Élisabeth Vigée-Lebrun, *Souvenirs de Mme. Louise-Élisabeth Vigée-Le Brun: notes et portraits, 1755–1789*, ed. Pierre de Nolhac, 2 vols. (Paris: A. Fayard, 1835), 1:113.
2. See, for example, Mary D. Sheriff, *The Exceptional Woman: Elisabeth Vigée-Lebrun and the Cultural Politics of Art* (Chicago: University of Chicago Press, 1997); Laura Auricchio, "Self-Promotion in Adélaïde Labille-Guiard's 1785 *Self-Portrait with Two Students*," *The Art Bulletin* 9, no. 1 (March 2007): 45–62.
3. This antagonism became first evident in the decision, in 1706, to exclude women from membership completely. This rule, however, was never validated by royal decree and thus was not strictly followed. In 1770, Jean-Baptiste Pierre limited the number of women accepted to four. This was reinforced after the acceptance of Vigée-Lebrun and Labille-Guiard. See Sheriff, *The Exceptional Woman*, 78–79; Laura Auricchio, *Adélaïde Labille-Guiard: Artist in the Age of Revolution* (Los Angeles: J. Paul Getty Museum, 2009), 29; Séverine Sofio, *Artistes femmes. Parenthèse enchantée XVIII–XIXe siècle: La parenthèse enchantée XVIIIe–XIXe siècles* (Paris: CNRS Éditions, 2016); Paris Amanda Spies-Gans, "Exceptional, but Not Exceptions: Public Exhibitions and the Rise of the Woman Artist in London and Paris, 1760–1830," *Eighteenth-Century Studies* 51, no. 4 (2018): 404–6.
4. On this point, see Melissa Hyde, "Women and the Visual Arts in the Age of Marie-Antoinette," in *Anne Vallayer-Coster: Painter to the Court of Marie-Antoinette*, ed. Eik Kahng (New Haven, CT: Dallas Museum of Art and Yale University Press, 2002), 75–93. For a broader view of women artists in the eighteenth century, see Sofio, *Artistes femmes. Parenthèse enchantée XVIII–XIXe siècle*.
5. Hannah Williams and Chris Sparks, *Artists in Paris: Mapping the Eighteenth-Century Art World*, www.artistsinparis.org (accessed October 13, 2019).
6. Spies-Gans, "Exceptional, but Not Exceptions."
7. Vigée-Lebrun famously exhibited history paintings at her first Salon in 1783, which has been addressed by Mary Sheriff in *The Exceptional Woman*, 120–29.
8. "Ces deux rivales marchent à grands pas vers la perfection." *Le Véridique au Sallon* (Paris: Chez Cailleau; Chez Petit, 1783), 19, https://catalogue.bnf.fr/ark:/12148/cb33640088w.
9. Sheriff, *The Exceptional Woman*, 185–89; Auricchio, *Adélaïde Labille-Guiard*, 24. There was a third woman showing alongside Vigée-Lebrun and Labille-Guiard, Anne Vallayer-Coster, but Vallayer-Coster's earlier acceptance in the Academy—thirteen years before Labille-Guiard and Vigée-Lebrun—seems to have separated her from her more junior female colleagues.
10. Hannah Williams, *Académie Royale: A History in Portraits* (Burlington, VT: Ashgate, 2015), 284–92.
11. Melissa L. Hyde, "Élisabeth Vigée-Lebrun (review)," *Early Modern Women*, 11, no. 2 (Spring 2017): 189.
12. "Je n'ignorais pas qu'une femme artiste, qui s'est toujours montrée mon ennemie, je ne sais pourquoi, avait essayé, par tous les moyens imaginables, de me noircir dans l'esprit de ces princesses..." Vigée-Lebrun, *Souvenirs*, 2:143.

13 Hyde, "Élisabeth Vigée-Lebrun," 189.
14 On these debates, see Christine Roulston, "Separating the Inseparables: Female Friendship and Its Discontents in Eighteenth-Century France," *Eighteenth-Century Studies* 32, no. 2 (Winter 1998/1999): 215–31; David Garrioch, "From Christian Friendship to Secular Sentimentality: Enlightenment Re-Evaluations," in *Friendship: A History*, ed. Barbara Caine (London: Equinox, 2009), 165–214; Julie Candler Hayes, "Friendship and the Female Moralist," *Studies in Eighteenth-Century Culture* 39, no. 1 (March 2010): 171–89; Lewis C. Seifert and Rebecca May Wilkin, eds., *Men and Women Making Friends in Early Modern France* (Burlington, VT: Ashgate, 2015).
15 "Besides, to tell the truth, the ordinary capacity of women is inadequate for that communion and fellowship which is the nurse of this sacred bond; nor does their soul seem firm enough to endure the strain of so tight and durable a knot." Michel de Montaigne, "Of Friendship," in *The Complete Essays of Montaigne*, trans. Donald M. Frame (Stanford, CA: Stanford University Press, 1965), 138.
16 "[E]lles s'unissent par nécessité, et jamais par goût." Anne-Thérèse de Marguenat de Courcelles, "De l'amitié," in *Avis d'une mère a son fils et a sa fille, et autres ouvrages de Madame la Marquise de Lambert; avec un abregé de sa vie* (Paris: Chez Jean Neaulme, 1748), 28.
17 "Une honnête femme a les vertus des hommes, l'amitié, la probité, la fidélité à ses devoirs: une femme aimable doit avoir non seulement les grâces extérieures, mais les grâces du cœur et des sentiments." Ibid., 68.
18 Anne Vincent-Buffault, *L'exercice de l'amitié: pour une histoire des pratiques amicales aux XVIIIe et XIXe siècles* (Paris: Éditions du Seuil, 1995), 91–92. As Julie Candler Hayes notes, Thiroux d'Arconville believed that friendship between men and women was only possible in old age or in other situations in which passion was no longer an issue. Hayes, "Friendship and the Female Moralist," 180.
19 See here especially the essays in Seifert and Wilkin, *Men and Women Making Friends in Early Modern France*.
20 Roulston, "Separating the Inseparables," 217.
21 Given that Labille-Guiard's family home was listed on the Rue Neuve des Petits Champs and she was baptized in the parish of Saint Eustache, her family home must have been on the blocks between Rue Richelieu and Place des Victoires, as Rue Richelieu was the boundary for the parish. The domicile was likely on the south side of the street, as much of the north side was occupied by royal and religious buildings.
22 Auricchio, *Adélaïde Labille-Guiard*, 8–11.
23 Joachim Lebreton, *Nécrologie. Notice sur Madame Vincent, née Labille, peintre* (Paris, 1803), 1.
24 On debt and the fashion industry in eighteenth-century Paris, see Clare Haru Crowston, *Credit, Fashion, Sex: Economies of Regard in Old Regime France* (Durham, NC: Duke University Press, 2013).
25 "Vente de fonds de Boutique Claude Edme Labille à Josephe Blondelu 18 septembre 1761," Minutier Central, MC/ET/LXXXIV/478, Archives nationales, Paris. The first reference to Labille as a *receveur* is in a report in the *Gazette de Paris* on April 29, 1758, about the first drawing of the lottery, wherein winning tickets were described as having been purchased "at the Bureau of sieur Labille, rue Neuve des Petits-Champs" ("pris au

Bureau du sieur Labille, rue Neuve des Petits-Champs"). Labille is mentioned again as having sold tickets for the drawing on June 19, 1761, in the Minutier Central, MC/ET/LXXXIV/47712.

26. The first year of the lottery had sales of two million livres, two-thirds of which were from Paris. The average receiver in Paris would have made about 833 livres a year from the lottery in the first year, and sales would nearly double over the next twenty years. On the *lotérie*, see Robert Kruckeberg, "The Wheel of Fortune in Eighteenth-Century France: The Lottery, Consumption, and Politics" (PhD diss., University of Michigan, 2009).

27. Auricchio, *Adélaïde Labille-Guiard*, 11; Anne-Marie Passez, *Adélaïde Labille-Guiard, 1749–1803; biographie et catalogue raisonné de son œuvre* (Paris: Arts et métiers graphiques, 1973), 8.

28. Auricchio, *Adélaïde Labille-Guiard*, Chapters 1 and 2; Elizabeth Mansfield, *The Perfect Foil: François-André Vincent and the Revolution in French Painting* (Minneapolis: University of Minnesota Press, 2012), Chapter 5.

29. Auricchio, *Adélaïde Labille-Guiard*, 11.

30. Joseph Baillio and Xavier Salmon, eds., *Élisabeth Louise Vigée Le Brun* (Paris: Réunion des musées nationaux, 2015), 13–14.

31. "During this time, my father brought together many artists and some men of letters in the evenings ..." ("A cette époque, mon père réunissait les soirs plusieurs artistes et quelques gens de lettres ...") Ibid., 14.

32. "From the age of fifteen, I was accepted into high society; I knew our greatest artists, ensuring that I received invitations everywhere. I remember well the first time I dined at the sculptor Lemoyne's house who had a great reputation at that time." ("Dès l'âge de quinze ans, j'avais répandue dans la haute société; je connaissais nos premiers artistes, en sorte que je recevais des invitations de toutes parts. Je me souviens fort bien que j'ai dîné en ville pour la première fois chez le sculpteur Lemoyne, alors en grande réputation.") Vigée-Lebrun, *Souvenirs*, 1:39. On Lemoyne's addresses, see Hannah Williams and Chris Sparks, *Artists in Paris*.

33. Bernadette Fort, "Les *Souvenirs* d'Élisabeth Vigée-Lebrun: distinction and sociabilité dans une *Vie* d'artiste," in *Artistes, savants et amateurs: art et sociabilité au XVIIIe siècle (1715–1815)*, eds. Jessica L. Fripp, Amandine Gorse, Nathalie Manceau, and Nina Struckmeyer (Paris: Mare et Martin, 2016), 249–63.

34. See Sofio, *Artistes femmes*, 63–70; Auricchio, *Adélaïde Labille-Guiard*, 8–11, 26–30.

35. Anatole de Montaiglon, *Procès-verbaux de l'Académie royale de peinture et de sculpture 1648–1793* (Paris: Libraires de la société, 1889), 9:152–53.

36. Ibid., 9:154.

37. Sheriff, *The Exceptional Woman*, 73–99.

38. Vigée-Lebrun wrote in her *Souvenirs*, "M. Pierre then spread rumors that it was by an order of the Court that I was received. I think that the King and Queen had been good enough to want to see me enter the Academy, but that is all." Quoted in Sheriff, *The Exceptional Woman*, 76. For a recent example of a straightforward acceptance of the royal order/voting process story, see Xavier Salmon, *Pastel du Musée du Louvre XVIIe–XVIIIe siècles* (Paris: Musée du Louvre; Éditions Hazan, 2018), 154.

39. "[R]epoussa avec force ce moyen oblique, declarant qu'elle voulait être jugée et non protégée." Lebreton, *Nécrologie*, 4, 7.

40 This point is made apparent by the majority of catalogue raisonnés of male artists, which rarely—if ever—describe their receptions in comparison to other artists. Furthermore, the idea of the "surprise invader," as described by Thomas Crow, celebrates the unusual receptions of artists, such as Antoine Watteau and Jean-Baptiste Greuze, rather than calling them into question. Thomas E. Crow, *Painters and Public Life in Eighteenth-Century Paris* (New Haven, CT: Yale University Press, 1985).

41 Mansfield, *The Perfect Foil*, 1–21.

42 "Lemoyne était d'une simplicité extrême; mais il avait le bon goût de rassembler chez lui une foule d'hommes célèbres et distingués; ses deux filles faisaient parfaitement les honneurs de sa maison.... C'est chez Lemoyne que j'ai connu Gerbier, le célèbre avocat; sa fille, Mme de Roissy, était fort belle, et c'est une des premières femmes dont j'aie fait le portrait. Nous avions souvent, à ces dîners, Grétry, Latour, fameux peintre au pastel; on rirait, on s'amusait." Vigée-Lebrun, *Souvenirs*, 1:39–40.

43 "le double intérêt qu'il présente, en offrant les traits d'un Artiste qui s'est fait admirer successivement aux dernier Salons, par les statues de Bossuer [sic], Descartes et Pascal et ceux du célèbre Lemoine, dont M. Pajou fut l'élève & l'ami, & dont il est en effet l'émule." *Nouvelles de la république des lettres et des arts* (February 26, 1783), 69.

44 The portrait was always listed under this title, never as *Portrait de M. Pajou*. See the *Nouvelles de la république des lettres et des arts* for February 12, 19, and 22, 1783, and entry no. 125 in the 1783 Salon *livret*.

45 "O le beau buste que celui de Monsieur Lemoyne, il vit, il pense, il regarde, il voit, il entend, il va parler." Quoted in Passez, *Adélaïde Labille-Guiard*, 109.

46 James David Draper, et al., *Pajou: sculpteur du Roi, 1730–1809* (Paris: Réunion des musées nationaux, 1997), 70.

47 Malcolm Baker, *The Marble Index: Roubiliac and Sculptural Portraiture in Eighteenth-Century Britain* (New Haven, CT: Yale University Press, 2014), 101–2.

48 Ronit Milano has argued that using modern clothing or drapery was common on sculptures that were meant to remain in the private realm. See Milano, *The Portrait Bust and French Cultural Politics in the Eighteenth Century* (Leiden: Brill, 2015), Chapter 1.

49 Vigée-Lebrun's *Self-Portrait in a Straw Hat*, for example, references but is by no means a copy of Peter Paul Rubens's *Portrait of Susanna Lunden* (*Le Chapeau de Paille*). See Sheriff, *The Exceptional Woman*, 208–15.

50 "Sans pinceau, le doigt seul place & fond chaque teinte." Claude-Henri Watelet, *L'art de peindre, poëme avec des Réflexions sur les différentes parties de la peinture* (Paris: H.-L. Guérin et L.-F. Delatour, 1760), 52.

51 "... ils la travailloient, ainsi que les modernes, avec l'ébauchoir: mais il se servoient aussi des doigts, et même des ongles, pour rendre les parties les plus délicates.... Quand on vouloit exprimer que l'opération la plus difficile étoit terminer, on disoit, *le moment où la terre glaise est sous* l'ongle." Claude-Henri Watelet and Pierre-Charles Lévesque, *Dictionnaire des art de peinture, sculpture et gravure* (Paris: Prault, 1792), 5: 549–50.

52 "On n'a pas besoin de beaucoup d'outils; car c'est avec ses mains qu'on commence & qu'on avance le plus son ouvrage." "Modeler en terre ou en cire," in *Encyclopédie, ou dictionnaire raisonné des sciences, des arts et des métiers, etc.*, eds. Denis Diderot and Jean le Rond d'Alembert. University of Chicago, ARTFL Encyclopédie Project (Autumn 2017 Edition), eds. Robert Morrissey and Glenn Roe, http://encyclopedie.uchicago.edu/.

53. Mary D. Sheriff, *Moved by Love: Inspired Artists and Deviant Women in Eighteenth-Century France* (Chicago: University of Chicago Press, 2004), 137–41.
54. Quoted in James David Draper and Guilhem Scherf, *Playing with Fire: European Terracotta Models, 1740–1840* (New Haven, CT: Metropolitan Museum of Art; Réunion des Musées Nationaux; Yale University Press, 2004), 2.
55. Ewa Lajer-Burcharth, *The Painter's Touch: Boucher, Chardin, Fragonard* (Princeton, NJ: Princeton University Press, 2018), 3.
56. See especially her discussion of Boucher's copies. Ibid., 13–22.
57. Melissa Hyde, "The Make-Up of the Marquise," in *Making Up the Rococo: François Boucher and His Critics* (Los Angeles: Getty Publishing, 2006), 83–106. Ewa Lajer-Burcharth, "Pompadour's Touch: Difference in Representation," *Representations* 73, no. 1 (2001): 54–88.
58. Sheriff, *The Exceptional Woman*, 185–89.
59. Most notably, Vigée-Lebrun's history paintings were used to view her (and all women painters) as hermaphrodites; in other words, as monstrous. Ibid., 189–95.
60. She had previously exhibited a number of these portraits, as well as portraits of François-André Vincent, at the Salon de la Correspondance. For provenance and display histories of these works, see Passez, *Adélaïde Labille-Guiard*.
61. Ibid., 16.
62. Sophie Join-Lambert and Anne Leclair, *Joseph-Benoît Suvée 1743–1807* (Paris: Arthena, 2017), 23–24.
63. Ibid., 32.
64. Passez, *Adélaïde Labille-Guiard*, 151; Neil Jeffares, "Carraux de Rosemond, Marie-Marguerite, Mme Jean-Guillaume Bervic," in *Dictionary of Pastellists before 1800* (online), updated Feburary 19, 2019, http://www.pastellists.com/Articles/Carreaux.pdf.
65. "Observations sur les ouvrages de peinture et sculpture exposés au Salon du Louvre, le 25 août 1783," *L'année littéraire*, no. 6 (1783): 262–66.
66. Allan Silver, "Historical Moments of Friendship Ideals: David & Jonathan, Montaigne, Adam Smith," in *Conceptualizing Friendship in Time and Place*, eds. Carla Risseeuw and Marlein Raalte (Leiden: Brill, 2017), 132–39.
67. Dena Goodman, *The Republic of Letters: A Cultural History of the French Enlightenment* (Ithaca, NY: Cornell University Press, 1996), 54–56. See also Silver, "Historical Moments of Friendship Ideals," 135.
68. Roulston, "Separating the Inseparables," 217.
69. Sheriff, *The Exceptional Woman*, 47–48.
70. Vigée-Lebrun, *Souvenirs*, 1:98–103.
71. Sheriff, *The Exceptional Woman*, 175. See also Roulston, "Separating the Inseparables," 224–27; and Meredith Martin, *Dairy Queens: The Politics of Pastoral Architecture from Catherine de' Medici to Marie-Antoinette* (Cambridge, MA: Harvard University Press, 2011), 164–66.
72. On Labille-Guiard's acceptance, see Auricchio, *Adélaïde Labille-Guiard*, 29.
73. Chevalier Louis de Jaucourt, "Display, Testimony of Friendship," *The Encyclopedia of Diderot & d'Alembert Collaborative Translation Project*, trans. Warren Roby and Martha Zumack (Ann Arbor: Michigan Publishing, University of Michigan Library, 2011), http://hdl.handle.net/2027/spo.did2222.0002.598 (accessed November 4, 2018).

Originally published as "Démonstration, Témoignage d'amitié," *Encyclopédie ou Dictionnaire raisonné des sciences, des arts et des métiers*, 4:822 (Paris, 1754).
74 Auricchio, *Adélaïde Labille-Guiard*, 34–37.
75 *Nouvelles de la république des lettres et des arts* 12 (March 19, 1783): 94–95.
76 These were portraits of the Comtesse de Flahaut and her son, Madame Dupin de Saint-Julien, and the Comtesse de Clermont Tonnere. See Passez, *Adélaïde Labille-Guiard*, 142–44, and Auricchio, *Adélaïde Labille-Guiard*, 39–40.
77 "C'est un homme que cette femme-là, étend-je dire sans cesse à mon Oreille." *Avis important d'une Femme, sur le Sallon de 1785. Par Madame E.A.R.T.L.A.D.C.S. Dédié aux femmes* (1785), 30, https://catalogue.bnf.fr/ark:/12148/cb443108228.
78 "Ce portrait, composé dans le genre de l'histoire, et dans lequel on reconnaît une touche vigoureuse, fait honneur au talent de l'Artiste." *Observations critiques sur les tableaux du Sallon, de l'année 1785 pour servir de suite au discours sur la peinture* (Paris: Chez les Marchands de Nouveautés, 1785), 19, https://catalogue.bnf.fr/ark:/12148/cb44309328x.
79 Laura Auricchio, "Self-Promotion in Adelaide Labille-Guiard's 1785 *Self-Portrait with Two Students*," *Art Bulletin* 89, no. 1 (2007): 45–62; Auricchio, *Adélaïde Labille-Guiard*, 47.
80 Arnauld Doria, *Gabrielle Capet* (Paris: Les Beaux-arts, 1934), 3; Jeffares, "Carraux de Rosemond."
81 "[A]u nombre de neuf, toutes jolies et aimables forment entre elles l'assemblage de neuf muses au berceau dont Mme Guyard est l'institutrice." Quoted in Passez, *Adélaïde Labille-Guiard*, 21.
82 Roulston, "Separating the Inseparables," 218.
83 Detroit Institute of the Arts, *French Painting 1774–1830: The Age of Revolution* (Detroit: Wayne State University Press, 1975), 557; Auricchio, *Adélaïde Labille-Guiard*, 43.
84 Two versions of the bust exist. The marble version was in Labille-Guiard's collection at the time of her death, eventually ending up in the hands of Pajou's son Jacques-Augustin Catherine, who was a student of Vincent's. The terracotta model for this bust was in the collection of the grandson of one of Pajou's students, Augustin Dumont. Draper, et al., *Pajou*, 258–59.
85 "À ton père, Guyard, j'avois jeté des fleurs"; "(On a été heureux de render cet homage au père d'une artiste aussi aimable que sensible.) C'est bien lui prouver qu'on s'occupoit d'elle." Antoine-Joseph Gorsas, *Deuxième promenade de Critès au Sallon* (London, 1785), 36, https://catalogue.bnf.fr/ark:/12148/cb44309388s.
86 Auricchio, *Adélaïde Labille-Guiard*, 47; Auricchio, "Self-Promotion in Adélaïde Labille-Guiard's 1785 *Self-Portrait with Two Students*." On Gorsas's politics and criticism, see Crow, *Painters and Public Life in Eighteenth-Century Paris*, 184.
87 Draper, et al., *Pajou*, 258–59.
88 Kathryn Tempest, *Cicero: Politics and Persuasion in Ancient Rome* (London: Bloomsbury Academic, 2014), 63.
89 See the chronology in Draper, et al., *Pajou*, 389, 393.
90 "She was provisionally accepted and fully accepted the same day and the portrait of Monsieur Pajou served as her reception piece, but her noble ambition was not yet satisfied, she asked the Academy, as a favor, to give her permission to make a large portrait in oil of one of its members, of the assembly's choice, to which they agreed."

("[E]lle a été agréé et reçue le même jour et le portrait de Mr Pajou en demeure pour morceau de réception, mais sa noble ambition n'étant pas encore satisfaite, elle a demandé a l'académie comme faveur qu'il lui fut permis de faire, à l'huile un portrait en grand d'un de ses members, au choix d'assemblee, ce qui lui a été accordé . . .") François-André Vincent to Saint Ours, 15 June 1783, published in Jean Pierre Cuzin, *Vincent entre Fragonard et David* (Paris: Arthena, 2013), 536.

91 "Ce Tableau appartient à M. Cochin"; "Ce Tableau appartient à M. Vernet." *Explication des peintures, sculptures et gravures, de Messieurs de l'Académie royale* (Paris: Veuve Héissant, 1785), cat. nos. 99 and 100.

92 "[The portrait of] M. Vanloo has great beauty, a firm and bold touch. This artist had very distinguished and very rare talents, because she knows how to combine the grace of her sex with the vigor and force that characterize the works of men." ("Celui de M. Vanloo est d'une grande beauté, d'une touche ferme et hardie. Cette Artiste est d'une mérite très distingué et très rare, puisqu'elle a su joindre aux grâce de son sexe la vigueur et la force caractérisent les Ouvrages de l'homme.") *Le peintre anglais au salon de peintures, exposées au Louvre en l'année 1785* (1785), 24, https://catalogue.bnf.fr/ark:/12148/cb44306614b; "Among all the portraits of Mme Guiard, the ones of M. Vernet and M. Amedée Vanloo have inspired all the applause. M. Vanloo speaks, reacts and truly emerges from her painting." ("Parmi tous les Portraits de Mme Guiard, celui de Mr. Vernet et celui de Mr Amedée Vanloo ont excité tous les applaudissements. Mr. Vanloo parle, agit et sort vraiment de son Tableau.") Louis Bonnefoy de Bouyon, *Minos au Sallon, ou La Gazette infernale: Par M. L. B. D. B.* (Gattieres, 1785), 22, https://catalogue.bnf.fr/ark:/12148/cb44310875v.

93 "[C'est aujourd'hui madame Guyard dès-lors la serrant de près] qui triomphe et fait entourer ses productions avec ces cris de surprise et de ravissement involontaires qui ne s'arrachent que par un mérite réel et éclatant." "Seconde lettre," *Mémoires secrets* 30 (September 1785): 160.

94 "Les autres portraits fait par cette académicienne caractérisent un pinceau sévère, plus propre à rendre les têtes pesantes et profondément occupée que les affections frivoles des gens du monde. Elle nous offre un Amedée Vanloo, un Vernet, un Cochin, trois artistes qui prêtent rien moins qu'aux grâces et à la gentillesse du faire, mais exigeant une touche réfléchie et vigoureuse." Ibid., 160–61.

95 "Il n'en est pas de même de madame le Brun, se vouant aux plus jolies femmes de la cour, aux plus galantes et les servant de tous les agréments de son pinceau." Ibid., 161.

96 Nina Kushner, *Erotic Exchanges: The World of Elite Prostitution in Eighteenth-Century Paris* (Ithaca, NY: Cornell University Press, 2016), 3–6.

97 "Il y a encore moins qui ont l'art d'enchanter autant la public par de séduisantes productions." Abbé de Fontenay, *Observations sur le Sallon de 1785. Extraites du Journal général de France* (1785), 18, https://catalogue.bnf.fr/ark:/12148/cb44309607s.

98 See the following volumes of the *Mémoires secrets*: 30 (February 8, 1786): 90–91; 32 (August 14, 1786): 268–69; 33 (October 10, 1786): 100; and 34 (April 1787): 388.

99 On Calonne and France's finances leading to the Revolution, see Vivian R. Gruder, *The Notables and the Nation: The Political Schooling of the French, 1787–1788* (Cambridge, MA: Harvard University Press, 2007).

100 On the Diamond Necklace Affair, see Sara Maza, "The Diamond Necklace Affair

101 "C'est dans cette occasion qu'elle s'est rendue la plus entièrement maîtresse de son sujet." *Avis important d'une Femme*, 30. See the discussion in Sheriff, *Exceptional Woman*, 187. Rumors of her sexual impropriety also involved her relationship with the painter Guillaume Ménageot, who rented lodging from the Lebruns. One critic did not even discuss Vigée-Lebrun's works at the 1785 Salon, instead only rehashing comments made about her 1783 work. He ended with the comment, "but when I see Mme Le Brun paint history, I think I see the club of Hercules tied by the hand of the graces" ("... mais lorsque je vois Mme. Le Brun peindre l'histoire, je crois voir la massue d'Hercule souliée par la main des grâces"). This is possibly a reference to Ménageot, who displayed *Alceste rendue à son mari par Hercule* at the Salon of 1785 (n. 20). *Discours sur l'origine, les progress et l'état actuel de la peinture en France* (Paris: les Marchands de Nouveautés, 1785), 28, https://catalogue.bnf.fr/ark:/12148/cb33350789v.

102 "Mistress signifies girls and women who are sought after for marriage or simply the loves of someone." ("Maîtresse se dit Des filles & des femmes qui sont recherchées en mariage, ou simplement aimées de quelqu'un.") *Le Dictionnaire de l'Académie française*. Quatrième Édition. T.2 1762, https://artfl-project.uchicago.edu/content/dictionnaires-dautrefois (accessed November 8, 2018).

103 For example, Lajer-Burcharth, "Pompadour's Touch"; Sheriff, *Moved by Love*; Mechthild Fend, *Fleshing Out Surfaces: Skin in French Art and Medicine, 1650–1850* (Manchester: Manchester University Press, 2017).

104 Sheriff, *Moved by Love*, 201–40.

105 See Lajer-Burcharth, "Pompadour's Touch"; Hyde, "The 'Make-Up' of the Marquise."

106 "Bien que d'un bel objet l'amour prenne naissance, L'œil ne peut toutesfois contanter un Amant; Car de celle qu'il sert cherchant la jouissance, Il n'y peut arriver que par l'Attouchement."

107 "[D]e tous les artistes que j'ai connus, Robert était le plus répandu dans le monde." Vigée-Lebrun, *Souvenirs*, 1:234.

108 Pontus Grate, "Hubert Robert et l'iconographie d'Augustin Pajou," *Gazette des beaux-arts* (July/August 1985): 7–14; Guillaume Faroult and Catherine Voiriot, *Hubert Robert, 1733–1808: un peintre visionnaire* (Paris: Somogy, 2016), 121.

109 Auricchio, *Adélaïde Labille-Guiard*, 49–50.

110 See Mary Vidal, "The 'Other Atelier': Jacques-Louis David's Female Students," in *Women, Art and the Politics of Identity in Eighteenth-Century Europe*, eds. Melissa Hyde and Jennifer Milam (Burlington, VT: Ashgate, 2003), 237–62.

Chapter 4
FRIENDSHIP ABROAD

1 Numbers 189–201 in *Explication des peintures, sculptures et gravures, de Messieurs de l'Académie Royale* (Paris, Veuve Herissant, 1777).

2 "Destiné à faire de grandes choses, je crains qu'il ne perde son tems à faire des Portraits." *La Prêtresse ou nouvelle manière de prédire ce qui est arrivé* (Rome and Paris: les Marchands de Nouveautés, 1777), 20, http://catalogue.bnf.fr/ark:/12148/cb42340521f.

3 The Prix de Rome was originally for painters and sculptors only. A prize in architecture was added in 1717. Reed Benhamou, *Charles-Joseph Natoire and the Académie de France in Rome: A Re-evaluation* (Oxford: Voltaire Foundation, 2015), 61–62. For a more general history of the Rome Academy, see Henry Lapauze, *Histoire de l'Académie de France à Rome: 1666–1801* (Paris: Plon, 1924), 2 vols.; Jean Paul Alaux, *Académie de France à Rome, ses directeurs, ses pensionnaires* (Paris: Éditions Duchartre, 1933).

4 Benhamou, *Charles-Joseph Natoire*, 62.

5 "S. Vincent a fait quelques portraits dernièrement d'un très bon goût; il me paroît que ce sera la partie où il voudra le plus s'occuper." Anatole de Montaiglon and Jules Guiffrey, *Correspondance des directeurs de l'Académie de France à Rome avec les surintendants des bâtiments*, vol. 13 (Paris: Jean Schemit, 1904), 63. As has been noted, Natoire's dislike for Vincent may also have been caused by Vincent's Protestantism, which had not been revealed to the director until the artist's arrival in Rome. Vincent most likely kept his faith a secret, as it would have made him ineligible to win the Prix de Rome. Pierre-Jean-Baptiste Chaussard, *Le Pausanias français; État des Arts du Dessin en France à l'Ouverture du XIXe Siècle* (Paris: Imprimerie de Demonville, 1806), 99.

6 Elizabeth Mansfield, *The Perfect Foil: François-André Vincent and the Revolution in French Art* (Minneapolis: University of Minnesota, 2012), 55–56.

7 Benhamou, *Charles-Joseph Natoire*, 95. According to Henry Lapauze, the first group of *pensionnaires*, sent in the 1660s, were married. But married *pensionnaires* were rare in the eighteenth century—so much so that the married painter and Prix de Rome winner Jean-Baptiste Frédéric Desmarais wrote to the Comte D'Angiviller in 1783 to remind the *surintendant des bâtiments* that there was no law against married men staying as a *pensionnaire*. See Lapauze, *Histoire de l'Académie de France à Rome*, 1:395. On the homosocial context of Rome, see Eugenio Sonnino, "In the Male City: The 'Status Animarum' of Rome in the Seventeenth Century," in *Socio-Economic Consequences of Sex-Ratios in Historical Perspective, 1500–1900*, eds. Antoinette Fauve-Chamoux and Sølvi Sogner (Milan: Università Bocconi, 1994), 23; Eugenio Sonnino, "The Population in Baroque Rome," in *Rome–Amsterdam: Two Growing Cities in Seventeenth-Century Europe*, ed. Peter van Kessel (Amsterdam: Amsterdam University Press, 1997), 65–66.

8 William M. Reddy, *The Navigation of Feeling: A Framework for the History of Emotions* (Cambridge: Cambridge University Press, 2001), 149; Alexandra Shepard, *Meanings of Manhood in Early Modern England* (Oxford: Oxford University Press, 2003), 96.

9 "Je serais trop heureux si tous pouvaient être persuadés de la sincérité des sentiments qu'ils m'ont inspiré … Adieu, mon cher ami je t'embrasse de tout mon cœur et suis pour la vie ton ami." Henry Lemonnier, "Suvée et ses amis à l'école de Rome," *Gazette des beaux-arts* 30 (August 1903): 103.

10 "Combien de fois je les ai vus, dans un âge avancé et rassemblés tous trois, comme à Rome dans l'atelier de l'un d'eux ou plus souvent encore dans un joyeux dîner, rire aux éclats au récit de leur mille folies et même de leurs amours …" Charles-Nicolas Duchange, "Berthélemy, peintre Laonnois (1743–1811)," *Bulletin de la Société académique de Laon*, 3: séance du 4 janvier 1853, 1854, 90.

11 On misrule, see Natalie Zemon Davis, "The Reasons of Misrule: Youth Groups and Charivaris in Sixteenth-Century France," *Past and Present* 50, no. 1 (1971): 41–75; Robert Darnton, *The Great Cat Massacre and Other Episodes in French Cultural History*

(New York: Basic Books, 1984), 75–106; Alexandra Shepard, *Meanings of Manhood in Early Modern England* (Oxford: Oxford University Press, 2003), 93–126.

12 Shepard, *Meanings of Manhood*, 96.

13 Jean-Pierre Cuzin, *François-André Vincent 1746–1816 entre Fragonard et David* (Paris: Arthéna, 2013), 358–61; 387–404. Cuzin first wrote on these drawings in an article, "Les caricatures de Vincent," *L'Information d'histoire de l'art* 16 (1971): 91–94. See also Mansfield, *The Perfect Foil*, 57–60.

14 Suzanne Boorsch, "The *Recueil de Caricatures* by La Live de Jully after Saly," *Yale University Art Gallery Bulletin* (2004): 69–83; Perrin Stein, "Etching in the Eternal City," in Perrin Stein, ed., *Artists and Amateurs: Etching in Eighteenth-Century France*, exh. cat. (New York: Metropolitan Museum of Art, 2013), 142. On Ghezzi, see Anthony M. Clark, "Pier Leone Ghezzi's Portraits," in Edgar Peters Bowron, ed., *Paragone* 165, no. 14 (1965): 11–21; Michael Benisovich, "Ghezzi and French Artists in Rome," *Apollo* 85 (May 1967): 340–47; Edward J. Olszewski, "The New World of Pier Leone Ghezzi," *Art Journal* 43, no. 4 (December 1983): 325–30.

15 The sole original caricature drawing by Jean-Baptiste Stouf is in the Musée d'art et d'archéologie, Besançon (collection Pâris, D.2994). There exists no biographical information on Moricaud Franconville, and these etchings are the only known examples of his work.

16 Ségolène Le Men, ed., *L'art de la caricature* (Paris: Presses universitaires de Paris-Ouest, 2011); Nadine Orenstein, *Infinite Jest: Caricature and Satire from Leonardo to Levine* (New York: Metropolitan Museum of Art, 2011); Todd Porterfield, ed., *The Efflorescence of Caricature, 1759–1838* (Burlington, VT: Ashgate, 2011); Colin Jones and Emily Richardson, eds., *The Saint-Aubin* Livre de caricatures*: Drawing Satire in Eighteenth-Century Paris* (Oxford: Voltaire Foundation, 2012); Elizabeth Mansfield and Kelly Malone, eds., *Seeing Satire in the Eighteenth Century* (Oxford: Voltaire Foundation, 2013).

17 Laurent Baridon and Marial Guédron, for example, mention Vincent's caricatures in *L'Art et l'histoire de la caricature des origines à nos jours* (Paris: Citadelle et Mazenod, 2009), and in "Caricaturer l'art: usages et fonctions de la parodie" in Le Men, *L'art de la caricature*, 87–108.

18 Cuzin, *Françoise-André Vincent*, 67

19 Thomas E. Crow, *Emulation: Making Artists for Revolutionary France* (New Haven, CT: Yale University Press, 1995); Nicholas Mirzoeff, "Revolution, Representation, Equality: Gender, Genre and Emulation in the Académie Royale de Peinture et Sculpture, 1785–1793," *Eighteenth-Century Studies* 31, no. 2 (1997): 153–74; Laura Auricchio, "The Laws of Bienséance and the Gendering of Emulation in Eighteenth-Century French Art Education," *Eighteenth-Century Studies* 36, no. 2 (2003): 231–40; John Iverson, "Emulation in France, 1750–1800," *Eighteenth-Century Studies* 36, no. 2 (2003): 217–30.

20 See Crow, *Emulation*.

21 See especially her discussion of Vincent and Joseph-Benoît Suvée in Mansfield, *The Perfect Foil*, 37–39.

22 "... en disent beaucoup sur l'homme, son esprit amical, confraternel, qui veut assurer la mémoire d'un milieu, celui qui va devenir le milieu 'Beaux-Arts', blagueur, frondeur,

mais profondément attaché au respect des hiérarchies. Les médailles, les prix, le rôle des professeurs lié à l'esprit de group et même de caste, entraînent un esprit de solidarité. Celui-ci est bien caractéristique de Vincent avec un côté 'premier de la classe,' chaleureux et bien élevé à la fois, dont les caricatures représentent, sans contradiction, l'autre versant." ("... say much about the man [Vincent], his friendly confraternal spirit, [a man] who wanted to remember his milieu, one that would become the milieu of the 'Beaux-Arts'—a joker and troublemaker, but deeply attached to the respect of hierarchies. The sense of group and even of privilege linked to the medals, the competitions, [and] the role of professors entailed a sense of solidarity. The latter is very characteristic of Vincent's 'first-in-class' side, warm and well raised, of which the caricatures represent the other side with no inconsistency.") Cuzin, *François-André Vincent*, 67.

23 Cuzin notes, "La caricature apparaît ainsi presque pédagogique, educative, car elle permet de montrer l'éventail le plus complet et le plus varié de l'humaine condition grâce à l'attention caustique et bienveillante qu'elle porte à l'individu, ses particularités physiques, ses accoutrements, ses expressions passagères—rires et grimaces." ("Caricature thus appeared almost pedagogical, educational, as it demonstrated the most complete and most varied range of the human condition thanks to the caustic and kindly attention brought to the individual, the physical particularities, the clothing, the passing expressions—laughs and grimaces.") Ibid.

24 "... en exagèrent les caractères, les usages et les mœurs de ses compatriotes, eut, sans doute, intention de les corriger." Claude Henri Watelet, *Dictionnaire des arts de peinture, sculpture et gravure* (Paris: L. F. Prault, 1792), 1:311.

25 "... ridiculiser plutôt les formes que le caractère moral." Ibid., 1:312.

26 "Quelques maîtres exhortent les Peintres à porter toujours avec eux des tablettes ou de petits cahiers, et à tracer les caractères des physionomies, et les expressions qui les frappent. Il est naturel, dans ces sortes d'études passagères, et qui ne permettent qu'un instant, que l'Artiste charge plus ou moins, pour mieux graver dans son esprit ce qu'il a observé. Ces espèces de caricatures sont destinées à être en quelque sorte secrets et au seul usage de l'Artiste qui les fait." Ibid., 1:309–14.

27 On the *Livre de caricatures*, see Jones and Richardson, *The Saint-Aubin* Livre de caricatures; Emily Richardson "'Tu n'as pas tout vü!': Seeing Satire in the Saint-Aubin *Livre de Caricatures*," in Mansfield and Malone, eds., *Seeing Satire in the Eighteenth Century*, 81–106; Melissa Hyde, "Needling: Embroidery and Satire in the Hands of Charles-Germain de Saint-Aubin," in Mansfield and Malone, eds., *Seeing Satire in the Eighteenth Century*, 107–30.

28 Jones and Richardson, *The Saint-Aubin* Livre de caricatures, 35–36, 39–40.

29 Nathalie Volle, *Jean-Simon Berthélemy, 1743–1811: peintre d'histoire* (Paris: Arthéna, 1979), 108, cat. no. 121.

30 Cuzin, *François-André Vincent*, 307.

31 Melissa Percival, *The Appearance of Character: Physiognomy and Facial Expression in Eighteenth-Century France* (London: W. S. Maney & Son for the Modern Humanities Research Association, 1999), 104–8.

32 The *têtes d'expression* were executed typically in up to three colors. See ibid., 101.

33 Ibid., 104.

34 Denis Diderot, "Salon of 1767," in *Diderot on Art*, trans. John Goodman, vol. 2 (New Haven, CT: Yale University Press, 1995), 131.
35 Ibid., 132.
36 Percival, *The Appearance of Character*, 98.
37 Elizabeth Mansfield and Kelly Malone, "Introduction: Seeing Satire in the Age of Reason," in Mansfield and Malone, eds., *Seeing Satire in the Eighteenth Century*, 1–11.
38 Ibid., 2.
39 Ibid., 3.
40 Antoine Cahen, "Les Prix de Quartier à l'Académie royale de peinture et de sculpture," *Bulletin de la société de l'histoire de l'art français* (1993): 61–62; Emmanuel Brugerolles, ed., *L'Académie mise à nu: L'École du modèle à l'Académie royale de peinture et de sculpture* (Paris: Beaux-arts de Paris, 2009); Susanna Caviglia, "Life Drawing and the Crisis of Historia in French Eighteenth-Century Painting," *Art History* 39, no. 1 (February 2016): 40–69.
41 See Lapauze, *Histoire de l'Académie de France à Rome*, 8; Benhamou, *Charles-Joseph Natoire*, 61; on copying, see 66–68.
42 Benhamou, *Charles-Joseph Natoire*, 104.
43 Mansfield, *The Perfect Foil*, 55–60; Cuzin, *François-André Vincent*, 29. On Natoire's directorship, see also Susanna Caviglia, "La sociabilité à l'Académie de France à Rome sous le directorat de Charles-Joseph Natoire (1752–1775)," in *Artistes, savants et amateurs: art et sociabilité au XVIIIe siècle (1715–1815)*, eds. Jessica L. Fripp, Nathalie Manceau, Nina Struckmeyer, and Amandine Gorse (Paris: Mare & Martin, 2016), 77–86.
44 Cuzin, *François-André Vincent*, 29.
45 Diderot, "Salon of 1767," 11.
46 Suvée's drawing is reproduced in Sophie Join-Lambert and Anne Leclair, *Joseph-Benoît Suvée 1743–1807* (Paris: Arthéna, 2017), D.236. Vincent's drawing is reproduced in Cuzin, *Francois-André Vincent*, 60D.
47 "Caricature," in ARTFL-FRANTEXT, The Project for American and French Research on the Treasury of the French Language (ARTFL), University of Chicago, accessed April 6, 2018, http://artfl-project.uchicago.edu/content/artfl-frantext.
48 "Charge," in ibid.
49 "We also call *charge*, in the language of Painting, what the Italians call caricature." ("Nous nommons aussi *charge*, en langage de Peinture, ce que les Italiens nomment *caricatura*...") Watelet, *Dictionnaire*, 1:310.
50 "Charges are often a game of painting.... they prove, independent of great talent, a sharp acuity for capturing characters and expressions." ("Les charges sont quelquefois des jeux de la Peinture ... elles prouvent, indépendamment d'une grande facilité, une sagacité fine à saisir les caractères et les expressions.") Ibid., 1:312.
51 "However, the adjective *chargé* is used most often in a sense which is most connected to art pedagogy." ("Cependant l'adjectif chargé est pris le plus souvent dans un sens qui a plus de rapport au didactique de l'Art.") Ibid., 1:326.
52 "... lorsqu'on dit qu'un trait, qu'un contour est chargé, qu'un figure, qu'une expression est chargé, on a pour objet seulement de blâmer une incorrection de l'Artiste, qui n'est relative qu'à sa negligence ou à quelque fausse idée qui l'a égarée. Ainsi le Professeur dit

très-sérieusement à un Elève qui dessine d'après le modele, soyez plus correct, plus exact." Ibid.
53 Ibid., 1:327.
54 Cuzin, *François-André Vincent*, 311.
55 Ibid.; Volle, *Jean-Simon Berthélemy*, 29.
56 Watelet, *Dictionnaire*, 1:329–30.
57 "Cette circonstance rend la *charge* non-seulement excusable, mais même nécessaire en plusieurs circonstances, et jusqu'à un certain point." Watelet, *Dictionnaire*, 1:330.
58 ["Quelquefois il les chargeoit dans les parties dont le ridicule étoit plus sensible, moins par jeu, que pour se les imprimer dans la mémoire avec des caractères inaltérables."] Pierre-Jean Mariette, "Lettre sur Léonard," in Anne Claude Philippe de Caylus, *Recueil de testes de caractere & de charges, dessinées par Lonard de Vinci, florentin & gravées par M. le c. de C* (Paris: J. Mariette, 1730), 12.
59 Cuzin, *François-André Vincent*, 399 n244D. Metropolitan Museum of Art, New York, Accession Number 1986.176.
60 Cuzin, *François-André Vincent*, 68, 392; "Suite de dessins en feuilles, croquis, études, académies, d'après la nature et l'antique; têtes d'expression, etc. par feu M Vincent, Item 78, trente trois pièces différents sujets et caricatures." *Notice des tableaux, dessins, estampes sous verre et en feuilles composant la cabinet et les études de feu, François-André Vincent: Vente à Paris, les 17, 18 et 19 Octobre 1816*, S. L., 1816. A number of the other *pensionnaires* of Vincent's cohort were awarded medals. See Cahen, "Les Prix de Quartier," 75.
61 Cuzin, *François-André Vincent*, 68, 392. See also Anatole de Montaiglon, *Correspondance des directeurs de l'Académie de France à Rome avec les surintendants des bâtiments* (Paris: J. Schemit, 1902), 12: 263, 314, 321, 402. An additional group of annotated *portraits-charges* by Vincent, also counterproofs, in the form of large medallion profile portraits, can be found in the collection of the Musée Carnavalet.
62 Cuzin, *François-André Vincent*, 399 n244D; 400 n247D; 409 n286D; 410 n287D.
63 "[i]ls faisaient l'un de l'autre ou des portraits remarquables, ou des charges pétillantes de verve et d'esprit." ["... dessinée à la plume et ombrée à la sepia, dans laquelle Vincent a exagéré de la manière plus plaisante la grande taille et la maigreur de son ami."] ["... une autre charge, aussi de Vincent, faisant le pendent de celle-ci."] Duchange, "Berthélemy, peintre Laonnois (1743–1811)," 89–90.
64 "[U]ne caricature, figure d'homme assis." Item 36, *Catalogue de tableaux, dessins, et sculptures après le décès de Feu M. Moitte*, Mfilm 35 1807 08 20, Bibliothèque de l'Institut national d'histoire de l'art, Paris. This inventory was published in Gisela Gramaccini, "L'inventaire après-décès de Jean-Guillaume Moitte (1746–1810)," *Gazette des Beaux Arts* (January 1992): 31–47.
65 Items 90, 92, and 93, in *Catalogue de tableaux, miniatures et dessins, etc., après le décès de Mr. Suvée, peintre*, Mfilm 35 1807 11 04, Bibliothèque de l'Institut national d'histoire de l'art, Paris.
66 Cuzin, *François-André Vincent*, 400 n 249D and 251D.
67 According to Thomas Arnauldet, there exists at least one more complete, inscribed version, which was sold in 1854. Arnauldet, *Notes sur les estampes satiriques bouffonnes ou singulières relatives à l'art et aux artistes français pendant les XVIIe et XVIIIe siècles* (Paris: J. Claye, 1859), 31.

68 An inventory made in 1781 by Joseph-Marie Vien noted the presence of "a press for counterproofing the drawings of the *pensionnaires*" among the Academy's belongings. Stein, "Etching in the Eternal City," 104–6, especially 215 n8. On exchange and counterproofing, see Jean-François Méjanès, *Les collections du comte d'Orsay: dessins du Musée du Louvre* (Paris: Éditions de la Réunion des musées nationaux, 1983), 130–31.

69 "C'est la representation sur la toile ou le papier, par le moyen des couleurs, d'une personne, d'une action, ou plus généralement d'un sujet, dans laquelle la vérité & la ressemblance exactes ne sont altérées que par l'excès du ridicule." Denis Diderot, "Charge," in Denis Diderot and Jean le Rond d'Alembert, eds., *Encyclopédie, ou dictionnaire raisonné des sciences, des arts et des métiers, etc.*, University of Chicago, ARTFL Encyclopédie Project (Spring 2013 Edition), Robert Morrissey, ed., accessed April 6, 2018, http://encyclopedie.uchicago.edu.

70 "... si vous chargez, & qu'il ne soit pas évident que vous en avez eu le dessein, l'être auquel on compare votre description n'étant plus celui que vous avez pris pour modèle, votre ouvrage reste sans effet." Diderot, "Charge," http://encyclopedie.uchicago.edu.

71 Nationalmuseum Sweden, NMG 183/1876.

72 Pierre Rousseau (born in Nantes 1751; died in Rennes 1829) was a pensioner in Rome from 1773 to 1775, leaving Rome early because of ill health. He is best known for his work on the Hôtel de Salm, which was destroyed during the French commune and rebuilt. Currently it is the Musée de la Légion d'honneur. See Michel Gallet, *Les architectes parisiens du XVIII siècle dictionnaire biographique et critique* (Paris: Éditions Mengès, 1995), 433–36.

73 We know very little about the Flemish painter Philippe-Henri Coclers van Wyck (born in Liège 1738; died, possibly in Marseille, 1803 or 1804). He came from a long line of Liègois painters, and we have some information about his grandfather, father, and brothers. Coclers van Wyck's career remains somewhat of a mystery, most likely because he was the most itinerant of his family. He resided in Rome between 1758 and 1772. He was *agréé* in the Royal Academy of Marseille in 1772, and was its director from 1785 until its dissolution in 1793. The most thorough biography of Coclers van Wyck can be found in Min Ae Étienne, "Un peintre liégeois meconnu: Philippe-Henri Coclers," *Le Vieux-Liège* 15, no. 315 (2006): 94–108.

74 Cuzin, *François-André Vincent*, 410.

75 Étienne, "Un peintre liégeois meconnu."

76 Mansfield, *The Perfect Foil*, 68–73.

77 On representations of the family, see Orest Ranum, "Intimacy in French Eighteenth-Century Family Portraits," *Word & Image* 6, no. 4 (1990): 351–67; Kate Retford, *The Art of Domestic Life: Family Portraiture in Eighteenth-Century England* (New Haven, CT: Yale University Press, 2006).

78 While not pertinent to the discussion here, it is important to note that, in both cases, there is a distinct separation of the arts along gender lines; in all three family portraits, the visual arts are the realm of the men, while musical talents belong to the women.

79 Xavier Salmon, *Jean-Marc Nattier: 1685–1766*, exh. cat. (Paris: Réunion des musées nationaux, 1999), 293–95.

80 There are two versions of this painting attributed to Baldrighi—one in the National Gallery of Parma, the other in the National Gallery of Canada. A third copy, currently

attributed to Pietro Melchiore Ferrari, is also at the Galleria Nazionale di Parma. Amalia Pacia, "Alexandre Roslin et Guiseppe Baldrighi entre Parme et Paris," in *De soie et de poudre: portraits de cour dans l'Europe des Lumières*, ed. Xavier Salmon (Versailles: Actes Sud, 2003), 45–46.

81 Amalia Pacia has convincingly argued for the identity of the central figure as Roslin. Although the identity of the figure to the right has been identified as Joseph-Marie Vien, Pacia disagrees, preferring to identify the man as Jean-Baptiste Boulard. Based on the biographic evidence Pacia presents, the identity of the third man being Boulard is more likely than Vien. See ibid., 48–57.

82 Roslin encouraged his cousin to visit Parma, instructing him to pass his greetings onto "M. Baldrighi, Ier Peintre de l'Infant, qui est un de mes anciens amis." Ibid., 59.

83 Cécile Beuzelin, "Le double portrait de Jacopo Pontormo: vers une histoire du double portrait d'amitié à la Renaissance," *Studiolo* 7 (2009): 80, 85.

84 For more on the Renaissance origins of the friendship portrait, see ibid.; Clovis Whitfield, "Portraiture: From the 'Simple Portrait' to the 'Ressemblance Parlante,'" in *The Genius of Rome 1592–1623*, ed. Beverly Louise Brown, exh. cat. (London: Royal Academy of Arts, 2001), 140–71.

85 Beuzelin, "Le double portrait," 94.

86 Both Cuzin and Mansfield have noted the formal similarities of Vincent's portrait to the genre scenes of Caravaggio and his followers because of the three-quarter-length figures set against an ambiguous background. The figures all wear a variety of costumes and the scene centers around one central gesture, the clasped hands of Vincent and Coclers van Wyck with brushes between them. Vincent looks out to the viewer deliberately, inviting us into the scene and reproducing a visual trope found in many Caravaggesque genre scenes. Mansfield points to Caravaggio's *Fortune Teller*, a painting that had been in the Royal Collection since 1665, and a subject oft-repeated by Caravaggio's followers. Vincent was undoubtedly exposed to a number of works by Caravaggio and his followers, as he spent much of the last two years of his Italian stay in Naples, a city where artistic production had been particularly influenced by Caravaggio. Cuzin, *François-André Vincent*, 140–42; Mansfield, *The Perfect Foil*, 69.

87 The correct identities of these figures were not discovered until the 1960s. See Oliver Millar, "Notes of Three Pictures by Van Dyck," *The Burlington Magazine* 111, no. 796 (July 1969): 414–17; Susan J. Barnes, ed., *Van Dyck: A Complete Catalogue of the Paintings* (New Haven, CT: Yale University Press, 2004), catalogue no. II.42.

88 Hans Vlieghe, "A propos d'un portrait de trois hommes par Simon de Vos (1603–1676) au Louvre," *Revue du Louvre* 38, no. 1 (1988): 38.

89 Alain Mérot, *Eustache Le Sueur: 1616–1655* (Paris: Arthena, 1987), 27.

90 Ibid.

91 See, for example, Leon Battista Alberti's famous self-portrait, although Vincent's use of white is in stark opposition to the Renaissance artist's discussion of color.

92 On the *costume espagnole*, see Emma Barker, "Mme Geoffrin, Painting and Galanterie: Carle Van Loo's Conversation Espagnole and Lecture Espagnole," *Eighteenth-Century Studies* 40, no. 4 (2007): 587–614; Melissa Percival, *Fragonard and the Fantasy Figure: Painting the Imagination* (Farnham, UK: Ashgate, 2012), 161–70.

93 On Fragonard's sketches for the portraits, see Carole Blumenfeld, *Une facétie de Fragonard*

les rélévations d'un dessin retrouvé (Montreuil: Gourcuff Gradenigo, 2013); Yuriko Jackall, ed., *Fragonard: The Fantasy Figures* (Chicago: Lund Humphries, 2017).

94 Cuzin, *Francois-André Vincent*, 82, cat. no. 291.
95 On the fantasy portraits, see Mary Sheriff, *Fragonard: Art and Eroticism* (Chicago: University of Chicago Press, 1990); Percival, *Fragonard and the Fantasy Figure*; Blumenfeld, *Une facétie de Fragonard*; and Jackall, *Fragonard: The Fantasy Figures*.
96 Percival, *Fragonard and the Fantasy Figure*, 84.
97 On masked balls, see Aileen Ribeiro, *The Dress Worn at Masquerade in England, 1730–1790, and Its Relation to Fancy Dress in Portraiture* (New York: Garland Publishing, 1984).
98 "Rien ne ressemble mieux à des étoffes et à des broderies magnifiques." Montaiglon and Guiffrey, *Correspondance des directeurs*, 10:142.
99 Stein, "Etching in the Eternal City," 115–20. A second series of drawings of the costume are possibly by Guillaume Voiriot. Jacob Brian and Lawrence Turcic, *Fifteenth–Eighteenth Century Drawings in the Metropolitan Museum of Art* (New York: Metropolitan Museum of Art, 1986), 286.
100 Joseph-Marie Vien, *Caravane du Sultane à la Mecque* (Paris: Chez Basan et Poignant Marchands d'estampes rue et hôtel Serpente, 1748).
101 Stein, "Etching in the Eternal City," 108.
102 Cuzin, "Les caricatures de Vincent," 91. Pierre-Adrien Pâris mentions in his journal entry for November 28, 1772, that he helped Vincent hang a number of drawings on the walls of his friend's studio, although he does not mention the subject of the drawings. Pâris, *Journal de mon sejour à Rome*, Ms. Pâris 6, Bibliothèque municipale de Besançon Etude et conservation, Besançon.

EPILOGUE

1 "The makeup of the Academy is wonderful for stimulation emulation … It's like watching a clever coquette play the field with her lovers: by means of progress and skill, she inflames desires and pushes passions to their highest pitch." ("La constitution de l'Académie est merveilleuse pour exciter l'émulation.... Il me semble voir une coquette habile qui dispute le terrain à ses Amans: A force de gradations et d'adresse, elle irrite les désirs, et porte les passions à leur comble.") Charles Mathon de La Cour, *Lettres à Monsieur *** sur les peintures, les sculptures, et les gravures, exposées au Sallon du Louvre en 1765. Seconde Lettre* ([Paris.]: De l'Imprimerie de d'Houry, Imprimeur de Mgr. le Duc d'Orléans, [1765]), 4, https://catalogue.bnf.fr/ark:/12148/cb423343340x.
2 Marisa Linton, "Fatal Friendships: The Politics of Jacobin Friendship," *French Historical Studies* 31, no. 1 (2008): 51–76. See also Kenneth Loiselle, "Living the Enlightenment in an Age of Revolution: Freemasonry in Bordeaux (1788–1794)," *French History* 24, no. 1 (2009): 60–81.
3 Linton, "Fatal Friendships," 56–58.
4 Laura Auricchio, *Adélaïde Labille-Guiard: Artist in the Age of Revolution* (Los Angeles: Getty Publications, 2009), 69–72. See also Nicholas Mizroeff, "Revolution, Representation, Equality: Gender, Genre, and Emulation in the Académie Royale de Peinture et Sculpture, 1785–93," *Eighteenth-Century Studies* 31, no. 2 (1997/1998): 153–74.

5 Jean-Pierre Cuzin, *François-André Vincent, 1746–1816: entre Fragonard et David* (Paris: Arthéna, 2013), 169–200; Elizabeth Mansfield, *The Perfect Foil: François-André Vincent and the Revolution in French Art* (Minneapolis: University of Minnesota, 2012), 146–57. On David's circle and his role in the restructuring of the Academy, see Thomas E. Crow, *Emulation: Making Artists for Revolutionary France* (New Haven, CT: Yale University Press, 1995); and Mizroeff, "Revolution, Representation, Equality."

6 Mansfield, *The Perfect Foil*, 151. See also Mizroeff, "Revolution, Representation, Equality."

7 Mansfield, *The Perfect Foil*, 151–52.

8 Auricchio, *Adélaïde Labille-Guiard*, 70–71.

9 It is also worth noting here that David was fairly antagonistic to Vincent and his circle during the Revolution. David denounced Vincent for not properly supporting the Revolution. David also accused Joseph-Benoît Suvée of being an aristocrat, and had him imprisoned for corresponding with his family in Belgium. See Auricchio, *Adélaïde Labille-Guiard*, 91; Mansfield, *The Perfect Foil*, 160.

10 The French Revolution drastically changed artistic practice and life in France, and the challenges artists faced as a result have been well addressed. See David Dowd, "The French Revolution and the Painters," *French Historical Studies* 1, no. 2 (1959); Albert Boime, *The Academy and French Painting in the Nineteenth Century* (New Haven, CT: Yale University Press, 1986); Philippe Bordes and Régis Michel, eds., *Aux armes et aux arts! Les arts de la Révolution 1789–1799* (Paris: Biro, 1988); Raphael Cardoso Denis and Colin Trodd, eds., *Arts and the Academy in the Nineteenth Century* (Manchester: Manchester University Press, 2000). On portraiture specifically, see Tony Halliday, *Facing the Public: Portraiture in the Aftermath of the French Revolution* (Manchester: Manchester University Press, 1999), 48–82; and Amy Freund, *Portraiture and Politics in Revolutionary France* (University Park: The Pennsylvania State University Press, 2014).

11 Halliday, *Facing the Public*, 47.

12 Freund, *Portraiture and Politics*.

13 Bauffremont was arrested for counterrevolutionary activity in 1793. Laura Auricchio has argued that although Labille-Guiard's portrait of him represents the apogee of her pre-Revolutionary career, the work and its sitter did not suit the politics of the day. Auricchio, *Adélaïde Labille-Guiard*, 76–77.

14 Neil Jaffares, "Boquet, Jeanne-Angélique, Mme Jean Charn," in *Dictionary of Pastellists before 1800* (online), updated June 18, 2018, http://www.pastellists.com/Articles/Bocquet.pdf. David Dowd claimed no artists were executed, but he appears to have been looking exclusively at members of the Academy. Dowd, "The French Revolution and the Painters," 133.

15 Sophie Join-Lambert and Anne Leclair, *Joseph-Benoît Suvée 1743–1807* (Paris: Arthena, 2017), 154–57.

16 Auricchio, *Adélaïde Labille-Guiard*, 91–93. Vincent's brother, Marie-Alexandre-François Vincent, and another student of Labille-Guiard's, Marie-Victoire d'Avril, also retreated to Labille-Guiard and Vincent's house.

17 Vincent and Labille-Guiard were married in 1800. After Labille-Guiard's death in 1803, Capet took care of Vincent during the remaining years of his life. Ibid., 107–8. For more on Capet, see Arnauld Doria, *Gabrielle Capet* (Paris: Les Beaux-arts, 1934).

18 Doria, *Gabrielle Capet*, cat. nos. 62, 64, 66, 67, 71, 72, 75, 76, 80.
19 "Dès exposition de 1796, on vit de bons portraits en miniature, au pastel et à l'huile, par Mlle Capet. Elle s'est surpassée depuis dans les portraits de MM Suvée, Houdon, Meyner, de Vandœuvre et de Mme Vincent, dont elle est l'élève la plus distinguée." Joachim Le Breton, *Rapports à l'Empereur sur le progrès des sciences, des lettres et des arts depuis 1789* (Paris: Belin. Delaporte, 1812), 127. This report was penned by François-André Vincent. Capet's inclusion was by no means coincidental; Vincent and Lebreton were undoubtedly promoting her. As Darcy Grimaldo Grigsby has argued, the 1808 report explicitly promoted Vincent and his circle over David, who was first painter to the Emperor. Grigsby, "Classicism, Nationalism and History: The Prix Decennaux of 1810 and the Politics of Art under Post-Revolutionary Empire" (PhD diss., University of Michigan, 1995), 79–99.
20 *Un Tableau représentant feue Mme Vincent (élève de son mari). Elle est occupée à faire le portrait de M. Le Sénateur Vien, comte de l'Empire et membre de l'Institut de France, régénérateur de l'École française actuelle, et maître de M. Vincent. L'auteur, qui s'est représenté chargeant sa palette, a placé dans ce tableau les principaux élèves de M. Vincent.* Number 89 in the catalogue. Societé des artiste français, *Explication des ouvrages de peinture et dessins, sculpture, architecture et gravure, des artistes vivans, exposés au Musée Napoléon le 14 octobre 1808* (Paris: Imprimerie des sciences et des arts, 1808), 13.
21 Given the reference to Labille-Guiard's students as "the nine muses," which included Capet (see Chapter 3), one wonders if Capet's choice of nine students was a pointed one.
22 Susan Siegfried, *The Art of Louis-Léopold Boilly: Modern Life in Napoleonic France* (New Haven, CT: Yale University Press, 1995), 96.
23 Thomas Gaehtgens, "Eine gemalte Künstlergenealogie. Zu Marie-Gabrielle Capets Atelierszene in der Münchener Neuen Pinakothek," *Niederdeutsche Beiträge zur Kunstgeschichte* 38 (1999): 209–19.
24 Bruno Foucart, "L'artiste dans la société de l'Empire: sa participation aux honneurs et dignités," *Revue d'histoire moderne et contemporaine* 17, no. 3 (1970): 714.
25 "M. Vien broke rank to regenerate the arts." ("M. Vien sortit des rangs pour régénérer les arts.") Breton, *Rapports à l'Empereur*, 19. On the celebration of Vien, see David O'Brien, *After the Revolution: Antoine-Jean Gros, Painting and Propaganda Under Napoleon* (University Park: The Pennsylvania State University Press, 2006), 72. On the politics of the *Rapport*'s introduction, see Grigsby, "Classicism, Nationalism and History," 86–90.
26 Séverine Sofio, "Gabrielle Capet's Collective Self-Portrait: Women and Artistic Legacy in Post-Revolutionary France," *Journal18*, Issue 8, *Self/Portrait* (Fall 2019), http://www.journal18.org/4397.
27 Heather Belnap Jensen, "Picturing Paternity: The Artist and Father-Daughter Portraiture in Post-Revolutionary France," in *Interior Portraiture and Masculine Identity in France, 1789–1914*, eds. Temma Balducci, Heather Belnap Jensen, and Pamela J. Warner (Burlington, VT: Ashgate, 2010), 39–42.
28 Ibid., 34.
29 Ibid., 41; Sofio, "Gabrielle Capet's Collective Self-Portrait."
30 Sarah Horowitz, *Friendship and Politics in Post-Revolutionary France* (University Park: The Pennsylvania State University Press, 2013), 1–20.

Bibliography

Archival Collections

Académie des sciences, belles-lettres et arts de Lyon, Lyon.
Archives nationales, Paris. Minutier central.
Bibliothèque municipale de Besançon etude et conservation, Besançon.
Bibliothèque de l'Institut national d'histoire de l'art, Paris.
Bibliothèque Nationale de France, Collection Deloynes, Paris.

Printed Primary Sources

Caylus, Anne Claude Philippe de. *Recueil de testes de caractere & de charges, dessinées par Lonard de Vinci, florentin & gravées par M. le c. de C.* Paris: J. Mariette, 1730.
Courcelles, Anne-Thérèse de Marguenat de. *Avis d'une mere a son fils et a sa fille, et autres ouvrages de Madame la Marquise de Lambert; avec un abregé de sa vie.* La Haye: Chez Jean Neaulme, 1748.
Coypel, Antoine. *Discours prononcez dans les Conférences de l'Académie royale de peinture et de sculpture.* Paris: Impr. de J. Collombat, 1721.
Coypel, Charles. *Discours sur la peinture, prononcez dans les Conférences de l'Académie royale de peinture et sculpture.* Paris: Chez P. J. Mariette, 1732.
———. "Vie d'Antoine Coypel." In *Vies des Premiers peintres du Roi, depuis M. Le Brun jusqu'à présent*, vol. 1. Edited by François-Bernard Lépicié, 1–41. Paris: Chez Jombert, 1752.
Explication des peintures, sculptures, et autres ouvrages de Messieurs de l'Académie Royale. Paris: J. J. E. Collombat, 1753.
Explication des peintures, sculptures et gravures, de Messieurs de l'Académie Royale. Paris: Veuve Herissant, 1777.
Explication des peintures, sculptures et gravures, de Messieurs de l'Académie Royale. Paris: l'Imprimerie de la Veuve Hérissant, 1785.
Grimm, Friedrich Melchior, and Denis Diderot. *Correspondance littéraire, philosophique et critique de Grimm et de Diderot depuis 1753 jusqu'en 1790, Vol. 1.* 15 vols. Paris: Furne, 1829.
Jombert, Charles-Antoine. *Catalogue de l'oeuvre de Ch. Nic. Cochin fils; écuyer, chevalier de l'Ordre du roy.* Paris: Prault, 1770.

La Font de Saint-Yenne, Étienne. *Reflexions sur quelques causes de l'état présent de la peinture en France . Avec un examen des principaux Ouvrages exposés au Louvre le mois d'Août 1746.* La Haye: Chez Jean Neaulme, 1747.

La Rochefoucauld, François de. *Réflexions, sentences et maximes morales.* Paris: E. Ganeau, 1714.

Lebreton, Joachim. *Nécrologie. Notice Sur Madame Vincent, Née Labille.* Paris, 1803.

———. *Rapports à l'Empereur sur le progrès des sciences, des lettres et des arts depuis 1789.* Paris: Belin. Delaporte, 1812.

L'année littéraire

Mercure de France

Mémoires secrets

Nouvelles de la république des lettres et des arts.

Richelet, Pierre. *Dictionnaire de la langue françoise ancienne et moderne. Tome 2, I–Z, vol. 2.* 2 vols. Amsterdam: aux dépens de la Compagnie, 1732.

Rousseau, Jean-Jacques. *Les confessions de J. J. Rousseau, citoyen de Genève,* vol. 4 (Lyon: Chez J. S. Grabit, 1793).

Sacy, Louis de. *Traité de l'amitié.* Paris: Chez Jean Moreau, 1704.

Societé des artiste français. *Explication des ouvrages de peinture et dessins, sculpture, architecture et gravure, des artistes vivans, exposés au Musée Napoléon le 14 octobre 1808.* Paris: Imprimerie des sciences et des arts, 1808.

Tocqué, Louis. *Le Discours de Tocqué sur le genre du portrait.* Edited by Arnauld Doria. Paris: J. Schemit, 1930.

Watelet, Claude-Henri. *L'art de peindre, poëme avec des réflexions sur les différentes parties de la peinture.* Paris: H.-L. Guérin et L.-F. Delatour, 1760.

———, and Pierre-Charles Lévesque. *Dictionnaire des art de peinture, sculpture et gravure.* 5 vols. Paris: Prault, 1792.

Vien, Joseph-Marie. *Caravane du Sultane à la Mecque.* Paris: Chez Basan et Poignant Marchands d'estampes rue et hôtel Serpente, 1748.

Vigée-Lebrun, Louise-Élisabeth. *Souvenirs de Mme. Louise-Élisabeth Vigée-Le Brun: notes et portraits, 1755–1789.* 2 vols. Paris: A. Fayard, 1835.

Databases

Dictionnaire Vivant de la Langue Française, https://dvlf.uchicago.edu.

Project for American and French Research on the Treasury of the French Language. "The ARTFL Encyclopédie," http://encyclopedie.uchicago.edu/.

Project for American and French Research on the Treasury of the French Language. "Dictionnaires d'autrefois," https://artfl-project.uchicago.edu/content/dictionnaires-dautrefois.

The Encyclopedia of Diderot & d'Alembert Collaborative Translation Project. Ann Arbor: Michigan Publishing, University of Michigan Library, https://quod.lib.umich.edu/d/did/.

Williams, Hannah, and Chris Sparks. *Artists in Paris: Mapping the Eighteenth-Century Art World,* www.artistsinparis.org

Secondary Sources and Works in Translation

Alaux, Jean Paul. *Académie de France à Rome, ses directeurs, ses pensionnaires.* Paris: Éditions Duchartre, 1933.

Allard, Sébastien, and Guilhem Scherf, eds. *Portraits Publics, Portraits Privés, 1770–1830.* Paris: Réunion des Musées nationaux, 2006.

Ariès, Philippe, and Georges Duby, eds. *A History of Private Life III: Passions of the Renaissance.* Translated by Arthur Goldhammer. Cambridge, MA: Harvard University Press, 1989.

Arnauldet, Thomas. *Notes sur les estampes satiriques, bouffonnes ou singulières relatives a l'art et aux artistes francais pendant les XVIIe et XVIIIe siècles.* Paris: J. Claye, 1859.

Auricchio, Laura. *Adélaïde Labille-Guiard: Artist in the Age of Revolution.* Los Angeles: J. Paul Getty Museum, 2009.

———. "The Laws of Bienséance and the Gendering of Emulation in Eighteenth-Century French Art Education." *Eighteenth-Century Studies* 36, no. 2 (2003): 231–40.

———. "Pahin de La Blancherie's Commercial Cabinet of Curiosity (1779–87)." *Eighteenth-Century Studies* 36, no. 1 (2002): 47–61.

———. "Self-Promotion in Adelaide Labille-Guiard's 1785 Self-Portrait with Two Students." *Art Bulletin* 89, no. 1 (2007): 45–62.

Bailey, Colin. *Patriotic Taste: Collecting Modern Art in Pre-revolutionary Paris.* New Haven, CT: Yale University Press, 2002.

Baillio, Joseph, and Xavier Salmon. *Elisabeth Louise Vigée Le Brun.* Paris: Réunion des Musées nationaux, 2015.

Baker, Malcolm. *Fame and Friendship: Pope, Roubiliac and the Portrait Bust.* New Haven, CT: Yale Center for British Art, 2014.

———. *The Marble Index: Roubiliac and Sculptural Portraiture in Eighteenth-Century Britain.* New Haven, CT: Yale University Press, 2014.

Baridon, Laurent, and Martial Guédron. *L'Art et l'histoire de la caricature des origines à nos jours.* Paris: Citadelle et Mazenod, 2009.

Barker, Emma. "Mme Geoffrin, Painting and Galanterie: Carle Van Loo's Conversation Espagnole and Lecture Espagnole." *Eighteenth-Century Studies* 40, no. 4 (2007): 587–614.

Barnes, Susan J., ed. *Van Dyck: A Complete Catalogue of the Paintings.* New Haven, CT: Yale University Press, 2004.

Bean, Jacob, and Lawrence Turcic. *15th–18th Century French Drawings in the Metropolitan Museum of Art.* New York: Metropolitan Museum of Art, 1986.

Bell, David. *The Cult of the Nation in France: Inventing Nationalism, 1680–1800.* Cambridge, MA: Harvard University Press, 2003.

Belnap Jensen, Heather. "Picturing Paternity: The Artist and Father-Daughter Portraiture in Post-Revolutionary France." *Interior Portraiture and Masculine Identity in France, 1789–1914*, edited by Temma Balducci, Heather Belnap Jensen, and Pamela J. Warner, 31–46. Burlington, VT: Ashgate, 2010.

Benhamou, Reed. *Charles-Joseph Natoire and the Académie de France in Rome: A Re-Evaluation.* Oxford: Voltaire Foundation, 2015.

———. "Discipline and Punishment in the Académie Royale de Peinture et de Sculpture." In *Institutional Culture in Early Modern Society*, edited by Anne Goldgar and Robert I. Frost, 247–77. Bedfordshire, UK: Brill, 2004.

———. *Regulating the Académie: Art, Rules and Power in Ancien Régime France*. Oxford: Voltaire Foundation, 2009.

Benisovich, Michael. "Ghezzi and French Artists in Rome." *Apollo* 85 (May 1967): 340–47.

Besnard, Paul Albert. *La Tour: La Vie et l'oeuvre de l'oeuvre de l'artiste*. Paris: Les Beaux-arts, 1928.

Berger, Jr., Harry. *Fictions of the Pose: Rembrandt Against the Italian Renaissance*. Stanford, CA: Stanford University Press, 2000.

Beuzelin, Cécile. "Le Double Portrait de Jacopo Pontormo: vers une histoire du double portrait d'amitié à La Renaissance." *Studiolo. Revue d'histoire de l'art de l'Académie de France à Rome* 7 (2009): 77–99.

Blumenfeld, Carole. *Une facétie de Fragonard les révélations d'un dessin retrouvé*. Montreuil: Gourcuff Gradenigo, 2013.

Boime, Albert. *The Academy and French Painting in the Nineteenth Century*. New Haven, CT: Yale University Press, 1986.

Bonnet, Jean-Claude. *Naissance du Panthéon, Essai sur le cultes des grands hommes*. Paris: Fayard, 1998.

Boorsch, Suzanne. "The Recueil de Caricatures by La Live de Jully after Saly." *Yale University Art Gallery Bulletin* (2004), 69–83.

Bordes, Philippe and Régis Michel, eds. *Aux armes et aux arts! Les arts de la Révolution 1789–1799*. Paris: Biro, 1988.

Boucher, François. "An Episode in the Life of the Académie de France a Rome: An Eighteenth-Century Masquerade 'à l'orientale.'" *The Connoisseur*, no. 596 (October 1961): 88–91.

Braudy, Leo. *The Frenzy of Renown: Fame and Its History*. Oxford: Oxford University Press, 1986.

Brian, Jacob, and Lawrence Turcic. *Fifteenth–Eighteenth Century Drawings in the Metropolitan Museum of Art*. New York: Metropolitan Museum of Art, 1986.

Brilliant, Richard. *Portraiture*. London: Reaktion Books, 1991.

Brissaud, Jean-Baptiste. *Manuel d'histoire du droit français*. Paris: A. Fontemoing, 1908.

Brugerolles, Emmanuelle, Georges Brunel, and Camille Debrabant, eds. *The Male Nude: Eighteenth-Century Drawings from the Paris Academy*. London: Paul Holberton Publishing, 2013.

Burke, Jill. "Patronage and the Art of Friendship: Piero Del Pugliese's Patronage of Filippino Lippi." In *Changing Patrons: Social Identity and the Visual Arts in Renaissance Florence*, 85–101. University Park: Pennsylvania State University Press, 2004.

Cabezas, Hervé. "Voltaire, ses portraits, par Maurice-Quentin de La Tour et Joseph Rosset, et leur reproduction, au Musée Antoine Lécuyer de Saint Quentin." *Bulletin de La Société de l'histoire de l'art Français Année 2009* (2011): 175–202.

Cahen, Antoine. "Les prix de quartier à l'Académie royale de peinture et de sculpture." *Bulletin de la Société de l'histoire de l'art français année 1993* (1994): 61–84.

Caradonna, Jeremy L. *The Enlightenment in Practice: Academic Prize Contests and Intellectual Culture in France, 1670–1794*. Ithaca, NY: Cornell University Press, 2012.

Catroux, Claude. "Hubert Robert et Mme Geoffrin." *Revue de l'art ancien et moderne* 40, no. 227 (1921): 30–40.

Catroux, R. Claude. *Catalogue de huit tableaux par Hubert Robert; quarante-trois dessins par Cochin, portraits du XVIIIe siècle provenant du salon de Madame Geoffrin et appartenant au comte de la Bedoyère.* Paris: Henri Baudoin et Jules Féral, 1921.

Caviglia, Susanna. "Life Drawing and the Crisis of Historia in French Eighteenth-Century Painting." *Art History* 39, No. 1 (February 2016): 40–69.

Charpentier, Jeanne, and Michel Charpentier. *L'Encyclopédie.* Paris: Éditions Bordas, 1967.

Chaussard, Pierre-Jean-Baptiste. *Le Pausanias français: état des arts du dessin en France à l'ouverture du XIXe siècle.* Paris: Imprimerie de Demonville, 1806.

Cicero. *On Friendship.* Translated by W. A. Falconer. Cambridge, MA: Harvard University Press, 1923.

Clark, Anthony M. "Pier Leone Ghezzi's Portraits." Edited by Edgar Peters Bowron. *Paragone* 165, no. 14 (1965): 11–21.

Clements, Candace. "The Duc d'Antin, the Royal Administration of Pictures, and the Painting Competition of 1727." *The Art Bulletin* 78, no. 4 (1996): 647–62.

Crowston, Clare Hare. *Credit, Fashion, Sex: Economies of Regard in Old Regime France.* Durham, NC: Duke University Press, 2013.

Crow, Thomas E. *Emulation: Making Artists for Revolutionary France.* New Haven, CT: Yale University Press, 1995.

———. *Painters and Public Life in Eighteenth-Century Paris.* New Haven, CT: Yale University Press, 1985.

Curran, Stuart. "Dynamics of Female Friendship in the Later Eighteenth Century." *Nineteenth-Century Contexts* 23 (2001): 221–39.

Cuzin, Jean-Pierre. "Les caricatures de Vincent." *L' Information d'histoire de l'art* 16 (1971): 91–94.

———. "De Fragonard à Vincent." *Bulletin de la Société de l'Histoire de l'Art Français* année *1981* (1983): 103–24.

———. *François-André Vincent, 1746–1816: entre Fragonard et David.* Paris: Arthéna, 2013.

D'Alembert, Jean le Rond. *Preliminary Discourse to the Encyclopedia of Diderot.* Translated by Richard N. Schwab and Walter E. Rex. Chicago: University of Chicago Press, 1995.

Darnton, Robert. "Workers Revolt: The Great Cat Massacre of the Rue Saint-Séverin." In *The Great Cat Massacre and Other Episodes in French Cultural History,* 75–106. New York: Basic Books, 1984.

Daumas, Maurice. *L'affaire d'Esclans: les conflits familiaux au XVIIIe siècle.* Paris: Seuil, 1988.

Davis, Natalie Zemon. "The Reasons of Misrule: Youth Groups and Charivaris in Sixteenth-Century France." *Past & Present* 50, no. 1 (1971): 41–75.

Debrie, Christine, and Xavier Salmon. *Maurice-Quentin de La Tour: prince des pastellistes.* Paris: Somogy, 2001.

Denis, Raphael Cardoso, and Colin Trodd, eds. *Arts and the Academy in the Nineteenth Century.* Manchester: Manchester University Press, 2000.

Detroit Institute of Arts, *French Painting 1774–1830*. Detroit, MI: Wayne State University Press, 1975.

Desmaze, Charles. *Le Reliquaire de M. Q. de La Tour, peintre du roi Louis XV, sa correspondance et son œuvre*. Paris: Ernest Leroux, 1874.

Dewald, Jonathan. *Aristocratic Experience and the Origins of Modern Culture: France, 1570–1715*. Berkeley: University of California Press, 1993.

Diderot, Denis. *Diderot on Art*. Translated by John Goodman. New Haven, CT: Yale University Press, 1995.

Doria, Arnauld. *Gabrielle Capet: biographie et catalogue critiques*. Paris: Les Beaux-arts, Édition d'études et de documents, 1934.

Dowd, David. "The French Revolution and the Painters." *French Historical Studies* 1, no. 2 (1959): 127–48.

Draper, James David, and Guilhem Scherf, eds. *Pajou: sculpteur du Roi, 1730–1809*. Paris: Réunion des musées nationaux, 1997.

———, eds. *Playing with Fire: European Terracotta Models, 1740–1840*. New Haven, CT: Metropolitan Museum of Art, Réunion des Musées Nationaux, and Yale University Press, 2004.

Duchange, Jean-Charles-Nicolas. "Berthlémy, peintre Laonnois (1743–1811)." *Bulletin de la société académique de Laon* III, séance du 4 janvier 1853 (1854): 81–121.

Étienne, Min Ae. "Un Peintre liégeois meconnu?: Philippe-Henri Coclers." *Le Vieux-Liège* 15, no. 315 (2006): 94–108.

Faroult, Guillaume, and Catherine Voiriot, eds. *Hubert Robert, 1733–1808: un peintre visionnaire*. Paris: Somogy, 2016.

Fend, Mechthild. *Fleshing Out Surfaces: Skin in French Art and Medicine, 1650–1850*. Manchester: Manchester University Press, 2017.

Flandrin, Jean-Louis. *Families in Former Times: Kinship, Household and Sexuality*. Translated by Richard Southern. Cambridge: Cambridge University Press, 1979.

Fontaine, André. *Les collections de l'Académie royale de peinture et de sculpture*. Paris: H. Laurens, 1910.

Fort, Bernadette. "Voice of the Public: The Carnivalization of Salon Art in Prerevolutionary Pamphlets." *Eighteenth-Century Studies* 22, no. 3 (1989): 368–94.

Foucart, Bruno. "L'artiste dans la société de l'Empire: sa participation aux honneurs et dignités." *Revue d'histoire moderne et contemporaine* 17, no. 3 (1970): 709–19.

Freund, Amy. *Portraiture and Politics in Revolutionary France*. University Park: The Pennsylvania State University Press, 2014.

Fripp, Jessica L., Nathalie Manceau, Nina Struckmeyer, and Amandine Gorse, eds. *Artistes, savants et amateurs: art et sociabilité au XVIIIe siècle (1715–1815)*. Paris: Mare & Martin, 2016.

Furber, Donald. "The Myth of *amour-propre* in La Rochefoucauld." *The French Review* 43, no. 2 (December 1969): 227–39.

Gaehtgens, Thomas W. "Du Parnasse Au Panthéon?: La Représentation Des Hommes Illustres et Des Grands Hommes Dans La France Du XVIIIe Siècle." In *Le Culte des Grands Hommes, 1750–1850*, edited by Thomas W. Gaehtgens and Gergor Wedekin, 135–71. Paris: Maison des sciences de l'homme, 2009.

———. "Eine gemalte Künstlergenealogie. "Eine gemalte Künstlergenealogie. Zu Marie-Gabrielle Capets Atelierszene in der Münchener Neuen Pinakothek." *Niederdeutsche Beiträge zur Kunstgeschichte*, 38 (1999): 209–19.

Gallet, Michel. *Les Architectes parisiens du XVIII siècle dictionnaire biographique et critique*. Paris: Éditions Mengès, 1995.

Garrioch, David. "From Christian Friendship to Secular Sentimentality: Enlightenment Re-Evaluations." In *Friendship: A History*, edited by Barbara Caine, 165–214. London: Equinox, 2009.

Gerson, Frédérick. *L'Amitié au XVIIIe siècle*. Paris: la Pensée universelle, 1974.

Goldgar, Anne. *Impolite Learning: Conduct and Community in the Republic of Letters, 1680–1750*. New Haven, CT: Yale University Press, 1995.

Goodman, Dena. "Public Sphere and Private Life: Toward a Synthesis of Current Historiographical Approaches to the Old Regime." *History and Theory* 31, no. 1 (1992): 1–20.

———. *The Republic of Letters: A Cultural History of the French Enlightenment*. Ithaca, NY: Cornell University Press, 1996.

Gordon, Daniel. *Citizens without Sovereignty: Equality and Sociability in French Thought, 1670–1789*. Princeton, NJ: Princeton University Press, 1994.

Gramaccini, Gisela. "L'inventaire Après-Décès de Jean-Guillaume Moitte (1746–1810)." *Gazette Des Beaux Arts* 119, no. 134 (January 1992): 31–47.

Grate, Pontus. "Hubert Robert et l'iconographie d'Augustin Pajou." *Gazette Des Beaux Arts* (July/August 1985): 7–14.

Greene, Vivien. "Un espace d'expérimentations: le portrait d'artiste." In *Portraits publics, portraits privés, 1770–1830: exposition au Grand Palais*, edited by Sébastien Allard, 180–203. Paris: Réunion des Musées nationaux, 2006.

Grigsby, Darcy Grimaldo. "Classicism, Nationalism and History: The Prix Decennaux of 1810 and the Politics of Art under Post-Revolutionary Empire." PhD diss., University of Michigan, 1995.

Gruder, Vivian R. *The Notables and the Nation: The Political Schooling of the French, 1787–1788*. Cambridge, MA: Harvard University Press, 2007.

Guichard, Charlotte. *Les amateurs d'art à Paris au XVIIIe siècle*. Paris: Champ Vallon, 2008.

———. "Taste Communities: The Rise of the Amateur in Eighteenth-Century Paris." *Eighteenth-Century Studies* 45, no. 4 (2012): 519–47.

Habermas, Jürgen. *The Structural Transformation of the Public Sphere: An Inquiry into a Category of Bourgeois Society*. Translated by Thomas Burger and Frederick Lawrence. Cambridge, MA: MIT Press, 1991.

Halliday, Tony. *Facing the Public: Portraiture in the Aftermath of the French Revolution*. Manchester: Manchester University Press, 1999.

Hamerton, Katharine J. "Rousseau and the New Domestic Art of Women's Taste." *Proceedings of the Western Society for French History* 37 (2009): 99–115.

Hamon, Maurice. *Madame Geoffrin: Femme d'influence, femme d'affaires au temps des Lumières*. Paris: Fayard, 2011.

Hayes, Julie Candler. "Friendship and the Female Moralist." *Studies in Eighteenth-Century Culture* 39, no. 1 (2010): 171–89.

Hoisington, Rena M. "Maurice-Quentin de La Tour and the Triumph of Pastel Painting in Eighteenth-Century France." PhD diss., New York University, 2006.

Horowitz, Sarah. *Friendship and Politics in Post-Revolutionary France*. University Park: The Pennsylvania State University Press, 2013.

Hunt, Lynn. *The Family Romance of the French Revolution*. Berkeley: University of California Press, 1992.

Hyatte, Reginald. *The Arts of Friendship: The Idealization of Friendship in Medieval and Early Renaissance Literature*. Leiden: Brill, 1994.

Hyde, Melissa Lee. *Making up the Rococo: François Boucher and His Critics*. Los Angeles: Getty Publications, 2006.

———. "Élisabeth Vigée-Lebrun (review). *Early Modern Women* 11, no. 2 (Spring 2017): 179–91.

———. "Under the Sign of Minerva: Adélaïde Labille-Guiard's Portrait of Madame Adélaïde." In *Women, Art and the Politics of Identity in Eighteenth-Century Europe*, edited by Melissa Lee Hyde and Jennifer Milam, 139–63. Burlington, VT: Ashgate Publishing, 2003.

———. "Women and the Visual Arts in the Age of Marie-Antoinette." In *Anne Vallayer-Coster, Painter to the Court of Marie-Antoinette*, edited by Eik Kahng, 75–93. New Haven, CT: Dallas Museum of Art and Yale University Press, 2002.

Iverson, John. "Emulation in France, 1750–1800." *Eighteenth-Century Studies* 36, no. 2 (2003): 217–30.

Jackall, Yuriko, ed. *Fragonard's Fantasy Figures*. London: Lund Humphries Publishers, Limited, 2017.

Jeffares, Neil. *Dictionary of Pastellists before 1800* (online), http://www.pastellists.com.

Join-Lambert, Sophie, and Anne Leclair. *Joseph-Benoît Suvée 1743–1807*. Paris: Arthéna, 2017.

Jones, Colin, and Emily Richardson, eds. *The Saint-Aubin Livre de Caricatures: Drawing Satire in Eighteenth-Century Paris*. Oxford: Voltaire Foundation, 2012.

Jones, Emrys. *Friendship and Allegiance in Eighteenth-Century Literature: The Politics of Private Virtue in the Age of Walpole*. Basingstoke, UK: Palgrave Macmillan, 2013.

Jones, Jennifer M. *Sexing La Mode: Gender, Fashion and Commercial Culture in Old Regime France*. Oxford: Berg, 2004.

Kettering, Sharon. *Patronage in Sixteenth- and Seventeenth-Century France*. Burlington, VT: Ashgate, 2002.

Kruckeberg, Robert. "The Wheel of Fortune in Eighteenth-Century France: The Lottery, Consumption, and Politics." PhD diss., University of Michigan, 2009.

Kushner, Nina. *Erotic Exchanges: The World of Elite Prostitution in Eighteenth-Century Paris*. Ithaca, NY: Cornell University Press, 2016.

Lajer-Burcharth, Ewa. *Necklines*. New Haven, CT: Yale University Press, 1999.

———. *The Painter's Touch: Boucher, Chardin, Fragonard*. Princeton, NJ: Princeton University Press, 2018.

———. "Pompadour's Touch: Difference in Representation." *Representations* 73, no. 1 (2001): 54–88.

Lapauze, Henry. *Histoire de l'Académie de France à Rome: 1666–1801*, 2 vols. Paris: Plon, 1924.

La Volpa, Anthony J. *The Labor of the Mind: Intellect and Gender in Enlightenment Cultures*. Philadelphia: University of Pennsylvania Press, 2017.

Le Marie Chevalier de Valory, Jules-Hippolyte. "Jean-François de Troy." In *Mémoires inédits sur les membres de l'Académie royale de peinture et de sculpture*, edited by Louis Dussieux, Eudor Soulié, Philippe de Chennevières, Paul Mantz, and Anatole de Montaiglon, 2:255–88. Paris: J. B. DuMoulin, 1854.

Le Men, Ségolène, ed. *L'art de la caricature*. Paris: Presses universitaires de Paris-Ouest, 2011.

Lemonnier, Henry. "Suvée et ses amis à l'Ecole de Rome." *Gazette des Beaux Arts* 554 (August 1903): 97–110.

Leribault, Christophe. *Jean-François de Troy, 1679–1752*. Paris: Arthéna, 2002.

Lichtenstein, Jacqueline. "L'ignorant ou le spectateur désintéressé." In *Les raisons de l'art. Essai sur les limites de l'esthétique*, 81–110. Paris: Editions Gallimard, 2014.

———, and Christian Michel, eds. *Les Conférences de l'Académie Royale de Peinture et de Sculpture*. 8 vols. Paris: École nationale supérieure des beaux-arts, 2006–12.

Lilti, Antoine. *Figures publiques: l'invention de la célébrité, 1750–1850*. Paris: Fayard, 2014.

———. *Le Monde des salons: Sociabilité et mondanité à Paris au XVIIIe siècle*. Paris: Fayard, 2005.

Linton, Marisa. *Choosing Terror: Virtue, Friendship, and Authenticity in the French Revolution*. Oxford: Oxford University Press, 2015.

———. "Fatal Friendships: The Politics of Jacobin Friendship." *French Historical Studies* 31, no. 1 (2008): 51–76.

———. *The Politics of Virtue in Enlightenment France*. New York: Palgrave, 2001.

Lloyd, Genevieve. *The Man of Reason: "Male" and "Female" in Western Philosophy*. New York: Routledge, 2002.

Lochman, Daniel, Maritere López, and Lorna Hutson, eds. *Discourses and Representations of Friendship in Early Modern Europe, 1500–1700*. Burlington, VT: Ashgate, 2011.

Locquin, Jean. "La Lutte des critiques d'art contre les portraitistes au XVIIIe siècle," *Archives de l'Art Français* 7 (1913): 309–20.

———. *La peinture d'histoire en France de 1747 à 1785: étude sur l'évolution des idées artistiques dans la seconde moitié du XVIIIe siècle*. Paris: Arthéna, 1978.

Loiselle, Kenneth. *Brotherly Love: Freemasonry and Male Friendship in Enlightenment France*. Ithaca, NY: Cornell University Press, 2014.

———. "Friendship and Loyalty in Early Modern Europe." In *Face of Communities: Social Ties between Trust, Loyalty and Conflict*, edited by Anna Feickert, Anna Haut, and Kathrin Sharaf, 121–36. Göttingen: V&R University Press, 2014.

———. "Living the Enlightenment in an Age of Revolution: Freemasonry in Bordeaux (1788–1794)." *French History* 24, no. 1 (2009): 60–81.

Lytle, Guy Fitch. "Friendship and Patronage in Renaissance Europe." In *Patronage, Art and Society in Renaissance Italy*, edited by F. W. Kent and Patricia Simons, 47–62. Oxford: Clarendon Press, 1987

Mangano, Bryan. *Fictions of Friendship in the Eighteenth-Century Novel*. Cham, Switzerland: Palgrave Macmillan, 2017.

Mansfield, Elizabeth. *The Perfect Foil: François-André Vincent and the Revolution in French Painting*. Minneapolis: University of Minnesota Press, 2012.

———, and Kelly Malone, eds. *Seeing Satire in the Eighteenth Century*. Oxford: Voltaire Foundation, 2013.

Martin, Meredith. *Dairy Queens: The Politics of Pastoral Architecture from Catherine de'Medici to Marie-Antointette*. Cambridge, MA: Harvard University Press, 2011.

———. "Tipu Sultan's Ambassadors at Saint-Cloud: Indomania and Anglophobia in Pre-Revolutionary Paris." *West 86th* 21, no. 1 (Spring–Summer 2014): 37–68.

Maza, Sara. "The Diamond Necklace Affair Revisited (1785–1786): The Case of the Missing Queen." In *Marie-Antoinette: Writings on the Body of a Queen*, edited by Dena Goodman, 73–98. New York: Routledge, 2003.

McClellan, Andrew. "D'Angiviller's 'Great Men' of France and the Politics of the Parlements." *Art History* 13, no. 2 (June 1990): 175–92.

McPherson, Heather. *Art and Celebrity in the Age of Reynolds and Siddons*. University Park: The Pennsylvania State University Press, 2017.

Méjanès, Jean-François. *Les Collections du comte d'Orsay: dessins du musée du Louvre*. Paris: Éditions de la Réunion des musées nationaux, 1983.

Mérot, Alain. *Eustache Le Sueur: 1616–1655*. Paris: Arthéna, 1987.

Michel, Christian. *The Académie royale de peinture et de sculpture: The Birth of the French School, 1648–1793*. Translated by Chris Miller. Los Angeles: Getty Publications, 2018.

———. *Charles-Nicolas Cochin et l'art des lumières*. Rome: École française de Rome, 1993.

Milano, Ronit. *The Portrait Bust and French Cultural Politics in the Eighteenth Century*. Leiden: Brill, 2015.

Millar, Oliver. "Notes on Three Pictures by Van Dyck." *The Burlington Magazine* 111, no. 796 (1969): 414–18.

Mirzoeff, Nicholas. "Revolution, Representation, Equality: Gender, Genre and Emulation in the Académie Royale de Peinture et Sculpture, 1785–1793." *Eighteenth-Century Studies* 31, no. 2 (1997): 153–74.

Montaiglon, Anatole de. *Procès-verbaux de l'Académie royale de peinture et de sculpture (1648–1792)*. 10 vols. Paris: J. Baur, 1875.

Montaiglon, Anatole de, and Jules Guiffrey, eds. *Correspondance des directeurs de l'Académie de France à Rome avec les surintendants des bâtiments*, 17 vols. Paris: J. Schemit, 1904.

Montaigne, Michel de. *The Complete Essays of Montaigne*. Translated by Donald M. Frame. Stanford, CA: Stanford University Press, 1965.

Müller, Michael. "Sans nom, sans place et sans mérite'? Réflexions sur l'utilisation du portrait en France au XVIIIe siècle." In *L'art et Les Normes Sociales Au XVIIIe Siècle*. Edited by Thomas W. Gaehtgens, Christian Michel, and Martin Schieder, 383–402. Paris: Éditions de la Maison des sciences de l'homme, 2001.

O'Brien, David. *After the Revolution: Antoine-Jean Gros, Painting and Propaganda Under Napoleon*. University Park: The Pennsylvania State University Press, 2006.

O'Donnell, Katherine, and Michael O'Rourke, eds. *Love, Sex, and Intimacy and Friendship Between Men, 1550–1800*. Baskingstoke, UK: Palgrave MacMillan, 2007.

Olszewski, Edward J. "The New World of Pier Leone Ghezzi." *Art Journal* 43, no. 4 (December 1983): 325–30.

Orenstein, Nadine. *Infinite Jest: Caricature and Satire from Leonardo to Levine*. New York: Metropolitan Museum of Art, 2011.

Österberg, Eva. "Challenging the Private–Public Dichotomy: Friendship in Mediaeval and Early Modern Society." In *Friendship and Love, Ethics and Politics: Studies in Mediaeval and Early Modern History*, 23–90. Budapest: Central European University Press, 2010.

Pacia, Amalia. "Alexandre Roslin et Guiseppe Baldrighi entre Parme et Paris." In *De Soie et de poudre: portraits de cour dans l'Europe des Lumières*, edited by Xavier Salmon, 45–74. Versailles: Actes Sud, 2003

Passez, Anne-Marie. *Adélaïde Labille-Guiard, 1749–1803; biographie et catalogue raisonné de son œuvre*. Paris: Arts et métiers graphiques, 1973.

Percival, Melissa. *The Appearance of Character: Physiognomy and Facial Expression in Eighteenth-Century France*. London: W. S. Maney and Son, 1999.

———. *Fragonard and the Fantasy Figure: Painting the Imagination*. New York: Routledge, 2012.

Perry, Gill. *Spectacular Flirtations: Viewing the Actress in British Art and Theatre, 1768–1820*. New Haven, CT: Yale University Press, 2007.

Pointon, Marcia. *Hanging the Head: Portraiture and Social Formation in Eighteenth-Century England*. New Haven, CT: Yale University Press, 1997.

Poniotowski, Stanislas Auguste, and Marie-Thérèse Rodet Geoffrin. *Correspondance inédite du roi Stanislas-Auguste Poniatowski et de Madame Geoffrin (1764–1777)*. Edited by Charles Moüy. Genéve: Slatkine Reprints, 1970.

Porterfield, Todd, ed. *The Efflorescence of Caricature, 1759–1838*. Burlington, VT: Ashgate, 2011.

Rabbe, F. "Pahin de La Blancherie et Le Salon de La Correspondance." *Bulletin de la société historique du VIe arrondissement de Paris* II (1899): 30–52.

Ranum, Orest. "Intimacy in French Eighteenth-Century Family Portraits." *Word & Image* 6, no. 4 (1990): 351–67.

Reddy, William M. *The Navigation of Feeling: A Framework for the History of Emotions*. Cambridge: Cambridge University Press, 2001.

Retford, Kate. *The Art of Domestic Life: Family Portraiture in Eighteenth-Century England*. New Haven, CT: Yale University Press, 2006.

Ribeiro, Aileen. *The Dress Worn at Masquerades in England, 1730 to 1790, and Its Relation to Fancy Dress in Portraiture*. New York: Garland Publishing, 1984.

Roach, Joseph. "Celebrity Erotics: Pepys, Performance, and Painted Ladies." *The Yale Journal of Criticism* 16, no. 1 (2003): 211–30.

———. *It*. Ann Arbor: University of Michigan Press, 2007.

Roche, Daniel. *France in the Enlightenment*. Translated Arthur Goldhammer. Cambridge, MA: Harvard University Press, 1998.

———. *Le Siècle des Lumières en Province: Académies et académiciens provinciaux, 1680–1789*, 2nd ed., 2 vols. Paris: Éditions de l'École des hautes études en sciences sociales, 1989.

Rojek, Chris. *Celebrity*. London: Reaktion, 2010.

Rosenberg, Pierre. "Le Concours de Peinture de 1727." *Revue de l'art*, no. 37 (1977): 29–42.

Roulston, Christine. "Separating the Inseparables: Female Friendship and its Discontents in Eighteenth-Century France." *Eighteenth-Century Studies* 32, No. 2 (Winter 1998/1999): 215–31.

Rousseau, Jean-Jacques. *A Discourse on Inequality*. Translated by Maurice Cranston. London: Penguin Books, 1984.

———. "Discourse on the Sciences and the Arts." In *The Basic Political Writings (Second Edition)*, edited by Donald A. Cress and David Wootton, 1–26. Indianapolis: Hackett Publishing Company, 2011.

———. *Politics and the Arts: Letter to M. D'Alembert on the Theatre*. Translated by Allan Bloom. Ithaca, NY: Cornell University Press, 1968.

Salmon, Xavier. *Jean-Marc Nattier: 1685–1766*. Paris: Réunion des musées nationaux, 1999.

———. *Maurice Quentin de La Tour: le voleur d'âmes*. Versailles: Artlys, 2004.

———. *Pastels Du Musée Du Louvre XVIIe–XVIIIe Siècles*. Paris: Éditions Hazan, 2018.

Seifert, Lewis C., and Rebecca May Wilkin, eds. *Men and Women Making Friends in Early Modern France*. Burlington, VT: Ashgate, 2015.

Sharp, Ronald. *Friendship and Literature: Spirit and Form*. Durham, NC: Duke University Press, 1986.

Shelford, April. *Transforming the Republic of Letters: Pierre-Daniel Huet and European Intellectual Life, 1650–1720*. Rochester, NY: University of Rochester Press, 2007.

Shepard, Alexandra. *Meanings of Manhood in Early Modern England*. Oxford: Oxford University Press, 2003.

Sheriff, Mary D. *The Exceptional Woman: Elisabeth Vigée-Lebrun and the Cultural Politics of Art*. Chicago: University of Chicago Press, 1997.

———. *Fragonard: Art and Eroticism*. Chicago: University of Chicago Press, 1990.

———. *Moved by Love: Inspired Artists and Deviant Women in Eighteenth-Century France*. Chicago: University of Chicago Press, 2004.

Siegfried, Susan. *The Art of Louis-Léopold Boilly: Modern Life in Napoleonic France*. New Haven, CT: Yale University Press, 1995.

Silver, Allan. "Historical Moments of Friendship Ideals: David & Jonathan, Montaigne, Adam Smith." In *Conceptualizing Friendship in Time and Place*, edited by Carla Risseeuw and Marlein Raalte, 119–42. Leiden: Brill, 2017.

Sofio, Séverine. *Artistes femmes: la parenthèse enchantée XVIIIe–XIXe siècles*. Paris: CNRS Editions, 2016.

———. "Gabrielle Capet's Collective Self-Portrait: Women and Artistic Legacy in Post-Revolutionary France," *Journal18* Issue 8, *Self/Portrait* (Fall 2019).

Sonnino, Eugenio. "In the Male City: The 'Status Animarum' of Rome in the Seventeenth Century." In *Socio-Economic Consequences of Sex-Ratios in Historical Perspective, 1500–1900*, edited by Antoinette Fauve-Camoux and Sølvi Sogner, 19–30. Milan: Università Bocconi, 1994.

———. "The Population in Baroque Rome." In *Rome–Amsterdam: Two Growing Cities in Seventeenth-Century Europe*, edited by Peter van Kessel and Elisja Schulte, 50–70. Amsterdam: Amsterdam University Press, 1997.

Spies-Gans, Paris Amanda. "Exceptional, but Not Exceptions: Public Exhibitions and the Rise of the Woman Artist in London and Paris, 1760–1830." *Eighteenth-Century Studies* 51, no. 4 (2018): 393–416.

Stein, Perrin, ed. *Artists and Amateurs: Etching in Eighteenth-Century France*. New York: Metropolitan Museum of Art, 2013.

Stiker-Métral, Charles-Olivier. *Narcisse contrarié: l'amour propre dans le discours moral en France, 1650–1715*. Paris: Honoré Champion, 2007.

Sutcliffe, Adam. "Friendship and Materialism in the French Enlightenment." In *Representing Private Lives of the Enlightenment*, edited by Andrew Kahn, 251–68. Oxford: Voltaire Foundation, 2010.

Tadmor, Naomi. *Family and Friends in Eighteenth-Century England: Household, Kinship and Patronage*. Cambridge: Cambridge University Press, 2011.

Tempest, Kathryn. *Cicero: Politics and Persuasion in Ancient Rome*. London: Bloomsbury Academic, 2014.

Todd, Janet M. *Women's Friendship in Literature*. New York: Columbia University Press, 1980.

Vidal, Mary. "The 'Other Atelier': Jacques-Louis David's Female Students." In *Women, Art and the Politics of Identity in Eighteenth-Century Europe*, edited by Melissa Hyde and Jennifer Milam, 237–62. Burlington, VT: Ashgate, 2003.

Vincent-Buffault, Anne. *L'exercice de l'amitié: pour une histoire des pratiques amicales aux XVIIIe et XIXe siècles*. Paris: Editions du Seuil, 1995.

Vlieghe, Hans. "A Propos d'un portrait de trois hommes par Simon de Vos (1603–1676) au Louvre." *Revue du Louvre* 38, no. 1 (1998): 37–38.

Volle, Nathalie. *Jean-Simon Berthélemy, 1743–1811: peintre d'histoire*. Paris: Arthéna, 1979.

West, Shearer. *Portraiture*. Oxford: Oxford University Press, 2004.

Whitfield, Clovis. "Portraiture: From the 'Simple Portrait' to the 'Ressemblance Parlante." In *The Genius of Rome 1592–1623*, edited by Beverly Louise Brown, 140–71. London: Royal Academy of the Arts, 2001.

Williams, Hannah. *Académie Royale: A History in Portraits*. Burlington: Ashgate, 2015.

———. "The Mysterious Suicide of François Lemoyne." *Oxford Art Journal* 38, no. 2 (June 2015): 225–45.

Wrigley, Richard. *The Origins of French Art Criticism: From the Ancien Régime to the Restoration*. Oxford: Oxford University Press, 1993.

Index

Page numbers in italics refer to illustrations.

Académie de Saint-Luc, 16, 82, 85, 86
Académie française, 1, 16, 19, 47, 51, 69, 195n3
  See also *Dictionnaire de l'académie française*
Alaux, Jean, 187
Alembert, Jean le Rond d', 51, 208n51, 210n69
  Cochin's portrait of, 64
  Encyclopédie, 3, 35, 51
  La Tour's portrait of, 47, 51, *52*, 65
  Rousseau's criticism of, 29, 102
amateur, 51, 58, 113, 127, 136, 146
  as engravers of Cochin's medallions, 74, 77
  as immortalized in Cochin's medallions, 65, 74
  rise of, 4, 27, 200n67
  role in the Academy, 13, 14, 22, 23, 27, 30–32, 196n5, 197n22
ami, 3, 11, 24–25
amitié, 11, 24, 25
  See also "De l'amitié"; friendship; *Traité d'amitié*; *Traité sur l'amitié*
amour-propre, 13, 17–18, 22, 198n41
Angiviller, comte d'
  Grands hommes, 26, 69, 73, 194n26
  surintendent des bâtiments, 69, 87, 104, 222n7
Angiviller, comtesse d', 104
Ansiaux, Jean-Joseph, 187

Antin, duc d', 19, 20
Arconville, Thiroux d', 84, 215n18
aristocrats
  critiques of aristocratic friendships, 102, 103, 106
  Labille-Guiard's portraits of, 104, 118
  Vigée-Lebrun's aristocratic network, 85, 87, 95, 102–4, 106, 113–14
Aristotle, 2, 12, 15–16, 161, 197–98n30
Artists' Portraits as Smokers and Drinkers (Vos), *165*, 167
Artist's touch. See *touche*
Avis important d'une femme (1785), 106, 114–18, 221n101

Bachaumont, Louis Petit de, 47, 55
Bachelier, Jean-Jacques, 97
  Labille-Guiard's portrait of, 95–97, *99*
Baillet de Saint-Julien, Louis-Guillaume, 39, 46, 47, 68
Baldrighi, Giuseppe
  Triple Portrait of Artists, 154–55, *158*, 161, 227–28n80, 228n82
Barbault, Jean, 178
Barry, James
  Self-Portrait with James Paine and Dominique Lefèvre, 155, *159*, 161
Bartolozzi, Francesco, 155, *160*
Beaufort, Jacques-Antoine, 95
Bergeret de Grancourt, Pierre-Jacques-Onésyme, 123, 174
Bernard, Jeanne, 97
Berthélemy, Jean-Simon, 77, 142, 146

Berthélemy, Jean-Simon (*continued*)
   caricature of Vincent, 127, *129*, 135–37, 143
   as *pensionnaire*, 123–25, 135
   Vincent's caricatures of, 143–46
black chalk, 125, 137
Blancherie, Pahin de la, 82, 89, 104
Bocquet, Jeanne-Angélique, 84
Boilly, Louis-Léopold
   Gathering of Artists in the Studio of Isabey, A, 154, 187–89, *188*
   Sculptor's Studio: Picture of a Family, A, 190
Bonafous, Louis-Abel de, 114
Boquet, Simon, *149*, 150
Bosse, Abraham
   Touch, from *The Five Senses*, 116–18, *117*
Bossuet, Jacques Bénigne, 26, 89
Boucher, François, 194n31, 204n2, 210n69
   Cochin's portraits of, 68, 210n69, 212n91
   portraits of Madame de Pompadour, 95
Boulard, Jean-Baptiste, 155, 228n81
Bounieu, Michel-Honoré
   La Gaîté, *134*
Bourdieu, Pierre, 4
Bretèche, Louis Richard de La, *173*, 174
Brizard, Jean-Baptiste, 95, 104
Brongniart, Alexandre-Théodore, 118
Brongniart, Alexandrine-Émilie, 118
Brouwer, Adrien
   Smokers, The, *166*, 167
bust, 36
   of Cicero, 107–10, *109*
   of Diderot (Houdon), 107
   of Labille (Pajou), 107–10, *108*, 219n84
   of La Tour (Lemoyne), 39, *44*
   of Lemoyne (Pajou), 89–93, *91*, *92*, 119, 217n48
   of Robert (Pajou), 118, 119, *121*, 124
Bust of Maurice Quentin de La Tour (Lemoyne), 39, *44*

Calonne, Charles-Alexandre de, 81, 114–16, *115*
Capet, Marie Gabrielle, 186–87, 230n17, 231n19
   Studio Scene: Adelaide Labille-Guiard Painting the Portrait of Joseph-Marie Vien, 187–90, *188*, 231n21
   See also *Self-Portrait with Two Pupils*
Caravaggio, 161, 228n86
   Fortune Teller, The, 161, 228n86
Caravane du Sultan à la Mecque (Vien), 178, *179*, 180
caricature, 6, 9, 127, 130
   Diderot on, 136, 137
   Watelet's discussions of, 130–32, 135, 137, 141–42, 225nn49–51
   See also Vincent, François-André
Caricature of François-André Vincent (Labille-Guiard), 97, *101*
Caricature of the Painter Pierre-Charles Jombert (Vincent), 125–27, *126*, 132–35, 143, 150
Caricatures (Stouf), 127, *128*, 146, *147*, 150, 223n15
Carlini, Agostino, 155, *160*
Carl Vanloo and his Family (L-M. Vanloo), 154, *156*
Carriera, Rosalba, 36
Cars, Laurent, 65, *67*, 73
Caylus, Comte de, 49, 65, 210n69
   Prix Caylus, 130, 135–37, 142
   Recueil de testes de caractère et de charges, dessinées par Léonard de Vinci, 142–43
celebrity
   artists' use of, 8, 37, 49–50, 55, 58, 68–69, 78, 81, 183
   new concept of, 37, 48–49, 58, 79, 207n37
   of Rousseau, 54, 211n87
   See also fame
censorship, 12, 51
Chambré, Anne de, 167–69, *168*
Chamfort, Nicolas, 48
Chardin, Jean-Siméon, 204n2

Cochin's portrait of, *66*, *67*, 68, 73, 212n91
La Tour's portrait of, *63*, 64, 76
Charles-Roger, Prince de Bauffremont, 186
Cicero
  bust of, 107–10, *109*
  On Friendship, 2, 12, 16–17, 107, 161
Cipriani, Giovanni Battista, 155, *160*
Clermont Tonnere, Comtesse de, 219n76
Clodion, 26, 110
Cochin, Charles-Nicolas, 6, 8, 35–36, 77, 102, 124, 183, 212n100
  Labille-Guiard's portrait of, 97, 110–13
  medallion portraits, 64–69, 77–78, 219n73
    Chardin, *66*, *67*, 68, 73, 212n91
    Cochin's hoped-for donation to the Academy, 75–77
    critics' reactions to, 65, 68, 74
    engravings of, 65, 69, 73, 74, 77, 210n69, 210n73, 212n90, 213n105
    Geoffrin's salon and, 65–68, 73–75, 78, 212nn90–91
    at the Salon of 1753, 35–37, 64, 77–79, 186
  Menu plaisirs du roi, 35, 74
Coclers van Wyck, Philippe-Henri, 227n73
  See also *Portrait de trois hommes*
Colbert, Jean-Baptiste, 22, 200n66
commerce, sociable, 3, 38–39, 46–47
commissions, 1, 37, 49, 50, 75, 102, 118, 167, 186, 191n6
  courtly, 6, 74, 206n25
  See also Angiviller, comte d': *Grands hommes*
community. See Royal Academy of Painting and Sculpture
competition. See Royal Academy of Painting and Sculpture
Condamine, Marquis de la, 47, 50
Confessions (Rousseau), 54, 211n87
copying, 88, 93, 94–95, 137, 155

Cossiers, Jan, 167
costume. See dress
counterrevolution, 9, 185, 230n13
Coypel, Antoine, 13, 19, 30–32, 196n14, 197n22
  Épître à mon fils, 12–19, 20, 196n16
    "Critique of Bias," 18–19
    "Idea of the Perfect Painter," 18
    "A Painter's Advisers," 13–15, 21, 23, 26–27, 185
Coypel, Charles, 19, 30, 302
  "Discourse on the Necessity of Receiving Advice," 12, 19–22, 185
  exchange with La Font, 22–23, 200n67
  Vie d'Antoine Coypel, 197n22
criticism, friendship and, 7, 10, 12–13, 23, 24, 185
  See also Coypel, Antoine; Coypel, Charles; *Le visionnaire*
Crow, Thomas, 5–6, 12, 217n40

Dandré-Bardon, Michel-François, 212n95
David, Jacques-Louis, 77, 194n31
  antagonism toward Vincent, 87, 189, 230n9, 231n19
  atelier, 122, 130
  dissident circle, 185, 186
Davidsz de Heem, Jan, 167
"De l'amitié" (Montaigne), 3, 83, 215n15
Demarteau, Gilles, 141
Descamps, Jean-Baptiste, 75–76
déshabille, 58, 64, 150
Desmarais, Jean-Baptiste Frédéric, 222n7
Dictionnaire de l'académie française, 3, 27, 141, 207n35, 221n102
Dictionnaire des arts de peinture, sculpture et gravure
  "caricature," 130–35, 137, 141
  clay modeling, 94
Diderot, Denis, 89
  debates on fame, 73, 211n87
  Encyclopédie, 3, 35, 146, 150
  Houdon's portrait of, 107

Diderot, Denis (*continued*)
  "Salon of 1767," 136, 137
  "terracotta is the concern of genius," 94, 119
directeur des bâtiments, 19
Discourse on Inequality (Rousseau), 30, 51
"Discourse on the Necessity of Receiving Advice" (C. Coypel), 12, 19–22, 185
Discours sur l'inégalité. See *Discourse on Inequality*
Discours sur les sciences et les arts (Rousseau), 28–29, 51
distinterestedness
  in criticism, 22–23, 32, 200n67
  in friendship, 2, 4–5, 8, 13, 14–15, 17, 22, 33, 47
drawing
  life drawing, 135, 137–41, 142, 150, 192n11
  tête d'expression, 113, 135–36, 143, 169
  See also caricature; Cochin, Charles-Nicholas: medallion portraits
dress
  bonnet de coton, 127, 150
  classicizing, 169
  costume espagnole, 169, 174, 178–80
  déshabille and, 59, 64, 150
  travestissement, 174–78, 180
Duchange, Charles-Nicolas, 125, 143–46
Duclos, Charles Pinot, 47, 50
Dupin de Saint-Julien, Madame, 219n76
Dupouch, Claude, 39, *42*
Durameau, Louis Jean-Jacques, 26
Dyck, Anthony van, 39
  Portrait of George Gage with Two Servants, 164, 167, 228n87

École des beaux-arts, 76, 82
École des élèves protégés, 135, 142
Edelinck, Gerard
  Pierre Mignard, 72
Émile (Rousseau), 3, 102
emulation, 1, 17, 82, 130, 199n52, 229n1

Encyclopédie (Diderot and Alembert), 3, 35, 46, 51, 94, 103, 146
encyclopédistes, 3, 51, 213n103
engraving, 36, 49, 50, 94, 110, 141, 204n6, 210n69
  of Cochin's medallions, 65, 69, 73, 74, 77, 210n69, 210n73, 212n90, 213n105
  of *grands hommes*, 69, 73
  of Labille-Guiard's portrait of Vien, 185–86
  of La Tour's portrait of Voltaire, 36
Enlightenment. See celebrity; disinterestedness; friendship; sociability
expression study. See *tête d'expression*

Falconet, Étienne, 73, 94, 211n87
fame, 48–49, 69–73, 78–79
  debates on the nature of, 73, 211n87
  friendship as linked to, 22, 30
  synonyms for, 48, 207n35
fancy dress. See *travestissement*
fantasy figure, 169–74, 178
Fantin-Latour, Henri, 154
Favart, Madame, 210n69, 213n105
Ferrand, Mademoiselle, 47, 78
Ficquet, Étienne, *34*
Filleul, Rosalie, 84, 186
Flahaut, Comtesse de, 219n76
Forbonnais, François Véron Duverger de, 213n103
Fort, Bernadette, 86, 201n76
Fortune Teller, The (Caravaggio), 161, 228n86
Fragonard, Jean-Honoré, 116
  fantasy portraits, 169–74, *173*
Franconville, Moricaud, 127, *128*, 146, *147*, 223n15
fraternité, 4, 9
Frémin, René, 39, *43*, 64
French Academy, Paris. See Académie française
French Academy, Rome, 124, 127, 180
French art, promotion and revival of, 17, 22, 33, 183, 187, 189–90

French Revolution
  arrest or execution of artists, 186, 230n9, 230n14
  dissolution of the Academy, 3, 81
  distrust of friendship, 9–10, 183–85
  fraternité, 4, 9
  Jacobins, 4, 183–85
  Palais Mancini's brief closure, 123
  reform of the Academy, 81–82, 185
French school. *See* French art
friendship
  as aristocratic, 102, 103, 106
  classical ideals of, 2–3, 5, 12, 16–17, 32, 107, 119, 183
  distrust of, 9–10, 183–85
  female, 82–85, 97, 102–3, 106–7, 110, 114, 122
  friendship portraits, 6, 113, 161
  as kinship, 4, 14, 110, 124
  male, 2, 9, 15–16, 29, 33, 81, 102, 104, 106, 125
  mixed-sex, 82–84, 97, 103, 113, 215n18
  patron-artist, 14, 38–39, 205n14
  See also *ami*; *amitié*; criticism; disinterestedness; sociability

Gabriel, Mademoiselle, 47
Gage, George, *164*
Garrigues, abbé, 65, 68
Gathering of Artists in the Studio of Isabey, A (Boilly), 154, 187–89, *188*
Gaultier, Denis, 167, *168*
Geerloff, Johan, 167
Geli, Madame de, 47, 213n106
genre painting, 36, 76, 167
  Caravaggesque, 161, 228n86
genres
  hierarchy of, 5
  "minor," 6, 35–36, 76–77
Geoffrin, Madame (Marie-Thérèse)
  Cochin"s medallions and, 65–68, 73–77, 211n76, 212nn90–91
  illness, 75, 212n93
  king of Poland and, 75, 212n92
  Robert's scenes of home, 68, *70*, *71*
  salon gatherings, 35, 36, 48, 69, 78
Ghezzi, Pier Leone, 127
Gois, Étienne-Pierre-Adrien, 95–97
Goodman, Dena, 8, 46, 102, 194–95n34
Gorsas, Antoine-Joseph, 107
gout (taste), 14, 15, 20, 27, 55, 88, 124, 136, 200n67
  See also *Le visionnaire*
Grand, Catherine (née Noël Catherine Verlée), 95, *96*
grands hommes, 5, 37, 68–69, 76, 194n26, 194n31
  Angiviller's series, 26, 69, 73, 194n26
  La Live de Jully's engravings, 69, 73
  Perrault's illustrations, 69, *72*, 73
Greuze, Jean-Baptiste, 217n40
  portrait of Watelet, 58, *61*
Grimou, Alexis, 174
Grollier, Marquise de, 84
group portrait, 6, 9, 143, 154–55, 167–69
  See also *Portrait de trois hommes*; *Studio Scene*
Guiche, marquise de la, 95, 102, 103
guillotine, 186, 230n14

Habermas, Jürgen, 49
  See also public sphere
Helvétius, Claude-Adrien, 102
Henri IV, 169
hero, 9, 48, 51, 69, 73
Hervey, Lady, 210n69, 213n105
history painting, 6, 169
  Academy and
    emphasis and promotion of, 19, 22, 37–38, 76, 77, 194n26
    occupying highest ranks, 3, 36, 123, 191n2, 192n11
  decline of, 38, 205n10
  portraits by history painters, 6, 39, 123, 124, 125, 135, 136, 143, 194n31
  Vigée-Lebrun and, 95, 113, 214n7, 218n59
  Vincent and, 123–24
Hogarth, William, 130–32
hommes illustres. *See grands hommes*

Horace, 18
Houdon, Jean-Antoine, 107, 187
Huet, Madame, 47
Hume, David, 73, 211n87
Huquier, Jacques-Gabriel, 65

Imperial Academy, St. Petersburg, 195n3
informality. See *déshabille*
Institut de France, 81–82, 189

Jacobins, 4, 183–85
Jaucourt, Louis de, 103–4
Jean-Siméon Chardin (Cochin), 65, 67, 68, 73, 212n91
Jeaurat, Étienne, 204n2
Joly, Hugues-Adrien, 65–68, 74
Jombert, Pierre-Charles, 210n73
  Vincent's caricatures of, 125–27, *126*, 132–35, 143, *145*, 150
Julie, ou la nouvelle Héloïse (Rousseau), 51

Kauffman, Angelica, 84

Labille, Claude-Edmé, 85, 86
  as lottery *receveur*, 85–86, 215–16n25
  Pajou's bust of, 107–10, *108*, 219n84
Labille-Guiard, Adélaïde, 6, 8, 77, 78, 85–86, 183, 215n21
  acceptance into the Academy, 8, 82, 86, 87, 95–97, 119, 122, 203n101, 212–13n101, 214n3, 214n9
  Capet's portrait of, 187–90, *188*, 231n21
  critics' reactions to, 82, 85, 95, 97–107, 112, 113–14, 186
  painter of the aunts of Louis XVI, 104, 118
  portrait of Bachelier, 95–97, *99*
  portrait of Bauffremont, 186, 230n13
  portrait of Brizard, 95, 104
  portrait of Charles-Roger, 186
  portrait of Pajou, 89–94, *90*, 107–10, 119, 219–20n90
  portrait of Vanloo, 110, *111*, 113, 220n92
  portrait of Vernet, 110–13, *112*, 220n92
  portrait of Vien, 95–97, *98*, *184*, 185–86
  portrait of Vincent, 97, *101*
  portraits of National Assembly, 186
  portraits of Suvée, 95–97, *100*, 187
  relationship with Vincent, 86, 97, 104, 107, 110, 186, 189, 218n60, 219–20n90, 230n17
  self-portrait with Capet and Rosemond, 104–10, *105*, 118
  supposed rivalry with Vigée-Lebrun, 8, 82–88, 95
  as teacher, 84, 97, 106, 110, 186, 230n16, 230n21
Laborde, Jean-Joseph de, 118
Lacombe, Jacques, 5, 50, 681
La conversation espagnole (C. Vanloo), 174, *176*
La Font de Saint-Yenne, Étienne
  on the Salon of 1746, 22–23, 37–38, 200nn67–68, 205n11
  on the Salon of 1753, 48, 49, 50, 55, 74, 78, 79, 207n29
La Gaîté (Bounieu), *134*
La justification de Suzanne (Menageot), 27–28
La lecture espagnole (C. Vanloo), 174, *177*
La Live de Jully, Ange-Laurent, 69, 73, 210n69, 211n82
Lamballe, Madame de, 102
Lambert, Madame de, 3, 83–84, 97, 103, 113
Lancret, Nicolas, 116
Largillière, Nicolas de, 21
L'Art de peindre (Watelet), 55–58, 93
La Tour, Maurice Quentin de, 6, 8, 36, 102, 124, 183, 194n31, 206n27
  accolades, 206n25
  déshabille and looser style, 55–64, 65
  Lemoyne's bust of, 39, *44*
  pastellist, 35, 36, 47

portrait of Alembert, 47, 51, *52*, 65
portrait of Chardin, *63*, 64, 76
portrait of Dupouch, 39, *42*
portrait of Frémin, 39, *43*, 64
portrait of Lemoyne, 39–47, *40*, 64, 88, 93
portrait of the Marquis de Voyer, 47, 50, 51, 55, *56*, 65, 78, 210n69
portrait of Parrocel, *45*, 46, 206n17
portrait of Restout, 39, *41*
portrait of Silvestre, 47, 50, 55–58, *57*, 59–64, 65, 78
portraits bequeathed to other artists, 77, 213n103
portraits of Rousseau, 47, 51–54, *53*, 78, 208n51
at the Salon of 1747, 23, 39–46
at the Salon of 1753, 35–37, 47–55, 64–65, 77, 78–79, 186, 208n46, 213n106
Voltaire à 41 ans, *34*, 36, 49
La véridique au Salon (1783), 82
Le Bas, Jacques-Philippe, 204n2
Leblanc, abbé
  La Tour's portrait of, 23, 210n69
  on the Salon of 1747, 23, 201n71
  on the Salon of 1753, 50, 55, 65, 68, 208n43
Le Bouteux, Joseph Barthélémy, 146
  caricature of Vincent, 127, *131*
  Vincent's caricatures of, 132, *133*, *140*, 141, 150
Lebreton, Joachim, 85, 87, 189, 231n19
Lecomte, Marguerite, 47, 65, 210n69, 213n105
Le déjeuner de Madame Geoffrin (Robert), 68, *70*
Lefèvre, Dominique, 155, *159*
Le Guay, Étienne Charles, 68
Lemonnier, Anicet-Charles-Gabriel, 124–25, 143
  portrait of the artist's brother, 180, *181*
  Vincent's caricatures of, *140*, 141, 143–46
Lemoyne, François, 20

Lemoyne, Jean-Baptiste II, 86, 87–89, 216n32
  bust of La Tour, 39, *44*
  bust of Parrocel, 76
  La Tour's portrait of, 39–47, *40*, 46–47, 64, 88, 93
  Pajou's busts of, 89–93, *91*, *92*, 119
  Vigée-Lebrun's portrait of, *80*, 88, 93, 119
  See also *Portrait of Pajou Modeling the Portrait of His Teacher, Lemoyne*
Le pourquoi ou l'ami des artistes (1781), 31–32
Le Riche de la Pouplinière, Alexandre-Jean-Joseph, 36, 48
Les Hommes illustres qui ont paru en France pendant ce siècle (Perrault), 69, *72*, 73
Le Sueur, Eustache
  Réunion d'amis, 167–69, *168*
Lettre à M. D'Alembert (Rousseau), 29, 102, 208n51
Lettre critique à un ami sur les ouvrages de MM de l'Académie exposés au Sallon de Louvre (1759), 23
Lettres à Monsieur *** sur les peintures, les sculptures, et les gravures, exposées au Sallon du Louvre en 1765 (Mathon de la Cour), 1–3, 183, 229n1
Lettre sur l'exposition des ouvrages de peinture, sculpture, etc. de l'année 1747 (Leblanc), 23, 201n71
Le visionnaire, ou Lettres sur les Ouvrages exposés au Sallon (1779), 24–31, 201n77, 202n88, 203n101
Lichtenstein, Jacqueline, 11–12, 13, 20, 22–23, 197n22, 200n67
life drawing, 135, 137–41, 142, 150, 192n11
Lilti, Antoine, 48, 49, 54, 68, 73
L'impartialité au Sallon (1783), 32
Lives of the Artists (Vasari), 205n14
Louis XIV, 38
Louis XVI, 83, 87, 104, 114, 118, 169

Louvre, 76, 85, 119, 213n106
  Academicians' lodgings and studios, 2, 81, 86, 88, 122, 191n7, 206n25
  Apollo gallery, 19
  salon carré, 7, 12
  See also *Le visionnaire*
Lundberg, Gustaf, 136
Luxembourg, Maréchal de, 54

Manelli, Pietro, 47, 51, 208n46
Marat, Jean-Paul, 4
Marcus Tullius Cicero (106–43 B.C.), 107–10, *109*
Marie-Antoinette, 86, 87, 95, 102–3, 114, 216n38
Mariette, Pierre-Jean, 23, 142–43, 206n27
Marigny, Madame de, 58, *60*
Marigny, Marquis de, 58, *60*, 124, 210n69
Marmontel, Jean-François, 51–54, 206n27, 208n51
masonic lodges, 4, 17
Massé, Jean-Baptiste, 204n2
Mathon de la Cour, Charles-Joseph, 1–3, 183, 229n1
Mayer, Constance, 190
medallion portrait, 6, 69
  Vincent and, 125, 169, 226n61
  See also Cochin, Charles-Nicolas
Members of the Society of Dilettanti (Reynolds), 169, *170*, *171*
Mémoires secrets, 113–14
Ménageot, François-Guillaume
  La justification de Suzanne, 27–28
  as *pensionnaire*, 124, 125, 146
  Vigée-Lebrun's rumored affair with, 81, 221n101
Mérimée, Jean-François-Leonor, 187
Messieurs, ami de tous le monde (1783), 32
Meynier, Charles, 187
Michel, Christian, 11–12, 13, 35–36, 197n22, 204n2, 210n73, 212n91
Miger, Simon-Charles, *184*, 185
Mignard, Pierre, *72*
miniature, 77, 187
Mirabeau, Marquis de, 47

Mitoire, Madame, 95, 110
Moitte, Guillaume, 146
Mondonville, Madame de, 47
Montaigne, Michel de, 3, 83, 215n15
Montalembert, Marquis de, 47, 50–51
Montesquieu, 26
Mosnier, Jean-Laurent, 107

Napoleon, report to, 187, 189, 231n19
National Assembly, 186
Natoire, Charles-Joseph, 124, 125, 137, 222n5
Nattier, Jean-Marc, 194n31
  Portrait of the Artist and his Family, 154, *157*
Nazarenes, 161
Nécrologie (Lebreton), 85, 87, 189, 231n19
Nivelle de la Chaussée, Pierre-Claude, 47, 50
Nollet, abbé, 47, 50
Nonnotte, Donat, 38–39
nude, 137, 141

Observations sur les ouvrages de MM. de l'Academie de peinture et de sculpture (Leblanc), 50, 55, 65, 68, 208n43
oil portrait, 6, 88, 93, 110, 119, 187, 189
On Friendship (Cicero), 2, 12, 16–17, 107, 161

Paine, James, 155, *159*
Painters and Public Life in Eighteenth-Century France (Crow), 5–6, 12, 217n40
Pajou, Augustin
  bust of Labille, 107–10, *108*, 219n84
  bust of Lemoyne (bronze), *92*, 93
  bust of Lemoyne (terracotta), 89–93, *91*, 119
  bust of Robert, 118, 119, *121*, 124
  Labille-Guiard's portrait of, 89–94, *90*, 107–10, 119, 219–20n90
  statue of Bossuet, 26, 89
  See also *Studio Scene*

Pajou, Catherine-Flore, 107–10
Palais Mancini, 97, 118, 123–24, 130, 150, 151
   Pensionnaires' caricatures, 125–50
      counterproofs, 143, 146, 182, 226n61, 227n68
      as parodies of life drawing, 127–30, 137–43, 150
      as souvenirs, 143–46, 182
   See also *Portrait de trois hommes*
Pallière, Étienne, 187
Pallière, Léon, 187
Parrocel, Charles, 204n2, 210n69
   La Tour's portrait of, *45*, 46, 206n17
   Lemoyne's bust of, 76
Pasha Having a Mistress's Portrait Painted, A (C. Vanloo), 174, *175*
pastel, 6, 7, 35
   Labille-Guiard's handling of, 93–94
   La Tour's focus on and handling of, 36, 47, 55, 59, 64, 65
   Vigée-Lebrun's handling of, 93
   Watelet's poem on, 55–58, 93
pensionnaire. See Palais Mancini
Perrault, Charles
   Les Hommes illustres qui ont paru en France pendant ce siècle, 69, *72*, 73
philosophes, 4, 48, 51
Picot, François-Édouard, 187
Pierre, Jean-Baptiste, 30, 68, 214n3
Pierre Mignard (Edelinck), *72*
Pigalle, Jean-Baptiste, 29, 77
Piles, Roger de, 13
Pliny the Elder, 161
Poland, king of, 50, 75, 212n92
Polignac, duchesse de, 95, 102
Pompadour, Madame de, 95
Pontormo, Jacopo
   Portrait of Two Friends, 161, *162*
portrait
   donations to the Academy, 76–77, 212n94
   exchange, 5, 6, 39, 46, 75, 77, 83, 107, 110, 113, 146, 183
   family portrait, 154, 161, 227n78
   formats
      bust-length, 37, 39, 64, 65, 110
      full-length, 59, 69, 110, 125, 127, 137, 142, 161
      half-length, 39, 59, 64, 89, 119, 161, 167
      profile, 65, 125, 137, 141, 143, 169, 226n61
   friendship portrait, 6, 113, 161
   as gift, 54, 74–77, 88, 107, 212n94
   greed and vanity as linked to, 5, 8, 37, 48, 79, 102
   miniature, 77, 187
   reception portrait, 59, 76–77, 110, 212n100
   reciprocal portrait, 39, 88
   self-portrait, 77, 82, 84, 95, 103, 110, 113, 169–74, 186, 228n91
   See also bust; fantasy figure; group portrait; medallion portrait; triple portrait
Portrait Bust of Claude-Edmé Labille (Pajou), 107–10, *108*, 219n84
Portrait Bust of Hubert Robert (Pajou), 118, 119, *121*, 124
Portrait Bust of Jean-Baptiste II Lemoyne (Pajou), 89–93, *91*, *92*, 93, 119
Portrait-charge of François-André Vincent (Le Bouteux), 127, *131*
Portrait-charge of the Architect Rousseau (Vincent), *148*, 150
Portrait-charge of the Painter Jombert (Vincent), *145*, 150
Portrait-charge of the Painter Le Bouteux (black chalk) (Vincent), *140*, 141, 150
Portrait-charge of the Painter Le Bouteux (pen and ink) (Vincent), 132, *133*, 150
Portrait-charge of the Painter Lemonnier (Vincent), *140*, 141
Portrait-charge of the Painter Suveé (counterproof) (Vincent), *139*, 141, 150
Portrait-charge of the Painter Suveé (Vincent), *138*, 141, 150

Portrait-charge of the Sculptor Boquet (Vincent), *149*, 150
Portrait de Chardin (Cochin), 65, *66*, 68, 73, 212n91
Portrait de trois hommes (Vincent), 9, 124, 151–67, *152*, 169, 182, 222n86
Portrait of Carle Vanloo and His Family (Louis-Michel Vanloo), 154, *156*
Portrait of Charles-Alexandre de Calonne (Vigée-Lebrun), 81, 114–16, *115*
Portrait of Claude-Henri Watelet (Greuze), 58, *61*
Portrait of Francesco Bartolozzi, Agostino Carlini, and Giovanni Battista Cipriani (Rigaud), 155, *160*, 161
Portrait of François-André Vincent (Berthélemy), 127, *129*, 135–37, 143–46
Portrait of George Gage with Two Servants (Dyck), *164*, 167, 228n87
Portrait of Hubert Robert (Vigée-Lebrun), 104, 118, *120*
Portrait of Jean-Baptiste II Lemoyne (Vigée-Lebrun), *80*, 88
Portrait of Jean-Jacques Bachelier (Labille-Guiard), 95–97, *99*
Portrait of Jean-Jacques Rousseau (La Tour), 47, 51–54, *53*, 208n51
Portrait of Jean Le Rond d'Alembert (La Tour), 47, 51, *52*, 65
Portrait of Joseph-Benoît Suvée (Labille-Guiard), 95–97, *100*
Portrait of Joseph-Marie Vien (Labille-Guiard), 95–97, *98*, *184*, 185–86
Portrait of Joseph Vernet (Labille-Guiard), 110–13, *112*, 220n92
Portrait of Louis de Silvestre (La Tour), 47, 50, 55–58, *57*, 59–64, 65, 78
Portrait of Louis Richard de La Bretèche (Fragonard), *173*, 174
Portrait of Madame Grand (Vigée-Lebrun), 95, *96*, 102
Portrait of Marquis Marc-René de Voyer d'Argenson (La Tour), 47, 50, 51, 55, 56, 65, 78, 210n69

Portrait of Pajou Modeling the Portrait of His Teacher, Lemoyne (Labille-Guiard), 89–94, *90*, 107–10, 119, 219–20n90
Portrait of Pierre Rousseau (Vincent), *153*, 154
Portrait of Susanna Lunden (Rubens), 217n49
Portrait of the Artist and His Family (Nattier), 154, *157*
Portrait of the Artist in His Studio (Mosnier), 107
Portrait of the Artist's Brother in Fancy Dress (Lemonnier), 180, *181*
Portrait of the Marquis de Marigny and his Wife (L-M. Vanloo), 58, *60*
Portrait of the Painter Charles-Amédée-Philippe Vanloo (Labille-Guiard), 110, *111*, 113, 220n92
Portrait of the Painter Charles Parrocel (La Tour), *45*, 46, 206n17
Portrait of the Painter Claude Dupouch (La Tour), 39, *42*
Portrait of the Painter Jean Baptiste Chardin (La Tour), *63*, 64, 76
Portrait of the Painter Jean Restout (La Tour), 39, *41*
Portrait of the Painter Louis de Silvestre (Valade), 59, *62*
Portrait of the Sculptor Jean-Baptiste II Lemoyne (La Tour), 39–47, *40*, 64, 88, 93
Portrait of the Sculptor René Frémin (La Tour), 39, *43*, 64
Portrait of Two Friends (Pontormo), 161, *162*
Preisler, John-Martin, 204n2
premier peintre du roi, 20, 38, 189, 231n19
Présentation d'un tableau à Madame Geoffrin (Robert), 68, *71*
Prix Caylus, 130, 135–37, 142
Prix de quartier, 19, 130, 142
Prix de Rome, 19, 97, 123, 130, 135, 150, 222n3, 222n5, 222n7
See also Palais Mancini

public sphere, 4, 6, 12, 23, 49, 84

quarrel of the ancients and the moderns, 69

Recueil de testes de caractère et de charges, dessinées par Léonard de Vinci (Caylus), 142–43
Réflexions sur quelques causes de l'état présent de la peinture en France (La Font de Saint-Yenne), 22–23, 37–38, 200nn67–68, 205n11
Renaissance, 123, 161, 169, 228n91
Republic of Letters, 11, 17, 51, 84
Restout, Jean, 39, 41, 204n2
Réunion d'amis (Le Sueur), 167–69, 168
Reynolds, Joshua, 169, 170, 171
Richelet, Pierre, 37
Rigaud, Hyacinthe, 21
Rigaud, Jean-François
  Portrait of Francesco Bartolozzi, Agostino Carlini, and Giovanni Battista Cipriani, 155, 160, 161
rivalry, 6, 20, 21, 82, 130
  supposed, between Labille-Guiard and Vigée-Lebrun, 8, 82–88, 95
Robert, Hubert
  Pajou's bust of, 118, 119, 121, 124
  scenes of Madame Geoffrin's home, 68, 70, 71
  Vigée-Lebrun's portrait of, 104, 118, 120
Rochefoucauld, François de La, 102
Romain, Jacques Dumant le, 76
Rome. *See* Palais Mancini
Rosemond, Marie Marguerite Carreaux de. See *Self-Portrait with Two Pupils*
Roslin, Alexandre, 76, 86, 124, 194n31, 212n95
  See also *Triple Portrait of Artists*
Roslin, Marie-Susanne (née Giroust), 76, 203n101
Rousseau, Jean-Jacques, 51, 103, 106
  Confessions, 54, 211n87
  critiques of women, 28–30, 102

Discours sur les sciences et les arts, 28–29, 51
Discours sur l'inégalite, 30, 51
Émile, 3, 102
  falling-out with Hume, 211n87
  on fame, 73, 211n87
  Julie, ou la nouvelle Héloïse, 51
  La Tour's portraits of, 47, 51–54, 53, 78, 208n51
  Lettre à M. D'Alembert, 29, 102, 208n51
  Rousseau, juge de Jean-Jacques, 54
Rousseau, Marie-Andrienne (née Potain), 118
Rousseau, Pierre, 227n72
  Vincent's caricature of, 148, 150
  Vincent's portrait of, 153, 154
  See also *Portrait de trois hommes*
Royal Academy, London, 49, 155
Royal Academy of Marseille, 154, 227n73
Royal Academy of Painting and Sculpture, Paris (Academy)
  amateurs' role in, 13, 14, 22, 23, 27, 30–32, 196n5, 197n22
  community, 2, 7, 8, 13, 27, 82, 199–22
  competition, 1–2, 17, 19–21, 22, 82, 122, 130, 142, 150, 182, 199n52, 224n22
  Prix Caylus, 130, 135–37, 142
  Prix de quartier, 19, 130, 142
  Prix de Rome, 19, 97, 123, 130, 135, 150, 222n3, 222n5, 222n7
  conférences, 11–14, 21–22, 195–96n5, 196n14, 196n16, 197n22
  directors of, 13, 19, 20, 47, 50 185, 189, 195–96n5
  dissolution of, 81, 87, 137, 214n3
  emulation, 1, 17, 82, 130, 199n52, 229n1
  founding of, 3, 16, 81, 137, 195n5, 214n3
  hierarchy of, 1, 2–3, 16, 76, 77, 191n2
  Louvre lodgings, 2, 81, 86, 88, 122, 191n7, 206n25

Royal Academy of Painting and
    Sculpture, Paris (*continued*)
  morceaux de réception, 46, 59, 76–77,
    89, 110, 119, 212n10
  portrait donations to, 76–77, 212n94
  premier peintre du roi, 20, 38, 189
  reform of, 81–82, 185
  sociability, 7–8, 22–23, 85, 122, 151,
    169
  statutes, 11, 16, 76, 137, 192n11,
    195–95n
  successor of, 81–82, 189
  women in, 81–82, 83, 214n3
  See also Palais Mancini
Royal Academy of Sciences, Paris, 47, 51
Rubens, Peter Paul, 39
  Portrait of Susanna Lunden, 217n49
  *Self-Portrait in a Circle of Friends from
    Mantua*, 163, 167

Sacy, Louis de, 16–17, 18
Saint-Aubin, Augustin de, 211n82
Saint-Aubin, Charles-Germain, 132
Salon
  livret, 46, 49, 55, 64, 69, 78, 118, 187,
    189, 201n71, 204n6, 209n60
  opening to all artists, 9, 186
  percentage of portraits, 36
  of 1737, 7–8, 12
  of 1743, 43
  of 1746, 22, 38
  of 1747, 39, 46, 47, 48, 64, 88
  of 1748, 44, 46, 47
  of 1753, 35–37, 47–54, 55, 64, 65, 69,
    77, 78–79, 186
  of 1759, 23, 54, 89, 93
  of 1761, 64, 177
  of 1763, 44, 46, 64, 88, 89
  of 1765, 1, 183
  of 1767, 136, 137
  of 1777, 123, 154
  of 1779, 24
  of 1783, 32, 82, 85, 95, 104, 113, 118,
    185, 186, 214n7, 217n44
  of 1785, 97, 104–18, 122, 221n101
  of 1787, 118
  of 1789, 104, 118
  of 1791, 186
  See also La Font de Saint-Yenne,
    Étienne; *Le visionnaire*
Salon de la Correspondance, 82, 89, 93,
    97, 104, 218n60
salon gatherings, 28, 36, 48, 65, 102
Saly, Jacques, 127
sanguine, 125, 135, 136
Schmidt, George Frederick, 204n2
Sculptor's Studio: Picture of a Family, A
    (Boilly), 190
sculpture. *See* Angiviller, comte d':
    Grands hommes; bust
Self-Portrait (Vincent), 169–74, 172
*Self-Portrait in a Circle of Friends from
    Mantua* (Rubens), 163, 167
Self-Portrait with Artist's Father
    (Mayer), 190
*Self-Portrait with James Paine and
    Dominique Lefèvre* (Barry), 155, 159,
    161
Self-Portrait with Two Pupils
    (Labille-Guiard), 104–10, 105, 118
Sergel, Johan Tobias, 146
Silvestre, Louis de
  La Tour's portrait of, 47, 50, 55–58,
    57, 59–64, 65, 78
  Valade's portrait of, 59, 62
Slodtz, Michel-Ange, 204n2
Smokers, The (Brouwer), 166, 167
sociability, 27
  Academic, 7–8, 22–23, 85, 122, 151,
    169
  Enlightenment, 3–5, 38–39, 46–47,
    102, 174, 185
Society of Dilettanti, 169, 170, 171
Souvenirs (Vigée-Lebrun), 81, 83, 84,
    86, 87, 88, 97, 102, 104, 118, 216n32,
    216n38
still life, 36, 76, 154
Stouf, Jean-Baptiste
  Caricatures, 127, 128, 146, 147, 150,
    223n15

Studio in Batignolles (Fantin-Latour), 154
Studio Scene: Adélaïde Labille-Guiard Painting the Portrait of Joseph-Marie Vien (Capet), 187–90, *188*, 231n21
surintendant des bâtiments, 22, 69, 87, 222n7
Sur la peinture (1782), 29
Suvée, Joseph-Benoît, 122
   collection, 97, 146
   imprisonment, 186, 230n9
   Labille-Guiard's portraits of, 95–97, *100*, 187
   as *pensionnaire*, 97, 124–25
   Vincent's caricatures of, *138*, *139*, 141, 143, 146, 150

taste. See *goût*
terracotta, 93–94, 118–19, 219n84
tête d'expression, 113, 135–36, 143, 169
Therbusch, Anna Dorothea, 203n101
Thévenin, Charles, 187
Tocqué, Louis, 38–39
Tomkins, Charles Algernon, *170*, *171*
Touch, from *The Five Senses* (Bosse), 116–18, *117*
touche, 58, 59–64, 65, 93–95
Tournehem, Charles-François Le Normand de, 37
Tournement, Lenormant de, 22
Traité d'amitié (Sacy), 16–17, 18
Traité sur l'amitié (Madame de Lambert), 3, 83–84, 97, 103, 113
travestissement, 174–78, 180
triple portrait, 154–55, 161–67
   See also *Portrait de trois hommes*; *Triple Portrait of Artists*
Triple Portrait of Artists (Baldrighi), 154–55, *158*, 161, 227–28n80, 228n82
Troy, Jean-François de, 20, 21, 65, 137, 178, 210n69

Valade, Jean
   Louis de Silvestre, 59, *62*
Vallayer-Coster, Anne, 29, 84, 113, 122, 214n9

Vanloo, Carle, 95, 210n69
   Labille-Guiard's portrait of, 110, *111*, 113, 220n92
   La conversation espagnole, 174, *176*
   La lecture espagnole, 174, *177*
   L-M. Vanloo's portrait of, 154, *156*
   Pasha Having a Mistress's Portrait Painted, A, 174, *175*
Vanloo, Christine (née Soumis), 154, 174
Vanloo, Louis-Michel
   Carl Vanloo and His Family, 154, *156*
   Portrait of the Marquis de Marigny and His Wife, 58, *60*
Vasari, Giorgio, 205n14
Vernet, Joseph, 68, 86
   Labille-Guiard's portrait of, 110–13, *112*, 220n92
   Ports of France, 110
   Vigée-Lebrun's portrait of, 86, 104
Vien, Joseph-Marie, 23, 77, 86, 97, 124, 201n73, 227n68, 228n81, 231n25
   as Academy's director, 185–86, 189
   accolades, 189
   Caravane du Sultan à la Mecque, 178, *179*, 180
   Cochin's portrait of, 68, 212n91
   Labille-Guiard's portrait of, 95–97, *98*, *184*, 185–86
   See also *Studio Scene*
Vien, Marie-Thérèse (née Reboul), 84, 203n101
Vigée, Louis, 86
Vigée-Lebrun, Élisabeth, 6, 77–78, 82, 85–86
   acceptance into the Academy, 6, 82, 86–88, 104, 203n101, 212–13n101, 214n3, 214n9, 216n38
   aristocratic network, 85, 87, 95, 102–4, 106, 113–14
   critics' reactions to, 82, 85, 95, 97–104, 106, 113–14
   flight from Paris, 87, 186
   history paintings, 95, 113, 214n7, 218n59
   portrait of Calonne, 81, 114–16, *115*

Vigée-Lebrun, Élisabeth (*continued*)
  portrait of Lemoyne, *80*, 88
  portrait of Madame Grand, 95, *96*, 102
  portrait of Marie-Antoinette
    en chemise, 95, 103
  portrait of Robert, 104, 118, *120*
  portrait of the Marquise de la Guiche
    as a milkmaid, 95, 102, 103
  portrait of Vernet, 86, 104
  rumors surrounding, 81, 114–18, 183,
    216n38, 221n101
  self-portraits, 82, 95, 118, 217n49
  Souvenirs, 81, 83, 84, 86, 87, 88, 97,
    102, 104, 118, 216n32, 216n38
  supposed rivalry with Labille-Guiard,
    8, 82–88, 95
Villemert, Boudier de, 28
Vincent, François-André, 6, 77, 183,
  185, 186–87
  accolades, 123, 142, 150, 222n5, 226n60
  Berthélemy's caricature of, 127, *129*,
    135–37, 143–46
  caricature of Boquet, *149*, 150
  caricature of Le Bouteux
    (black chalk), *140*, 141, 150
  caricature of Le Bouteux
    (pen and ink), 132, *133*, 150
  caricature of P. Rousseau, *148*, 150
  caricature of Suveé, *138*, 141, 150
  caricature of Suveé (counterproof),
    139, 141, 150
  caricatures of Jombert, 125–27, *126*,
    132–35, 143, *145*, 150
  caricatures of Lemonnier, *140*, 141,
    143–46
  history painting and, 123–24
  Labille-Guiard's portrait of, 97, *101*
  Le Bouteux's caricature of, 127, *131*
  pensionnaire caricatures, 9, 123, 124–50
    counterproofs, 143, 146, 226n61
    as parodies of life drawing, 130, 141,
      142, 150
    as *portrait charges*, 141–42, 143–50,
      226n61
    as souvenirs, 143–46

Portrait de trois hommes, 9, 124,
  151–67, *152*, 169, 182, 222n86
portrait of P. Rousseau, *153*, 154
relationship with Labille-Guiard, 86,
  97, 104, 107, 110, 186, 189, 218n60,
  219–20n90, 230n17
report to Napoleon, 187, 189, 231n19
self-portrait, 169–74, *172*
supposed rivalry with David, 87, 189,
  230n9, 231n19
as teacher, 86, 187, 189, 219n84
Vincent, François-Élie, 86
Voiriot, Guillaume, 95–97, 229n99
Voltaire à 41 ans (La Tour), *34*, 36, 49
Vos, Simone de
  Smokers, The, *165*, 167
Voyer, Marquis de, 50, 51, 210n69
  La Tour's portrait of, 47, 50, 51, 55, *56*,
    65, 78, 210n69

Watelet, Claude-Henri, 47, 50, 51, 65,
  210n69, 213n105
  Dictionnaire de l'Académie française,
    141–42
  *Dictionnaire des arts de peinture,
    sculpture et gravure*, 94, 130–32,
    135, 137
  Greuze's portrait of, 58, *61*
  L'Art de peindre, 55–58, 93
  La Tour's portrait of, 47, 50, 51, 65
  Moulin Joly, 114
Watteau, Antoine, 217n40
Wellington, Duke of, 109
white chalk, 135, 136
Williams, Hannah, 6, 46, 76, 82, 193n15,
  203n102
women
  in the Academy, 81–82, 83, 214n3
  aristocratic, 85, 102, 104
  friendship between, 82–85, 97, 102–3,
    106–7, 110, 114, 122
  Rousseau's critiques of, 28–30, 102
  as *salonnières*, 28, 36, 48, 102

Yvon, Claude, 3

THE TYPOGRAPHY AND ORNAMENTATION featured in *Portraiture and Friendship in Enlightenment France* are adapted from original Rococo designs by Pierre-Simon Fournier (1712–1768), the foremost type founder in eighteenth-century France. Known as Fournier le Jeune (to distinguish from his typographer father Jean-Claude Fournier), he was a progressive Parisian thinker during the Enlightenment and his many technical innovations include the point measurement system to standardize type font sizes. His specimen books *Modèles des caractères de l'imprimerie* (1742) and *Manuel typographique* (1764–66) are considered by many the most elegant ever published in France. Influenced by the royal *Romain du Roi* typefaces of the previous century, the Fournier designs show greater delicacy and refinement, and are distinguished by their legibility and readability, particularly in regard to italic fonts. The twentieth century witnessed a revival of the Fournier types with new releases by Deberny & Peignot in 1913 and Monotype in 1925.